1095

THE GENIUS OF JOHN

The Genius of John

A COMPOSITION-CRITICAL COMMENTARY ON THE FOURTH GOSPEL

Peter F. Ellis

THE LITURGICAL PRESS
Collegeville, Minnesota

First printing, November 1984
Second printing, June 1985

Cover design by Ann Blattner. Adapted from a sixth-century mosaic in the Basilica of S. Vitale, Ravenna.

Library of Congress Cataloging in Publication Data

Ellis, Peter F., 1921–
    The genius of John.
    Bibliography: p.
    1. Bible. N.T. John—Commentaries. I. Title.
BS2615.3.E45   1984   228'.07   84-23333
ISBN 0-8146-1328-4 (pbk.)

TO
John Gerhard, S.J.

Contents

PART V: THE HOUR OF GLORY (12:12–21:25)   195

Preface

Through no merit of my own, this is a different kind of commentary. Other commentaries divide John's Gospel into a Book of Signs (chs 1–12) and a Book of Glory (chs 13–21), presuppose it was written according to the laws of narrative, and take for granted a series of authors and editors, each of whom in one way or another either rewrote, supplemented, or redacted a primitive Johannine manuscript.

In 1975, in a doctoral dissertation John Gerhard, S.J., proposed the startling hypothesis that the Gospel was not the work of many but of one author, that it was a unified manuscript from beginning to end, and that it was written according to the laws of parallelism rather than the laws of narrative. After testing out the Gerhard hypothesis, I became convinced that Gerhard was correct and that his revolutionary discovery called for a new approach to the study of the Fourth Gospel. This commentary is a first-fruits result of that new approach. It is based upon Gerhard's discovery, and in all that pertains to the architectonic structure of the Gospel it is totally indebted to him. The commentary itself is my own, along with whatever mistakes have been made in the application of Gerhard's hypothesis to the text of the Gospel.

Scholars will notice that little is said about source, form, and redaction criticism. This is intentional. The emphasis is upon composition and narrative criticism. The major commentaries deal at length with the former; this commentary deals almost exclusively with the latter.

I welcome this opportunity to express my gratitude to John Gerhard and to those many others who helped me along the way, especially my graduate students at Fordham University; my friends Fathers Francis X. Murphy, William B. Biffar, Joseph C. Rowan, Matthew Meehan, and Jack Spicer; and finally, my wife, Judy. Her intuition in matters of structure and composition saved me from numerous blunders and contributed substantially to whatever may be of lasting value in this commentary.

Fordham University
August 1, 1983

Abbreviations

BOOKS OF THE BIBLE

Acts	Acts of the Apostles	1 Kgs	1 Kings
Am	Amos	2 Kgs	2 Kings
Bar	Baruch	Lam	Lamentations
1 Chr	1 Chronicles	Lk	Luke
2 Chr	2 Chronicles	Lv	Leviticus
Col	Colossians	Mal	Malachi
1 Cor	1 Corinthians	1 Mc	1 Maccabees
2 Cor	2 Corinthians	2 Mc	2 Maccabees
Ct	Canticle of Canticles	Mi	Micah
Dn	Daniel	Mk	Mark
Dt	Deuteronomy	Mt	Matthew
Eccl	Ecclesiastes	Na	Nahum
Eph	Ephesians	Neh	Nehemiah
Est	Esther	Nm	Numbers
Ex	Exodus	Ob	Obadiah
Ez	Ezekiel	Phil	Philippians
Ezr	Ezra	Phlm	Philemon
Gal	Galatians	Prv	Proverbs
Gn	Genesis	Ps(s)	Psalms
Hab	Habakkuk	1 Pt	1 Peter
Hag	Haggai	2 Pt	2 Peter
Heb	Hebrews	Rom	Romans
Hos	Hosea	Ru	Ruth
Is	Isaiah	Rv	Revelation
Jas	James	Sir	Sirach
Jb	Job	1 Sm	1 Samuel
Jdt	Judith	2 Sm	2 Samuel
Jer	Jeremiah	Tb	Tobit
Jgs	Judges	1 Thes	1 Thessalonians
Jl	Joel	2 Thes	2 Thessalonians
Jn	John	Ti	Titus
1 Jn	1 John	1 Tm	1 Timothy
2 Jn	2 John	2 Tm	2 Timothy
3 Jn	3 John	Wis	Wisdom
Jon	Jonah	Zech	Zechariah
Jos	Joshua	Zeph	Zephaniah
Jude	Jude		

OTHER SOURCES

AER	*American Ecclesiastical Review*
Ant.	Josephus, *Antiquities of the Jews*
CBQ	*Catholic Biblical Quarterly*
ETL	*Ephemerides theologicae lovanienses*
HUCA	*Hebrew Union College Annual*
Int	*Interpretation*
JBL	*Journal of Biblical Literature*
JHS	*Journal of Hellenic Studies*
NAB	New American Bible
NTS	*New Testament Studies*
RSV	Revised Standard Version
RThom	*Revue thomiste*

Introduction

The genius of John resides in his ability to penetrate to the theological foundations that undergird the events of Jesus' life. His mind reaches to the deeper meaning of the events, to the relationships of the Father, the Son, and the Holy Spirit in the work of redemption, and to the Trinitarian love for humanity which generated that work and which seeks through the gospel to bring within that sublime circle of indwelling love all who respond to Jesus with faith.

John deals with the same revealed truth as Matthew, Mark, Luke, and Paul. His way of speaking about that truth, however, is different. Like waters from the same source, the Johannine, Pauline, and synoptic traditions all come from the same historical Jesus but flow through different lands, pick up different textures, and emerge as observably different rivers.

The Johannine river, as the reader quickly perceives, flows through a theological Shangri-la—an almost mystic world, a world with its own language, its own symbolism, and its own unique theological viewpoint. The reader who enters this world senses immediately how different it is from the world of Paul and the Synoptics. In short order, however, the reader grasps the central concepts of Johannine theology, acquires a feeling for its innate consistency, and enjoys a provocative theological experience.

Before entering this world, something must be said about the date, the author, and the sources of the Fourth Gospel. In addition, something must be said about the audience and purpose of the author, his literary techniques, and the structure of his Gospel. These points belong to what is known as introduction. The better they can be established and described, the easier it is to understand and appreciate the Gospel. As we shall see, it is not easy to establish the date, the author, and the sources of the Fourth Gospel. Fortunately, these are of less importance than the more easily identified audience, purpose, literary techniques, and structure.

85 - 100 AD

Date

Internal evidence suggests that the Gospel was written after 85 A.D. External evidence points to a date not later than 110 A.D. The allusion to Peter's martyrdom in 21:18–19 demands a date after 64 A.D. Three references to excommunication from the synagogue (9:22; 12:42; 16:2) allude to the *Birkat ha-minim,* a "Test Benediction" used by the rabbis to exclude from the synagogue all heretics and perhaps especially Christians. Since the "Test

1

Benediction'' was instituted in the mid eighties, it is reasonable to conclude
that the Gospel was written sometime after 85 A.D.

How long after is impossible to determine. But external evidence in the
form of papyrus fragments found in Egypt suggests some ten or fifteen years
later, i.e., between 85 and 100 A.D. The Rylands papyrus, the papyrus Eger-
ton 2, P^{66}, and P^{75} all date to approximately 150 A.D. These papyrus finds
prove that the Gospel existed in Egypt in the first half of the second century.
If one allows forty or fifty years for the Gospel to become known and copied
in Egypt, one comes on the basis of external evidence to the same conclusion suggested by the internal evidence, i.e., 85–100 A.D. for the date of the
Gospel.

The author

Whoever the author of the Fourth Gospel was, one thing is certain: he
wanted to remain anonymous. He wanted only to be known as the disciple
whom Jesus loved. He speaks about himself in 13:23 as the one who at the
Last Supper "was lying close to the breast of Jesus"; in 19:23-26, 35, as the
disciple who stood beneath the cross, was given the care of Jesus' mother,
and witnessed the death of Jesus; in 20:2-10, as the disciple who ran with
Peter to the tomb on Easter morning and, upon seeing the burial cloths,
believed; in 21:7, as the disciple who alone recognized the stranger on the
shore as Jesus; and in 21:20-23, as the disciple about whom Jesus said to
Peter; "If it is my will that he remain until I come, what is that to you?"

It is probable that he is the "disciple . . . known to the high priest" who
spoke to the maid and had Peter admitted to the court of Annas (18:15-16).
It is quite probable that he was one of the two unnamed disciples of John
the Baptist who followed Jesus at the beginning of his public life (1:35-39),
and equally probable that he was one of the two unnamed disciples who accompanied Peter in the boat on the Lake of Galilee after the resurrection
(21:2).

What is certain is that the Gospel itself declares the Beloved Disciple to
be "the disciple who is bearing witness to these things, and who has written
these things . . . ." (21:24). The meaning of this statement is hotly debated.
It asserts at a minimum that the Beloved Disciple is the author of at least
ch 21; at a maximum, it asserts that he is the author of the entire Gospel.
The reasons for these conclusions will be explained in the commentary on
21:24-25.

However much the Gospel says about the Beloved Disciple, it nowhere
identifies him by name. Tradition, via Polycarp, Polycrates, and Irenaeus,
testifies to the belief of the Church in the early second century that John,
the son of Zebedee, was the Beloved Disciple.[1] This belief perdured until
the twentieth century and was defended as recently as the sixties by such
renowned Johannine scholars as R. Schnackenburg and R. E. Brown. Brown,

however, in his more recent *The Community of the Beloved Disciple,* has abandoned it and now goes along with the modern trend of dissociating John, the son of Zebedee, and the Beloved Disciple.[2]

Contemporary scholars see the Beloved Disciple as a disciple of Jesus, but not one of the Twelve, a disciple who formed and led his own Christian community sometime after the resurrection and became for that community a living link with the teaching of Jesus. They see him also as the leading figure in a school of interpreters who preserved his teaching and expanded it as the years went on, until a genius member of the school at the end of the first century authored the Gospel as we know it now.[3] His identity, however, remains a mystery. Considering the paucity of the evidence, it will probably always remain a mystery. C. K. Barrett is undoubtedly correct, however, in minimizing the importance of finding a solution. He says:

> It is more important to understand the theological task achieved by him than to know his name, and more important to know the materials with which he worked, and the way he used them, than to know the date and place at which he wrote. In fact, with the evidence at present at our disposal, it is impossible to determine name, date, and place with any confidence.[4]

The sources of the Gospel

A Gospel that, according to most scholars, is not the work of an eyewitness and that was composed or at least completed as late as sixty or seventy years after the resurrection had to be based on either written or oral source materials. Since the Gospel combines a large amount of discourse material with a small amount of narrative material, scholars have focused their attention alternately on the possibility of written sources for either the narrative or the discourse material. The results have not been gratifying.

For the narrative material, some opt for a knowledge of Mark and Luke. Others deny that John even knew the Synoptics. No solution seems possible. Apart from the Synoptics as sources, R. Bultmann and more recently R. Fortna have maintained that the narrative material in John is dependent upon what Fortna calls "The Gospel of Signs," a written narrative which, Fortna claims, began with John the Baptist, contained a series of seven miracle stories, climaxed with an account of the passion and resurrection, and concluded with the words of Jn 20:30-31.[5] J. L. Martyn, along with many others, is inclined to agree with Fortna.[6] B. Lindars disagrees, and with good reasons.[7] As we shall see in the commentary, there are more compelling reasons against the cogency of Fortna's hypothesis than for it.

With regard to sources for the Johannine discourses, Bultmann contended that John was dependent on what Bultmann called Gnostic "revelation discourses." Few now agree with him. Lindars, with somewhat better reason, hypothesizes that many of the discourses were based upon homilies by the Beloved Disciple that were later incorporated into the Gospel at strategic points.[8] This hypothesis squares well with the consistency of John's style, vocabulary, and theology, but not, as we shall see, with the structure of the Gospel. In short, whatever the postulated sources, whether written or oral, John has so Johannized his material from tradition that any clear indications of distinct source materials have been so homogenized as to be virtually undetectable. It is much more probable that the Gospel as a whole is a pristine theological creation flowing from a genius theologian who required no sources beyond the broad oral traditions of the community in which he lived.

Where this community was located has never been adequately identified. Most scholars, following early Church tradition, opt for Ephesus; others opt for Alexandria or Antioch. C. K. Barrett rightly concludes: "It is impossible to make out a satisfactory and conclusive case for any of the three great cities, Ephesus, Alexandria, and Antioch, as the place of origin of the fourth gospel."[9]

As we have seen, it is difficult to establish with any certitude either the date, the author, or the sources of the Fourth Gospel. We come now to questions about the audience for whom John wrote, the purpose for which he wrote, the literary techniques he utilized to put across his message, and the architectural structure he designed for his Gospel in order to give it unity, artistry, and consistency. Here we can speak with less difficulty and more certitude.

The audience and purpose of the Gospel

John's Gospel is intensely polemical. The polemic begins in the prologue with the author's bitter observation that though Jesus "came to his own home . . . his own people received him not" (1:11). In 2:24-25, the author goes out of his way to remark that while many in Jerusalem believed in Jesus when they saw the signs he did, "Jesus did not trust himself to them." In 3:11, he records Jesus' words to Nicodemus and those like Nicodemus: "Truly, truly, I say to you, we speak of what we know, and bear witness to what we have seen; but you do not receive our testimony." In chs 5–10, he shows Jesus angrily refuting the accusations of the Jews and repeats regularly the words "the Jews sought to kill him" (5:18; 7:1, 19, 25; 8:37, 40, 59; 10:31, 39). In 9:39–10:21, he recounts how Jesus accuses the Pharisees of moral blindness and brands them as thieves and robbers. In 11:45-54, he convicts the Jewish leaders of plotting the death of Jesus. In 15:13-25 and 16:2ff, he accuses them of hating not only Jesus but his followers as well. Finally, in his passion account (chs 18–19), he goes out of his way to place the major blame for Jesus' death on the Jews by recording Jesus' words to Pilate: ". . . he who delivered me to you has the greater sin" (19:11).

So persistent a polemic leaves no doubt that John wrote his Gospel *against* the Jews.[10] But *for* whom did he write it? To begin with, such a barrage of accusations against the synagogue Jews surely indicates that he did not write for his enemies. He could hardly have expected many, if any, of them to read his Gospel. What the barrage does indicate is that whoever his audience was, he thought it necessary to warn them against the synagogue leaders, to fortify their faith by providing them with theological arguments to refute the Jewish objections to Christ and Christianity (5:19-47; 6:32-70; 7:1-8:59; 9:39-10:39), and to encourage and strengthen them in a time of hardship and persecution brought upon them by the opposition of the synagogue.

If we ask who would need such warnings, refutations, encouragement, and strengthening, we come to one reasonable conclusion: John wrote his Gospel primarily for Jewish Christians whose faith was wavering, who were under attack by the synagogue for believing in Jesus, and who, because of Jewish persecution, were tending to either remain in or return to the synagogue and thereby apostasize from their faith in Jesus. In brief, John's primary audience was that group of Christian Jews who were straddling the fence between the Christian community and the Jewish synagogue. John's own expression of his purpose in 20:31 should therefore be translated: ". . . that you may (not simply believe but) continue to believe that Jesus is the Christ, the Son of God, and that believing you may have life in his name."

John's secondary audience was that group of Jewish Christians who belonged to Christian communities but who were wavering in their faith because of persecution and the threat of death (16:1-4). For these he records the words of Jesus: "I have said all this to you to keep you from falling away" (16:1). All, or at least some, of these may be the "other sheep" mentioned in 10:16, of whom Jesus says, "And I have other sheep, that are not of this fold; I must bring them also, and they will heed my voice. So there shall be one flock, one shepherd."[1]

Brown identifies six groups in the Gospel who are outside the Johannine community: (1) the world—those who prefer darkness to light; (2) the Jews— synagogue leaders who excommunicated and persecuted other synagogue Jews who believed in Jesus; (3) the adherents of John the Baptist—those who argued that the Baptist and not Jesus was God's prime envoy to his people; (4) the crypto-Christians—Christian Jews who did not have the courage to publicly profess their faith in Jesus; (5) Jewish Christians—Christians who had left the synagogue but whose faith in Jesus was inadequate for one reason or another; (6) Christians of the apostolic churches—followers of Peter and the other apostles who, according to John, "did not fully understand Jesus or the teaching function of the Paraclete"—with whom the Johannine Christians prayed for unity.[12]

It would seem clear that John writes *against* groups 1, 2, 3, and *for* at least groups 4 and 5. The Gospel responds to their theological needs, calls them to a definitive decision for Christ, and provides them with a theological armory against the arguments of the anti-Christian Jewish theologians. In the Gospel as a whole, Nicodemus typifies the crypto-Christians (cf. 3:1-21; 7:50-52; 19:38-42). The disciples who abandon Jesus after his Eucharistic discourse typify the Jewish Christians whose faith was inadequate (cf. 6:60-68 and 8:31). Caiaphas typifies all the Jewish leaders who opposed and persecuted the Johannine community (cf. 11:45-53). And the Beloved Disciple typifies, we may be sure, the faithful members of John's own Christian community.

In conclusion, we may be reasonably sure that John wrote his Gospel for weak Christians both in his own community and in the synagogue. His purpose was to call to a definitive decision for Christ those Christian Jews (crypto-Christians) who were straddling the fence between Jesus and the synagogue (1) because they feared excommunication from the synagogue (cf. 9:22; 12:37-43; 16:2); (2) or because they found Jesus' teaching about the Eucharist a hard saying and could not accept the Eucharist as truly the flesh and blood of Jesus (cf. 6:59ff); (3) or because they could not accept the high Christology of John and his community (cf. 5:1-47; 7:1–8:59, especially 8:31; 10:22-29; and perhaps 2:23-25; 11:46); (4) or, possibly but not certainly, because they had been disciples of John the Baptist and could not easily accept Jesus as greater than the Baptist (cf. 1:19-34; 3:22–4:3). For all of these, the Gospel as a whole, with its massive emphasis on witness to Jesus and response of faith in Jesus, provided a powerful appeal for a definitive decision concerning Christ and the Christian community. To all of these equally, the words of Jesus would apply: "I have said all this to you to keep you from falling away" (16:1).

John's literary techniques

Few things are more helpful for readers of John's Gospel than an appreciation of his literary techniques.[13] These are for the most part the techniques of a dramatist. They include the technique of using stories to set up scenes; the use of discourses, dialogues, and monologues to expound Jesus' teaching; the use of misunderstanding and double-meaning words to emphasize important elements of Jesus' teaching; and the use of such other techniques as the rule of two, explanatory comments, irony, foreshadowing, inclusion, and the chiastic arrangement of parts, sequences, and sections of the Gospel. All of these call for some explanation.

1. STORIES. John uses stories to set up scenes, discourses, and dialogues. The following are good examples. In 1:19-51, the story of Jesus' coming to John the Baptist at the Jordan sets the scene for the parade of witnesses who testify successively to Jesus as Lamb of God, Messiah, King of Israel, Son of God, and Son of Man.

In 2:13-25, the story of the cleansing of the temple sets the scene for Jesus' dialogue with the Jews concerning his words "Destroy this temple [he means his body], and in three days I will raise it up." In 3:1-21, the story of

Nicodemus' coming to Jesus at night sets the scene for Jesus' dialogue with Nicodemus about being "born again" (3:5), just as in 4:4ff, Jesus' meeting with the Samaritan woman sets the scene for his dialogue with her about the water that will become "a spring of water welling up to eternal life" (4:14).

John uses the same technique in ch 5, where the cure of the paralytic (5:1-18) sets the scene for the long monologue of 5:19-47; in ch 6, where Jesus' discussion with the Jews about signs (6:22-31) sets the theme for Jesus' homily on "the true bread from heaven" (6:32-58); in chs 7-8, where Jesus' secret trip to Jerusalem sets the scene for a series of debates with the Jews; in ch 9, where the cure of the man born blind sets the scene for the discourse on the good and the bad shepherds (10:1-21); in 10:22-39, where Jesus' appearance at the feast of the Dedication leads to his final dispute with the Jews; and lastly in chs 13-17, where the washing of the feet (13:1-32) sets the scene for Jesus' Last Supper discourse. In all these examples, the stories are secondary to the dialogues, monologues, and discourses for which they prepare the way. They are clearly the work of a superb dramatist.

2. DISCOURSES, DIALOGUES, AND MONOLOGUES. As C. H. Dodd has pointed out,[14] the typical Johannine discourse (e.g., in 3:1-21; 4:4-38; 5:1-47; 6:22-58; 9:39-10:21; 10:22-39; 13:33-16:33) follows a distinctive pattern. (a) It begins with a solemn declaration by Jesus, often in lapidary terms (e.g., 3:3; 4:10; 5:17; 6:32; 7:16; 9:39; 10:25; 13:13). (b) It is frequently followed by an objection or question based upon a misunderstanding of Jesus' words (e.g., 3:4; 4:11; 5:18; 6:41-42; 7:20; 9:40; 10:6; 10:31; 13:36). (c) There then follows Jesus' discourse clarifying the misunderstanding or the objection. The discourse is sometimes interrupted by further questions and objections (e.g., 4:4-38; 6:33-58; 15:33-16:33) and at other times consists entirely of a long monologue (e.g., 3:11-21; 5:19-47; 10:7-18).

John is justified in taking the liberty of composing these discourses. As he explains in 15:26; 16:13-14, it is really the Paraclete who is behind the discourses. Thus the Paraclete, through John, is explaining Jesus' words according to the needs of the Church at the time of the author.

3. MISUNDERSTANDING AND DOUBLE-MEANING WORDS. Misunderstanding is a dramatist's technique whereby the author represents a person as misunderstanding either the actual words of the speaker or the meaning of his or her words in order to give the speaker (in this case Jesus) the opportunity to explain himself or herself more fully. This frequently comes about because the author uses double-meaning words, i.e., words that have one meaning for Jesus and quite another for the person or persons to whom he is speaking.

There are many examples of double-meaning words in this Gospel. When Jesus says, "Destroy this temple, and in three days I will raise it up" (2:19), the Jews think he means the temple of Jerusalem, but Jesus means his own body put to death and later raised from the dead. When Jesus says to

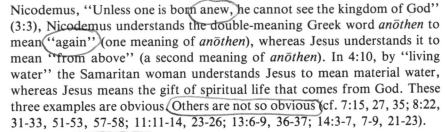

Nicodemus, "Unless one is born anew, he cannot see the kingdom of God" (3:3), Nicodemus understands the double-meaning Greek word *anōthen* to mean "again" (one meaning of *anōthen*), whereas Jesus understands it to mean "from above" (a second meaning of *anōthen*). In 4:10, by "living water" the Samaritan woman understands Jesus to mean material water, whereas Jesus means the gift of spiritual life that comes from God. These three examples are obvious. Others are not so obvious (cf. 7:15, 27, 35; 8:22, 31-33, 51-53, 57-58; 11:11-14, 23-26; 13:6-9, 36-37; 14:3-7, 7-9, 21-23).

4. THE RULE OF TWO. Storytellers and dramatists try to limit dialogue to two persons at any one time. Others on stage are either provided with exit cues or reduced to simple bystanders. This is what is meant by the rule of two, and John uses it regularly. Three examples are noteworthy: the staging of the scene with the Samaritan woman in 4:4-38; the staging of the scene at Bethany when Jesus comes to raise Lazarus; and the staging of Jesus' trial before Pilate.

In the first example, the disciples go into town for food (4:8), leaving the stage to Jesus and the Samaritan woman. When they return (4:27), the woman exits (4:28), leaving the stage to Jesus and his disciples. In the second, when Jesus arrives at Bethany, Martha comes to Jesus first and dialogues with him (11:20-27). She then departs off stage to call Mary (11:18), and Mary comes on stage to speak with Jesus (11:32). In the third, the trial before Pilate, it is notable that Pilate speaks outside to the Jews, inside to Jesus alone. In all three of these exquisitely staged stories, John scrupulously observes the dramatist's rule of two.

5. EXPLANATORY COMMENTS. These are used to explain or clarify a statement and sometimes to correct wrong impressions a reader might derive from a statement. Today most of them would be put in footnotes. Some examples: comments explaining symbols (2:21; 12:33; 18:9; 21:9); comments reminding the reader of something that happened previously (3:24; 11:2); comments correcting misapprehensions (4:2; 6:6).

6. IRONY. John has certain persons, most frequently opponents, make statements about Jesus that they think are correct and that John's readers know are correct, but in a different and sometimes far deeper sense. The following are good examples. In 4:12, the Samaritan woman asks Jesus, "Are you greater than our father Jacob . . .?" She thinks not; the reader knows that Jesus is inestimably greater than Jacob.

The Jews ask, "Has not the scripture said that the Christ is descended from David, and comes from Bethlehem, the village where David was?" (7:42). Their question implies that they deny Jesus' Davidic descent and birth in Bethlehem. The reader knows the opposite is true.

Caiaphas declares, "You do not understand that it is expedient for you that one man should die for the people, and that the whole nation should not perish" (11:50). Caiaphas means that the execution of Jesus as a revolutionary will save the Jews from the wrath of Rome. The reader knows that Caiaphas, without being conscious of it, has prophesied the death of Jesus for the spiritual redemption not only of the Jews but of the whole world!

When Pilate asks, "What is truth?" (18:38), his question implies that one cannot find the truth. John's readers know that the truth Pilate despairs of finding stands before him in the person of Jesus, "the way, and the truth, and the life" (cf. 14:6).

Finally, when the soldiers mock Jesus as king (19:2-3), John's readers grasp the double irony: he whom the soldiers ironically declare to be king is, ironically, truly a king!

7. FORESHADOWING. This is a storyteller's technique whereby knowledge of the future is given in advance in order to arouse anticipation and suspense, and at the same time prepare the audience to look for an interconnection of the parts of the story with the whole.[15] There are several excellent examples of foreshadowing in John's Gospel. In the prologue, John says, "He came to his own home, and his own people received him not" (1:11). Hearing these words, the reader is led to anticipate both the rejection of Jesus by the Jews and his eventual death on the cross.

When Jesus looks at Peter and says to him, " 'So you are Simon the son of John? You shall be called Cephas' (which means Peter)" (1:42), the reader, who already knows the significance of Simon's nickname, Peter (cf. Mt 16:17-19), is led to anticipate what actually only happens at the end of the Gospel, namely, Jesus' designation of Peter to be vicar-shepherd in charge of his flock (21:15-19).

A classic example of foreshadowing occurs in 11:4. Jesus responds to Martha and Mary's message about Lazarus' illness by declaring, "This illness is not unto death; it is for the glory of God, so that the Son of God may be glorified by means of it." Lazarus' illness is not unto death because Jesus will raise him. And because Jesus raises him, the Jewish leaders will plot and bring about Jesus' death. Thus, Lazarus' illness is "for the glory of God," because it leads to Jesus' death-glorification on the cross. Simpler foreshadowings are found in 11:50; 12:33; 13:36; 16:32; 21:18.

8. INCLUSION. Known among classical scholars as "ring composition," inclusion is a storyteller's technique in which what is said at the beginning of a piece is repeated at the end. The repetition forces the reader's attention back to the beginning and thus serves as a frame for the piece as a whole. John frames his whole Gospel by repeating in ch 21 words and names used in 1:19-51 (note the return in ch 21 of the names Simon son of John, Nathanael, the two unnamed disciples, the words "follow me," and the commissioning of Peter as vicar-shepherd of the sheep, a commissioning already implicit in the change of Simon's name to Peter in 1:42).

In addition to framing the Gospel as a whole, John frames each individual sequence of his Gospel. Two examples will suffice: 2:1-12 (note how vv 11-12

1226 A.D.   Stephen Langton

repeat names and places in vv 1-2); 20:1-18 (note how the sequence begins and ends with the full name of Mary Magdalene). Recognition of inclusions is important for the interpreter. More than anything else, inclusions clearly indicate beginnings and endings and thus help the exegete to divide the Gospel into distinct parts, sequences, and sections. In modern terms, inclusions divide the written Gospel into parts, chapters, and paragraphs. The importance of this becomes obvious when the reader realizes that ancient manuscripts like John's Gospel were regularly written almost entirely without indications of, or divisions into, parts, chapters, and sections.

Recognition of John's inclusions becomes all the more important when one realizes that the present division of the Gospel into twenty-one chapters, as found in all modern Bible translations, goes back to the twelfth century[16] and was done with complete disregard for John's use of inclusions to divide his Gospel into individual parts, sequences, and sections. As we shall see when we deal with the structure of the Gospel, John uses inclusions regularly, skillfully, and abundantly in the composition of his Gospel.

9. CHIASM. Chiasm is a development of inclusion. Instead of simply ending and beginning in the same way, chiasm extends the balancing of the first and the last by balancing the second and the fourth (thus, *abcb'a'*, or *ab—b'a'*). In John's Gospel, the author uses the five-member chiasm in every part, sequence, and section. Since the Gospel is filled with chiastically structured parts, sequences, and sections, and since we shall be seeing all of these in the course of our commentary, we give here only one example—the chiastic structure of 2:1-12. In the text that follows, the reader should note how the boldfaced words in (a) are repeated in (a'), and the boldfaced words in (b) are repeated in (b').

(a)   On the **third day** there was a marriage at **Cana in Galilee,** and the **mother** of **Jesus** was there; **Jesus** also was invited to the marriage, with his **disciples.**

(b)   When the **wine** failed, the mother of Jesus said to him, "They have no **wine.**" And Jesus said to her, "O woman, what have you to do with me? My hour has not yet come." His mother said to the **servants,** "Do whatever he tells you."

(c)   Now six stone jars were standing there, for the Jewish rites of purification, each holding twenty or thirty gallons. Jesus said to them, "Fill the jars with water." And they filled them up to the brim. He said to them, "Now draw some out, and take it to the steward of the feast." So they took it.

(b')   When the steward of the feast tasted the water now become **wine,** and did not know where it came from (though the **servants** who had drawn the water knew), the steward of the feast called the bridegroom and said to him, "Every man serves the good **wine** first; and when men have drunk freely, then the poor **wine;** but you have kept the good **wine** until now."

(a′)   This, the first of his signs **Jesus** did at **Cana in Galilee,** and manifested
his glory; and his **disciples** believed in him. After this he went down to Capernaum, with his **mother** and his brothers and his **disciples;** and there they
stayed for a few **days.**

The use of chiasm in the writings of the Old and the New Testaments
and in the writings of the Greeks and Romans has been amply documented.[17]
Its use by John, as we shall see, is the key to the structure of his Gospel
as a whole and to the structure of each individual sequence and section.

The structure of the Gospel

The search for the structure of John's Gospel has been long and
dishearteningly unsuccessful. Forty years ago, Bultmann proposed that the
Gospel as it stands is not the Gospel as it came from the hand of the author,
but the poor attempt of editors to put back in order an originally well-
arranged manuscript that was either damaged or disarranged as early as the
autograph stage. In 1963, D. M. Smith, Jr., made a study of Bultmann's
theses regarding the order of John and came to the conclusion that in almost
every instance Bultmann's reconstruction raised as many problems as it provided solutions.[18] Smith himself came to the conclusion that it was "quite
possible, indeed probable, that the Fourth Gospel has been left to us in an
unfinished stage."[19]

Brown begins his section on the unity and composition of the Gospel with
the question: "Is the fourth gospel as it now stands the work of one man?"[20]
His answer, like that of all modern commentators with the exception of
Lagrange and Hoskyns, is an emphatic denial. Despite the fact that there
is absolutely no textual witness to any other order than the one we find now
in the Gospel, almost all commentators take for granted that there were at
least two hands at work in the composition of the Gospel and that the Gospel
as it stands now is in a state of great disorder.

The great commentators since Bultmann (Dodd, Barrett, Brown,
Schnackenburg, Lindars, and Marsh) all call attention to the difficulties with
Bultmann's reconstruction but do little more toward reconstructing the so-
called original Gospel beyond suggesting a series of inept redactors who have
distorted the original order of the Gospel by introducing new material at
several points and by adding to what is considered the original ending of
the Gospel (20:30-31) a new concluding chapter (ch 21). To explain the alleged
disorder, they propose variant versions of the following hypotheses: (1)
hypotheses of accidental displacements; (2) hypotheses of multiple sources
ineptly melded together; (3) hypotheses of successive redactions of an earlier
Gospel supplemented and re-edited later by incompetent redactors and
editors. Despite these and other hypotheses, what H. M. Teeple said in 1962
remains true: "No one yet has demonstrated convincingly that the gospel
has been disarranged."[21]

More recently, John Gerhard, S.J., has proposed the hypothesis that the Gospel has suffered neither displacements nor disarrangements but stands now as it came from the hand of the author.[22] Gerhard bases this proposition on the contention amply demonstrated in his thesis that the Gospel was composed according to the laws of chiastic parallelism rather than according to the ordinary laws of narrative. He contends that the Gospel appears to be in a state of disarrangement only if one presupposes that the author composed it according to the ordinary laws of narrative composition. If one presupposes, on the contrary, that the Gospel was composed according to the laws of chiastic parallelism, every part, sequence, section, and element is precisely where it belongs.

Gerhard's hypothesis, in brief, asserts that the Gospel as it now stands is the work of one man; that it has suffered no displacements; that it has a clear and easily demonstrable chiastic structure from beginning to end; and that it exists now in our New Testament (with the exception of the adulteress pericope and a few insignificant glosses) exactly as it came from the author. In sum, Gerhard finds to be absolutely true the conclusion Strauss came to many years ago when he declared that the Gospel "was like the seamless robe of which it spoke (Jn 19:23-24), which one may cast lots for, but cannot divide."[23]

The heart of Gerhard's hypothesis resides in its fundamental presupposition—a presupposition diametrically opposed to the fundamental presupposition of all previous authors. Gerhard presupposes that John wrote his Gospel according to the laws of chiastic parallelism and not according to the laws of narrative. He points out that in a Gospel written according to the laws of narrative, the reader would rightly expect a logical and chronological succession of events without violent changes of geography, situation, time, and content.[24] He readily admits that if this narrative presupposition were true, scholars would be correct in deducing that John's Gospel has suffered displacements, rearrangements, supplementary interpolations, and even several redactions.

The following would be the most obvious of these displacements and rearrangements: (1) the cleansing of the temple (2:13-25), which is out of place and should be transposed to some point closer to the passion account; (2) 3:27-36, which is misplaced and should be rearranged to follow either 1:19-34 or perhaps 3:19; (3) chs 5–7, which are not in correct order and should be rearranged so that ch 5 and ch 7 go together, with ch 6 preceding them; (4) parts of 10:22-39 (the shepherd and sheep parts), which are misplaced and should go somewhere in 10:1-21; (5) 12:44-50, which floats and can find no good resting place anywhere in the Gospel; (6) chs 15–17, which should be treated as supplementary material added to the Last Supper discourse by one or more redactors; and (7) ch 21, which gives the appearance of being a supplement added to the Gospel as an epilogue by the final editor.

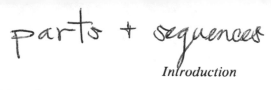
parts + sequences

The above-mentioned displacements and rearrangements have been hypothesized on the premise, rarely if ever questioned, that the Gospel was written according to the laws of narrative. If this premise were true, logic would demand that some hypothesis of displacements, rearrangements, and redactions must be found, even though it reduces the Gospel as it stands to a hodgepodge of material put together by remarkably incompetent authors, editors, and redactors. Reflecting on this situation, C. H. Dodd thirty years ago remarked, "Unfortunately, when once the gospel has been taken to pieces, its reassemblage is liable to be affected by individual preferences, preconceptions, and even prejudices."[25] That this has been the unenviable fate of the Fourth Gospel during the last fifty years needs no documentation.

If, on the other hand, the narrative premise is false, as Gerhard contends, then the situation is entirely different. There remains the possibility that the Gerhard hypothesis is true and that the Gospel was indeed written according to the laws of parallelism rather than according to the laws of narrative. That this is more than a mere possibility may be deduced from the fact that chiastic parallelism as a structural principle in ancient Middle Eastern books has been amply documented in the last fifty years for both classical[26] and biblical[27] authors. C. H. Talbert is undoubtedly correct in his contention that books in the ancient Middle East were frequently written according to the laws of chiastic parallelism, and in his subsequent judgment that ". . . the very law of duality (i.e., parallelism) by which one part is made to correspond to another by being either analogous or contrasting seems deeply rooted in Near Eastern mentality."[28]

The uniqueness of John's structure, according to the Gerhard hypothesis, is not simply that the Gospel as a whole is constructed according to the laws of chiastic parallelism but that each of the five major parts and each of the twenty-one individual sequences of the Gospel is constructed according to the laws of chiastic parallelism. We will begin by demonstrating the chiastic parallelism of the Gospel as a whole; then in the commentary we will demonstrate the chiastic parallelism within each of the twenty-one individual sequences of the Gospel.

As we shall see, John creates his parallelisms most often by repeating either the same words or the same content (concepts). Occasionally he creates parallelisms by means of antithetic parallelism, i.e., by contrasting a negative with a positive or a positive with a negative situation or concept. On rare occasions he not only parallels words and content (concepts) but even the literary form of a sequence.[29]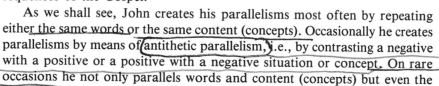

Chiastic parallelism of the Gospel as a whole

In the outline of the Gospel on p. 14, the reader will notice that the Gospel is divided into twenty-one sequences rather than into the usual twenty-one chapters. This has been done because each sequence constitutes a well-defined

1226

unit either because of unity of place or time or theme or situation. Ideally these sequences should take the place of the old chapter arrangement of the Gospel that comes from Stephen Langton, who in 1226 divided the Gospel into its present very poor arrangement of chapters and verses.

The original Gospel, like almost all ancient books, contained neither chapters nor verses nor even paragraphing. Scholars are agreed that Langton's division is almost entirely arbitrary, and they have attempted to rectify the situation by retaining Langton's chapters and verses but adding titles or headings to indicate where they believe John would have begun new chapters and paragraphs if he were writing his Gospel today.

The outline presented here follows the outline of the Gospel discovered by John Gerhard. According to Gerhard, John divided his Gospel into twenty-one sequences, with the first mirrored back by the twenty-first, the second mirrored back by the twentieth, the third by the nineteenth, and so through the whole Gospel, with the eleventh sequence (6:16-21) standing alone in the middle.

In the outline, because of limitation of space, only the most obvious parallels of persons, places, and situation can be shown. Following the commentary on each sequence, beginning with the fourth, the reader will find a listing of the full range of parallels John has created in order to compose his Gospel according to the laws of parallelism.

PART I: 1:19–4:3
WITNESS AND DISCIPLESHIP

Seq. 1 (1:19-51): At the Jordan. Jesus' **first coming.** Baptist and disciples **witness. Simon** is called **Peter** (Rock). **Two unnamed disciples** and **Nathanael** are present.

Seq. 2 (2:1-12): **Mary** at Cana. "**Woman,** what have you to do with me?" **Nuptial** situation. **Water** to wine.

Seq. 3 (2:13-25): "**Destroy** this temple (Jesus' **body**) . . . ."

Seq. 4 (3:1-21): Discourse at **night** to Nicodemus on **eternal life, discipleship, water,** and the **Spirit.**

Seq. 5 (3:22–4:3): The Baptist repeats his **witness** to Jesus.

PART II: 4:4–6:15
RESPONSE: POSITIVE AND NEGATIVE

Seq. 6 (4:4-38): Samaritan **woman.** Jesus is the **Messiah.**

PART V: 12:12–21:25
WITNESS AND DISCIPLESHIP

Seq. 21 (20:19–21:25): At the Lake. Jesus' **second coming** is discussed. Thomas **witnesses. Simon Peter** is told: "Feed my sheep." **Two unnamed disciples** and **Nathanael** are present.

Seq. 20 (21:1-18): **Mary** at the tomb. "**Woman,** why are you weeping?" **Nuptial** language from Song of Songs.

Seq. 19 (chs 18–19): Jesus' **body** is **destroyed** in the passion.

Seq. 18 (chs 13–17): Supper discourse at **night** on **washing** of feet, **discipleship, eternal life,** and the **Spirit.**

Seq. 17 (12:12-50): Palm Sunday, crowd **witnesses** to Jesus.

PART IV: 6:22–12:11
RESPONSE: POSITIVE AND NEGATIVE

Seq. 16 (10:40–12:11): Bethany **women** (Martha and Mary). Jesus is the **Messiah.**

Seq. 7 (4:39-45): Samaritan men **hear,** believe, and profess: "You are the **Savior** of the world."

Seq. 8 (4:46-52): **Pagan official** does not **see** but **believes.**

Seq. 9 (5:1-47): At **feast,** Jesus cures a **paralytic** and makes himself **equal to the Father.**

Seq. 10 (6:1-15): Multiplication of the **loaves** near **Passover.**

Seq. 15 (10:22-39): Jesus declares: "My sheep **hear** my voice . . . they shall never **perish.**"

Seq. 14 (9:1-10:21): The **Pharisees** refuse to **see** and **believe.**

Seq. 13 (7:1-8:58): At **feast,** Jesus refers to cure of **paralytic** and makes himself **equal to the Father.**

Seq. 12 (6:22-72): The **loaves** are explained as the Eucharist near **Passover.**

PART III: 6:16-21

THE NEW EXODUS

Jesus walks on the sea, declares "I am he" and brings the new Israel to the other shore of the sea.

Chiastic parallelism of each of the five major parts of the Gospel

The five major parts of the Gospel are: part I: 1:19–4:3; part II: 4:4–6:15; part III: 6:16-21 (the center); part IV: 6:22–12:11; part V: 12:12–21:25. Each of these five major parts has five sequences, with the fifth mirroring the first and the fourth mirroring the second. What is true of part I, arranged here according to the laws of parallelism, will be found to be true of the four other major parts of the Gospel (see pp. 65, 107, 113, 195).

Part I (1:19–4:3): Witness to Jesus

Seq. 1 (1:19-51):   The **Baptist** and the disciples **witness** to Jesus.
Seq. 2 (2:1-12):   **Water** of the old covenant is changed into wine of the new covenant.
Seq. 3 (2:13-25):   "Destroy this temple, and in three days I will raise it up."
Seq. 4 (3:1-21):   **Water** of the new covenant and rebirth to eternal life
Seq. 5 (3:22–4:3):   The **Baptist** reiterates his **witness** to Jesus.

The significance of noting the inclusion-conclusion with which each major part of the Gospel ends consists in the clear indication it gives the reader that John has indeed divided his Gospel into five major parts, each consisting of five sequences. How much this assists the reader in understanding the Gospel as a whole will become evident in the course of our commentary. In brief, and prescinding from other minor themes, the reader will see that part I (1:19–4:3) and part V (12:12–21:25) not only parallel each other but concentrate on the same themes, namely, witness to Jesus and discipleship. In like manner, part II (4:4–6:15) and part IV (6:22–12:11) not only parallel each other but concentrate in a similar manner on the same major themes, namely, response to Jesus both positive and negative and a theological defense of Jesus' divinity. These themes—witness to Jesus, response to Jesus, and discipleship—constitute the major themes of the Fourth Gospel.

The rewards of parallelism

Studying the chiastic outline of John's Gospel on p. 14, the reader will notice that the author has paralleled in a chiastic structure part with part, sequence with sequence, and section with section. The total effect of such a structure when it is presented to the eye is similar to the effect of an elaborate mosaic or a large Persian rug.

Richard Greene Moulton, the last of the nineteenth-century school that followed Robert Lowth's principles of parallelism in the study of the Bible, emphasizes the importance of printing the text in such a way that the chiastic structure can be seen visually and thus adverted to: "The essential thing is that the verse structure should be represented to the eye by proper printing of the text. Where this is done further explanation is superfluous; where structural arrangement is wanting, no amount of explanation is likely to be of much avail."

Admittedly, such a structure is alien to modern experience and difficult to appreciate. But for the reader who is willing to study the principles of parallel structure and apply them to the Gospel of John as a whole, the aesthetic, literary, and theological rewards are considerable.

Leaving aside the aesthetic rewards, which are too subjective to be adequately described, and leaving until later the theological rewards, the literary rewards can be described briefly.

First, sequences of the Gospel and sections of sequences which seem to Bultmann and others to be out of their original place in the Gospel and which they accordingly move either backward or forward in the book to achieve a more flowing and continuous narrative are seen to be precisely where the laws of chiastic parallelism require them to be (e.g., 2:13-25; 3:22-36; chs 5, 6, 7).

Second, sections of the Gospel which are considered by many to be doublets of earlier sections, and which are therefore deduced to be the work of inept redactors or editors, are seen to be artistic and necessary parallels of their chiastic counterparts when judged according to the laws of chiastic parallelism (e.g., 3:22-36 parallels 1:19-31 and chs 16–17 parallel 13:1–14:31).

Third, individual sequences and sections of sequences whose beginnings and ends are difficult to determine when one expects them to follow the laws of narrative are seen to have clear and definite beginnings and endings when one reads them according to the laws of chiastic parallelism.

Fourth, such pericopes as 2:13-25 (the cleansing of the temple), 11:1-54 (the Lazarus story and the priests' plot), to name but two, have always posed problems for those who read John according to the laws of narrative. According to the laws of parallelism, both pericopes are exactly where they belong, the temple pericope balancing the passion narrative (the destroying of the body of Jesus) and the Lazarus pericope balancing the "bread of life" promise in 6:32-58.

Fifth, commentators down through the centuries have been all too content to laud John's Gospel for its theological depth and for its occasional brilliant literary sorties. But on the whole, they have apologized for the seemingly pedestrian literary gifts of the author. When John is seen through the focus of chiastic parallelism, this judgment has to be revised. Any author who could compose so elaborate a structure with such artistic attention to detail and over so long an opus deserves to be ranked with the best of antiquity's literary artists.

Lastly, many have adverted to what has been called the "spiral" movement of John's thought. They have seen this spiral movement, however, as peculiar, confusing, and repetitive. When the spiral movement is seen as part and parcel of John's chiastic parallelism, it ceases to be peculiar and becomes artistic; it ceases to be confusing and serves to clarify; it ceases to be repetitious and becomes balanced and supportive.

For the reader who wishes to read the Fourth Gospel with appreciation for the author's artistry and with a view to sharpening the focus with which to look at the Gospel as a whole and in its parts, the following exercises are suggested in discovering parts, sequences, sections, and elements and in setting criteria for distinguishing and determining distinct sequences according to the laws of chiastic parallelism.

1) Make a preview of what appears to be a unit, e.g., 2:1-12; 18:1-12; 19:31-42.

2) Make a study of its components or what look to be its components.

3) Review the unit with all parallels in mind and then apply the following criteria for distinguishing and determining distinct parts, sequences, sections, and elements:

a) Is there a change of time, place, subject matter, speakers?

b) Is there a balance of parts, e.g., part one with part five, part two with part four?

c) Are there any inclusion-conclusions by way of names, places, ideas, key words?

Finally, one may ask, why did John intentionally arrange his composition according to the laws of parallelism? Some answers are: (1) in order that the work might be the more easily memorized; (2) in order that corresponding parts might help to interpret one another; (3) in order to give to his grand theme a suitable artistic form in the same way that Vergil chose dactylic hexameters for his theme; (4) in order to present his work to the world in the same parallel literary pattern used so extensively in the Old Testament and other epic works of Middle Eastern authors.

We conclude, therefore, that neither interpreters of the Fourth Gospel nor translators should ignore the help given to them by an author when he chooses parallelism as his method of composition.

In the commentary that follows, the reader is advised to attend first to the structure of each sequence, then to the text itself, in which the most obvious parallels are indicated by the words in boldface type, and finally to the commentary itself. We begin with the prologue (1:1-18), which, like each of the twenty-one sequences that make up the Gospel as a whole, is structured according to a five-section parallel structure (*abcb'a'*).

THE PROLOGUE

1:1-18

The function of the prologue

John's prologue serves as an overture to his Gospel. It is written in stately and solemn prose and summarizes the quintessential message of the Gospel.[1] It testifies to the Johannine community's belief in the divinity of Jesus, his pre-existence, his function in the creation of the world, and his function in the Father's plan for the salvation of humanity. It schematizes in five steps the movement of Jesus' life and mission: (1) his coming into the world as the life and light of the world (vv 1-8); (2) the rejection of him by his own people (vv 9-11); (3) his effect on all those who believe in him (vv 12-13); (4) the acceptance of him by those who saw his glory and believed in him (v 14); (5) his gifts to the world of grace and truth and knowledge of the Father (vv 15-18). The prologue thus sounds the central themes that will be developed at length in the Gospel as a whole.

The background of the prologue

The thought-world of the prologue has been discussed for decades.[2] Some scholars have located it in early Jewish Gnosticism, others in Hellenistic philosophy, and still others in the writings of the Qumran community. More recently scholars have turned to the Old Testament as the thought-world of John's prologue. They have noted the relationship of the prologue to Genesis, especially Gn 1, and to the wisdom literature, especially Prv 8:22-30; Wis 7:22–8:1; 8:10; 9:9-13; Sir 1:20-30; 24:3-21. As we shall see in our commentary, these texts provide a more than adequate thought-world for the statements John makes about Jesus in his prologue. On the influence of Gnosticism, philosophy, and the Qumran community on the prologue, much has been said but little that commands assent. Most scholars would now agree with the judgment of Brown:

> In sum, it seems that the Prologue's description of the Word is far closer to biblical and Jewish strains of thought than it is to anything purely Hellenistic. In the mind of the theologian of the Prologue the creative word of God, the word of the Lord that came to the prophets, has become personal in Jesus who is the embodiment of divine revelation. Jesus is divine Wisdom, pre-existent, but now come among men to teach them and give

19

them life. Not the Torah but Jesus Christ is the creator and source of light and life. He is the *Memra,* God's presence among men. And yet, even though all these strands are woven into the Johannine concept of the Word, this concept remains a unique contribution of Christianity. It is beyond all that has gone before, even as Jesus is beyond all who have gone before.[3]

The structure of the prologue

John structures each of the twenty-one sequences of his Gospel according to a chiastic format. Not surprisingly, the prologue follows the same format. That the prologue is chiastic in format has been recognized by many.[4] That it follows an *abcb'a'* pattern, however, rather than any other chiastic pattern should be credited entirely to Gerhard as an original discovery. His discovery, as we shall see, reinforces the opinion of those who consider the prologue a unity and, at the same time, clarifies considerably the thought-content of the prologue as a whole.[5]

Parallel structure of the prologue

(a) **Through the pre-existing Word,** all things **came to be** (1:1-8).
(b) The true light is **rejected** by his own (1:9-11).
(c) To all who believe, power is given to become children of God (1:12-13).
(b') The Word become flesh is **accepted** by those who beheld his glory (1:14).
(a') **Through Jesus Christ,** grace and truth **came to be** (1:15-18).

Text

(a)   1:1 **In the beginning was the Word,** and the Word **was with God,** and the Word was **God.** [2]He was in the beginning with **God;** [3]**all** things were made **through him,** and without him was not anything made that was made. [4]In him was life, and the life was the light of men. [5]The light shines in the darkness, and the darkness has not overcome it. [6]There was a man sent from **God,** whose name was **John.** [7]He came for testimony, to **bear witness** to the light, that **all** might believe through him. [8]He was not the light, but came to **bear witness** to the light.

(b)   [9]The true light that enlightens every man was coming into the world. [10]He **was in the world,** and the world was made through him, yet **the world knew him not.** [11]He came to his own home, and **his own people received him not.**

(c)   [12]But to all who received him, who believed in his name, he gave power to become children of God; [13]who were born, not of blood nor of the will of the flesh nor of the will of man, but of God.

(b')   [14]And the Word became flesh and **dwelt among us,** full of grace and truth; **we have beheld his glory,** glory as of the only Son from the Father.

(a')   [15]**(John bore witness** to him, and cried, "This was he of whom I said, 'He who comes after me ranks before me, for **he was before me.'** ") [16]And from his fulness have we **all** received, grace upon grace. [17]For the law was given through Moses; grace and truth came **through Jesus Christ.** [18]No one

has ever seen **God;** the only Son, who is **in the bosom of the Father,** he
has made him known.

John creates parallelism between (a) and (a') by mentioning the witness
of the Baptist in v 7 and returning to it in v 15; by re-emphasizing, in the
Baptist's words "he was *before me"* in v 15b, Jesus' pre-existence, first mentioned in v 1; by paralleling "through him," i.e., the Word, in v 3 with
"through Jesus Christ" in v 17; and finally, by paralleling "the Word was
with God" in v 1 with "the only Son, who is *in the bosom of the Father"*
in v 18.

He creates antithetic parallelism in (b) and (b') by contrasting the rejection of Jesus by "his own"—the Jews—in vv 9-11 with the acceptance of
him by those among whom Jesus dwelt and who "beheld his glory" in v 14.

The center (c) deals with the central contention of the Fourth Gospel,
namely, that those who believe in Jesus are born anew and become the
children of God (vv 12-13; cp. 3:5, 16-17; 20:30-31).

Commentary

(a) Through the pre-existing Word, all things came to be (1:1-8).

1:1 In the beginning was the Word. With its manifest allusion to
Gn 1 concerning the creation of all things and especially life and light (vv
3 and 4), these words situate the existence of the Word as prior to creation
(cf. the parallel in v 15b: "he was before me"; see also 8:56-58: "before
Abraham was, I am"). The emphasis of the verb "was" (*ēn* in the Greek)
implies continuing existence, i.e., "was and still is." **And the Word was with
God.** These words imply close union of the Word with God. The Greek for
"with God" is *pros theon* and expresses the movement of the Word "toward"
God. The parallel expression in v 18, "in the bosom of the Father" (*eis ton
kolpon tou patros*), implies the same. **And the Word was God.** These words
testify to the divine nature of the Word. In the Greek (*kai theos ēn ho logos*),
no article is used before the word "God." John eliminates the article in order
to prevent identification of the Word with the Father, to whom the title *ho
theos* properly belongs. In 5:19-30 and 10:29-39, he will make a similar subtle distinction between the Son and the Father.

1:2 He was in the beginning with God. These words reiterate and emphasize the truth enunciated in v 1. The Word existed before creation (cf.
17:4, where Jesus speaks about returning to the position of glory he had with
the Father "before creation").

Concerning the use of the term "the Word" (*Logos*) to describe the pre-
existent Son of God, it should be noted that while "the Word" is used only
here in the prologue, it is nevertheless only one of the expressions used by
John to describe Jesus. In the course of the Gospel, John will speak of Jesus
as "the bread of life" (6:32-58 *passim*); "the light of the world" (8:12); the

"door" of the sheepfold (10:7); the "resurrection and the life" (11:25-26); and "the way, and the truth, and the life" (14:6).

In the context of Gn 1, the term "the Word" is a particularly apt title for Jesus, since God is there described as bringing about all creation through his word alone, e.g., "He said, 'Let there be light, and there was light'" (Gn 1:3). There are allusions here as well to wisdom as spoken about in Prv 8:22, Sir 24, and Wis 7-9. There may even be an echo here of Is 55:11, where God says of his word that "it shall not return to me empty, but it shall accomplish that which I purpose, and prosper in the thing for which I sent it." Finally, it was through his word that God revealed himself to his prophets, and through them to Israel. If a synonym were to be used here for "the Word," the best term would probably be "the revealer." Jesus through his words and his deeds reveals the nature of the Father as one who loves the world (cf. 3:16). In v 18, the chiastic parallel to vv 1-2, it is significant that the prologue concludes with the statement that it is Jesus, "the only Son," who "has made him [the Father] known."

1:3 all things were made through him. Since all things have been given physical existence and life through Jesus, the Word, it will follow in the Gospel that all are called to believe in Jesus in order to receive spiritual, i.e., eternal, life (cf. 3:16-17; 4:10-14; 5:19-30; 6:47-58; 8:12; 10:10, 27; 11:25-26). The emphasis in v 3 is on the agency of Jesus in the creation of the physical universe. In the chiastic parallel of v 17, the emphasis will be on the agency of Jesus in bringing to all humanity God's spiritual gifts of "grace and truth." Here, as in vv 1-2, the reader will find echoes of what was said in Prv 8:30 and Wis 7:12 concerning the role of wisdom in the creation of the world. **And without him was not anything made that was made.** In Hebrew poetry, antithetic parallelism frequently consists in saying the same thing positively and then again negatively. Here John says negatively what he had said positively in v 3a: "all things were made through him."

1:4 In him was life, and the life was the light of men. As the Word, i.e., as the revealer, Jesus communicated the knowledge-love about God necessary for eternal life (cf. 17:3: "And this is eternal life, that they know thee the only true God, and Jesus Christ whom thou hast sent"). It can be said, therefore, that in Jesus one finds life inasmuch as he is the source of life. As revealer of God, Jesus' life in the world made him "the light," i.e., the source of knowledge about God and about eternal life for all humanity (cf. 8:12; 12:34-36). John prefaces this statement to v 5 because in v 5 he is preparing to introduce for the first time a reference to the historical existence of Jesus.[6]

1:5 The light shines in the darkness, and the darkness has not overcome it. That the darkness did not overcome the light is a general statement about the negative response of the Jews to Jesus and about the climax of that negative response—the crucifixion. The Jews thought they had "overcome"

Jesus when they had him put to death, but the resurrection proved that "the darkness" had not overcome the light.

The theme of the opposition between the light and the darkness in relation to the Jewish enemies of Jesus surfaces verbally in 3:19-21; 12:35-36; and 16:3, but it runs throughout the Gospel. The Jews' rejection of Jesus will be stated explicitly in vv 9-11 (b) and contrasted with the acceptance of Jesus by those who believed in him in v 14 (b'). Barrett points out that the verb for "overcome" can also mean to "seize," in the sense of "comprehend" or "understand."[7] Since John likes to use double-meaning words and since the theme of the Jews' refusal to understand Jesus runs throughout the Gospel (cf. 12:37-44), it is quite probable that John is using the verb in both of its meanings. The Jews neither understood Jesus nor succeeded in overcoming him.

1:6-8   There was a man sent from God. A reference to John the Baptist ends section (a), and another reference to him will begin section (a'). What John emphasizes here is the vast difference between Jesus and the Baptist. The Baptist came *only as a witness* (cf. 3:27-36, where the Baptist himself harps upon this difference); Jesus alone is the light. The Baptist came so that through his witness to Jesus, all might believe in Jesus. In 1:35-42, John will describe how Jesus' first disciples came to believe in him as a result of the Baptist's witness to him.

(b) The true light is rejected by his own (1:9-11).

1:9   The true light that enlightens every man. Jesus is the source of light, and therefore of revelation and life for all men. John prefaces this statement about the universality of Jesus' impact on humanity because he is about to contrast here in (b), by antithetic parallelism, the rejection of Jesus by his own people, the Jews, with the acceptance of Jesus by believers in section (b').

1:10   He was in the world. The word "world" has a double meaning in this verse. The words "and the world was made through him" clarify the first meaning as referring to the physical world and humanity as a whole in the sense already expressed in vv 3-4. It is this world of all humanity that God "so loved that he gave his only Son" (3:16). "World," however, in the words "yet the world knew him not" has a more restricted meaning. It refers in a general sense to all who are opposed to Jesus, to all at any time who prefer the darkness to the light (cf. 3:19-21). More specifically, as v 11 shows, "world" refers to the Jews of the synagogue who rejected Jesus and brought about his death (cf. 15:18-25).

1:11   his own people received him not. These John's saddest words, encapsulate a theme that runs from beginning to end of his Gospel (cf. 1:19-28; 2:13-25; 3:11; 5:18; 7:1, 20; 8:40; 9:40-41; 10:31; 11:45-54; 15:18-25; 19:4-16).

(c) To all who believe, power is given to become children of God (1:12-13).

Many who argue for a chiastic structure in the prologue rightly identify vv 12-13 or some section of vv 12-13 as the center of the chiasm.[8] They do so for several reasons: (1) vv 12-13 deal with *all* people and specify the crucial difference between believers and nonbelievers; (2) this crucial difference is spelled out in the verses on either side of vv 12-13, i.e., in vv 9-11 (b), where John deals with the nonbelievers, the Jews, and in v 14 (b'), where he deals with the believers; (3) vv 12-13 concentrate on an important theme of the Gospel, namely, the identity of the true versus the false children of God (cf. 3:3-21; 5:31-47; 6:59-69; 8:31-47; 10:25-29); (4) vv 12-13 do not properly parallel any other verses in the prologue, although this is disputed by some.[9]

1:12ab But to all who received him. To "receive," i.e., to believe in Jesus, is for John the key to eternal life (cf. 3:3-29 and *passim* throughout the Gospel). It is the key to eternal life for *all*. This general statement fits with the universal scope of Jesus' mission: he is "the Lamb of God, who takes away the sin of the world" (1:29); the "light of the world" (8:12); and when "lifted up from the earth," he will "draw all men to himself" (12:32).

1:12c he gave power to become children of God. The Old Testament often refers to the Israelites as the children of God (cf. Ex 4:22; Dt 14:1; Hos 11:1; Jer 3:19). The New Testament frequently uses the phrase or its equivalent in the context of a debate dealing with the question, Who are the true sons of God, i.e., who is it, the synagogue or the Christian Church, that constitutes the true Israel of God? (cf. Mt 3:9; 11:9; 21:28; Gal 3:25; 4:6-7; Rom 8:14-17, 21, 29; Eph 5:1, 8; 1 Jn 3:1-2, 10; 5:2). The theme of the true versus the false children of God is central to John's Gospel and is therefore fittingly given the central position in his prologue, in which he summarizes the major themes of his Gospel (for the theme "the children of God," cf. 3:3-21; 8:31-47; 11:52; 20:17; see also 14:18, 23).

Since John has already identified the false children of God as the Jewish nation in vv 9-11 (b) and will immediately designate the true children of God as the "us" and the "we" of v 14 (b'), it is readily understandable that a statement containing the criterion for determining the true "children of God" should find its logical position in vv 12-13 (c), between vv 9-11 (b) and v 14 (b'). From the beginning to the end of his Gospel, John insists on faith as the ultimate criterion for eternal life, union with Jesus, and discipleship. It is no accident that when he expresses the purpose for which he wrote his Gospel, he says, "These [things] are written that you may believe that Jesus is the Christ, the Son of God, and that believing you may have life in his name" (20:31).

1:13 who were born. The children of God are born by the will of God and not through any agency of man, i.e., by grace and not by nature. Jesus' discourse to Nicodemus deals precisely with the origin of the children of God and states unequivocally that they are born from above through water and the Holy Spirit (3:3-9). Supernatural life, in short, is a gift from God. **Not of blood.** These words rule out procreation through the blood of the father and mother, a popular ancient belief concerning the origin of life. **Nor of the will of the flesh.** These words probably refer to sexual desire, just as the following words, "nor of the will of man," probably refer to the initiation of human birth by the father. All these are ruled out because the initiative in the birth of the children of God comes from God alone.

(b') The Word become flesh is accepted by those who beheld his glory (1:14).

1:14a And the Word became flesh and dwelt among us. Without ceasing to be the divine Word, pre-existent with the Father (vv 1-2), the Word takes on human flesh and is henceforth both divine and human. To become flesh, therefore, is the equivalent of "to be born as a human being," although the verb used (*egeneto*) does not have the same strict meaning of "to be born" that it has in v 13 (*egennēthēsan*). The Word not only became flesh, he "dwelt among us." The verb for "dwelt" (*eskēnōsen*) is derived from the noun for "tent" (*skēnē*) and has the sense of "he pitched his tent among us." It re-echoes loudly God's coming to dwell with his people in the tabernacle, i.e., tent, as described in Ex 40:34-38. In v 11 (b), the Word "came to his own home [the Jewish nation], and his own people received him not." Here in (b'), John contrasts the reception of Jesus by the Christian community (v 14) with his rejection by the Jewish nation (v 11).

full of grace and truth. These words are best understood from their Old Testament Sinai covenant ambient, where they testify to God's grace and truth, i.e., his love and fidelity (Hebrew: *hesed w^eemeth*). That the Word "dwelt among *us*" emphasizes the Johannine contention that the Christian community alone, in contrast to the Jewish nation, which "received him not" (v 11), constitutes the true Israel of the new covenant. Recognition of the antithetic parallelism created by John between vv 9-11 (b) and v 14 (b') is essential for grasping the full import of John's statement in v 14.

1:14b we have beheld his glory. *"We,"* and not the Jewish nation, have beheld the glory of the incarnate God. The word "glory" *(doxa)*, from the Hebrew *chabod*, signifies the outward manifestation of inward divinity (cf. Is 6:3 and Jn 12:41; Mk 9:2-8; Phil 2:6-7). The statement testifies, therefore, to the Johannine community's belief in the divinity of the incarnate Word— that belief which the Jewish nation refused to accept. **Glory as of the only Son from the Father.** Jesus' glory comes from his relationship with the Father. He is one with the Father as God but distinct from him as a person. John will explain the relationship of the Son with the Father at length in 5:19-47; 7:1–8:59; 10:31-38. Throughout the Gospel, he will insist that the Jews have refused to see and accept the glory, i.e., the divinity, of Jesus as the only-begotten Son sent by the Father for the salvation of the world.

(a') Through Jesus Christ, grace and truth came to be (1:15-18).

1:15 John bore witness to him. By returning to the person (the Baptist) and the content (the Baptist's witness to Jesus) of vv 7-8 with which he concluded section (a), John signals the beginning of section (a') of his chiastic structure for the prologue. In vv 15-18 (a'), he repeats and at the same time goes beyond what he said about the Word in vv 1-8 (a). The Baptist's witness that "he who comes after me ranks before me, for he *was before me"* testifies directly to Jesus' pre-eminence and indirectly to his pre-existence, first mentioned in v 1. The Baptist will testify at length to Jesus' nature and power in 1:19-34 and 3:27-36.

1:16 And from his fulness have we all received, grace upon grace. It is important to note that John reintroduces the Baptist in v 15 not only because he wants to create a parallel with vv 7-8 (a), but also because the Baptist represents the Old Testament (he is the last of the Old Testament prophets); and John, in this verse and the verses that follow (vv 17-18), intends to contrast the great gift of the law given by God through Moses with the much greater gifts of grace and truth given by God through Jesus. Thus, while "grace upon grace" could mean grace after grace in a cumulative sense, it is far more likely that it means grace in place of grace, in the sense that the greater grace brought through Jesus and the new covenant surpasses abundantly the grace of the old covenant.

1:17 For the law was given through Moses. The contrast between Moses and Jesus is not meant to denigrate Moses but rather to extol Jesus. John is not against the law of Moses but against its interpretation by the Pharisees (cf. 5:1-18; 9:1-38). He sees the law as God's gift to Israel and recognizes Moses as a witness to Jesus (cf. 1:45; 5:45-47). The point he is trying to make here is that the "grace and truth" that come through Jesus far surpass the gift of the law given through Moses in the old covenant. Jesus, as the prologue stated in v 14, is "full of grace and truth." It should be noted that the words "grace and truth" here in the (a') section of the prologue parallel broadly the words "light and life" in vv 4-5 of the (a) section.

1:18a No one has ever seen God. It was popularly believed in the Old Testament that no one could see God and live (cf. Dt 4:12; Ps 97:2; Is 6:5). The contrast between Jesus and Moses is continued here. Moses never saw God. Jesus, on the contrary, as the only-begotten Son of God, is always in the presence of God and has not only seen him but "has made him known," i.e., he has revealed him to the world. In and through Jesus, the world hears, sees, and knows the Father (cf. 8:38; 12:45; 14:9). As Hoskyns puts it, "Sight comes to rest, not in a psychological, mystical experience, but in the historical relationship between the disciples and the man Jesus."[10] John does not explain here to whom Jesus "has made him [God] known." In v 14b, however, he stated, "We have beheld his glory, glory as of the only Son from the Father." The "we" refers to the disciples of Jesus and to the Johannine community. Thus, through the Christian community, God is revealed to the world through Jesus.

1:18b who is in the bosom of the Father. The metaphor attests to the intimacy of the Father and the Son and is best illustrated by John's remark about the Beloved Disciple in 13:23: "One of his disciples, whom Jesus loved, was lying close to the breast of Jesus."

The prologue concludes as it began. It began with Jesus called the Word (v 1); it concludes with Jesus declared to be the revealer of the invisible Father (v 18). It began with the statement that "the Word was God" (v 1); it ends with the only Son called God (v 18). It began with the observation that "the Word was with God" (v 1); it concludes with the only Son "in the bosom of the Father" (v 18).

The inclusions that link vv 1 and 18 have been noticed by many scholars. What has not been noticed is that vv 15-18 (a') parallel vv 1-8 (a), just as v 14 (b') parallels vv 9-11 (b). With vv 12-13 (c) in the center, the prologue has a clearly defined *abcb'a'* structure. As we shall see, this structure recurs in each of the twenty-one sequences of the Gospel and even in sections and subsections of sequences. It is so pervasive, so regular, so almost automatic that we might well speak of it not only as the most common of the Johannine rhetorical techniques but as the habitual and almost subconscious rhythmic movement of the Johannine thought-process.

Chiastic parallels in the prologue

(a) vv 1-8	*(a') vv 15-18*
v 1: In the beginning	v 15: He was before me
v 1: was the Word	v 18: He has made him known
v 1: The Word was with God	v 18: in the bosom of the Father
v 1: The Word was God	v 18: the only Son
v 3: All things made through him	v 17: grace and truth through Jesus Christ
v 4: life and light	v 17: grace and truth
vv 6-8: John . . . came . . . to bear witness.	v 15: John bore witness

(b) vv 9-11	*(b') v 14*
v 10: he was in the world	v 14a: The Word became flesh
v 11: his own people received him not.	v 14bc: He dwelt among us . . . we have beheld his glory.

(c) vv 12-13

v 12c: Power to become children of
God

When these parallels are placed side by side and their thought-content is compared and summarized, as they should be in a presentation according to the laws of parallelism, the reader is enabled to grasp the full meaning and thrust of John's theological message. Expressed according to the laws of narrative, the summarized content of (a) and (a′) and (b) and (b′) would read as follows:

> The Word, who is the only Son of God and who has made God known, existed in the beginning with the Father and in the bosom of the Father. He existed before creation just as he existed before the Baptist who bore witness to him. All things were made through him and came to be through him—light and life, grace and truth. He was indeed full of grace and truth.
>
> The Word became flesh and came into the world as the light of the world. The darkness of the world neither understood nor overcame him. He came to his own home, and his own people received him not. But he dwelt among us; we have beheld his glory, glory as the only Son from the Father, and we declare that "to all who received him, he gave power to become children of God, children who were born, not of blood nor of the will of the flesh nor of the will of man, but of God."
>
> Moses gave us God's gift of the law. But Jesus, who is full of grace and truth, has given us the greater gift—grace and truth. He has in addition revealed to us the Father.

Part I

WITNESS TO JESUS
1:19–4:3

Part I concentrates on Jesus' manifestation of himself to the world through the testimony of the Baptist, the Holy Spirit, the disciples, and his own works (signs) and words. The evangelist, in short, presents the credentials of Jesus for the reader's examination.

The whole of part I is framed chiastically by the witness of the Baptist, beginning with his witness to Jesus by the Jordan in sequence 1 (1:19-39) and ending with his final witness to Jesus at Aenon near Salim in sequence 5 (3:22–4:3). Thus the Baptist's witness forms a major inclusion-conclusion for the whole of part I.

In sequence 2 (2:1-12) and sequence 4 (3:1-21), the evangelist achieves chiastic parallelism by balancing the mysterious change of water into wine at Cana with the mysterious rebirth from on high brought about through water and the Holy Spirit in the Nicodemus narrative. In the center (c), Jesus in Jerusalem for the feast of the Passover speaks about his passion, death, and resurrection (2:13-25). The relationship of the sequences can be seen in the following outline of their parallel structure.

Parallel structure of part I

(a) *Sequence 1 (1:19-51):*   **The Baptist witnesses to Jesus.**
(b) *Sequence 2 (2:1-12):*   **Water** replaced by wine at Cana
(c) *Sequence 3 (2:13-25):*   Jesus cleanses the temple.
(b′) *Sequence 4 (3:1-21):*   Rebirth through **water** and the Spirit
(a′) *Sequence 5 (3:22–4:3):* **The Baptist witnesses to Jesus** again.

Sequence 1

THE BAPTIST WITNESSES TO JESUS

1:19-51

Parallel structure

(a) The Baptist **witnesses** to Jesus (1:19-39).

(b) Andrew **finds** Simon (1:40-41).

(c) Jesus changes Simon's name to Peter (1:42).

(b') Philip **finds** Nathanael (1:43-45).

(a') Nathanael **witnesses** to Jesus (1:46-51).

Text

(a)   1:19 And this is the testimony of John, when the Jews sent priests and Levites from Jerusalem to ask him, "Who are you?" ²⁰He confessed, he did not deny, but confessed, "I am not the Christ." ²¹And they asked him, "What then? Are you Elijah?" He said, "I am not." "Are you the prophet?" And he answered, "No." ²²They said to him then, "Who are you? Let us have an answer for those who sent us. What do you say about yourself?" ²³He said, "I am the voice of one crying in the wilderness, 'Make straight the way of the Lord,' as the prophet Isaiah said."

²⁴Now they had been sent from the Pharisees. ²⁵They asked him, "Then why are you baptizing, if you are neither the Christ, nor Elijah, nor the prophet?" ²⁶John answered them, "I baptize with water; but among you stands one whom you do not **know,** ²⁷even he who comes after me, the thong of whose sandal I am not worthy to untie." ²⁸This took place in Bethany beyond the Jordan, where John was baptizing.

²⁹The next day **he saw Jesus coming** toward him, and said, "Behold, the Lamb of God, who takes away the sin of the world! ³⁰This is he of whom I said, 'After me comes a man who ranks before me, for he was before me.' ³¹I myself did not **know** him; but for this I came baptizing with water, that he might be revealed to **Israel."** ³²And John bore witness, "**I saw** the Spirit **descend** as a dove from **heaven,** and it remained on him. ³³I myself did not **know** him; but he who sent me to baptize with water said to me, 'He on whom you see the Spirit **descend** and remain, this is he who baptizes with the Holy Spirit.' ³⁴And I have **seen** and have borne witness that this is the **Son of God."**

³⁵The next day again John was standing with two of his disciples; ³⁶and he looked at Jesus as he walked, and said, "**Behold,** the Lamb of God!" ³⁷The two disciples heard him say this, and they followed Jesus. ³⁸Jesus turned, and **saw** them following, and said to them, "What do you seek?"

30

And they said to him, **"Rabbi"** (which means Teacher), "where are you staying?" ³⁹He said to them, "Come and see." They came and **saw** where he was staying; and they stayed with him that day, for it was about the tenth hour.

(b)   ⁴⁰One of the two who heard John speak, and followed him, was **Andrew, Simon Peter's** brother. ⁴¹He first **found** his brother Simon, **and said to him, "We have found** the Messiah" (which means Christ).

(c)   ⁴²He brought him to Jesus. Jesus looked at him, and said, "So you are Simon the son of John? You shall be called Cephas" (which means Peter).

(b′)   ⁴³The next day Jesus decided to go to Galilee. And he **found** Philip **and said to him,** "Follow me." ⁴⁴Now Philip was from Bethsaida, the city of **Andrew** and **Peter.** ⁴⁵Philip **found** Nathanael, **and said to him, "We have found** him of whom Moses in the law and also the prophets wrote, Jesus of Nazareth, the son of Joseph."

(a′)   ⁴⁶Nathanael said to him, "Can anything good come out of Nazareth?" Philip said to him, **"Come and see."** ⁴⁷Jesus **saw Nathanael coming to him, and said of him, "Behold,** an Israelite indeed, in whom is no guile!" ⁴⁸Nathanael said to him, "How do you **know** me?" Jesus answered him, "Before Philip called you, when you were under the fig tree, I **saw** you." ⁴⁹Nathanael answered him, **"Rabbi, you are the Son of God!** You are the King of **Israel!"** ⁵⁰Jesus answered him, "Because I said to you, I **saw** you under the fig tree, do you believe? You shall **see** greater things than these." ⁵¹And he said to him, "Truly, truly, I say to you, you will see **heaven** opened, and the angels of God ascending and **descending** upon the Son of man."

The reader who compares the words in bold print in (a) and (a′) will notice that John has created chiastic parallels by repeating identical words and expressions in each. In v 29, John says the Baptist "saw Jesus coming toward him, and said, 'Behold, ...' "; in v 47, Jesus "saw Nathanael coming to him, and said of him, 'Behold, ...' " In v 32, the Baptist says, "I saw the Spirit descend as a dove from heaven . . . ."; in v 51, Jesus tells Nathanael, "You will see heaven opened, and the angels of God . . . descending upon the Son of Man." In v 34, the Baptist declares, "And I have . . . borne witness that this is the Son of God"; Nathanael, in v 49, repeats this witness by declaring, "You are the Son of God." In v 38, the two disciples address Jesus as "Rabbi"; similarly, in v 49, Nathanael addresses Jesus as "Rabbi." In v 39, Jesus says to the two disciples, "Come and see"; Philip, in v 46, says the same to Nathanael. Lesser parallels are the words "Israel," "see," "know," and "descending."

In (b) and (b′), John creates parallelism by mentioning Andrew and Simon Peter in both sections (vv 40 and 44) and by paralleling the actions of Andrew and Philip. In v 41, John writes: "[Andrew] first found his brother Simon, and said to him, 'We have found . . . .' "; and in v 45, using the identical words, he writes: "Philip found Nathanael, and said to him, 'We have found . . . .' "

The center (c) concentrates on Simon Peter and foreshadows his mission as the "Rock," the vicar of Christ. In sequence 21, Simon Peter, the "Rock," will be commissioned by Jesus to be the vicar-shepherd of his sheep (21:16-19).

Commentary

Following the prologue and serving as a more prosaic introduction to the Gospel as a whole, 1:19-51 deals immediately with the central theme of the Gospel—the Johannine community's witness to Jesus as the Redeemer of the world. Jesus is "the Lamb of God, who takes away the sin of the world," the pre-existent Son of God, the one upon whom the Spirit descends and remains, the one about whom Moses in the law and also the prophets wrote, the Messiah, the King of Israel, and the Son of Man.[1]

The witness to Jesus is massively theological and achieves its impact by means of two literary techniques: first, a parade of witnesses, led by the Baptist (1:19-34), includes the Holy Spirit (vv 32-33), the disciples Andrew (v 41), Philip (v 45), and Nathanael (v 49), and concludes with the witness of Jesus himself (v 51). Second, a heaping up of titles, which begins with the Baptist's testimony to him "who comes after me, the thong of whose sandal I am not worthy to untie" (1:27), includes the "Lamb of God" (vv 29-36), the pre-existent one (v 30), the one upon whom the "Spirit descends as a dove from heaven" (vv 32-33), and "the Son of God" (1:34), continues with Andrew's testimony that Jesus is the Messiah (v 41), Philip's testimony that Jesus is the one "of whom Moses in the law and also the prophets wrote" (v 45), and Nathanael's testimony, "You are the Son of God! You are the King of Israel!" (v 49). It concludes with Jesus' speaking about himself as "the Son of man" (v 51).[2]

We call the parade of witnesses and the heaping up of titles literary techniques because the author uses them for theological purposes rather than to describe what actually happened and what actually was said. Scholarly opinion is unanimous in agreeing that recognition of Jesus as the Messiah came late rather than early, and recognition of Jesus' divinity and pre-existence came even later.[3]

(a) The Baptist witnesses to Jesus (1:19-39).

The Baptist's witness unfolds over three days. On the first day, he witnesses before the priests and Levites sent from Jerusalem (vv 19-28); on the second day, he witnesses in the presence of Jesus (vv 29-34); and on the third day, he witnesses in the presence of his disciples (vv 35-39). His witness ends, fittingly, with two of his disciples leaving him to follow Jesus (vv 37-39). As John will later say, "He must increase, but I must decrease" (3:30).

1:19 the Jews. John regularly refers in this way both to the Jews opposed to Jesus and to the official leaders of Judaism, especially the Pharisees (cf. 2:18; 5:10, 18; 6:41, 52; 7:11; 8:22; 9:18). It is unusual that Pharisees should send an official delegation (1:24), since the priests had greater authority than the Pharisees. Probably the author reflects conditions at the end of the first century, when the Pharisees, rather than the priests, had become the official leaders of Judaism. This fits with the delegation's barely disguised hostility toward the Baptist, a hostility not nearly so manifest at the beginning of Jesus' ministry.

1:20 I am not the Christ. The Baptist's rejection of such titles as Messiah, Elijah, and the prophet both here and in 3:27-28 may well be, as many have suggested, part of a polemic against followers of the Baptist at the end of the first century. The evangelist's more immediate purpose, however, is to show the Baptist decreasing and Jesus by contrast increasing. This will be the central theme of sequence 5 (3:22-4:3), which is the chiastic parallel to sequence 1 in part I of the Gospel.

1:21 Are you Elijah? It was popularly believed that Elijah would return as the forerunner of the Messiah (cf. Mal 3:23; Mk 9:11-13). Some early Christians saw the Baptist in this way (cf. Mt 11:14; 17:12; Mk 9:13). Others, like John and his community, did not. **Are you the prophet?** On the basis of Dt 18:18 and perhaps 1 Mc 4:46; 14:41, some expected the Messiah to be the Mosaic prophet of the end-time.[4]

1:22-23 Who are you? The Baptist denies that he is the Messiah, Elijah, or the prophet and identifies himself as the forerunner of the Messiah by applying to himself the text of Is 40:3, in which "a voice cries: 'Prepare the way . . . in the desert.' " Since the Baptist preaches in the desert and declares himself the forerunner of the Messiah, the text from Isaiah is particularly appropriate to describe him and his function.

1:24-27 Then why are you baptizing? The official delegation, acting as watchdogs in religious matters, as they do throughout John's Gospel (cf. 2:18; 7:45-52; 8:13; 9:13-34), wants to know the religious significance of John's baptism. The question allows the Baptist to depreciate his own work and shift attention from himself to Jesus, the one whom the hostile officials will refuse to recognize (cf. 2:18ff; 3:11; 5:16-18; 7:11-30; 7:45-52 and *passim*). John baptizes with water; Jesus will baptize with water and the Holy Spirit (cf. 1:31-33; 3:5).

1:28 Bethany beyond the Jordan. The location of this place, also mentioned in 10:40-42, is disputed. It seems to have been somewhere east of the Jordan, a good distance from the Bethany of Mary, Martha, and Lazarus near Jerusalem (cf. 11:1ff), from which it is clearly distinguished in 10:40-42 and 11:5-6.

1:29 Behold, the Lamb of God. The theology of universal redemption involved in taking away the "sin of the world" is based on Jesus' death on the cross. The metaphorical name "Lamb of God" has a double background in Johannine theology: first, the Suffering Servant of Is 52:13-53:12, who is described as "like a lamb that is led to the slaughter" (Is 53:7 and cf. 1 Jn 3:5); second, the paschal lamb of the Jewish Passover. In 19:36, the evangelist sees fulfilled in Jesus' death the command of Ex 12:46: "Break none of his bones," a regulation concerning the sacrifice of the paschal lamb.

It is significant as well in regard to the death of Jesus at the Passover that the evangelist makes his first explicit reference to Jesus' death when Jesus declares at the Passover in Jerusalem: "Destroy this temple, and in three days I will raise it up" (2:18-21). In 6:4, where the evangelist again mentions the Passover, Jesus' death is implicit in the Eucharistic terminology used in telling the story of the multiplication of the loaves (6:11) and in the discourse on the bread of life (6:32-58) in Jesus' statement about eating the flesh of the Son of man and drinking his blood (6:53, 56). In the chiastic structure of the Gospel, it is no accident that sequences 1 and 21 both refer to taking away sin *(hamartia)*—here in 1:29, with the reference to the Lamb of God who takes away the sin of the world; and in 20:23, where the risen Lamb of God gives to his disciples the power to take away sins *(hamartias)*.

1:30　for he was before me. In these words the Baptist witnesses to Jesus' pre-existence, just as the evangelist does in the prologue (1:1-3) and as Jesus himself does in his words "Before Abraham was, I am" (8:58).

1:31　I came . . . that he might be revealed to Israel. The Baptist does not mean that he did not know Jesus at all but that he did not know him for who he truly was, the Lamb of God, etc. In line with his avowed purpose to decrease that Jesus may increase, the Baptist declares that his whole ministry has been carried out solely in preparation for the coming of Jesus.

1:32-33　I saw the Spirit descend . . . and it remained on him. The coming of the Spirit upon the Messiah had been foretold (cf. Is 11:2; 61:1). In 1:51, which belongs to the (a') section of sequence 1, the evangelist will parallel this descent *(katabainon)* of the Spirit upon Jesus with the angels descending *(katabainontas)* upon the Son of Man. In 3:34, speaking again about Jesus and the Spirit, the Baptist will say, ". . . it is not by measure that he [God] gives the Spirit." In each case the meaning is the same—Jesus has received the fullness of the Spirit.

1:34　the Son of God. The Baptist concludes his testimony by witnessing solemnly to the divinity of Jesus. Some translations (e.g., the New American Bible) prefer the reading "God's chosen one" *(eklektos tou theou)*, as do many commentators.[5] However, the reading "Son of God" *(ho huios tou theou)* is found in the majority of the manuscripts. Also, while one would ordinarily prefer the more difficult reading *(eklektos)*, since it is hard to imagine a scribe changing "Son of God" to "chosen one," in this case the clear parallel to 1:34 in Nathanael's statement "You are the Son of God" in 1:49 would indicate that the easier reading should indeed be preferred. The fact that 1:34 occurs in (a) and 1:49 in (a'), precisely where one would expect to find such parallels in a Gospel written according to the laws of parallelism, gives added support to the reading "Son of God." Thus, parallelism supports the reading found in the majority of the manuscripts.

1:35-37 two of his disciples. The Baptist's witness prompts two of his disciples to follow Jesus. It is clear from 1:40 that one of the two is Andrew, the brother of Peter. The other is not named and has sometimes been identified as Philip, who is mentioned along with Andrew in 6:5-9 and 12:22. More probably the second unnamed disciple is the Beloved Disciple, who in 21:7 (part of sequence 21, which is the chiastic parallel of sequence 1) points Jesus out to Peter, just as Andrew in 1:41 points Jesus out to Peter. Andrew tells Peter, "We have found the Messiah." The unnamed disciple in 21:7 tells Peter, "It is the Lord!" Parallelism suggests that the unnamed disciple in sequence 1 is the same as the unnamed disciple in sequence 21.

1:38-39 Come and see. Jesus' reply in 1:38 (a) will be paralleled in 1:46 (a') when Philip replies to Nathanael's skepticism about Jesus' origin from Nazareth with the same words: "Come and see." The tenth hour (4 P.M.) is perhaps mentioned (v 39) because of its importance for the disciples. With these two disciples, Jesus begins to gather his Twelve.

(b) Andrew finds Simon (1:40-41).

1:41 We have found the Messiah. The grounds for Andrew's startling conclusion are not clear. He has stayed with Jesus, and presumably Jesus has explained the scriptures to him (v 39). The evangelist, however, is interested only in Andrew's conclusion, not in how he arrived at it. In 1:43-45 (b'), Philip will find Nathanael and say to him, as Andrew said to Simon, "We have found . . . ."[6]

(c) Jesus changes Simon's name to Peter (1:42).

1:42 You shall be called Cephas. In the Scriptures, change of name signifies change of role or destiny in the history of salvation (cf. Gn 17:5; 32:28). The significance of the name Cephas ("rock") is explained ecclesiologically by Matthew (Mt 16:16-18). John takes for granted that his readers understand the meaning of the name. In 21:16-19, he will explain the ecclesiological importance of the change of name when he tells how Jesus commissions Peter to be shepherd of his sheep. The two episodes—the change of name in sequence 1 (1:42) and the appointment as shepherd of the sheep in sequence 21 (21:16-19)—are chiastically paralleled. They cannot, therefore, be the work of an ecclesiastical redactor, as so many have claimed after Bultmann.[7] Schnackenburg grasps the significance of the little episode when he says, ". . . the Johannine Jesus already has the vision of the later Church before his eyes as he gathers his first disciples around him."[8]

(b') Philip finds Nathanael (1:43-45).

1:43-44 he found Philip. As Andrew "found" Peter (v 41), Jesus finds Philip, who is from the same town as Andrew and Peter—Bethsaida, a town on the northeast shore of the Lake of Galilee. Jesus' intention of going to

Galilee (v 43a) and his immediate finding and calling of Philip (v 43b), who is from Galilee (v 44), may have some connection, but it is certainly not clear. The parallelism between vv 40-41 and 43-45 suggests that Philip may be the second of the two unnamed disciples in vv 35-37.

1:45 Philip found Nathanael. In a perfect parallel with v 41, Philip finds Nathanael, as Andrew "found" Peter, and repeats verbatim Andrew's first words to Peter: "We have found . . . ." Like the Baptist and Andrew before him, Philip witnesses to Jesus, testifying that he is the one about whom "Moses in the law and also the prophets wrote." His testimony is equivalent to saying that in Jesus the prophecies of the Old Testament have been fulfilled—a belief shared by all the writers of the New Testament (e.g., Mt 1-2 and *passim;* Lk 24:27). Nathanael, otherwise unknown in the New Testament, is mentioned twice by John—here in sequence 1 and again in 21:2, which is part of sequence 21, the chiastic parallel of sequence 1. Since some of the apostles had more than one name, it has been suggested that Nathanael may be another name for Bartholomew or perhaps Matthew, but these are conjectures, and the only good support for holding that Nathanael is one of the Twelve is the fact that he appears with other apostles in both sequence 1 and 21. He is not mentioned in the Synoptics' list of apostles (cf. Mk 3:16-19; Mt 10:2-4; Lk 6:13-16).

(a') Nathanael witnesses to Jesus (1:46-51).

We have begun section (a') at v 46 because, with the words "Come and see" in v 46, the evangelist begins to repeat a number of words and expressions that have an exact correspondence with words and expressions in 1:19-39, the (a) section.

1:46 Can anything good come out of Nazareth? Nazareth was unimportant religiously and politically and was nowhere mentioned in the Old Testament. With mixed disdain and doubt, therefore, Nathanael expresses his skepticism in a manner not unlike that of doubting Thomas in 20:24-29. Philip's response, "Come and see," parallels Jesus' response to the two unnamed disciples in 1:38. When Nathanael sees Jesus, his doubt, like that of Thomas, evaporates.

1:47a Jesus saw Nathanael coming to him. When the Baptist sees Jesus coming to him, he says, "Behold, the Lamb of God . . . ." (1:29); when Jesus sees Nathanael coming to him, he says, "Behold, an Israelite indeed, in whom there is no guile." In contrast to so many of the Jews in John's Gospel, Nathanael is refreshingly willing to "come and see." Because of his willingness, Jesus bestows on him the encomium "an Israelite indeed, in whom there is no guile."

1:47 in whom is no guile. This is possibly a comparison with guileful Jacob, the first to bear the name Israel (Gn 32:28-30, 35). Brown suggests the explanation that "Nathanael is the last of the disciples to be called, and in him is fulfilled the purpose for which John the Baptist had come: 'The very reason why I came and baptized with water was that he (Jesus) might be revealed to *Israel* (1:31).' "[9] The parallelism formed by "Israel" in 1:31 in (a) with 1:47 in (a') would support this suggestion.

1:48 How do you know me? Jesus' foreknowledge concerning Nathanael's being "under the fig tree" before Philip called him is characteristic of the Johannine Jesus, who knows all things (cf. 2:23-25; 3:14-18; 4:16-18; 13:1). In this case, such manifest foreknowledge, combined with Nathanael's willingness to come and see, is more than enough to elicit Nathanael's act of faith.

1:49 Rabbi, you are the Son of God! Nathanael, like the disciples in 1:38 (a), addresses Jesus as "Rabbi." He continues, however, with the astounding witness to Jesus, "You are the Son of God." In so doing, he repeats the Baptist's identical witness in 1:34 (a) and, equivalently, the witness of doubting Thomas in 20:28, "My Lord and my God," thereby creating parallels exactly where the reader should expect to find them: first, between (a') and (a) in sequence 1; second, between sequence 1 (1:19-51) and sequence 21 (20:19–21:25).

Some authors, e.g., Mowinckel,[10] understand "Son of God" in the diluted sense of the title found in such Old Testament texts as 2 Sm 7:14; Ps 2:6-7; Ps 89:27, where the Davidic king is spoken of as God's adopted son. In support, they adduce the companion title "You are the king of Israel." It is true that in the Old Testament texts the two titles would be equivalent. In John's Gospel, however, belief in Jesus' divinity and pre-existence has already been expressed in the prologue (1:1ff) and in the witness of the Baptist (1:30, 34). Considering the chiastic parallelism between 1:49 and 1:34, and between sequence 1 and sequence 21, in which Thomas' testimony "My Lord and my God" parallels the testimony in 1:34 and 1:49, there would seem little doubt that the title in 1:49 should be given its full weight.

1:50a Because I said to you, I saw you under the fig tree, do you believe? Jesus' reply to doubting Thomas in 20:29, "Have you believed because you have seen me," poses a similar question—a question that will recur throughout the Gospel, namely, what is the foundation or source of true, salvific faith? (cf. 2:23-25; 4:42; 4:48; 6:28-30; 9:40-41; 12:37-43).

1:50b You shall see greater things than these. The promise will be fulfilled in one way in the Gospel through the miracles (signs) that are recounted, beginning with the change of water into wine at Cana, Nathanael's hometown. It will be fulfilled in a far more complete way, however, through the revelatory discourses of Jesus with which the Gospel is filled. In the chiastic parallelism of sequence 21 with sequence 1, there is perhaps a faint echo of these "greater things" in the closing words of the Gospel: "But there are also many other things which Jesus did; were every one of them to be written, I suppose that the world itself could not contain the books that would be written'' (21:25 and cp. 20:30).

1:51   angels of God ascending and descending upon the Son of man. The symbolic imagery is based upon the vision of Jacob in Gn 28:12-17, in which he sees a stairway or ramp upon which angels are ascending and descending. ''Heaven opened'' is symbolic language for God revealing. The angels ascending and descending are symbolic of the union of Jesus and the Father and of their uninterrupted intercommunication. The symbolism of the ''angels ascending and descending *upon* the Son of man'' is to designate Jesus as the place (like Bethel—''house of God'') of God's full revelation.[11] As Jacob said of his dream, ''This is none other than the house of God, and this is the gate of heaven'' (Gn 28:17).

This intercommunication and mutuality of presence between Jesus and the Father is expressed even more cogently in the later words of Jesus: ''I know him, for I come from him, and he sent me'' (7:29), and ''Not that any one has seen the Father except him who is from God; he has seen the Father'' (6:46). What Nathanael and the others will ''see,'' therefore, in the signs that follow, and especially in the passion, is Jesus' union with the Father, the union of his manhood with the Father, the union that is the substance and cause of his ''glory.'' Jn 1:51 is programmatic in the sense that it announces the purpose of the ''signs,'' which is to reveal Jesus' union with the Father for those who have eyes (faith) to ''see.'' What they will see is Jesus' union with the Father, which constitutes his ''glory.'' The statement in 2:11 that Jesus ''manifested his glory'' in the Cana miracle should be read as a reference back to 1:51, which in turn looks forward to all the signs of the remainder of the Gospel and to the many texts referring to Jesus' glory, Jesus' hour, and Jesus' work. Dodd's observations indicate both the unity and the subtlety of John's thought-process:

> The whole series of 'signs' which follows, culminating in the supreme sign of the cross and resurrection, is the vision of the heaven opened and the angels of God ascending and descending upon the Son of Man. And these 'signs' are history. ''The Logos was made flesh—and we beheld His glory.'' Whatever else, therefore, the Gospel story is to be, it is to be a realized apocalypse. . . . There is a far-reaching equivalence of the two propositions: ''The Logos became flesh and dwelt among us, and we beheld His glory''; and ''You will see heaven opened and the angels of God ascending and descending on the Son of Man.'' Both of them contain in brief the substance of what the evangelist is now about to relate.[12]

Themes

The theme of witness dominates the sequence. The parade of witnesses and the heaping up of titles constitute, for all practical purposes, a summary of the christological beliefs of the Johannine Church at the end of the first century. These beliefs will be expressed more fully in the course of the Gospel, especially in 5:1-47; 7:1–8:52; 10:22-39; 13–17.

The theme of response is evident in the positive response of the disciples and in the implied negative response of the Jews. The replacement theme is at the most implicit, but for Christian readers at the end of the first century, the gathering of the first disciples and the fact that none of the Jewish delegation approaches Jesus would hint at least that Jesus was already turning away from official Judaism and concentrating on his own.

Sequence 2

WATER REPLACED BY WINE AT CANA

2:1-12

Parallel structure

(a) **Jesus,** his **mother,** and his **disciples** at **Cana** (2:1-2)
(b) **Wine** and **servants** (2:3-5)
(c) Water changed to wine (2:6-8)
(b') **Wine** and **servants** (2:9-10)
(a') **Jesus,** his **mother,** and his **disciples** at **Cana** (2:11-12)

Text

(a)   2:1 On the third **day** there was a marriage **at Cana in Galilee,** and the **mother** of **Jesus** was there; [2]**Jesus** also was invited to the marriage, with his **disciples.**

(b)   [3]When the **wine** failed, the mother of Jesus said to him, "They have no **wine.**" [4]And Jesus said to her, "O woman, what have you to do with me? My hour has not yet come." [5]His mother said to the **servants,** "Do whatever he tells you."

(c)   [6]Now six stone jars were standing there, for the Jewish rites of purification, each holding twenty or thirty gallons. [7]Jesus said to them, "Fill the jars with water." And they filled them up to the brim. [8]He said to them, "Now draw some out, and take it to the steward of the feast." So they took it.

(b')   [9]When the steward of the feast tasted the water now become **wine,** and did not know where it came from (though the **servants** who had drawn the water knew), the steward of the feast called the bridegroom [10]and said to him, "Every man serves the good **wine** first; and when men have drunk freely, then the poor **wine;** but you have kept the good **wine** until now."

(a')   [11]This, the first of his signs, **Jesus** did **at Cana in Galilee,** and manifested his glory; and his **disciples** believed in him. [12]After this he went down to Capernaum, with his **mother** and his brothers and his **disciples;** and there they stayed for a few **days.**

In sequence 2, John creates the simplest possible parallels. In (a) and (a'), he parallels the words "Jesus," "mother," "disciples," and "Cana in

Galilee." In (b) and (b'), he parallels the words "wine" and "servants." The center (c) deals with the changing of the water into wine.

Commentary

The Cana "sign" is not the simple miracle story it seems to be. A number of factors suggest depths of symbolic meaning not immediately evident to the eye: (1) Mary's provocative statement, "They have no wine"; (2) Jesus' mysterious reply, "My hour has not yet come"; (3) the abundance of the water changed to wine (120–180 gallons); (4) the steward's apparently joking remark about how wine is to be served at a banquet; (5) the observation that in this "sign" Jesus "manifested his glory; and his disciples believed in him"; (6) the remarkable parallels with the story of Mary at the tomb in 20:1-18.

(a) Jesus, his mother, and his disciples at Cana (2:1-2)

2:1 On the third day. Does this mean simply the third day after Philip's and Nathanael's call (1:43), or is there something more to it? Several explanations are possible. First, the simplest explanation is that the three days allow time for Jesus and his disciples to move from where John the Baptist was baptizing to Cana in Galilee.

Second, many commentators add the "third" day mentioned here to the four days mentioned earlier (1:19, 29, 35, 43) and arrive at seven days, indicating a "new week of creation," which is contrasted with the old week of creation in Gn 1. The new week of creation would symbolize the Christian dispensation in the same way that the miraculous wine symbolizes the Christian dispensation in contrast to the water of the old dispensation. In favor of this interpretation and symbolism is the fact that Matthew, Mark, and Luke begin their Gospels with references to the creation story: Matthew, with his words "The book of the *genealogy* of Jesus Christ . . ." (Mt 1:1); Mark, with his remark that Jesus "was with the wild beasts," presumably like the first Adam in the garden (Mk 1:13); Luke, with his genealogy of Jesus going back to Adam (Lk 3:23-38). John himself begins his prologue with the words "In the beginning . . ." and refers to Mary as the "woman" in 2:4 and 19:26 in a way that seems to reflect the "woman" of Gn 3:15.[1]

Third, the "third day" may be John's faint foreshadowing of the resurrection. Early Christians would immediately think of the resurrection when confronted with remarks about Jesus and the third day. In 2:19, Jesus will say, "Destroy this temple, and in three days I will raise it up." In Lk 24:21, the Emmaus disciples remark, ". . . and besides all this, it is now the third day since this happened." The reference in Jn 20:1 to the first day of the week (the third after Jesus' death), in addition to other parallels in 20:1-18 with 2:1-12 (e.g., recurrence of the title "woman" and recurrence of the same persons in both sequences: Mary, Jesus, the disciples, and the brothers), would give some support for this interpretation.

(b) Wine and servants (2:3-5)

2:3 They have no wine. Jewish wedding festivities lasted a week, and hosts were expected to supply abundant wine. Mary's remark looks to obviating the hosts' embarrassment and, as v 5 indicates, constitutes more than a hint that she expects Jesus to do something about it. Martha's request in 11:20-27 will be similarly imprecise and similarly rewarded.

2:4a O woman, what have you do to with me? The question (Greek: *ti emoi kai soi;* Hebrew: *mah li wa lak*) can mean: (1) "Why are you bothering me?" in an adversative sense, as in 1 Kgs 17:18; or (2) "That is your affair; how am I involved?" in a sense in which the speaker simply disengages himself without rebuke or objection, as in 2 Kgs 3:13. In the context, the second sense seems more reasonable. The meaning of the question may well be that no one, not even Jesus' mother, has any control over his purposeful advance to the "hour" of his destiny (cf. 10:17-18).

2:4b My hour has not yet come. In Johannine terminology, Jesus' "hour" refers to the time of his passion, death, and resurrection (cf. 7:6, 8, 30; 8:20; 12:12, 27; 13:1). Since the Father in union with Jesus has determined the hour of Jesus' death, the apparently negative answer does not mean that Jesus will do nothing, since he goes ahead and works the miracle, but makes it clear that flesh and blood cannot determine or control Jesus' work of redemption (cf. 10:17-18; 12:27). This answer fits with Jesus' attitude toward his mother in Mk 3:33-35 and Lk 2:49.

2:5 Do whatever he tells you. Despite Jesus' ambiguous reply, Mary clearly expects him to do something about the situation. The servants are not alerted for nothing, nor will Mary be disappointed.

(c) Water changed to wine (2:6-8)

2:6 stone jars . . . for the Jewish rites of purification. The reference to the jars is a key observation, since the water of purification is related to the old dispensation, and the miracle to the new dispensation, which replaces the old. The reference to the "good wine" in 2:10 will continue the contrast and the replacement, and is important for the "sign" value of the miracle, which contrasts new and old.

2:7 Fill the jars with water. Emphasis is placed not so much on the miracle itself as on the lavishness of Jesus' miraculous gift.

(b') Wine and servants (2:9-10)

2:9 steward . . . tasted the water now become wine. The miracle is verified through the steward and the reference to the servants who "knew" where the wine had come from. **Did not know where it came from.** In John's

Gospel, questions having to do with "origin," especially Jesus' origin (cf. 7:27f; 8:14; 9:29; 19:9), imply an answer that almost always has something to do with origin from God. In this case, the answer would be that the miracle has been brought about by God to manifest Jesus' glory.

2:10 good wine first. What appears to be a joking remark has a subtle Johannine double meaning. The good wine is the new Christian dispensation, which replaces the old dispensation, just as the wine replaced the water for purification in the stone jars. The "good wine" served last does not invalidate the "poor wine"; it replaces it.

(a') Jesus, his mother, and his disciples at Cana (2:11-12)

2:11 manifested his glory. The relationships between sign, glory, and belief in 2:11 are important, because the three are frequently associated in John's Gospel. It is no accident, therefore, that the climax of the story combines the three concepts. The sign-miracle testifies to the union of Jesus and the Father, and therefore to Jesus' glory, which will be revealed fully only in the "hour" of his passion, death, and resurrection (cf. 12:23; 13:1; 17:24). Jesus' glory is his total union with the Father. The miracle manifests this union inasmuch as it testifies to Jesus' oneness with the Father in the working of the sign. The belief of the disciples is related to their ability to see, inchoatively at least, that such a miracle involves the union of Jesus with the Father. It testifies, therefore, to the truth of Jesus' claims. The reference to the disciples recalls 2:2 and links the episode with 1:35-51 and especially with 1:51—the programmatic text for the remainder of the Gospel.

2:12 mother . . . brothers . . . disciples. The reference to Jesus' mother, to his disciples, and to "a few days" hark back to the introduction (2:1-2), where the same persons are mentioned, minus the brothers, and thus close the circle with a perfect inclusion-conclusion.[2] **Brothers.** The sudden appearance of Jesus' brethren is surprising. They will appear again in 7:3-8 and 20:17.[3]

Themes

Sequence 2 places major emphasis on the theme of replacement. The wine, symbolizing the new dispensation, replaces the water of the old dispensation. The messianic symbolism of the miracle becomes evident when the reader recalls that messianic days are described in the Old Testament as the days of God's new nuptials with Israel (cf. Hos 2:16-25; Is 54:4-8; 62:4-5; Mt 22:1-14; Jn 3:39; Rv 19:7-9). Abundance of wine is associated with messianic days in Gn 49:10-12; Am 9:13-14; Hos 14:7; Jer 31:12.[4]

In addition to the messianic symbolism, there is a possible wisdom symbolism. The motif of wisdom is suggested by a comparison with Prv 9:5, where wisdom prepares a banquet and invites people to eat of her bread and "drink of her wine," and with Job 28:12-20, where the question arises concerning the origin of wisdom. The remarks about the steward not knowing "where" the wine had come from (2:9-10) may reflect this motif (cf. 3:8, where the motif of origin crops up again in relation to the wind blowing where it will).

All things considered, the episode emphasizes the replacement of Jewish institutions by a new economy of salvation. The theme will be continued in the following sequence, where Jesus speaks of his body replacing the temple of Jerusalem (2:13-25); in Jesus' statement to the Samaritan woman concerning the hour when "neither on this mountain nor in Jerusalem will you worship the Father" (4:21); in the water that is superior to the water of Jacob's well (4:6-12); and in the bread that comes down from heaven and gives eternal life to those who believe (6:35-58). The replacement of the feasts of the Jews in chs 5–10 by the continuing feast of Jesus' "passing over" to the Father should likewise be understood as a continuation of this theme.

The other concentric themes are present but not central to the sequence. The working of the sign-miracle, by testifying to Jesus' power and to his unity with the Father, continues the theme of witness so central to sequence 1 (1:19-51). And the response of the disciples to the miracle (". . . his disciples believed in him") continues the theme of positive response on the part of the disciples already indicated in 1:35-51.

It must be confessed that modern readers would not as readily appreciate John's symbolism as Jewish-Christian readers would have at the end of the first century. For them, in a context of polemic with the synagogue concerning the validity of Jesus' and Christianity's claims, every aspect of the story and its symbolic content would be scrutinized and delighted in.

replacement theme

Sequence 3

JESUS CLEANSES THE TEMPLE

2:13-25

Parallel structure

(a) **Jesus** in **Jerusalem** at the **Passover** (2:13)
(b) His **disciples remember** the words of **scripture** (2:14-17).
(c) "Destroy this temple, and in three days I will raise it up" (2:18-21).
(b') His **disciples remember** the words of **scripture** (2:22).
(a') **Jesus** in **Jerusalem** at the **Passover** (2:23-25)

Text

(a)   2:13 The **Passover** of the Jews was at hand, and **Jesus** went up to **Jerusalem.**

(b)   ¹⁴In the temple he found those who were selling oxen and sheep and pigeons, and the money-changers at their business. ¹⁵And making a whip of cords, he drove them all, with the sheep and oxen, out of the temple; and he poured out the coins of the money-changers and overturned their tables. ¹⁶And he told those who sold the pigeons, "Take these things away; you shall not make my Father's house a house of trade." ¹⁷**His disciples remembered** that it was **written,** "Zeal for thy house will consume me."

(c)   ¹⁸The Jews then said to him, "What sign have you to show us for doing this?" ¹⁹Jesus answered them, "Destroy this temple, and in three days I will raise it up." ²⁰The Jews then said, "It has taken forty-six years to build this temple, and will you raise it up in three days?" ²¹But he spoke of the temple of his body.

(b')   ²²When therefore he was raised from the dead, **his disciples remembered** that he had said this; and they believed the **scripture** and the word which Jesus had spoken.

(a')   ²³Now when he was in **Jerusalem** at the **Passover** feast, many believed in his name when they saw the signs which he did; ²⁴but **Jesus** did not trust himself to them, ²⁵because he knew all men and needed no one to bear witness of man; for he himself knew what was in man.

As in 2:1-12, so in 2:13-25, John creates chiastic parallelism in the simplest possible manner. In (a) and (a'), he parallels the words "Jesus," "Jerusalem," and "Passover." In (b) and (b'), he parallels the words "his disciples remembered the scripture." The center (c) deals with the significance of Jesus' words "Destroy this temple, and in three days I will raise it up."

Commentary

According to the synoptic Gospels, the cleansing of the temple took place shortly before the passion (cf. Mt 21:2ff; Mk 11:11ff; Lk 19:45ff). John moves it up to the beginning of his Gospel to provide a chiastic parallel with sequence 19 (chs 18–19), the story of the destroying of the temple of Jesus' body in the passion.[1] Parallelism is achieved by way of the idea central to both sequences—the destroying of the body of Jesus, which is followed by the resurrection, so that henceforth the risen Jesus becomes the temple of the new dispensation. What would be almost impossible to explain according to the laws of narrative composition becomes perfectly intelligible when the Gospel is read according to the laws of parallelism.

It has been suggested that the prediction of Mal 3:1, "Behold, I send my messenger to prepare the way before me, and the Lord whom you seek [interpreted to refer to Jesus] will suddenly come to his temple," may have influenced the evangelist's placement of the cleansing immediately after the testimony of the Baptist in 1:19–34 instead of just before the passion, as it is in the Synoptics. This is possible, but the parallel structure of the Gospel as a whole explains the premature recounting of the incident more cogently and satisfactorily.[2]

By placing the cleansing where it is, John has not only provided a perfect chiastic balance with the passion narrative in chs 18–19, but he has also set the stage for his remarks about the "new worship" in 4:19-25 and for his motif of the replacement of the Jewish feasts (centered on the temple) by Jesus in chs 5–10. The perhaps more correct chronological order of the synoptic Gospels thus gives way to John's chiastic structure and theological order.

(a) Jesus in Jerusalem at the Passover (2:13)

2:13 The Passover of the Jews was at hand. "Passover of the *Jews*" may be meant in contradistinction to Passover of the *Christians*. It fits, moreover, with John's regular mention of Jewish feasts (cf. chs 5–10), which are to be replaced by the continuous feast of the Lamb of God sacrificed for the sin of the world. For those who read the Gospel according to the laws of narrative, John's Gospel appears to record three distinct Passover feasts: (a) the Passover mentioned here in 2:13; (b) another Passover mentioned in 6:4; (c) the Passover of Jesus' death mentioned in 12:1, 12, 20 and 13:1. On this basis, Jesus' public ministry is determined to have lasted at least two years. However, when the Gospel is read according to the laws of parallelism instead of the laws of narrative, the Passover in 2:13 may very well be the same as the Passover of Jesus' death mentioned in 1:1 and 13:1. The length of Jesus' public ministry cannot, therefore, be solidly based on the number of Passovers mentioned in John's Gospel.

(b) His disciples remember the words of scripture (2:14-17).

2:14 In the temple. From what follows, it is clear that the whole temple area, which embraced many buildings and extensive courtyards and not just the temple itself, is meant. The oxen, sheep, and pigeons were used in the Passover celebration and other rites. Money-changers did business changing foreign currency, forbidden in the temple area, into the shekels and half-shekels required for tribute.

2:15-16 drove them all . . . out of the temple. The removal of the sacrificial animals signals the end of temple sacrifice. The expulsion of the money-changers and the declaration "you shall not make my Father's house a house of trade" is a protest against the Jews' commercial abuse of the temple. Underlying Jesus' words is almost certainly the accusation of Jeremiah: "Has this house, which is called by my name, become a den of robbers in your eyes?" (Jer 7:11). The Synoptics record similar sentiments (cf. Mk 11:17; Mt 21:13; Lk 19:46). Theologically, the cleansing of the temple emphasizes the same theme as the miracle at Cana—the theme of replacement. What is new in John's account of the cleansing is the linking of the new dispensation with the death and resurrection of Jesus (cf. vv 18-22).

2:17 Zeal for thy house. The quotation is from Ps 69:9 and contrasts Jesus' attitude toward the temple with that of the Jews. It was only later, as mentioned in v 22, that the disciples remembered the text from Ps 69:9 and realized how fitting it was to describe Jesus' attitude toward the temple.

(c) "Destroy this temple, and in three days I will raise it up" (2:18-21).

2:18 What sign have you to show us for doing this? Jesus' actions and his claim that the temple is his Father's house presuppose extraordinary authority (cf. Mt 21:23; Mk 11:27) and call for proof supporting such authority. Since many false messiahs had arisen in the first century, the Jewish authorities rightly asked Jesus for a sign to confirm his authority. The sign Jesus will give is the sign of the resurrection (the sign that the Jews still refused to accept in John's time at the end of the first century). Jesus' words here are not unlike those of Mt 12:38-40, where Jesus, when asked for a sign by the Pharisees, gives the sign of Jonah, who was returned to dry land after three days in the stomach of a great fish.

2:19 Destroy this temple, and in three days I will raise it up. All the words in this statement are subject to double meanings. "Destroy" can refer to destruction of a building or to the dissolution of a human life. "Temple" can refer to a material edifice or to a human body. "Raise" can refer to rebuilding or resurrection. The Jews take the first meaning in every case; Jesus, as John explains in vv 21-22, intends the second. This leads to a massive misunderstanding and at the same time focuses the reader's attention on what is central to the evangelist's theological interests, namely, the passion, death, and resurrection of Jesus, which will be the subject of sequence 19 (chs 18–19), the chiastic parallel of sequence 3.

2:20   forty-six years to build this temple. Herod began his reconstruction of the temple in 20 B.C., and it was not fully completed until 63 A.D. Presumably the major work was finished in the first forty-six years of construction. The Jews' question, "Will you raise it up in three days?" indicates that they think Jesus is talking about the material temple.

2:21   But he spoke of the temple of his body. The evangelist clarifies the Jews' misunderstanding by reminding his readers at the end of the first century that Jesus was really talking about his death and resurrection. Implicit in Jesus' words and in the evangelist's clarification of what he meant is the replacement of the temple as God's place of worship by the crucified and risen body of Jesus, which is to become the temple of the new dispensation. In him, as the prologue so succinctly put this same truth (1:14), the Word "became flesh and dwelt among us."[3]

(b') His disciples remember the words of scripture (2:22).

2:22   When therefore he was raised from the dead. The evangelist wishes his readers to know that the disciples at the time of Jesus neither fully understood Jesus nor fully believed in him until after the resurrection. After the resurrection, they understood the scriptures in relation to Jesus in a way that was not possible before (cf. Lk 24:44-45). Nonetheless, he wishes to testify to Jesus' foreknowledge of his death and resurrection, and in this he is in full agreement with Mark (8:31; 14:58; 15:29); Matthew (16:21; 26:61; 27:39; 28:63); and Luke (9:22).

(a') Jesus in Jerusalem at the Passover (2:23-25)

2:23   when they saw the signs which he did. John presupposes the many miracles related in the synoptic Gospels. His theological reflection, however, deals not so much with miracles or signs, as he calls them, but with the nature of the faith that flows from them. As he will indicate in a number of places (cf. 4:42; 4:48; 6:14-15; 9:39-41; 12:37-43; 20:29), faith based on signs alone is not always genuine faith. This is clear in 4:48; 6:25-29; 6:60-67; 4:40-44; 20:26-29. What was said by Jesus about the sower and the seed and different kinds of soil the seed falls on (cf. Mk 4:3-20; Mt 13:4-23; Lk 8:5-15) is said in a different way in John's Gospel, but the teaching is the same, namely, not every faith-response to Jesus is a true faith-response!

2:25   he himself knew what was in man. These cryptic words deal with the theme of genuine faith-response and prepare the way for much that follows in the Gospel, beginning with the Nicodemus episode (3:1-21).

Themes

The central theme of the sequence is the theme of replacement—the replacement of the temple of Jerusalem and its sacrificial rites by the temple of Jesus' body and the continuous feast of the Passover of the Lamb of God sacrificed on the cross and risen from the tomb.

The conclusion (vv 23-25) heightens the theme of the Jews' negative response to Jesus insinuated in their reaction to Jesus' words "Destroy this temple, and in three days I will raise it up" (vv 18-21), and at the same time foreshadows the mystery of the Jews' rejection of Jesus, which will become so much a motif of the Gospel in later sequences (cf. especially 5:16-18; chs 7-8; 11:45-57; 12:37-50; 15:18-16:4).

The theme of witness is toned down from what it was in the first two sequences but surfaces in Jesus' own witness to his future resurrection and to his replacement in his own body of the sacrificial system of the Jews.

Sequence 4

REBIRTH THROUGH WATER AND THE SPIRIT

3:1-21

Parallel structure

(a) A **man** named Nicodemus **came to Jesus** by **night** and said, ". . . you are a teacher **come from God;** for no one can **do** these signs that you **do,** unless **God** is with him" (3:1-2).

(b) *Central question:* How can a man be born anew and enter the **kingdom of heaven?** (3:3-9).

(c) "Are you a teacher of Israel, and yet you do not understand this?" (3:10).

(b′) *Answer to central question:* "As Moses lifted up the serpent in the wilderness, so must the Son of man be lifted up, that whoever believes in him may have **eternal life.** For God so loved the world that he gave his only Son, that whoever believes in him should not perish but have **eternal life**" (3:11-18).

(a′) Jesus says: ". . . **men** loved **darkness** rather than **light.** . . . everyone who **does** evil hates the **light,** and does not **come to the light.** . . . But he who **does** what is true **comes to the light,** that it may be clearly seen that his **deeds** have been **wrought in God**" (3:19-21).

Text

(a)   3:1 Now there was a **man** of the Pharisees, named Nicodemus, a ruler of the Jews. ²This man **came to Jesus** by **night** and said to him, "Rabbi, we know that you are a teacher **come from God;** for no one can **do** these signs that you **do,** unless **God** is with him."

(b)   ³Jesus answered him, **"Truly, truly, I say to you,** unless one is born anew, he cannot see **the kingdom of God."** ⁴Nicodemus said to him, "How can a man be born when he is old? Can he enter a second time **into his mother's womb** and be born?" ⁵Jesus answered, **"Truly, truly, I say to you,** unless one is born of water and the Spirit, he cannot enter **the kingdom of God.** ⁶That which is born of the flesh is flesh, and that which is born of the Spirit is spirit. ⁷Do not marvel that I said to you, 'You must be born anew.' ⁸**The wind** blows where it wills, and you hear the sound of it, but you do not know whence it comes or whither it goes; so it is with every one who is born of the Spirit." ⁹Nicodemus said to him, "How can this be?"

(c)   ¹⁰Jesus answered him, "Are you a teacher of Israel, and yet you do not understand this?

(b′)   [11]**"Truly, truly, I say to you,** we speak of what we know, and bear witness to what we have seen; but you do not receive our testimony. [12]If I have told you **earthly things** and you do not believe, how can you believe if I tell you heavenly things? [13]No one has ascended **into heaven** but he who descended from heaven, the Son of man. [14]And as Moses lifted up the serpent in the wilderness, so must the Son of man be lifted up, [15]that whoever believes in him may have **eternal life.** [16]For God so loved the world that he gave his only Son, that whoever believes in him should not perish but have **eternal life.** [17]For God sent the Son into the world, not to condemn the world, but that the world might be saved through him. [18]He who believes in him is not condemned; he who does not believe is condemned already, because he has not believed in the name of the only Son of God.

(a′)   [19]**"And this is the judgment, that **the light has come** into the world, and **men** loved **darkness** rather than **light,** because their **deeds** were evil. [20]For every one who **does** evil hates the **light,** and does not **come to the light,** lest his **deeds** should be exposed. [21]But he who **does** what is true **comes to the light,** that it may be clearly seen that his **deeds** have been wrought in **God."**

The parallelism of sequence 4 is complicated because it is achieved primarily through a balancing of concepts and only secondarily through verbal repetitions. First, in (a) and (a′), John emphasizes the test of legitimacy propounded by Nicodemus: "We know that you are a teacher come from God; for no one can *do* these signs that you *do,* unless God is with him" (v 2). In 3:19-21 (a′), this same test is proposed—what a man *does* determines whether a man loves the darkness and does not come to the light, or loves the light and comes to the light. Second, there is the conceptual parallel between night in (a) and darkness in (a′). Third, there is the parallel between Nicodemus coming to Jesus, the light, out of the darkness of night in (a) and the repeated references to coming to the light that is Jesus (cf. 1:4: "In him was life, and the life was the light of men"; and 8:12: "I am the light of the world") in (a′). Fourth, there are such verbal parallels as "come," "do," "God."

In (b) and (b′), the parallelism is highly conceptual but still clear. In (b), the question is raised in vv 4 and 9: How can a man be born anew and enter the kingdom of heaven, i.e., eternal life? The question is answered by Jesus in (b′) when he speaks about his "being lifted up," meaning his death on the cross; about the love of the Father, who "gives" his Son to death; and about the necessity of believing in the name of the Son of man in order to have eternal life. In addition to this central conceptual parallel, there are a few verbal and equivalently verbal parallels: "Truly, truly, I say to you"; "eternal life" equivalent to "kingdom of God"; and "earthly things" in v 12 equivalent to "wind" in v 8.

In the center (c), Jesus' question "Are you a teacher of Israel, and yet you do not understand this?" forms a clear hinge or turning point between what Nicodemus does not understand in (b) and what Jesus will explain to him in (b′).

Commentary

With sequence 4, the reader faces a formidable challenge, for the simple reason that the Johannine discourses, of which this is the first, are far more difficult to follow and understand than the brief narrative sequences already encountered. The discourses, therefore, should be approached with the cautions of Hoskyns in mind:

> The reader of the gospel is now required to attend to the themes of a "Johannine discourse." If he is to understand the discourses, of which this (ch 3) is the first, he must understand them in their scriptural biblical setting. Unless he is to do grave violence to the text, he is not free to put them in any other setting, ancient or modern. The fourth gospel is a biblical book, and the first discourse is spoken to a Jewish Rabbi. If these discourses seem to us to be so full of gaps that they appear to leap rather than move; or if, alternatively they seem to us to be monotonous; if they seem to be set quite out of their context by the introduction of the Evangelist's own comments; we must not be satisfied with these judgments of ours, since the Evangelist most assuredly did not think that what he wrote was fragmentary or monotonous or inconstant. We must not rest from exegesis until the apparent gaps have been filled up so completely that each discourse moves step by step as an ordered, a theologically ordered, whole; until, that is to say, what is said becomes intelligible and coherent speech, and until, moreover, it coheres with the biblical Palestinian background upon which the Evangelist has set it. . . . This is the energy of understanding which the Evangelist demanded of his original readers; and his book still makes the same demand upon us.[1]

When looked at through the focus of parallelism, the reader can readily understand why the discourse seems, to the eyes of Hoskyns, to "leap rather than move." Hoskyns has recognized the peculiar leaping movement characteristic of this kind of parallel structure—a movement that seems to leave gaps, but only because it moves in a manner that seems to be continually rising and then circling back to the beginning.

In sequence 4, the movement proceeds from Nicodemus' admission that Jesus must be "a teacher come from God" (3:1-2) to Jesus' declaration that life eternal is a gift from above (3:3-9). Jesus then rebukes Nicodemus (3:10) and goes on to deal with the efficacity of his death for bringing about life from above for those who believe in him (3:11-18). He concludes with a challenge to the Jews and to all persons to respond to God's love for the world by abandoning the darkness and coming through faith in him to eternal life (3:19-21).

(a) Nicodemus comes at night (3:1-2).

3:1 Nicodemus. As a Pharisee and member of the ruling Sanhedrin, Nicodemus represents official Judaism. He has been impressed by Jesus' signs, but his faith, like the faith of those in Jerusalem who saw Jesus' signs and "believed," is suspect (cf. 2:23-25).[2] He comes "by night," either out of fear of his fellow Jews or perhaps out of zeal for the law, since zealous scribes were expected to study and discuss the law even deep into the night. More likely the author has him come at night in order to create a parallel with the Last Supper discourse (chs 13–17)[3] and with the "light" (antithetic parallelism) mentioned in vv 19-21.

3:2 a teacher come from God. Nicodemus' acknowledgment that Jesus is a teacher "come from God" is in marked contrast to the animosity of the Jewish leaders in general (cf. 5:16-18; 7:32, 45-52; 8:48-59; 9:39-41; 11:45-55). In 3:19-21, Jesus will speak of those who come into the light (like Nicodemus) and those who love the darkness (like the other Jewish leaders).

(b) Can he return to his mother's womb? (3:3-9).

Jesus' discourse to Nicodemus (vv 3-21) is really directed to those Jews at the end of the first century who, like Nicodemus, are on the fence, unable to make up their minds about leaving the synagogue and entering the Christian Church. The discourse is centered on the gratuitousness of God's gift of faith and eternal life, on how a man can be born again as a result of the Son of man's being "lifted up," and on the need to believe in Jesus and to "be born of water [baptism] and the Spirit" (v 5). In addition to parallelism, three Johannine literary techniques are important for a correct interpretation of the discourse.

First, there is the Johannine discourse format. As Dodd has pointed out, the typical Johannine discourse begins with a dialogue and then tapers off into a monologue. It usually has the following format: (1) an oracular statement by Jesus; (2) an objection to, or crass misunderstanding of, Jesus' words; (3) Jesus' monologue explaining the real meaning of his oracular statement.

Second, there is the Johannine technique of double-meaning words, which allows Jesus' dialoguer to understand the double-meaning word in one sense (the wrong sense) and Jesus to understand it in another sense (the right sense).

Third, there is the Johannine technique of misunderstanding on the part of Jesus' dialoguer. The author represents one party to the dialogue as failing (frequently in a crass manner) to understand the words of the speaker in order to allow the speaker (Jesus) the opportunity to explain himself more fully. To a certain extent the misunderstanding technique is used as a counterpart to either the double-meaning words or to the symbolic meaning of words (e.g., "temple" in 2:19ff; "born anew" in 3:3ff; "water" in 4:5ff; "work" in 3:34 and 5:18ff; "bread" in 6:32ff).

3:3 born anew. Jesus' dialogue with Nicodemus begins with an answer to a presupposed question on Nicodemus' part: "What must I do to gain eternal life?" The answer is in the form of an oracular statement in which the mysterious element is found in the double-meaning Greek word *anōthen*. The word, like our musical expression "from the top," can mean "from above" or "again," or "anew." Nicodemus understands it in the gross sense of "anew," i.e., to be born again physically. Jesus obviously means it in the sense of to be born again by the gift of life given "from above." The misunderstanding allows Jesus in vv 5ff to expound both the gratuity of God's gift of life from above and the need to be baptized (v 5) in order to enter into eternal life ("God's kingdom").

3:5 water and the Spirit. Bultmann suggested that the words "of water" (as a reference to baptism) are the interpolation of an ecclesiastical redactor. The words, however, are found in all the manuscripts, and baptism by water and the Spirit had been prepared for at least implicitly in the Baptist's words "he who sent me to baptize with water said to me, 'He on whom you see the Spirit descend and remain, this is he who baptizes with the Holy Spirit.' " (1:33).

Confirmation for the authenticity of the words as a reference to baptism is found in the parallelism between the Nicodemus discourse in ch 3 and the discourse to the Twelve in chs 13-17. Even Bultmann, in an offhand remark, notices the relationship between 3:1-21 and chs 13-17. He says: "The differences between the discourse of 3:1ff (together with the *related* farewell discourse) . . . ." (italics added).[5] Both discourses speak about baptism (cp. 3:5 with 13:4-11, where the account of the footwashing is almost universally admitted to have baptismal overtones);[6] about the Holy Spirit (cp. 3:5-8 with 14:16-17; 15:26; 16:7-16); about the "world" (cp. 3:16; 15:18ff); and about "love" (cp. 3:16 and 13-17 *passim*).

3:6-8 born of the flesh is flesh. The gratuity of God's gift of rebirth and eternal life is further emphasized by the obvious sense of "that which is born of the flesh . . ." (v 6) and by the parable of the wind (spirit-breath), the reality of which is a fact of experience, but the origin of which in pre-scientific times was a complete mystery.

3:9 How can this be? This critically important question, asked in (b), is answered in (b') when Jesus speaks about the Son of man who "must be lifted up," i.e., crucified, in 3:14; when he adds "that whoever believes in him may have eternal life" in 3:15; and finally when he declares in 3:16, "God so loved the world that he *gave* his only Son."

(c) "Are you a teacher of Israel, and yet you do not understand this?" (3:10).

Jesus' question to Nicodemus forms the turning point or hinge of the whole sequence. In section (b), Nicodemus' question had been: "How can a man be born anew and enter the kingdom of heaven?" In section (b'), Jesus will explain what he says here in (c). What Nicodemus does not understand is that a man can be born anew and enter the kingdom of God, i.e., achieve eternal life, through believing in Jesus whom the Father out of love gave up to death through the crucifixion, the "being lifted up" of v 14, so that "whoever believes in him should not perish but have eternal life" (v 16).

(b′) Answer to central question: "As Moses lifted up . . ." (3:11-18)

3:11 we . . . bear witness to what we have seen. In 3:11-12, John has Jesus speak through Nicodemus to his Jewish readers on the fence at the end of the first century. Nicodemus has twice asked about the "how" of the Christian claim that eternal life comes through rebirth by water and the Spirit (cf. 3:4, 9). Jesus replies to the question of "how" in vv 14-18. Here he accuses the Jews, through Nicodemus, of refusing to believe in him even though he testifies to what "we have seen." The "we" of v 11, as Schnacken-burg explains, is not unique in John's Gospel (cf. 1:14; 9:4). It is best explained as the response of the Christian Church, in union with Jesus, to the Jews' rejection of Jesus' claims.[7] This explanation fits with the plural (*lambanete*) of the following words, addressed to the Nicodemus circle: ". . . but you [plural] do not receive our testimony." In brief, the teaching of Jesus is unimpeachable because, as he says, "we speak of what we know, and bear witness to what we have seen" (v 11).

3:12 earthly things. Probably John refers to the little parable about the wind told by Jesus to Nicodemus in v 8.

3:13 No one has ascended into heaven. Jesus' explanation for the knowledge he claimed in v 11 is that he talks about what he knows and testifies to what he has seen because he alone has been in heaven. As Hoskyns puts it: "Though no man has ascended into heaven, yet God has willed that there should be a descent from heaven to earth; not an apparition or epiphany in the sky, but a real descent into human flesh. This descent is the mission of Jesus . . . ."[8]

3:14-15 And as Moses lifted up the serpent. The reference is to Nm 21:9 and is used to introduce what Luther called "the Gospel in miniature." Here Jesus gives his answer to Nicodemus' question "How can this be?" (v 9). What Jesus knows from being in heaven (v 13) is "how" men can be born again and thus "see the kingdom of God" (v 3). In order for men to "see the kingdom of God," which, as commentators agree, is the equivalent of having eternal life (v 15), the Son of man must be "lifted up," i.e., crucified (cf. 8:28; 12:23, 32-34), and men must believe in him. It is important to note at this point that vv 13-18 of (b′) balance with, and look back at, vv 3-9 of (b) by centering on the two subjects central to section (b), namely, eternal life, i.e., the kingdom of God, and the "how" (v 9) of achieving eternal life.

3:16 God so loved the world. Here, for the first time, John mentions the Father's personal initiative. Here, too, for the first time and in a single profoundly theological declaration, John encapsulates the core theology of his Gospel: God's love, expressed through the giving up to death of his only-begotten Son for the life of the world, is the reason behind all that is embraced in the "how" of Nicodemus' question and behind all that is new in the new covenant. In brief, the "work" of the Father is to manifest his love for the world by "giving" his Son; the "work" of the Son is to manifest his love for the Father and for the world by giving himself to death (cf. 4:34; 13:1-2; 17:1-4; 19:30); the "work" of the world is to believe in the only-begotten Son whom the Father has sent to reveal his love to the world (cf. 3:16b; 6:29; 17:20-25).

The choice of the word "gave" in 3:16 is unusual. John usually speaks of the Father "sending" the Son, as he does almost immediately in 3:17. The context, however, explains the choice of the word. Jesus had just said, "So must the Son of man be lifted up," an obvious reference to his crucifixion and death. Later Jesus will speak of his death as the completion of the "work" for which he had been sent into the world by the Father (cf. 17:4 and 19:30). The Father's "giving" of Jesus, therefore, is a giving over to death—a fittingly nuanced way of expressing what was implicit in the words "So must the Son of man be lifted up." He *must* be lifted up because his Father, out of love for the world, has "given" him up to death.

This richer interpretation of the verb "gave" is supported not only by the reference to the passion in v 14 but by the implicit allusion to the sacrifice of Isaac, the "only-begotten" son of Abraham. It is further supported by John's description of Jesus in the passion "bearing his own cross" (19:17) just as Isaac carried the wood for his own sacrifice (Gn 22:2-6).

The description of Jesus as the "only [begotten] Son" (*monogenē*) in 3:16 is probably an allusion to the Abraham-Isaac story of Gn 22, but it also serves as an antithetic reply to the words of Nicodemus in 3:2: "Rabbi, we know that you are a *teacher* come from God." Nicodemus spoke about Jesus as if he were just another teacher among many. On the contrary, as John so often makes clear—and never so clear as here—Jesus is not just another teacher, he is the unique and only Son of God!

3:17-18 He who believes in him. John returns here to the subject of eternal life, the central subject of section (b). The work of the Father and the Son is to save the world. The work of the world is to believe God's only Son and thus enter into eternal life (cf. 6:29 and 17:20-23).[9]

(a') Jesus says: ". . . men loved darkness rather than light . . ." (3:19-21).

Section (a') returns the reader's mind to section (a) and thus forms an inclusion. Section (a) spoke of Nicodemus coming to Jesus by night and applying to him the test of "deeds." In section (a'), Jesus will speak of those who come to the light and those who do not, and he will apply to them the test of "deeds."

3:19 this is the judgment. Jesus, the light of the world, has come to his own, but his own have not accepted him. The world has preferred the darkness. And the world has proved this by its deeds.

3:20 ˙ every one who does evil hates the light. Here John has Jesus say what wisdom teachers of the Old Testament would take for granted: Those who do good love the light and come to the light naturally; those who do evil love the darkness and fear to come to the light lest their evil deeds become known. There are, however, two difficulties with this explanation. First, Jesus seems to imply that a person's salvation—his or her coming or not coming to the light—is dependent on his or her situation and disposition *before* the coming of Jesus. However, if this were so, the gratuity of the gift of faith so emphasized in the dialogue with Nicodemus (3:3-9) would then make no sense. Thus, 3:3-9 would seem to eliminate effectively the first difficulty.

Taking for granted the gratuity of faith, there remains a second difficulty. John still seems to be dividing people into two classes—those predestined to come to the light and those predestined to love the darkness. The tension between this interpretation of vv 20-21 and v 16 is unbearable. How can God so love the world if he has predestined some members of the world to inevitably but certainly condemn themselves by refusing to come to the light?

We suggest that the solution to this second difficulty rests precisely in the tension between vv 20-21 and v 16. Some do love the darkness and do refuse to come to the light. But this is not because they have been predestined, but because they freely reject the gratuitous gift of faith offered to them. The refusal is grounded, not in a mystery of predestination, but in the mystery of free will and its exercise. The sequence as a whole is an explanation for, and an invitation to, John's audience—the Jews wavering between Christianity and the synagogue—to come to Jesus and believe in him and be saved. If John had believed that human beings are predestined, a great deal of his Gospel would make no sense. Indeed, the avowed purpose of the author would make no sense: "These [signs] are written that you may believe that Jesus is the Christ, the Son of God, and that believing you may have life in his name" (20:31). The same would be true of other invitations to faith in this Gospel (cf. 5:31-47; 6:25-29; 10:16, 38; 12:35-36; 17:20-25).

John's conclusion (3:19-21), therefore, is perfectly consistent with the rest of the sequence. Through Jesus' dialogue with Nicodemus, John expounds the central truths of Christianity—God's love for the world, Jesus' mission to save the world by dying, the need to believe in Jesus and to manifest that belief by accepting baptism in water and the Spirit. Section (a') is a fitting conclusion inasmuch as it urgently invites John's readers to come to the light and be saved because God "sent the Son into the world, not to condemn the world, but that the world might be saved through him" (3:17).

Themes

Apart from the prologue, no discourse in John contains so much sheer, concentrated theology as the discourse to Nicodemus. In this discourse, as Hoskyns says, Jesus "has nothing to hide: and He lays bare all the fundamental themes of his mission. The whole is in the parts, and what follows is not a discourse, but The Discourse, the subject-matter of which is repeated in all subsequent discourses.''[10] Here, as nowhere else in his Gospel, the profundity of the Johannine insight and the interrelationship of the concentric themes has the luminosity of lightning illuminating the surrounding darkness.

First, there is the theme of witness. Jesus witnesses to himself and to the source of his teaching: "We speak of what we know" (v 11). He knows because he is the one who "descended from heaven" (v 13). What he knows is the Father's love for the world and his plan for the world (v 16 in relation to vv 14-15). The salvific plan that flows from the Father's love for humankind impels him to manifest his love by sending his only-begotten Son to die. The Son will manifest his love for the Father and for humankind by dying and thus completing the work of the Father (cf. 4:34; 17:1-4; 19:30). For all who believe in Jesus as the manifestation of the Father's love, there is the promise of eternal life. Summed up under the heading of John's own favorite word, "work" (cf. 4:34; 5:17; 6:29; 17:4), God's plan begins with his own "work"—the sending and giving of his only-begotten Son. It is fulfilled by the "work" of the Son, who in his death manifests the love of the Father for humankind (cf. 4:34; 13:1-4; 17:4; 19:30). It is implemented by the salvation to eternal life of those who respond to the Father by believing in, and following the example of, the Son (13:15-17).

Second, the theme of response. To be born again to eternal life calls for a response of faith in Jesus (vv 18-21) and an acceptance of baptism (v 5 and cf. 13:8).

Third, the theme of replacement. The initiative of the Father in sending the Son makes all things new. Life eternal now depends on faith in Jesus, which completes and replaces all that the Jews had hitherto depended on for achieving eternal life. This faith is manifested through an acceptance of a new baptism that replaces the baptism of repentance preached by John the Baptist: "Unless one is born of water and the Spirit, he cannot enter the kingdom of God."

Chiastic parallels with sequence 2 (2:1-12)

Parallelism between sequence 4 (3:1-21) and sequence 2 (2:1-12) is achieved in three ways. First, by the centrality of "water" in both sequences—the water changed into wine in 2:6-9 and the water of baptism necessary for eternal life in 3:5. Second, by the parallelism of the word "mother," used four times in 2:1-12 (vv 1, 3, 5, 12) and once in 3:1-21 (v 4). Third, by the antithetic parallelism effected by the contrast between the disciples who "believed in him" (2:11) and the Jews who do not believe in him, of whom Jesus says to Nicodemus, "you [plural] do not receive our testimony" (3:11). In a wider sense the two sequences parallel each other in their central contention that the old order has passed away and the new is at hand—the wine of the new dispensation has replaced the water-purification of the old dispensation, and commitment to Jesus in faith manifested through baptism with water and the Spirit has replaced the commitment to God hitherto called for in the old dispensation.[11]

Sequence 5

THE BAPTIST WITNESSES TO JESUS AGAIN

3:22–4:3

Parallel structure

(a) Here he is **baptizing,** and **all are going to him** (3:22-26).

(b) No one can receive anything except what is given him **from heaven** (3:27-28).

(c) He must increase, but I must decrease (3:29-30).

(b′) He who comes **from heaven** is above all (3:31-36).

(a′) Jesus was making and **baptizing more disciples than John** (4:1-3).

Text

(a)   3:22 After this **Jesus** and **his disciples** went into the land of **Judea;** there he remained with them and **baptized.** ²³**John** also was **baptizing** at Aenon near Salim, because there was much water there; and people came and were **baptized.** ²⁴For **John** had not yet been put in prison. ²⁵**Now** a discussion arose between John's disciples and a Jew over purifying. ²⁶And they came to John, and said to him, ''Rabbi, he who was with you beyond the Jordan, to whom you bore witness, here he is, **baptizing,** and **all are going to him.''**

(b)   ²⁷John answered, ''No one can receive anything except what is **given** him **from heaven.** ²⁸You yourselves **bear me witness,** that I said, I am not the Christ, but I have been sent before him.

(c)   ²⁹''He who has the bride is the bridegroom; the friend of the bridegroom, who stands and hears him, rejoices greatly at the bridegroom's voice; therefore this joy of mine is now full. ³⁰He must increase, but I must decrease.''

(b′)   ³¹He who comes from above is above all; he who is of the earth belongs to the earth, and of the earth he speaks; he who comes **from heaven** is above all. ³²He **bears witness** to what he has seen and heard, yet no one receives his testimony; ³³he who receives his testimony sets his seal to this, that God is true. ³⁴For he whom God has sent utters the words of God, for it is not by measure that he **gives** the Spirit; ³⁵the Father loves the Son, and has **given** all things into his hand. ³⁶He who believes in the Son has eternal life; he who does not obey the Son shall not see life, but the wrath of God rests upon him.

(a′)   4:1 **Now** when the Lord knew that the Pharisees had heard that **Jesus**

60

was **making and baptizing more disciples** than **John** ²(although **Jesus** himself did not **baptize**, but only **his disciples**), ³he left **Judea** and departed again to Galilee.

In sequence 5, John creates parallelism by using both conceptual and verbal parallels. The central concept discussed in (a) and reiterated in (a′) is that Jesus is drawing larger crowds than the Baptist and is "baptizing more disciples than John" (3:26; cp. 4:1). Verbal parallels abound: "now," "Jesus," "his disciples," "Judea," "baptizing," "John," "John's disciples."

In (b) and (b′), the parallels are more complicated but nevertheless clear. In (b), John begins to explain why Jesus is superior to him: what Jesus has *received* is what "is given him from heaven" (v 27). Also, Jesus is the Messiah; John is the one who has "been sent before him" (v 28). In (b′), John explains at greater length why Jesus is superior to him. In addition to this basic conceptual parallel, there are the following verbal parallels: "given" (v 27; cp. vv 34 and 35); "from heaven" (v 27; cp. v 31); "witness" (v 28; cp. v 32).

In the center (c), the central theme of the whole sequence—Jesus' superiority—is summed up in the analogy of the bridegroom and the best man, and in the words "He must increase, but I must decrease" (v 30).

Commentary

(a) Here he is baptizing, and all are going to him (3:22-26).

3:22-24   went into the land of Judea. The introduction provides a transition from the scene in Jerusalem with Nicodemus to an indefinite place in Judea. It also sets the stage for the central theme of the sequence: John's witness to Jesus' superiority over himself, expressed succinctly in v 30: "He must increase, but I must decrease." In passing, it should be noted that the Fourth Gospel provides an item of historical information not found in the synoptic Gospels. According to John, there was a time before the arrest of the Baptist when Jesus and the Baptist carried out parallel baptizing ministries (vv 23-24).

3:25-26   a discussion. The dispute about purification between a certain Jew and the disciples of the Baptist leads to the first testimony witnessing to Jesus' superiority: "Rabbi, he who was with you beyond the Jordan, to whom you bore witness, here he is, baptizing, and all are going to him" (v 26). At the same time, the reference to Jesus as "he who was with you beyond the Jordan" harks back to sequence 1 (1:19-51), where John first testified to Jesus (1:19-34), and thus signals the reader by this inclusionary remark that part I (1:19–4:3) is coming to a conclusion.

(b) No one can receive anything except what is given him from heaven (3:27-28).

3:27   except what is given him from heaven. The statement of the Baptist's disciples about "all" going to Jesus (3:26) sets the stage for John's witness. John explains why it is that all are going to Jesus. It is because Jesus has something special "given him from heaven" (v 27).[1] This something given from heaven is not explained until vv 31-36 (b'), but John does give a reason why all are going to Jesus. Jesus is, as John had testified (cp. 3:28 with 1:20-27), "he who comes after me, the thong of whose sandal I am not worthy to untie" (1:27). Witness to Jesus' superiority, therefore, advances in (b) with John's implicit reference to the source of Jesus' greatness: "No one can receive anything except what is given him from heaven," and with John's reminder to his disciples that he had already testified concerning Jesus: "I am not the Christ, but I have been sent before him" (cp. 3:28 and 1:20, 30-31). The statement implies that Jesus is the Messiah.

(c) He must increase, but I must decrease (3:29-30).

3:29-30   the bridegroom. John's witness to Jesus' superiority reaches a climax with his declaration that Jesus is the messianic bridegroom of Israel and that henceforth he, like the groom's best man, must decrease while Jesus increases. The little parable about the bridegroom, the best man, and the bride reiterates John's testimony: "You yourselves bear me witness, that I said, I am not the Christ, but I have been sent before him" (v 28). The Old Testament had spoken about Israel as the bride of God (cf. Hos 2:21; Jer 2:2; 3:20; Is 62:4f; Ez 16:8), and the New Testament thought of the Church as the bride of Christ (cf. 2 Cor 11:2; Eph 5:25ff; Rv 21:2). In brief, the Baptist is saying that not he but Jesus is the messianic king of Israel.

(b') He who comes from heaven is above all (3:31-36).

3:31-33   He who comes from above. The evangelist now has the Baptist explain his mysterious statement of v 27, "No one can receive anything except what is given him from heaven," in a clear reference back to the subject of section (b), namely, the reason why "all are going" to Jesus. The reason given for Jesus' superiority is that Jesus "comes from above," in contrast to the Baptist, who "is of the earth . . . and of the earth he speaks" (v 31). It is not that the Baptist is earthly, in the sense of unspiritual, but that he is of the earth in contrast to Jesus, who comes "from above," from heaven. Jesus is the one "who comes from heaven" and testifies (in contrast to the "earthly" Baptist, who speaks on an earthly plane) to what he has seen and heard in heaven, so that as a result what he testifies to is by definition true and must be accepted (cf. 3:11-13).

3:34   utters the words of God. The mysterious something "given him from heaven" (v 27) is now explained. It is first of all Jesus' message—the words of God—which God has given him and which he speaks with the fulness of the Spirit, because "it is not by measure that he [God] gives the Spirit" to Jesus (cf. 1:33).

3:35-36 has given all things into his hand. The something "given him from heaven" is further explained in v 35: "The Father loves the Son," and because he loves him, he "has given all things into his hand." The extent of the "all things" is not defined, but the import of v 36 is that the "all things" has to do with the gaining of eternal life: "He who believes in the Son has eternal life. He who does not obey the Son shall not see life, but the wrath of God rests upon him." Jesus is superior to the Baptist, therefore, because of what has been given him from on high: first, his message (v 32); second, his power to bestow eternal life on those who believe in him (vv 35-36).

(a') Jesus was making and baptizing more disciples than John (4:1-3).

4:1-3 making and baptizing more disciples than John. These verses close the ring on the whole episode by repeating the gist of the introduction (3:22-26), which spoke of Jesus baptizing and about "all going to him" (3:26). They also serve as a transition to the dialogue with the Samaritan woman in 4:4-38 by giving the reason for Jesus' departure from Judea: "Now when the Lord knew that the Pharisees had heard that Jesus was making and baptizing more disciples than John . . . ,[2] he left Judea and departed again to Galilee." It should be noted that the first time he started out for Galilee was in 1:43: "The next day Jesus decided to go to Galilee." On that occasion he went unconstrained and was next seen at Cana of Galilee (2:1-12); here, there is constraint because of the Pharisees. The menace of the Pharisees will increase as the gospel advances (cf. 5:1-18; 7-8 *passim;* 9-12 *passim*).

Themes

The major theme of the sequence is the theme of witness to Jesus. It begins in (a) with the statement of the Baptist's disciples that "he who was with you beyond the Jordan . . . is baptizing, and all are going to him" (3:26). It advances in (b) with John's implicit reference to the source of Jesus' greatness, "No one can receive anything except what is given him from heaven" (3:27), and with John's reminding his disciples that he had already solemnly declared, "I am not the Christ, but I have been sent before him" (3:28 and cp. 1:20; 1:30-31). It reaches a climax in (c) with John's declaration that Jesus is the bridegroom of Israel and that henceforth he, John, must decrease while Jesus increases.

In (b'), the evangelist explains the meaning of the Baptist's mysterious remark in 3:27: "No one can receive anything except what is given him from heaven." Jesus is the one who comes from heaven and testifies to what he has seen and heard in heaven, so that his testimony is true and must be accepted. Moreover, what Jesus has been given has been given to him by the Father. The witness theme is concluded in (a') by the evangelist's remark about Jesus' learning that "the Pharisees had heard that Jesus was making and baptizing more disciples than John" (4:1).

The replacement theme is not present at all, unless one wishes to see it in Jesus' replacing the Baptist and in the Baptist's disciples' leaving him to follow Jesus. The theme of response is present in 3:32: "He bears witness to what he has seen and heard, yet no one receives his testimony"; and 3:36: "He who believes in the Son has eternal life; he who does not obey the Son shall not see life, but the wrath of God rests upon him."

Chiastic parallels with sequence 1 (1:19-51)

The fifth sequence (3:22–4:3) forms a major inclusion-conclusion with the first sequence (1:19-51) of part I (1:19–4:3) by bringing back the Baptist to reiterate the witness he gave to Jesus in 1:19-34 and by showing him now ready to fade from the scene as Jesus' manifestation of himself to Israel becomes an accomplished fact.

The inclusion-conclusion is achieved by returning to the scene many of the same persons—the Baptist and his disciples, Jesus and his disciples—and by highlighting once again the theme of baptism. In addition, the reader should attend to the other numerous verbal parallels indicated below.

Sequence 5	*Sequence 1*
3:23: **John** also was **baptizing** at Aenon near Salim.	1:25-26: They asked him, "Then why are you **baptizing** . . . .? **John** answered, I **baptize** with water . . ."
3:25: Now a discussion arose between **John's disciples** and a Jew . . .	1:35: The next day again John was standing with two of **his disciples** . . .
3:26: "Rabbi, he who was with you **beyond the Jordan** . . ."	1:28: This took place in Bethany **beyond the Jordan** . . .
3:28: "You yourselves bear me witness, that I said, **I am not the Christ,** but I have been **sent before him.**"	1:20: He confessed **"I am not the Christ."**
	1:30: "This is he of whom I said, 'After me comes a man who ranks **before** me, for he was **before** me.' "
	1:33: "He who **sent** me to baptize . . ."
4:1-3: Now when the **Lord** knew that the Pharisees had heard that Jesus was making and baptizing more disciples than John . . . he left Judea and departed **again to Galilee.**	1:23: ". . . make straight the way of the **Lord**"
	1:43: The next day Jesus decided to go **to Galilee.**

Part II

RESPONSE TO JESUS
4:4–6:15

In part II, which deals primarily with response to Jesus, the evangelist makes use of antithetic parallelism to balance sequence with sequence. He creates antithetic parallelism between (a) and (a') by contrasting the willing belief of the half-pagan Samaritan woman with the blind refusal of the Galilean Jews to accept and believe in Jesus. In (b) and (b'), he creates antithetic parallelism by contrasting the belief of the Samaritan townspeople, based only on the word of Jesus, with the unbelief of the Jerusalem Jews, even after Jesus had cured a paralytic practically before their eyes.

The center (c) also deals with the theme of response and shows a royal official (probably intended to represent the response of the pagans to Jesus) believing in Jesus even before he comes to find out that his son had been healed. Thus, all five sequences of part II deal with different kinds of response to the credentials of Jesus. By emphasizing the negative response of the Jews in sequences 9 and 10, the evangelist prepares for his turning point in part III (6:16-21).

Parallel structure of part II

(a) *Sequence 6 (4:4-38):*   The **Samaritan woman believes.**
(b) *Sequence 7 (4:39-45):*   The **Samaritan townspeople believe.**
(c) *Sequence 8 (4:46-52):*   The royal official believes.
(b') *Sequence 9 (5:1-47):*   The **Jerusalem Jews refuse to believe.**
(a') *Sequence 10 (6:1-15):* The **Galilean Jews refuse to believe.**

Sequence 6

THE SAMARITAN WOMAN BELIEVES

4:4-38

Parallel structure

(a) Jesus, **wearied** (*kekopiakōs*), sits at the well (4:4-6).
(b) The Samaritan woman is **surprised** (4:7-18).
(c) Worship in spirit and truth (4:19-24)
(b′) The apostles are **surprised** (4:25-34).
(a′) Others have **labored** *(kekopiakasin),* and you have entered into their **labor** *(kopon)*—(4:35-38).

Text

(a)   4:4 He had to pass through Samaria. ⁵So he came to a city of Samaria, called Sychar, near the **field** that Jacob gave to his son Joseph. ⁶Jacob's well was there, and so Jesus, **wearied** as he was with his journey, sat down beside the well. It was about **the sixth hour.**

(b)   ⁷**There came a woman of Samaria** to draw water. Jesus said to her, "Give me a drink." ⁸For **his disciples had gone away into the city to buy food.** ⁹The Samaritan woman said to him, **"How is it that you, a Jew, ask a drink of me, a woman of Samaria?"** For Jews have no dealings with Samaritans. ¹⁰Jesus answered her, "If you knew the gift of God, and **who it is** that is saying to you, 'Give me a drink,' you would have asked him, and he would have given you living water." ¹¹The woman said to him, "Sir, you have nothing to draw with, and the well is deep; where do you get that living water? ¹²Are you greater than our father Jacob, who gave us the well, and drank from it himself, and his sons, and his cattle?" ¹³Jesus said to her, "Every one who drinks of this water will thirst again, ¹⁴but whoever drinks of the water that I shall give him will never thirst; the water that I shall give him will become in him a spring of water welling up to eternal life." ¹⁵The woman said to him, "Sir, give me this water, that I may not thirst, nor come here to draw."

    ¹⁶Jesus said to her, "Go, call your husband, and come here." ¹⁷The woman answered him, "I have no husband." Jesus said to her, "You are right in saying, 'I have no husband'; ¹⁸for **you have had five husbands,** and he whom you now have is not your husband; this you said truly."

(c)   ¹⁹The woman said to him, "Sir, I perceive that you are a prophet. ²⁰Our fathers worshiped on this mountain; and you say that in Jerusalem is the place where men ought to worship.'' ²¹Jesus said to her, ''Woman, believe me, the hour is coming when neither on this mountain nor in Jerusalem will you worship the Father. ²²You worship what you do not know; we worship what we know, for salvation is from the Jews. ²³But the hour is coming, and now is, when the true worshipers will worship the Father in spirit and truth, for such the Father seeks to worship him. ²⁴God is spirit, and those who worship him must worship in spirit and truth.''

(b')   ²⁵The woman said to him, ''I know that Messiah is coming (he who is called Christ); when he comes, he will show us all things.'' ²⁶Jesus said to her, **''I who speak to you am he.''**

²⁷Just then **his disciples came. They marveled that he was talking with a woman,** but none said, ''What do you wish?'' or, ''Why are you talking with her?'' ²⁸So **the woman** left her water jar, and **went away into the city,** and said to the people, ²⁹''Come, see a man who told me **all that I ever did.** Can this be the Christ?'' ³⁰They **went out of the city** and were coming to him.

³¹Meanwhile the **disciples** besought him, saying, ''Rabbi, **eat.''** ³²But he said to them, ''I have **food** to eat of which you do not know.'' ³³So the **disciples** said to one another, ''Has any one brought him **food?''** ³⁴Jesus said to them, ''My **food** is to do the will of him who sent me, and to accomplish his work.

(a')   ³⁵''Do you not say, 'There are yet **four months,** then comes the harvest'? I tell you, lift up your eyes, and see how the **fields** are already white for harvest. ³⁶He who reaps receives wages, and gathers fruit for eternal life, so that sower and reaper may rejoice together. ³⁷For here the saying holds true, 'One sows and another reaps.' ³⁸I sent you to reap that for which you did not **labor;** others have **labored,** and you have entered into their **labor.''**

The evangelist creates parallelism between (a) and (a') in several ways: (1) by the repetition of different forms of the Greek word for ''labor'': *kekopiakōs* in (a), and *kekopiakasin* and *kopon* in (a'); (2) by the repetition of the word ''field'' (*chōriou*) in v 5 and in v 35 (*chōras*); and (3) by a time reference in each section (cf. 4:6b and 35b).

The evangelist has (b') look back at (b) in several ways. First, in (b) he has the woman come and the disciples leave; in (b') he has the disciples come and the woman leave (cp. 4:7-8 with 4:27-28). Second, in (b) he has the woman express her surprise that Jesus, a Jew, should speak to her, a Samaritan and a woman; in (b') he has the disciples express their surprise that Jesus should be found talking to a woman (cp. 4:9 with 4:27). Third, in (b) Jesus raises the question of his identity by saying, ''If you knew the gift of God, and *who it is* that is saying to you, 'Give me a drink . . .''' (4:10); in (b') the evangelist has Jesus respond to the woman's statement ''I know that Messiah is coming'' by identifying himself as the Messiah with the words ''I who speak to you am he'' (cp. 4:19, 26 with 4:10). Fourth, in (b) the evangelist has Jesus express his knowledge about the Samaritan woman's private marital situation (4:17-18); in (b') he has the woman announce to the people: ''Come, and see a man who told me all that I ever did'' (cp. 4:29 with 4:17-18). Finally, the disciples, who had departed the scene in 4:8 to buy *food,* return to engage Jesus in a discussion about *food* in 4:31-34.

The center (c) in 4:19-24 is clearly set off from (b) and (b') by its subject matter—the place and nature of true worship—and by the tenfold concatenation of the word "worship" (vv 20, 21, 22, 23, 24).

Commentary

A commentary on any part of John's Gospel requires a good control of John's literary techniques. In the sequence of the Samaritan woman, the literary and dramatic techniques the evangelist uses are so varied, abundant, and artistic that they represent practically a showcase of his talent. It will be helpful, therefore, to stop a moment and advert to some of the techniques the evangelist utilizes in this artfully told story.

First, there is the usual Johannine dialogue technique, which begins with the oracular statement of Jesus in 4:10, continues with a first misunderstanding on the part of the woman (v 11), followed by Jesus' explanation of what she has failed to understand (vv 13-14), and later a second misunderstanding (v 15). Unlike Jesus' dialogue with Nicodemus, his dialogue with the Samaritan woman does not tail off into a monologue.

Second, the use of the "rule of two." The dramatist's rule of two makes it desirable that as often as feasible no more than two speakers appear and speak in any one scene. It is a technique derived from the folk-tale and is scrupulously followed by John in this sequence. At the very beginning, John studiously gets the disciples off the stage when Jesus begins his dialogue with the Samaritan woman (cf. 4:8) and just as studiously gets the woman off the stage when the disciples return (cf. 4:27-28).

Third, the technique of double-meaning words. John regularly uses words that have one meaning for the characters in his story and another for Jesus or for the evangelist's readers. The following are notable in 4:4-38: "living water" (4:10); "not thirst" (4:15); "food" (4:32); and "harvest" (4:35).

Fourth, the misunderstanding technique. The technique is used twice with the woman (4:11-15) and once with the disciples (4:31-33), in each case allowing Jesus to correct the misunderstanding and thus by contrast express his real meaning more emphatically.

Fifth, the use of "stages." John uses three stages in this sequence. He has a front stage for Jesus and the Samaritan woman, a back stage in town for the disciples' quest for food and for the Samaritan woman's dialogue with her townspeople, and an in-between stage for the townspeople coming out to meet Jesus (cf. 4:30).

(a) Jesus, wearied *(kekopiakōs),* sits at the well (4:4-6).

4:4 He had to pass through Samaria. This was not a geographical necessity, since there were other routes available, but the same kind of necessity as in 3:14—a necessity in some way associated with God's plan to bring all who believe in Jesus to eternal life.[1]

4:5 Sychar. Probably Askar, a town at the foot of Mount Ebal, about three quarters of a mile from the well; possibly the ruins of ancient Shechem, a very short distance from the well. The field given to Joseph is a reference to Gn 48:22: "I give to you, as to the one above his brothers, Shechem . . . ."

4:6 sat down . . . about the sixth hour. The scene is reminiscent of the scene in Ex 2:15, in which Moses sits at the well. The reference to the "sixth hour" is dubious as a reference to the passion (19:14—"the sixth hour"), unless the reference to "thirst" is meant to prepare the reader for the words of Jesus on the cross: "I thirst" (19:14). In both cases, the dubious allegorical association would have to do with Jesus' thirst to complete his work of salvation.

(b) The Samaritan woman is surprised (4:7-18).

4:7-8 a woman of Samaria. With the Samaritan woman on stage and ready for the dialogue with Jesus, the evangelist removes the disciples by having them go into town to buy food, thus preserving the rule of two and at the same time setting the stage for the return of the disciples and their subsequent discussion with Jesus about food in vv 31-34 of (b′).

4:9 Jews have no dealings with Samaritans. The opposition between Jews and Samaritans had roots going back to the time of the Judges (cf. Jgs 6-9). Later, following the division of Solomon's kingdom in 922 B.C. into a northern kingdom (Israel) and a southern kingdom (Judah), Samaria became the capital of the rebel northern kingdom. After the destruction of Samaria by the Assyrians in 722, the city became half Israelite and half pagan when the Assyrians repopulated it with pagans deported from other parts of the empire (cf. 2 Kgs 17:24ff).

When the Jews returned from the Babylonian exile in 537, they rebuilt the temple but refused to let the Samaritans collaborate in the rebuilding on the score that they were a mongrel race tainted by pagan blood and pagan religion. The active animosity between Jews and Samaritans probably dates from this period, though it could have begun even later when the Samaritans built their own temple on Mount Gerizim about 315 B.C. in opposition to the temple of Jerusalem. The destruction of the Samaritan temple (c. 128 B.C.) by the Maccabean king John Hyrcanus did nothing toward assuaging the religious and national animosity of the two peoples. In the course of time, the rabbis came to treat all Samaritans as unclean, i.e., as people whom Jews could not associate with, come into contact with, or share drinking vessels with, as in this case, without becoming unclean.[2]

4:9b How is it that you, a Jew, ask a drink of me? Jesus, as his manner of acting here indicates, is not concerned with rules of uncleanness (cf. Mk 7:1-15). Nor is he concerned about the impropriety of speaking with a woman—a matter that surprises his apostles (cf. vv 27-28). As the Savior of the world, he is concerned with all men and women, regardless of social distinctions.

4:10 If you knew the gift of God. In characteristic Johannine style, Jesus gives the dialogue a theological turn by means of a mysterious and almost oracular statement that sums up both the content and the purpose of the conversation that is to follow. What Jesus really is saying is: "If only you recognized God's gift (eternal life) and who it is (the Savior of the world) that is asking you for a drink, you would have asked him instead, and he would have given you the living water of eternal life."

4:11 living water. As in 3:5ff, where Nicodemus was made to misunderstand Jesus' words about being "born anew," so here the Samaritan woman is made to misunderstand Jesus' words about living water. Jesus means the water of eternal life (cf. 3:5; 7:39; 19:34); she thinks he means flowing (living) water as opposed to cistern (dead) water (cf. Jer 2:13; Zech 14:8; Ez 47:9). **Sir.** The woman uses titles indicating her growing respect for Jesus, addressing him successively as "you, a Jew" (v 9), "Sir" (*Kyrie*)—(v 11), "prophet" (v 19), and "the Christ" (v 29).

4:12 Are you greater than our father Jacob? The irony of the question is typically Johannine. The woman is made to speak the truth but without realizing it: Jesus in infinitely greater than Jacob.

4:15 Sir, give me this water, that I may not thirst. Again the woman is made to misunderstand, thinking that getting "this water" will save her tiresome trips to the well, whereas Jesus is speaking, as before, of the water of eternal life.

4:16-18 Go, call your husband. Jesus' supernatural knowledge has already been demonstrated (cf. 1:48), and the point made here about the woman's five husbands may simply be another example of the same (cf. v 29: "Come, see a man who told me all that I ever did"). Nevertheless, in the immediate sequel to the discussion about the woman's marital status, Jesus speaks about true and false worship and expressly refers to the Samaritan temple on nearby Mount Gerizim. The context of worship suggests that the references to the "five husbands" may be better understood as a veiled allusion to the pagan peoples, mentioned in 2 Kgs 17:24, who had come to Samaria with their false gods. The one who "is not your husband," therefore, is probably an equally veiled allusion to the false religion of the Samaritans or, more properly, to the Samaritans' false worship of the true God. The irony would not have been lost on John's Jewish-Christian readers.

(c) Worship in spirit and truth (4:19-24)

4:19 a prophet. The woman's acknowledgment of Jesus as a prophet looks back for its justification to the supernatural knowledge about her life that Jesus had manifested, but at the same time it leads the way to the discussion about worship that follows, since it was a popular opinion that a prophet was needed in order to decide upon matters of worship (cf. 1 Mc 4:46). In view of the subsequent discussion in 4:25ff about the Messiah, it may be that the woman is making a veiled reference to the Samaritans' expectation that the prophet predicted by Moses in Dt 18:15 would be the Messiah.

4:20-24 worship. In 2:13-25, Jesus had already implied that the temple of his body would replace the temple of Jerusalem. Here he reiterates that contention. The hour (v 21) that is coming is the hour of Jesus' death, which will terminate any legitimacy heretofore claimed by either the Jewish temple in Jerusalem or the Samaritan temple on Mount Gerizim.

4:22 salvation is from the Jews. Jesus confirms the election of Israel and the divine source of her revelation, but he does so in such a way that his subsequent statement in v 23 about the hour coming when "the true worshipers will worship the Father in spirit and truth" implies the end of Israel's privileged status and the replacement of Israel by the community of Christians—the "true worshipers . . . in spirit and truth." The sense of "the hour coming" that "now is" means that in Jesus the type of perfect worship sought by the Father is already present! The idea is similar to that expressed in 2:13-25 and 11:25.

4:24 God is spirit. John uses the term "spirit" in the Old Testament sense of life-giving spirit or influence. Since Christians share this life-giving spirit, they are those who "worship in spirit and truth." **Spirit and truth.** The terms are almost equivalent. The spirit is the source of divine life-giving vitality; the truth is the divine reality revealed by Jesus. Thus, it follows that true worshipers are those born of the spirit, as in 3:5-8 and 3:31.[3]

(b') The apostles are surprised (4:25-34).

4:25 I know that Messiah is coming. The reference is to the promised prophet of Dt 18:15, whom the Samaritans (who accepted as inspired only the Pentateuch and not the rest of the Old Testament) spoke of as the *taheb,* i.e., the "one who returns," rather than as the Messiah. Little is known about messianic expectations among the Samaritans, but John here makes it clear that Jesus is the fulfillment of whatever the Samaritans expected in the way of a Messiah.

In the (b) section, Jesus had made a mysterious reference to himself in v 10: "If you knew the gift of God, and *who it is* that is saying to you, 'Give me a drink' . . . ." Here, in response to the woman's remark about the Messiah's coming, Jesus explains "who he is." He is the Messiah. This flashback to v 10 concludes Jesus' dialogue with the woman. At the same time, the disciples, who had been removed from the stage in v 8 by going into town to buy food, now return, and the Samaritan woman departs—in perfect observance of the rule of two. John, who had begun the (b) section

with the departure of the disciples to buy food (4:8), will now terminate the
(b') section (4:25-34) with the return of the disciples and with their discussion with Jesus about food.

4:27 They marveled that he was talking with a woman. The surprise of
the disciples balances with the surprise of the Samaritan woman in v 9, just
as the woman's statement to the people of the town, "Come, see a man who
told me *all that I ever did"* (v 29), balances with Jesus' statement to the
woman about *the five husbands in her personal life* in v 18.

4:30 They went out of the city and were coming to him. The Samaritan
townspeople do not actually meet Jesus until the following sequence (4:39-45),
but the evangelist is not just preparing for the next sequence—he is setting
the scene for the conclusion of the whole Samaritan-woman sequence. Here,
for the first time, the three stages upon which the action of the sequence
is acted out are visible at the same time: (1) the rear stage, which is in the
town; (2) the intermediate stage, upon which the Samaritans are seen walking toward Jesus; (3) the center stage, upon which the disciples are seen
discoursing with Jesus about food and the harvest (4:31-38).

4:31 Meanwhile. Barrett correctly observes that "the scene between the
disciples and Jesus (vv 31-38) takes place *between* the departure of the woman
and the arrival of the men of Sychar."[4] The evangelist's remark thus
associates the two scenes, and the reader is enabled to see at the same time
the center stage, where Jesus is discoursing with his disciples, and the intermediate stage, where the Samaritans, who have left the town (the rear
stage), are now visible coming out to meet Jesus. The fact that Jesus and
his disciples can see the Samaritans approaching prepares the reader to understand the otherwise mysterious words of Jesus in vv 35ff as referring to the
approaching Samaritans: "Lift up your eyes, and see how the fields are
already white for harvest." Jesus has brought the Samaritan woman to believe
in him. In the next sequence (4:39-45), the townspeople, who "are already
white for harvest" will be brought to believe in Jesus too.

4:31-34 the disciples besought him, saying, "Rabbi, eat." In his
characteristic manner, the evangelist clarifies the whole situation by having
the disciples misunderstand what Jesus means by "food." This gives Jesus
the opportunity to explain to them the real meaning of what he has been
about in his dialogue with the Samaritan woman. Jesus' food is the work
of salvation—bringing men and women to believe in him and thereby bringing them to eternal life (cf. 17:4 and 19:30). That is the way he "accomplishes" the work of the Father, who "so loved the world that he gave
his only Son, that whoever believes in him should not perish but have eternal life" (3:16). The technique of using a double-meaning word, followed
by a misunderstanding in which the hearer understands the word on a shallow
or mundane level, followed by Jesus' explanation of the word on an infinitely
deeper level, had already been used in Jesus' dialogue with Nicodemus (3:5-10)

and in his dialogue with the Samaritan woman (4:10-15). Thus, as so often in John's Gospel, it is the misunderstanding technique that gives the clue to his meaning.

Popular interpretation of this sequence has frequently centered interest on the Samaritan woman. The evangelist, however, is interested in far more than the woman. The sequence moves ahead continually from its depiction of the woman's gradual movement toward belief in Jesus as prophet (v 19) and possibly as Messiah (v 30) to her telling the townspeople about Jesus and their setting out from the town to meet Jesus (v 29) and eventually coming to believe in him, not on the word of the Samaritan woman, but on his word alone (4:39-45).

The evangelist reveals his overall interest and purpose for the sequence as a whole here in 4:31-34, where everything comes together with the disciples' misunderstanding about "food" and Jesus' clarification: "My food is to do the will of him who sent me, and to accomplish his work" (v 34). In the light of 3:15-17, where the evangelist pinpointed the work of God with the words "God so loved the world that he *gave* his only Son, that whoever *believes* in him should not perish but have eternal life," the Samaritan-woman sequence takes on a whole new aspect. It shows Jesus, the only-begotten Son of God, *doing* the *work* for which the Father *sent* him into the world. It shows him patiently leading the half-pagan Samaritan woman to *believe* in him, the source of the water that becomes a fountain "welling up to eternal life" (4:14). He had said, "If you knew the gift of God, and who it is that is saying to you, 'Give me a drink' . . . ." (4:10). Here in 4:32-34, he declares that he has done the work of the Father by bringing the Samaritan woman to believe in him, the source of living water and what that water signifies— eternal life, God's gift to all who believe in him.

(a') Others have labored (*kekopiakasin*), and you have entered into their labor (*kopon*)—(4:35-38).

The evangelist's inclusion-conclusion consists of a brief monologue on the subject of the harvest and the work entailed in reaping and harvesting.

4:35-36 Do you not say . . . ? Between sowing and reaping in Palestine there is ordinarily a period of four to six months, but the harvest of those who believe in Jesus is not dependent on time. Jesus and the apostles can see the Samaritans approaching. The sight prompts Jesus to say: "Lift up your eyes, and see how the fields are already white for harvest." Jesus has sown the word in the heart of the woman; the woman has sown the word in the hearts of her townspeople. The "reaper," who is certainly Jesus in this context, is about to gather "fruit for eternal life," inasmuch as the woman is already half converted and the townspeople will shortly come to believe in Jesus and say, "We know that this is indeed the Savior of the world" (4:42).

4:36b-37 One sows and another reaps. If Jesus is the reaper, who is the sower? In the immediate context of the sequence, it could be Jesus himself, who sowed the word in the heart of the woman, or the woman, who sowed the word in the heart of her townspeople, who are now approaching to hear and eventually believe in Jesus. In the context of the Gospel as a whole, however, the sower is much more likely the Father, who sent Jesus. Jesus himself, in v 34, had said, "My food is to do the will of him who sent me, and to accomplish his work." It is not too farfetched to see the work of the Father as sowing the seed of belief in the hearts of people, especially since elsewhere in the Gospel it is the Father who draws men and women to himself through Jesus (cf. 6:44, 65) and gives them to Jesus (cf. 6:37ff; 10:29; 17:6). Thus Jesus, as reaper, completes the work of his Father, the sower (cf. 4:34; 5:17; 17:4; 19:30).

4:38a I sent you to reap. The words presuppose that the apostles have already been commissioned by Jesus to sow the word and reap the crop of believers for whom they have been sent into the world, as Jesus was sent into the world by the Father. While such a mission seems premature this early in Jesus' ministry, especially in view of the fact that Jesus does not actually commission the apostles until after the resurrection (cf. 20:21-23; 21:15-19), it is nonetheless true that John gives little attention to chronology (probably because it could not be easily sustained in the chiastic structure of his Gospel) and frequently has Jesus speak before his death and resurrection in a manner more suitable to the situation that existed only after his resurrection (cf. the whole of the Last Supper discourse and especially ch 17). The words, therefore, should probably be interpreted as a brief instruction for the missionaries of the Johannine Church at the end of the first century. As such, the words would share the timelessness of John's Last Supper discourse (chs 13–17), which is also directed to the missionaries of the Johannine Church.

4:38b others have labored. In the immediate context of v 38, the "others" could be all those who sowed the word of the gospel before the time of the evangelist in the late first century. Some commentators would include the patriarchs, the prophets, and John the Baptist. The context of vv 34-37, however, with Jesus as the reaper and the Father as the sower, makes it more probable that the "others" are Jesus and the Father. Schnackenburg objects to including the Father with Jesus among the others who have labored. He says, "This might hold good for Jesus (cf. 4:6), but it would be quite out of place for the Father."[5] Schnackenburg may be correct; nevertheless, John regularly associates the Father and the Son in the work of salvation, most prominently in 5:17, where Jesus says, "My Father is working still, and I am working," but also elsewhere (cf. 5:19-21, 30, 36; 8:17-18; 28; 10:30, 37-38).

Themes

The themes of witness, response, and replacement seem evenly distributed throughout the sequence, but actually the major theme is the theme of response: we are shown how Jesus leads the Samaritan woman to respond to him with faith.

In part I of the Gospel (1:19–4:3), the witness theme dominated. The evangelist showed Jesus manifesting himself to the Jews through the witness of the Baptist, the Holy Spirit, the apostles, and the sign at Cana. These witnesses were followed by his declarations about the temple of his body in the sequence of the cleansing of the temple (2:13-25) and about the need for faith in him in his discourse to Nicodemus (3:1-21). Concomitant with his manifestation went a positive response from the Baptist and his disciples, and a lukewarm if not cold response from the Jews in the sequences of the cleansing of the temple and the discourse to Nicodemus.

In the whole of part II (4:4–6:15), the response theme, rather than the witness or replacement theme, is the major theme. In part II, Jesus begins to do the "work" for which the Father sent him into the world—the work of saving the world (3:16-18) by eliciting from men and women a positive response to himself, his words, and his signs.

He begins by revealing himself to the Samaritan woman, and she responds positively, prompting Jesus to say, "My food is to do the will of him who sent me, and to accomplish *his work"* (4:34). At the same time, he sees the Samaritans coming across the fields and, anticipating their conversion, declares, "The fields are already white for harvest" (4:35b). The Samaritans, as we see in sequence 7 (4:39-45), hear Jesus and believe even though they see no miracles nor hear Jesus reveal to them, as he had to the Samaritan woman, mysterious knowledge of their private lives.

The theme of positive response will be carried on in sequence 8 (4:46-54) when the words of the Samaritans, "We know that this is indeed the Savior of the world" (4:42b), are realized in the belief and conversion of the royal official and his family. The work of the Father who loves the world and gives his only-begotten Son to save the world is thus seen being carried out by the Son through his conversion of the half-Jewish Samaritans and the royal official and his family.

In sequence 9 (5:1-47)—the cure on the sabbath, followed by a revelatory and judgmental speech to the Jews—and in sequence 10 (6:1-15)—the account of the Galilean Jews' response to Jesus' multiplication of the loaves and fishes—the theme of response is continued, but in a negative vein. In contrast to the positive response of the Samaritans and the royal official, the Jews of Jerusalem and the Jews of Galilee neither listen to Jesus nor respond to his words and miracles. With the emphasis on the theme of response in part II of the Gospel, the movement of the Gospel accelerates. The negative response of the Jews will lead eventually to Jesus' rejection of the Jews, his formation of the Christian community, and his eventual passion, death, and resurrection.

The theme of replacement is not slighted, but neither is it emphasized. It is carried on from the previous sequences, where it was a major theme (in the Cana miracle and the cleansing episode), and repeated via the water analogy (4:7-15) and the discussion concerning the place and nature of the true worship (4:19-24). As R. H. Lightfoot observes:

> Both at the beginning and end of the Lord's conversation with the woman of Samaria, there is a contrast between the old order and the new order now coming into being (4:23): 1) the water drawn from Jacob's well is not to be compared with the water brought by the Lord (4:7-15); 2) both the Jewish worship in the temple at Jerusalem, and the Samaritan worship on Mount Gerizim, are to be, indeed, are being replaced by a worship which will have its seat neither in Jerusalem nor in Samaria.[6]

The theme of witness is continued through Jesus' witness to himself at the beginning and the end of the dialogue with the Samaritan woman and by her heaping up of titles for Jesus, beginning with "Sir" (v 11) and progressing through "prophet" (v 19) to Messiah (v 30). The title "Savior of the world" in 4:42 should probably be added to the heaping up of titles in this part of the Gospel.

Sequence 7

THE SAMARITAN TOWNSPEOPLE BELIEVE IN JESUS

4:39-45

Parallel structure

(a) Many **Samaritans from that city believed in him** because of the woman's testimony (4:39).

(b) **He stayed there two days** (4:40-41).

(c) This is indeed the Savior of the world (4:42).

(b') **After the two days he departed** to Galilee (4:43-44).

(a') The **Galileans welcomed him,** having seen all that he had done in Jerusalem at the feast (4:45).

Text

(a)   4:39 Many **Samaritans** from that city **believed in him** because of the woman's testimony, "He told me **all that I ever did.**"

(b)   ⁴⁰So when the Samaritans came to him, they asked him to stay with them; and **he stayed there two days.** ⁴¹And many more believed because of his word.

(c)   ⁴²They said to the woman, "It is no longer because of your words that we believe, for we have heard for ourselves, and we know that this is indeed the Savior of the world."

(b')   ⁴³**After the two days he departed** to Galilee. ⁴⁴For Jesus himself testified that a prophet has no honor in his own country.

(a')   ⁴⁵So when he came to Galilee, the **Galileans welcomed him,** having seen **all that he had done** in Jerusalem at the feast, for they too had gone to the feast.

The evangelist creates parallelism between (a) and (a') in two ways. First, he parallels the words "all that I ever did" (*panta hosa epoiēsa*) in v 39 with the words "all that he had done" (*panta hosa epoiēsen*) in v 45. Second, using a subtle form of antithetic parallelism, he contrasts the reception Jesus receives in v 39 from the Samaritans who believed in him (*episteusan eis auton*) with the cool reception he receives from the Galilean Jews, who are not said to believe in him but only to "welcome him" (*edexanto auton*) and, indeed,

77

to welcome him, "having seen all that he had done in Jerusalem at the feast" (v 45).

The center (c) emphasizes even more the faith of the Samaritans, who are said to believe in Jesus "because of his word"—a far cry from the inadequate faith of the Galilean Jews, who only welcome Jesus because they had seen what he had done at the feast in Jerusalem (cf. 2:13-25, but especially vv 23-25).

In (b) and (b'), the evangelist creates parallelism by repeating the words "two days" (vv 40 and 43). Also, he further emphasizes the Samaritans' warm reception of Jesus (they beg him to stay for two days) by contrasting it with the different kind of reception Jesus would receive in Galilee—"For Jesus himself testified that a prophet has no honor in his own country" (v 44).

Commentary

(a) Many Samaritans from that city believed in him because of the woman's testimony (4:39).

4:39 Samaritans . . . believed in him. Up to this point in the Gospel, the only ones said to have believed in Jesus (*episteusan eis auton*) without qualification are the disciples at Cana (2:11). Here the same is said of the Samaritans. The statement is strong because it is meant to point up a contrast to the statement of the inclusion (v 45) that "when he came to Galilee, the Galileans welcomed (better: "received") him." They welcomed or received him in contrast to the Samaritans, who "believed in him." That the Samaritans believed in him because of the woman's testimony: "He *told* me all that I ever did (*panta hosa epoiēsa*)," provides an even starker contrast to the Galilean Jews, who had *seen* "all that he had done (*panta hosa epoiēsan*) in Jerusalem at the feast" (cf. 2:23-25) and nevertheless did not believe but only "welcomed" ("received") him (v 45).

(b) And he stayed there two days (4:40-41).

4:40 they asked him. The contrast between the believing Samaritans and the welcoming Galilean Jews is further heightened by the eagerness of the Samaritans to hear Jesus. They "asked him" is in marked antithetic parallelism with Jesus' statement about the Galilean Jews in (b'): "a prophet has no honor in his own country" (v 44). The two days Jesus stayed with the Samaritans enhance even further his reception in Samaria in contrast with his reception in Galilee.

4:41 believed because of his word. Heightening the contrast to the Galilean Jews to the utmost, John uses the verb "believe" for a second (v 41: *episteusan*) and a third time (v 42: *pisteuomen*). In v 42, he will deliberately emphasize the nature of the Samaritans' faith. They believe in Jesus, not because of what the woman told them about Jesus' miraculous knowledge concerning her private life (4:17-18), but because "we have heard for ourselves." Unlike the Galilean Jews, who do not esteem "a prophet in his own country" (v 44) and who only "welcome" (better: "receive") him even after seeing all that he had done in Jerusalem (v 45), the Samaritans believe Jesus on his word alone! This is John's way of saying that faith terminates in the person of Jesus, not in dogmatic formulas or theological statements intellectually grasped. As Hoskyns cogently observes, "The pressing of faith to its proper resting place in the teaching of Jesus Himself and not merely in the teaching of his disciples conditions the form of the gospel throughout."[1]

(c) This is indeed the Savior of the world (4:42).

4:42 the Savior of the world. The title is surprising coming from the Samaritans after only two days with Jesus, but it is nonetheless thoroughly Johannine. The universalism of the title recurs in many places in the Gospel, e.g.: "Behold, the Lamb of God, who takes away the sin of the world!" (1:29); ". . . so must the Son of man be lifted up, that whoever believes in him may have eternal life" (3:14-15); "For God so loved the world that he gave his only Son . . ." (3:16); ". . . and I, when I am lifted up from the earth, will draw all men to myself" (12:32); ". . . for I did not come to judge the world but to save the world" (12:47); "He did not say this of his own accord, but being high priest that year he prophesied that Jesus should die for the nation, and not for the nation only, but to gather into one the children of God who are scattered abroad" (11:51).

While surprising coming from the Samaritans, the title "Savior of the world" is really no less surprising than the titles so quickly given to Jesus in his first encounter with the Baptist and his disciples in 1:19-52 (e.g., Lamb of God, Messiah, King of Israel, Son of God, Son of man) and in his encounter with the Samaritan woman in 4:4-24 (e.g., Sir, prophet, Messiah) and would seem in this instance to be another example of John's literary technique of "heaping up titles."[2] The title serves the further function of providing a significant parallel with 5:1-47, the chiastic counterpart of this sequence in part II of the Gospel. In 5:1-47, John stresses Jesus' power to save (judge) *all men* (5:19-30).

(b') After the two days he departed to Galilee (4:43-44).

4:43 two days. The tempo increases with Jesus' departure for Galilee after two days with the Samaritans (cf. the parallel "two days" in v 40).

4:44 a prophet has no honor in his own country. Jesus' own words (cf. Mt 13:57; Mk 6:4) are used to foreshadow the kind of welcome he will receive from his own, the Galilean Jews, in contrast with the welcome he had received from the half-pagan Samaritans. "His own country" is Galilee! It is possible, but not probable, that the words refer to the Samaritan woman in 4:42. Her fellow townspeople say to her: "It is no longer because of your words that we believe . . . ."

(a′) The Galileans welcomed him, having seen all that he had done in Jerusalem
   at the feast (4:45).

4:45   welcomed him. The welcome ("reception" would be a much better word) is not an acceptance of Jesus in the sense that the Galilean Jews
believe in Jesus as the Samaritans believed. It is quite the opposite. They
welcome him because they themselves had seen all that he had done in
Jerusalem at the feast. The ambiguity and inadequacy of the welcome can
be deduced from the reason for the welcome: they had "seen all that he had
done in Jerusalem." The reader is immediately reminded of the evangelist's
comments in 2:23-25: "Now when he was in Jerusalem at the Passover feast,
many believed in his name when they saw the signs which he did; but *Jesus
did not trust himself to them, because he knew all men* and needed no one
to bear witness of man; for *he himself knew what was in man.*"

John's intentional contrast between the reception Jesus received from the
believing Samaritans in (a) and the reception he received from the Galilean
Jews in (a′) suggests that 4:45 is meant in the same sense as 2:23-24. Both
texts foreshadow the Jews' rejection of Jesus. Schnackenburg does not really
know what to do with the text "Jesus himself testified that a prophet has
no honor in his own country." He says, "There is much to be said for the
idea that the verse is a redactional gloss, inserted in view of what actually
happened to Jesus (cf. 6:42) . . . ."[3] Nevertheless, Schnackenburg catches
perfectly the drift of the evangelist's mind in 4:44-45. He says:

> The reader has been told nothing so far of the Galileans' attitude to Jesus—
> not even after the first miracle at Cana. Hence the evangelist now notes
> that they did in fact "receive" Jesus (*dechesthai* occurs only here; under
> the influence of the proverb, v 44?), but only because they had seen all that
> he had accomplished in Jerusalem. This derogatory judgment is confirmed
> by Jesus' words in v 45: the response of the Galileans is as inadequate as
> that of the people of Jerusalem (2:23). Hence "receive" only means a
> welcome of a superficial type, not that "acceptance" (*lambanein tina*) which
> designates genuine faith (1:12; 5:43; cf. 3:11, 32f; 12:48; 13:20; 17:8). This
> is only an apparent correction of the saying quoted by Jesus in v 44; its
> real meaning is already confirmed.[4]

Themes

The theme of response, positive and negative, dominates sequence 7. The
Samaritan townspeople, like the Samaritan woman, respond positively to
Jesus. They are not Jews, not "his own" (1:11: "He came to his own home,
and his own people received him not"), but they accept him and believe in
him. In sequence 8 (4:46-54), the royal official, like the Samaritans not a
Jew, will receive and believe in Jesus and, as the Samaritans did, on Jesus'
word alone. Thus the first three sequences of part II (4:4–6:15) show Jesus
manifesting himself to non-Jews and receiving from all of them a response

of faith in his person without their having first seen him perform any signs or wonders.

The qualification is important because the evangelist will go on in the last two sequences (5:1-47 and 6:1-15) of part II to show that the Jews of Jerusalem would not believe in Jesus even after he cured a paralytic (5:1-47), and the Jews of Galilee would misconstrue his multiplication of the loaves and, instead of believing in him, would try to force him to become a nationalistic hero-king figure (6:1-15). The qualification is important for a second reason. It helps to explain the strange anomaly of Jesus' having "testified that a prophet has no honor in his own country" (4:44) immediately before John's statement "when he came to Galilee, the Galileans welcomed him" (4:45).

The theme of witness is brief but dramatic. The Samaritans witness to Jesus as "the Savior of the world." It is another way of witnessing to the truth proclaimed by the Baptist when he declared, "Behold, the Lamb of God who takes away the sin of the world" (1:29).

Sequence 8

THE ROYAL OFFICIAL BELIEVES

4:46-54

Parallel structure

(a) So he **came again** to Cana in **Galilee,** where he had **made the water wine** (4:46-47).

(b) Go; **your son will live** (4:48-50a).

(c) The man believed the word that Jesus spoke to him and went his way (4:50b).

(b′) The father knew that was the hour when Jesus had said to him, **"Your son will live"** (4:51-53).

(a′) This was now the **second sign** that Jesus did when he **had come from Judea to Galilee** (4:54).

Text

(a) 4:46 So he **came again** to Cana in **Galilee,** where he **had made the water wine.** And at Capernaum there was an official whose son was ill. [47]When he heard that Jesus **had come from Judea to Galilee,** he went and begged him to come down and heal his son, for he was at the point of death.

(b) [48]Jesus therefore said to him, "Unless you see signs and wonders you will not believe." [49]The official said to him, "Sir, **come down** before my **child** dies." [50a]Jesus said to him, "Go; **your son will live.**"

(c) [50b]The man believed the word that Jesus spoke to him and went his way.

(b′) [51]As he was **going down,** his servants met him and told him that his **son was living.** [52]So he asked them the hour when he began to mend, and they said to him, "Yesterday at the seventh hour the fever left him." [53]The father knew that was the hour when Jesus had said to him, **"Your son will live"**; and he himself believed, and all his household.

(a′) [54]This was now the **second sign** that Jesus did when he **had come from Judea to Galilee.**

The evangelist creates parallelism between (a) and (a′) by repeating the word "Galilee" in vv 46 and 54 and the words "had come from Judea to Galilee" in vv 47 and 54, and by paralleling the words "where he had made the water wine" (v 46) with the words "the second sign" in v 54. The exact words are not parallel, but the concept in each is the same, since the water made wine in v 46 is a clear reference to the "first sign" Jesus performed at Cana when he first came from Judea to Galilee (cf. 2:1-12).

In (b) and (b'), John creates parallelism by repeating the words "son" (*huios*) and "boy" (*pais, paidion*) in vv 49 and 50, and by repeating in vv 50 and 53 the identical words: "Your son will live." The center (c) emphasizes the royal official's belief in Jesus by showing that he believed in Jesus even *before* the miracle took place.

Commentary

(a) He came again to Cana in Galilee, where he had made the water wine (4:46-47).

4:46a   Cana in Galilee. John's reminder of what had happened on Jesus' first visit to Cana serves two purposes. First, it establishes a new scene for the sequence and gives it some distance from the previous scene in Samaria. Second, it recalls the faith-response of the disciples after seeing Jesus' first miracle at Cana (2:11) and thus prepares the reader for John's emphasis on the faith-response of the royal official, who will believe *on Jesus' word alone*. The reminder is important because it helps to distinguish those who believe in Jesus (the disciples in 2:11; the Samaritan woman in 4:29; and the people of Samaria in 4:42) from those who refuse to believe in him (the Jews of Jerusalem in 2:23-25 and 3:11) and those other Jews in the following sequences who will refuse to believe in him even after his cure of the paralytic (5:1-47) and his multiplication of the loaves (6:1-15).

4:46b   an official whose son was ill. It is not clear whether he is a Gentile, as in the Matthean (8:3-13) and Lukan 7:1-10) versions of the story, or a Jew, but probably John intends him to be taken as a Gentile.[1] The words "had come down from Galilee" remind the reader of the first Cana miracle that Jesus worked when he came from Judea to Galilee (cf. 1:42 and 2:1).

(b) Go; your son will live (4:48-50a).

4:48   Unless you see signs and wonders. The strangeness of Jesus' indignant rebuff in view of the official's obvious faith, and the fact that the verbs are in the plural (*edēte* and *pisteusēte*) lead some commentators to believe that John has added this rebuff to the traditional story (cf. Mt 8:5-13; Lk 7:1-10).[2] Like Jesus' statement to Nicodemus in 3:11d, ". . . but you do not receive (*lambanete*) our testimony," which is also in the plural even though Jesus is addressing only Nicodemus, just as he addresses only the official here, the charge has all the earmarks of an accusation made against the Jews of John's time rather than against the contemporaries of Jesus. The purpose of the remark is to emphasize that faith terminates in Jesus himself rather than in his miracles.[3] That this is a Johannine emphasis is apparent from other places where John highlights a faith that terminates in Jesus himself rather than in his miracles (cf. 4:41; 5:24; 11:25-27; 20:29, 31). John has little esteem for faith based on miracles alone (cf. 2:23-24; 6:2, 14).

(c) The man believed the word that Jesus spoke to him and went his way (4:50b).

4:50b The man believed the word. John's reason for using the story is found in these words. Without seeing a miracle, without knowing his son was cured, the official believed on Jesus' word alone. It is the kind of faith John looks for from those who hear the word of Jesus, the kind of faith that merits the praise: "Blessed are those who have not seen and yet believe" (20:29).[4]

(b') The father knew that was the hour when Jesus had said to him, "Your son will live" (4:51-53).

4:53 he himself believed; and all his household. Presumably the whole household believed on the word of the official about what Jesus had told him as well as upon the basis of the son's cure. In any event, John has made his point by means of vv 48 and 50b concerning the finer quality of the faith of those who believe even without seeing.

(a') This was now the second sign that Jesus did when he had come from Judea to Galilee (4:54).

4:54 second sign. There are seventeen references to signs in John's Gospel: 2:11, 18, 23; 3:2; 4:25, 48, 54; 6:2, 14, 26, 30; 7:4, 31; 9:16; 10:41; 11:47; 12:18, 37; 20:30. Of the seven or eight sign-miracles recounted, only two are numbered—the first Cana sign (2:11) and the second Cana sign (4:54).

Attempts to explain why only the two Cana signs were numbered are legion.[5] The simplest explanation, deducible from John's parallel structure in 4:46-54, is that the words "This was now the second sign" in 4:54 have been put here by the author to form an indirect parallel with the words "Cana . . . where he had made the water wine" in 4:46. Both miracles at Cana were performed "when he had come from Judea to Galilee" (cp. 4:54 with 1:43 and 2:1). The reason for numbering the first sign in 2:11 would be quite simply that the author wanted to say that the Cana miracle was the beginning of the "greater things" promised by Jesus to Nathanael when he said, "Because I said to you, I saw you under the fig tree, do you believe? You shall see greater things than these" (1:50). The enumeration of the second Cana sign, therefore, would not in any way indicate that originally all the signs were enumerated, as many have claimed. "Second" is mentioned only to provide a parallel between the introduction (v 46) and the inclusion-conclusion (v 54) and reflects back to the beginning of the story, as any good inclusion should.

In conclusion, the first three sequences of part II have shown Jesus doing the work of the Father, who "so loved the world that he gave his only

Son, that whoever believes in him should not perish but have eternal life'' (3:16). In sequence 6, Jesus brings the Samaritan woman to believe in him; in sequence 7, the Samaritan townspeople; in sequence 8, the royal official and his household. Thus, Jesus' ''food'' (4:43), which is to do the will of the Father by bringing people to believe in him and have eternal life, is central to all three sequences and introduces the theme of the work of the Father and the Son, which is central to the story of the cure of the paralytic in 5:1-18 and the subsequent discourse in 5:19-47.

Themes

Two themes, witness and response, stand out. The witness value of the miracle testifies to Jesus' power to give life. The response of the official testifies to the kind of faith Jesus seeks. Emphasis is on the theme of response, as in the previous two sequences. Outsiders like the Samaritans and the royal official believe on Jesus' word. As will be shown in the following sequences, neither Jesus' words nor his miracles can elicit from the Jews of Jerusalem and Galilee a positive response of faith.

Beyond the theme of response that dominates the sequence, there is the element of the symbolic that almost all commentators have noticed. It is probable that the cure (restoring the health of the boy) symbolizes the eternal life that Jesus gives in response to faith.[6] Thus the two themes emphasized are faith as the response to Jesus' word and Jesus' power to give life, a power that witnesses to his person and to his relation to the Father. The life or health given to the boy is a symbol of the eternal life given to those who believe in the Son.

Sequence 9

THE JEWS REJECT JESUS, AND JESUS
REJECTS THE JEWS

5:1-47

The healing of the paralytic (5:1-18) is the first of three sections in sequence 9 (5:1-47). It paves the way for the long discourse that follows in the second and third sections (section B: 5:19-30, and section C: 5:31-47), each of which has the usual Johannine parallel structure.

In addition to the parallel structure of the three sections of sequence 9, the reader should note the dramatic build-up to the passion that begins with the Jews' contesting Jesus' cure of the paralytic on the sabbath. The passion had already been alluded to in the words "My hour has not yet come" (2:4); "Destroy this temple, and in three days I will raise it up" (2:19); and in the mysterious words "As Moses lifted up the serpent in the wilderness, so must the Son of man be lifted up" (3:14). Beginning with sequence 9, however, there are regular direct references to the climax of the Gospel, and the references use such emotion-packed words as "kill," "hate," "fear," and "arrest" (cf. 5:16-18; 6:51; 7:1, 6-8, 13, 20, 25, 30, 32, 44; 8:20, 28, 37, 59; 9:1ff; 10:11, 15, 17-18, 31, 39; 11:46-53; 12:4, 7, 23, 32, 37-50).

Also, for the first time in the Gospel, the reader will note that the evangelist uses a new literary technique. He mates sign, feast, and discourse by making references in his discourses to both the sign worked and the feast mentioned. In sequence 9 (5:1-47), there are several references to the sabbath and what may be a few implicit references to the feast of Pentecost. In sequence 12 (6:22-71), he will mate the multiplication of the loaves with the feast of the Passover and the manna in the desert. And in sequence 13 (7:1–8:59), he will mate the long discourse of 7:1–8:58 with the feast of Tabernacles. In sequence 15 (10:22-39), he will mate a short discourse with the feast of the Dedication of the Temple. The technique is used to implement the theme of replacement: Jesus replaces all the feasts of the Jews!

Section A (5:1-18): Jesus heals a paralytic on the sabbath.

Parallel structure

(a) The **Jews** contest **Jesus'** healing a man **on the sabbath** (5:1-11).

(b) The **Jews** ask the **man** who it was that **healed** him (5:12-13).

(c) Jesus and the healed man in the temple (5:14)

(b′) The **man** tells the **Jews** that it was Jesus who **healed** him (5:15).

(a′) The **Jews** persecute **Jesus** because he healed a man **on the sabbath** (5:16-18).

Text

(a)   5:1 After this there was a feast of **the Jews,** and **Jesus** went up to Jerusalem. ²Now there is in Jerusalem by the Sheep Gate a pool, in Hebrew called Bethzatha, which has five porticoes. ³In these lay a multitude of invalids, blind, lame, paralyzed. ⁵One man was there, who had been ill for thirty-eight years. ⁶When Jesus saw him and knew that he had been lying there a long time, he said to him, "Do you want to be healed?" ⁷The sick man answered him, "Sir, I have no man to put me into the pool when the water is troubled, and while I am going another steps down before me." ⁸Jesus said to him, "Rise, take up your pallet, and walk." ⁹And at once the man was healed, and he took up his pallet and walked. Now that day was the **sabbath.** ¹⁰So **the Jews** said to the man who was cured, "It is the **sabbath,** it is not lawful for you to carry your pallet."

(b)   ¹¹But he answered them, **"The man who healed** me said to me, 'Take up your pallet, and walk.' " ¹²They asked him, "Who is **the man** who said to you, 'Take up your pallet, and walk'?" ¹³Now **the man** who had been **healed** did not know **who it was,** for **Jesus** had withdrawn, as there was a crowd in the place.

(c)   ¹⁴Afterward, Jesus found him in the temple, and said to him, "See, you are well! Sin no more, that nothing worse befall you."

(b′)   ¹⁵**The man** went away and told the Jews that **it was Jesus who had healed him.**

(a′)   ¹⁶And this was why the **Jews** persecuted **Jesus,** because he did this on the **sabbath.** ¹⁷But **Jesus** answered them, "My Father is working still, and I am working." ¹⁸This was why the **Jews** sought all the more to kill him, because he not only broke the **sabbath** but also called God his Father, making himself equal with God.

Parallelism is created in (a) and (a′) by repeating the words "Jesus," "Jews," and "sabbath," and this is done in the context of a dispute about healing on the sabbath that is common to both (a) and (a′).

In (b) and (b′), the evangelist creates a subtle parallelism by repeating the words "man" and "healed" in a context that deals in (b) with the question of who it was that healed the paralytic and in (b′) with the answer to the question, identifying Jesus as the healer.

The center (c) is neatly set off from (b) and (b′) by changing the scene. In (c), the scene is set in the temple, where the healed man meets Jesus and learns who it is that has healed him, thus enabling him in (b′) to answer the question put to him by the Jews in (b).

Commentary

(a) The Jews contest Jesus' healing a man on the sabbath (5:1-11).

5:1 a feast of the Jews. The nameless feast may be Pentecost, the feast of the law given at Sinai. In favor of the surmise are the references to Moses and the law in section C (5:31-32, 45-47). This would fit with John's technique of mating sign, feast, and discourse. On the other hand, John may have purposely omitted the name of the feast in order to draw attention to the sabbath, which is so central to the whole movement and action of the sequence. Barrett thinks that "John here introduces a feast simply in order to account for the presence of Jesus in Jerusalem" and adds, "If the article is read, the reference might be to the Passover or to Tabernacles, which was often known as 'the Feast' (*ha hag*)."[1] If John does want his readers to understand that he is talking about the feast of Tabernacles, then the feast in sequence 9 (5:1-47) is the same as the feast of Tabernacles in sequence 13 (7:1-8:59), the sequence that is the chiastic counterpart to sequence 9 (5:1-47).

5:2 five porticoes. It is possible that the five porticoes symbolize the five books of the Pentateuch and the giving of the law at Sinai, which was celebrated at the feast of Pentecost. The references to Moses and the scriptures in 5:41-47 would contribute to this symbolism and would help to indicate the connection between the sign, the feast, and the discourse of Jesus. Implicit would be the theme of replacement and the message that the pool-Pentateuch-law cannot give life and Israel must wait for something better. According to 5:41-47, Moses in the Pentateuch was pointing to Jesus as the giver of life. If this be reasonably close to the mark, then the cure of the man at the pool, in the light of the discourse that follows, symbolizes the gift of eternal life that Jesus gives.

5:5 thirty-eight years. The number may be an allusion to the (forty) years the Jews spent in the desert, according to Dt 2:14-15, and thus may symbolize Judaism's incapacity to do anything without Jesus.

5:8 Jesus said to him, "Rise . . . and walk." The words suggest that John's account may be dependent on either Mk 2:1-12 or Mt 9:1-8. Brown, however, does not consider the story a variant of either the Markan or the Matthean story, but claims it bears the marks of primitive Palestinian tradition, particularly in the excellent knowledge of the topography of Jerusalem, recently confirmed by the discovery of the five-porticoed pool of Bethzatha near the Sheep Gate in Jerusalem.[2]

5:10 It is the sabbath. The Jews' accusation of sabbath-breaking, which is expressly directed against the healed man but implicitly against Jesus, will boomerang when Jesus explains in 5:16-18 that he is no more bound by the sabbath laws than his Father: "My Father is working still, and I am working" (5:17). The charge of sabbath-breaking, therefore, is groundless when directed against Jesus. What John has accomplished in giving so brief an account of the cure (only vv 1-9) and immediately bringing up the sabbath-breaking charge is to prepare the way for the dispute in 5:10-18 and the discourse that follows in 5:19-47.

(b) The Jews ask the man who it was that healed him (5:12-13).

5:12-13 Who is the man. . . . ? The Jews do not ask, "Who is the man that healed you?" but "Who is the man who said to you, 'Take up your pallet, and walk?'" They are not interested in the miracle (cf. the same attitude in 9:1ff). They want to know who it was that instigated the breaking of the sabbath. As they said in v 10, "It is the sabbath, it is not lawful for you to carry your pallet."

(c) Jesus and the healed man in the temple (5:14)

5:14 Sin no more. Jesus' statement presupposes, as in the cure of the paralytic in Mk 2:1-12 and Mt 9:1-8, that Jesus has not only cured the man but forgiven his sins as well. While sin and sickness-punishment are frequently associated as cause and effect in both Testaments, Jesus, according to John in 9:1ff, will explicitly deny the connection. It might be inferred from the tension between 5:14 and 9:1-3 that Jesus sometimes associated sin with sickness-punishment and sometimes did not, or at least that the Johannine community thought that way.

(b′) The man tells the Jews that it was Jesus who healed him (5:15).

5:15 told the Jews that it was Jesus. As in (b), the speakers are the man and the Jews. In (b), the Jews ignored the miracle and tried to focus on Jesus' sabbath-breaking by asking, "Who is the man who said to you, 'Take up your pallet, and walk'?" Here in (b′), the man answers their question, but not in the terms in which they put it. He does not tell them that Jesus was the one who told him to pick up his pallet and thereby break the sabbath, but that it was Jesus who had *healed* him!

(a′) The Jews persecute Jesus because he healed a man on the sabbath (5:16-18).

5:16 because he did this on the sabbath. The inclusion-conclusion leads the reader's mind back to the introduction, where Jesus cured on the sabbath. In v 17, Jesus himself will shift attention from the cure to the significance of the cure by relating it to his work.

5:17 My Father is working still. The cure is a sign for those who have eyes to see that God is at work in the works of Jesus. The Jews, however, see Jesus as only a man. As a man, he is breaking the law made for men. Implicit in their misunderstanding of Jesus and his working on the sabbath is the fact that they would readily admit that God works on the sabbath. It would follow that if they knew who Jesus really is, namely, the only Son and equal with the Father, their objection would be groundless.

5:18 This was why the Jews sought all the more to kill him. Jesus' answer in v 17 implies that he works on the sabbath because he is God. The implication that he is "making himself equal with God" is picked up immediately by the Jews. They seek to kill him because they consider such a claim to be blasphemy. In the discourse that follows (5:19-47), Jesus will defend himself against this charge of blasphemy. In section B (5:19-30), he will develop the argument that the work he does, which is to give eternal life, is precisely the work of the Father. In section C (5:31-47), he will deal with the refusal of the Jews to respond to him. He will contend that the Jews refuse to see, i.e., to believe, despite the witness of John, the witness of Jesus' works, the witness of the Father, and the witness of the scriptures. They thus bring judgment upon themselves in refusing to honor the Son (5:22-23).

Concluding section A, two points are worthy of note. First, John has purposely placed his emphasis, not on the cure, but on the Jews' deliberate refusal to acknowledge the cure and its significance. John uses the miracle simply as a springboard to introduce the revelatory discourse that follows in sections B and C. Second, section A has emphasized the dual work of the Father and the Son. This work is a work of giving life. It was for this purpose that Jesus had come, saying, "My food is to do the will of him who sent me, and to accomplish his work" (4:34). Sequence 12 (6:22-71) will continue this theme of work but will put the emphasis on the other side of the coin—on the work of men and women and on the work of believing in the one the Father has sent (6:29), entering into union with him through the Eucharist (6:51), and thus living in union with the Father and the Son (6:56-57).

Section B (5:19-30): Jesus' right to judge, i.e., to give and refuse life

Parallel structure
   (a) The Son **can do nothing** of his own accord (5:19-23).
   (b) **The hour is coming when the dead will hear the voice** of the Son of God (5:24-25).
   (c) The Father gives the Son the power to judge (5:26-27).
   (b') **The hour is coming when all who are in the tombs will hear his voice** (5:28-29).
   (a') **I can do nothing** on my own authority (5:30).

Text

(a)   5:19 Jesus said to them, "Truly, truly, I say to you, **the Son can do nothing of his own accord,** but only what he sees the Father doing; for whatever he does, that the Son does likewise. [20]For the Father loves the Son, and shows him all that he himself is doing; and greater works than these will he show him, that you may marvel. [21]For as the Father raises the dead and gives them life, so also the Son gives life to whom he will. [22]The Father **judges** no one, but has given all **judgment** to the Son, [23]that all may honor the Son, even as they honor the Father. He who does not honor the Son does not honor the Father who sent him.

(b) ²⁴"Truly, truly, I say to you, he who hears my word and believes him who sent me, has eternal life; he does not come into judgment, but has passed from death to life. ²⁵Truly, truly, I say to you, **the hour is coming** and now is, **when the dead will hear the voice** of the Son of God, and those who hear will **live.**

(c) ²⁶"For as the Father has life in himself, so he has granted the Son also to have life in himself, ²⁷and has given him authority to execute judgment, because he is the Son of man.

(b′) ²⁸"Do not marvel at this; for **the hour is coming when all who are in the tombs will hear his voice** ²⁹and come forth, those who have done good, to the resurrection of **life,** and those who have done evil, to the resurrection of judgment.

(a′) ³⁰"**I can do nothing on my own authority;** as I hear, I **judge;** and my **judgment** is just, because I seek not my own will but the will of him who sent me."

Parallelism in (a) and (a′) is achieved by the repetition of the central idea of the whole section: "The Son can do nothing of his own accord." Also repeated is the idea that Jesus receives his right to judge from the Father: "[He] has given all judgment to the Son" (5:22) and "As I hear, I judge" (5:30).

In (b) and (b′), parallelism is achieved by the repetition of the words "the hour is coming" in vv 25 and 28, and the words "will hear his voice" in 5:25 and 5:28. The parallelism is perfect. The only difference is that in (b) Jesus speaks of realized eschatology and in (b′) of final eschatology. In (c), Jesus repeats the central idea of the whole section: "Just as the Father . . . so the Son" (5:26).

Commentary

The first part of Jesus' discourse following the cure of the paralytic and the Jews' charge that Jesus was thereby making himself God's equal is admirably explained by Barrett:

> The occasion of this discourse is the miracle of 5:2-9, the Jewish objection to what Jesus had done and commanded on the Sabbath, and the reply of Jesus, "My Father worketh hitherto, and I work," which was rightly understood by the Jews as a claim to equality with God. It was imperative that John should handle this claim without further delay. Already (even if the Prologue be excluded) he had made extensive claims on behalf of Jesus. He is greater than John the Baptist: he is the Lamb of God, the Son of God, the Messiah, the Son of man, the savior of the world. In the following chapters the great "I am" sayings occur: I am the bread of life, the light of the world, the good shepherd, the way, the truth, the life, etc. In what sense are these divine claims made? Is Jesus a man who exalts himself

to a position of divine authority? A demi-god, half human and half divine? Do his assertions imply any rivalry with the creator, the God of Israel and the Old Testament?[3]

(a) The Son can do nothing of his own accord (5:19-23).

5:19 Truly, truly, I say to you. Unlike the synoptic Gospels, in which dialogues regularly lead up to either a pronouncement or a lapidary statement, in John the lapidary statement is placed at the beginning (cf. 4:10, 13, 34; 6:32, 53; 7:37-38; 8:12; 10:7) and is then followed by a discourse or monologue. Here the lapidary statement that governs the whole section is briefly enunciated by Jesus: "Truly, truly, I say to you, the Son can do nothing of his own accord, but only what he sees the Father doing." The same thought is repeated in 5:30, forming an inclusion-conclusion for 5:19-30.

5:20 greater works than these. The statement prepares the reader for the contrast between what Jesus has done—the cure of the paralytic—and the overwhelming power he will demonstrate in giving life to all who hear his voice in the present (5:24-25) and in the future at the time of the general resurrection of the dead (5:28-29).

5:21-23 all judgment to the Son. In Ps 82, judges are called gods, because of their godlike power over life and death in the judgment tribunal. It is this power over life and death that the Father gives to the Son—a power more positively described in v 21: "For as the Father raises the dead and gives them life, so also the Son gives life to whom he wills." Since the Father has given this power to the Son, it follows that "he who does not honor the Son does not honor the Father who sent him" (v 23). The idea is central to John's theology, as it is to the Synoptics (cf. Mt 10:32-33; Mk 8:38; Lk 9:26). In John, as in the Synoptics, the statement is a challenge and a warning to the Jews at the end of the first century. In the present context, the declaration prepares the way for Jesus' condemnation of the Jerusalem Jews that will follow in section C (5:31-47).

(b) The hour is coming when the dead will hear the voice of the Son of God (5:24-25).

5:24 has eternal life. The present tense ("has") and the declaration of v 25 that "the hour is coming, and now is" indicate that the word "dead" in v 25 is to be understood of those spiritually dead. It is John's way of speaking about realized eschatology—believers already live with the eschatological life-force of the Spirit (cf. 3:5; 11:26). One who believes in Jesus already possesses the water of eternal life (4:10, 14) and the bread that gives life to the world (6:33, 47-51).

(c) The Father gives the Son the power to judge (5:26-27).

5:27 because he is the Son of man. In Dn 7:13, the Son of man is given "dominion, glory, and kingship" over all nations and peoples. In the present context of Jesus' receiving power from the Father to give life to both the spiritually dead (5:24-25) and to the physically dead (5:28-29), the reference to the Danielic Son of man who has universal power over all humankind makes excellent and cogent sense (cf. Jn 13:3; 17:2; Mt 13:41; 25:31; 28:18). Since the title "Son of man" is frequently used in John's Gospel in contexts that deal with the passion and death of Jesus (e.g., 3:14-17; 8:28; 12:31-34), it is not unlikely that the title is used here with the implication that it is through his passion and death that Jesus completes the work of the Father (cf. 4:34; 17:4; 19:30) and thus brings it about that all who believe in him can receive the gift of eternal life.

(b′) The hour is coming when all who are in the tombs will hear his voice (5:28-29).

5:28 all who are in the tombs. The passage duplicates with perfect parallelism the statements of 5:25.[4] It differs, however, in its basic thrust. In (b), John speaks of realized eschatology; in (b′), of final eschatology. In v 25, Jesus spoke of the "dead," i.e., the spiritually dead, and of an "hour [that] is coming, and now is." In v 28, the hour is coming; it has not come; and in place of the word "dead," Jesus uses the expression "all who are in the tombs." The voice that those in the tombs hear is the voice of the eschatological Son of man of v 27, just as in Mt 25:31ff those to be judged in the final judgment hear the voice of the Son of man say to them, "Come, O blessed of my Father" or "Depart from me, you cursed." The reference to those in the tombs re-echoes Dn 12:2: "Many of those who sleep in the dust of the earth shall awake, some to everlasting life, and some to shame and everlasting contempt." The whole passage clearly speaks of the final judgment at the end of time.[5]

(a′) I can do nothing on my own authority (5:30).

5:30a I can do nothing on my own authority. The words form a perfect inclusion-conclusion with v 19, ". . . the Son can do nothing of his own accord," and at the same time summarize the theme of judgment (giving and taking life), which has been so prominent in the whole of section B (5:19-30).

5:30b because I seek not my own will. Jesus' judgment is honest because it is not his own will but that of the Father that he carries out (cf. 4:34; 17:4; 19:30). If he were doing his own will, one might contest his honesty, since it might be said that he was seeking his own glory rather than that of the Father. This Jesus denies absolutely.

Section C (5:31-47): Jesus condemns the Jews of Jerusalem.

Parallel structure

(a) The testimony of "**another**" (5:31-32)
(b) The testimony of **the Baptist** (5:33-35)

(c) The testimony of the works, the Father, and the scriptures (5:36-40)

(b′) Jesus condemns the Jews who receive **the Baptist** but not him to whom **the Baptist testifies** (5:41-44).

(a′) **Moses** and the scriptures accuse the Jews (5:45-47).

Text

(a)   5:31 "If I bear witness to myself, my testimony is not true; ³²there is **another who bears witness to me,** and I know that the testimony which he bears to me is true.

(b)   ³³"You sent to **John,** and he has borne witness to the truth. ³⁴Not that the testimony which I **receive** is **from man;** but I say this that you may be saved. ³⁵He was a burning and shining lamp, and **you were willing to rejoice for a while in his light.**

(c)   ³⁶"But the testimony which I have is greater than that of John; for the works which the Father has granted me to accomplish, these very works which I am doing, bear me witness that the Father has sent me. ³⁷And the Father who sent me has himself borne witness to me. His voice you have never heard, his form you have never seen; ³⁸and you do not have his word abiding in you, for you do not believe him whom he has sent. ³⁹You search the scriptures, because you think that in them you have eternal life; and it is they that bear witness to me; ⁴⁰yet you refuse to come to me that you may have life.

(b′)   ⁴¹"I do not **receive** glory **from men.** ⁴²But I know that you have not the love of God within you. ⁴³I have come in my Father's name, and you do not **receive** me; **if another comes in his own name, him you will receive.** ⁴⁴How can you believe, who receive glory from one another and do not seek the glory that comes from the only God?

(a′)   ⁴⁵"Do not think that I shall accuse you to the Father; it is **Moses** who accuses you, on whom you set your hope. ⁴⁶If you believed **Moses,** you would believe me, for **he wrote of me.** ⁴⁷But if you do not believe his writings, how will you believe my words?"

In (a), Jesus speaks about "another who bears witness to me" (v 32). In the inclusion (vv 45-47), he says, "If you believed Moses, you would believe me, for he wrote of me" (v 46). Parallelism suggests that the unnamed "another" who testifies on Jesus' behalf is Moses, who, according to v 46, "wrote" about Jesus. According to v 32b, "the testimony which he [the "another" of v 32a] bears to me is true." The implication of v 47, "But if you do not believe his [Moses'] writings, how will you believe my words?" is that what Moses wrote is testimony that can be verified by reading the scriptures. Parallelism, therefore, in (a) and (a′) is achieved by paralleling the "another" with Moses.

In (b) and (b′), there is a clear reference to John the Baptist in v 33 and a parallel implicit reference in the words of v 43, "If *another* comes in his own name, him you will receive." That this "another" is the Baptist seems reasonably clear from the words of vv 34-35: "He [the Baptist] was a burning and shining lamp, and you were willing to rejoice for a while in his light." The "him" whom Jesus says "you receive" (v 43) strongly suggests the lamp in whose light the Jews rejoiced (v 34), namely, the Baptist.

Similarly parallel in (b) and (b') are the expressions "Not that the testimony which I receive is from man" (*ou para anthrōpou tēn martyrian lambanō*) in v 34 and "I do not receive glory from men" (*doxan para anthrōpōn ou lambanō*) in v 41; the same words, "*ou para anthrōpou(ōn) lambanō,*" are repeated in both statements. In (c), the subject matter that deals with the witness of the works, the Father, and the scriptures sets off (c) from (b').

Commentary

The whole of section C (5:31-47) from beginning to end deals with the obstinacy of the Jerusalem Jews who refuse to accept the multiple witness to Jesus that the Gospel up to this point has provided. They reject the testimony of Jesus himself, the testimony of the Baptist, and the testimony of Jesus' miracles (works). Since they will accept none of these witnesses nor even that of Moses in the scriptures, Moses himself will be their accuser!

(a) The testimony of "another" (5:31-32)

5:31 If I bear witness to myself. According to Dt 19:15, a man cannot be convicted on the testimony of a single witness. According to Dt 17:6 and Nm 35:30, several witnesses are required for a conviction in the case of a capital crime. In 5:31-47, Jesus is preparing a case for the condemnation of the Jews (a case similar to that presented in Mt 11:2–12:50 and 23:13-39). He begins, therefore, by adverting to the claims of the law, which did not recognize the testimony of a single witness. He will not prejudice his case by appealing to his own witness alone, even though, as he will say in 8:14, "Even if I do bear witness to myself, my testimony is true, for I know whence I have come and whither I am going."[6]

5:32 there is another who bears witness to me. The mysterious "another" has been identified by some as the Baptist and by others as the Father. The parallelism, however, between the introduction (5:31-32) and the inclusion (5:45-47) strongly suggests that the "another" is Moses. Jesus' assertion in 5:46 that "he [Moses] wrote of me" provides a good parallel with the words "There is another who bears witness to me" (5:32). Jesus says of this other's witness that it is true (5:32b). It is not surprising, therefore, that in 5:46 he appeals to Moses in the Torah—the validity of whose witness would be considered a priori verified by all Jews.

(b) The testimony of the Baptist (5:33-35)

5:33-34 You sent to John. The Gospel opened with the Jews sending a deputation to question John the Baptist (1:19ff). Jesus reminds them of this for two reasons. First, even though he does not need the human testimony of John the Baptist, since he has the witness of his works (v 36), of his Father (v 37), of the scriptures (v 39), and of Moses (vv 45-47), it is nevertheless true that the witness of the Baptist was valid and might have helped to bring the Jews to Jesus if they had accepted it. This is the meaning of the remark "I say this that you may be saved" (v 34b). If they had really listened to the Baptist, they would have come to Jesus.

5:35 He was a burning and shining lamp. The second reason why Jesus reminds the Jews that they had sent priests and Levites to the Baptist is because they had accepted the Baptist, at least for a while, as a true prophet: "you were willing to rejoice for a while in his light" (v 35). Jesus' implicit *ad hominem* argument is: "Since you accepted the Baptist as a true prophet, why did you not accept his witness about me?" Jesus will not let the Jews have it both ways.

5:35b you were willing to rejoice for a while in his light. The implication seems to be that while the Jews initially accepted John as a prophet, they eventually refused to accept him precisely because of his witness to Jesus. Thus, to reject Jesus' claims, the Jews were obliged, if they were to be consistent, to deny the Baptist as well (cf. Mt 11:16-19). The argument made more sense to the evangelist's contemporaries than it does to us. It is similar to the argument against the Jews in Mt 21:23-27, where the Jews question Jesus' authority and Jesus retorts by asking them, "The baptism of John, whence was it? From heaven or from men?" Matthew presents the Jews as saying to themselves, "If we say, 'From heaven,' he will say to us 'Why then did you not believe him?' But if we say 'From men,' we are afraid of the multitude; for all hold that John was a prophet" (Mt 21:25-26). In Mt 21:23-27 and Jn 5:33-35, the argument is the same: the leaders of the Jews were trying to have it both ways by accepting the Baptist at one time and then later reversing themselves when they realized the import of his witness to Jesus.

(c) The testimony of the works, the Father, and the scriptures (5:36-40)

5:36 testimony which I have is greater than that of John. The testimony is that of the works or miracles Jesus performed (v 36), the testimony of the Father (v 37), and the testimony of the scriptures (v 39). John mentions only a few of Jesus' miracles (2:1-12; 4:46-52; 5:1-9; 6:1-15; 9:1-38; 11:1-44; 21:1-14), and he downgrades belief that rests upon miracles (cf. 2:23-25; 4:45; 4:48; 20:26-31); but he makes it clear that Jesus' miracles were meant to testify to the truth of his claims (cf. 20:30-31). The Jews have refused to accept the witness of Jesus' miracles, just as they have refused to accept the witness of the Baptist.

5:37 the Father . . . has himself borne witness to me. No such witness is recorded in the Gospel, except indirectly. The Gospel's claim is that those who hear the Father hear the Son and vice versa. It would follow, then, that if the Jews would accept Jesus, they would be able to hear the testimony of the Father. The idea is expressed aptly in 1 Jn 5:9-10: "If we receive the testimony of men, the testimony of God is greater; for this is the testimony of God that he has borne witness to his Son. He who believes in the Son of God has the testimony in himself. He who does not believe God has made him a liar, because he has not believed in the testimony that God has borne to his Son." This testimony exists and is true, but it exists only for those who believe in Jesus. It follows then: "His voice you have never heard, his form you have never seen; and you do not have his word abiding in you, for you do not believe him whom he has sent" (vv 37b-38).

5:39 You search the scriptures. The witness of the scriptures constitutes another testimony to Jesus. At the same time, the statement looks forward to John's inclusion-conclusion, where he will identify the mysterious "another" of 5:31 with Moses' witness in the scriptures (5:45-47).

5:40 yet you refuse to come to me. The words are reminiscent of Mt 23:37-39: "Jerusalem, Jerusalem . . . how often would I have gathered your children together as a hen gathers her brood under her wings, and you would not!"

(b′) Jesus condemns the Jews who receive the Baptist but not him to whom the Baptist testifies (5:41-44).

5:41 I do not receive glory from men. In the same vein as Matthew's condemnation of the Pharisees (Mt 23:3-39), Jesus continues to attack the insincerity of the Jews. They are interested in human praise, and especially praise from one another (v 44); Jesus is not. The reason they are interested in human glory or praise and not "the glory [praise] that comes from God" (v 44) is because they "do not have the love of God" in their hearts (v 42). If they had the love of God in their hearts, they would seek the praise that comes from God (v 44). The contrast is severe. Jesus seeks only the approbation (praise-glory; the Greek *doxa* is the same in both places) of God, the Jews seek only the approbation of humans. This is proved by the fact that Jesus comes in his Father's name, yet they do not accept him precisely because they are more interested in human approbation than in God's approbation (v 43a).

5:43b if another comes in his own name. Parallelism with vv 33-35 suggests that this "another" is the Baptist, especially since both here ("him you will receive") and there ("you were willing to rejoice for a while in his light") the Jews are said to accept John at the same time that they reject Jesus. The difficulty is that this "another comes in his own name," which does not seem at first to be an accurate description of the Baptist. However, if Jesus is contrasting himself, who comes in the name of the Father, with John, who comes in his own name as a prophet and was received as such by the Jews, the difficulty is lessened. Most commentators understand this "another" to refer to general messianic claimants or to rabbis who make special claims for themselves as authoritative teachers (cf. Mt 23:3-12).

(a') Moses and the scriptures accuse the Jews (5:45-47).

5:45 it is Moses who accuses you. Parallelism suggests that "Moses" in v 45 is the same as the "another who bears witness to me" in vv 31-32. Here in vv 45-47, it is self-evident that the witness of Moses in the scriptures is, as v 32 puts it, "true" and can be verified. It is not clear to what scriptural testimony Jesus refers. Some think it is Dt 18:18, where there is a prediction of a future prophet like Moses. More likely it refers to the scriptures in general, which the early Christians saw fulfilled in Jesus and from which, as a consequence, they adduced a multitude of proof tests (cf. Mt 1–2 *passim* and Lk 24:25-29, 44-45).

In sequence 9 (5:1-47), John has made his first full-scale defense of Jesus' claims to divinity. He will return to a fuller defense of Jesus' claims in chs 7–8, the chiastic counterpart of 5:1-47 in John's Gospel. The historicity of such a defense can be somewhat defended from the similar apologias for Jesus in the synoptic Gospels. On this basis, Brown concludes:

> Therefore, it is plausible that the roots of this Johannine discourse may be found in the primitive tradition of Jesus' words. But it is obvious that nowhere in the Synoptic Gospels do we find such a logical and completely developed apologetic for Jesus' claims. We may well surmise, then, that what we have in John is the product of the apologetic of the Christian Church against the Jewish objections to Christ, an apologetic grounded in Jesus' own arguments, but now systematized. The whole of ch v fits in very well with the purpose of the Gospel to persuade Jewish Christians to leave the Synagogue and openly to profess their faith in Jesus.[7]

Themes

The themes of witness and response dominate sequence 9. Jesus witnesses to himself through the cure of the paralytic, through the testimony of Moses (5:31-32), John the Baptist (5:33-34), the Father, and the scriptures (5:36-40). The Jews' refusal to believe in Jesus despite all the witnesses he adduces discloses God's judgment on them. The discourse in 5:19-47 is like a playing out of the principle enunciated in 3:18-19: "He who believes in him is not condemned; he who does not believe is condemned already, because he has not believed in the name of the only Son of God. And this is the judgment, that the light has come into the world, and men loved darkness rather than light, because their deeds were evil."

It should be noted, however, that Jesus' condemnation of the Jews in 5:19-47 has about it a note of regret and thereby reflects the theology of

3:16-17: "For God so loved the world that he gave his only Son, that whoever believes in him should not perish but have eternal life. For God sent the Son into the world, not to condemn the world, but that the world might be saved through him."

Both sequence 9 (5:1-47) and sequence 10 (6:1-15) deal with the Jews' rejection of Jesus and Jesus' rejection of the Jews. Sequence 9 (5:1-47) is balanced antithetically in part II (4:4–6:15) with sequence 7 (4:39-45) by showing the Samaritans believing on the word of Jesus alone without seeing signs, while the Jews, who have the evidence of the paralytic's cure, do not believe on the evidence of the cure nor on the testimony of Jesus' word. The centrality of the theme of witness-response, and especially response, in part II of the Gospel is evident from the arrangement:

Sequence   6: The Samaritan woman believes and accepts Jesus (4:4-38).
Sequence   7: The Samaritans believe and accept Jesus (4:39-45).
Sequence   8: The royal official believes and accepts Jesus (4:46-52).
Sequence   9: The Jerusalem Jews reject Jesus (5:1-47).
Sequence 10: The Galilean Jews reject Jesus (6:1-15).

It should be noted as well that Jesus' condemnation of the Jews (5:1–6:15) comes just before the turning point of the Gospel in 6:16-21, just as it does in the Gospels of Matthew and Mark. Thus, the turning point in Matthew's Gospel comes in ch 13 and is immediately preceded by Jesus' twofold condemnation of the Jews in 11:6-24 and 12:22-45. The turning point in Mark's Gospel occurs at 8:31, where Jesus begins to concentrate on the instruction of his disciples, and is preceded by Jesus' condemnation of the Jews in 7:1-23 and 8:11-21.

Chiastic parallels with sequence 7 (4:39-45)

Balance between 5:1-47 and 4:39-45 is achieved primarily by antithetic parallelism. In 4:39-45, the non-Jewish Samaritans believe on Jesus' word alone. In 5:1-47, Jesus' own people, the Jews of Jerusalem, far from believing on Jesus' word alone, refuse to believe even when Jesus cures the paralytic. The antithetic parallelism of the two sequences is the same as that between the positive response of the Samaritan woman in 4:4-38 and the negative response of the Galilean Jews in 6:1-15.

In addition to the antithetic parallelism, there is the broad synonymous parallelism between the title the Samaritans give to Jesus in 4:42 ("We know that this is indeed the Savior of the world") and the thematic of 5:1-30, which deals with Jesus' power to save. Jesus' discourse in 5:19-30 is for all practical purposes a theological explanation of his power to save all who believe in him. The key declarations are the following: "For as the Father raises the dead and gives them life, so also the Son gives life to whom he will" (5:21), and "He who hears my word [as the Samaritans did] and believes him who sent me, has eternal life" (5:24).

Sequence 10

THE GALILEAN JEWS REFUSE TO BELIEVE

6:1-15

Parallel structure

(a) Followed by the **multitude, Jesus** goes up into **the hills** (6:1-3).
(b) The multitude is **hungry** (6:4-9).
(c) The multitude is seated (6:10).
(b') The multitude is **filled** (6:11-13).
(a') Misinterpreted by the **multitude, Jesus** flees again to **the hills** (6:14-15).

Text

(a)   6:1 After this Jesus went to the other side of the Sea of Galilee, which is the Sea of Tiberias. ²And a **multitude** followed him, **because they saw the signs which he did** on those who were diseased. ³**Jesus** went up into **the hills,** and there sat down with his disciples.

(b)   ⁴Now the Passover, the feast of the Jews, was at hand. ⁵Lifting up his eyes, then, and seeing that a multitude was coming to him, Jesus said to Philip, "How are we to buy **bread,** so that these people may **eat?**" ⁶This he said to test him, for he himself knew what he would do. ⁷Philip answered him, "Two hundred denarii would not buy enough **bread** for each of them to get a little." ⁸One of his **disciples,** Andrew, Simon Peter's brother, said to him, ⁹"There is a lad here who has **five barley loaves** and two **fish;** but what are they among so many?"

(c)   ¹⁰Jesus said, "Make the people sit down." Now there was much grass in the place; so the men sat down, in number about five thousand.

(b')   ¹¹Jesus then took the **loaves,** and when he had given thanks, he distributed them to those who were seated; so also the **fish,** as much as they wanted. ¹²And when they had **eaten** their fill, he told his **disciples,** "Gather up the fragments left over, that nothing may be lost." ¹³So they gathered them up and filled twelve baskets with fragments from the **five barley loaves,** left by those who had **eaten.**

(a')   ¹⁴When **the people saw the sign which he had done,** they said, "This is indeed the prophet who is to come into the world!" ¹⁵Perceiving then that they were about to come and take him by force to make him king, **Jesus** withdrew again to **the hills** by himself.

100

John creates parallelism in (a) and (a′) by paralleling the personages (Jesus and the multitude); the place (the hills, vv 3 and 15); and the phrase "because they saw the signs which he did" (*hoti heōrōn ta sēmeia ha epoiei*) in v 2 with the phrase "the people saw the sign which he had done" (*idontes ho epoiēsen sēmeion*) in v 14. In (b) and (b′), the personages are the same: Jesus, the multitude, and the disciples. There is antithetic parallelism between the multitude that is hungry in (b) and filled in (b′). There is in addition the repetition of such words as "five barley loaves" (vv 9 and 13), "fish" (vv 9 and 11), "disciples" (vv 8 and 12), and "eat" (vv 5 and 12). In the center (c), John has placed the little scene in which Jesus has the multitude seated—perhaps an allusion to the Eucharistic table.

Commentary

It is presupposed in this commentary that the miracle of the loaves happened only once; that the synoptic accounts, where doubled, are different versions of the same event; that John's account is another version of the traditional story first recounted by Mark (6:32-44) and later retold by Matthew (14:13-21) and by Luke (9:10-17). John's account would appear closest to Mk 6:32-44 but is not dependent upon it.[1]

It is also presupposed that the Eucharistic motif (probably by way of the Christian Passover liturgy) had influenced the telling of the story almost from the beginning. Thus, the synoptic accounts as well as the Johannine account stemmed from traditions of the event that already incorporated the Eucharistic motif.[2] The essential liturgical expressions are: "took the loaves" (*elaben tous artous*), "gave thanks" (*eucharistēsas*), and "distributed them" (*diedōken*).[3]

Redactionally speaking, i.e., comparing John's story with the Synoptics' accounts and noting the differences, John has Johannized the whole account. He has kept what he needed from the traditional story and rejected what did not fit with his theological purposes. In addition, he has added what was required to make his account a perfect springboard for the sequences that follow: Jesus on the waters (6:16-21) and the great Eucharistic discourse (6:22-71). The significant additions are: the hills in vv 3 and 15; the Passover timing of the multiplication in v 4; the references to Jesus as prophet and king in vv 14-15; and the Galilean Jews' misunderstanding of Jesus' sign in vv 14-15. John has also moved up the number five thousand from the end in the synoptic accounts to the middle of his story (v 10) in order to take the emphasis off the miracle and put it on the reaction-rejection of the Galilean Jews.

(a) Followed by the multitude, Jesus goes up into the hills (6:1-3).

6:1 went to the other side of the Sea of Galilee, which is the Sea of Tiberias. However one solves the vexed question of where the multiplication of the loaves took place, whether near the city of Tiberias, as 6:22-24 indicates, or someplace on the Transjordan side of the lake, which seems more probable,⁴ the purpose of the introduction is clear. John wants to establish an exodus setting for the multiplication of the loaves (6:5-15), the crossing of the sea (6:16-21), and the discourse on the bread as the Eucharistic bread of the new covenant people of God (6:22-71). **Saw the signs which he did.** Note the parallel with v 14.

6:3 went up into the hills. To establish the exodus setting, John notes that Jesus went up into the hills as Moses did in Ex 19:24; 32-34.

(b) The multitude is hungry (6:4-9).

6:4 the Passover . . . was at hand. This significant temporal comment is used, like "the hills" in v 3, to help establish an exodus setting. In passing, it should be noted that the theological purposes of John in mentioning the Passover make it difficult to use this reference to the Passover as chronological evidence for the duration of Jesus' public ministry. Reading John's Gospel according to the laws of parallelism rather than according to the laws of strict narrative makes it even more difficult.

6:5 Jesus said to Philip. John's account of the preparation for the miracle of the loaves differs in typical Johannine fashion from the account in the Synoptics. In Mt 14:15 and Mk 6:35, the apostles take the initiative. In Jn 6:5, Jesus as usual takes the initiative (cf. 3:7; 3:3; 4:7; 5:6; 9:6; 11:34-44; 13:3; 18:4).

6:6 he himself knew what he would do. In typical Johannine fashion again, the Johannine Jesus has supernatural knowledge of the future, and John as usual goes out of his way to point this out (cf. 1:42, 48, 51; 2:24; 3:11-13; 4:17-18; 5:6; 6:15; 13:1; 18:4).

(c) The multitude is seated (6:10).

6:10 five thousand. In the Synoptics, the number of those fed is mentioned at the end of the account in order to enhance the wonder of what Jesus had done and to focus the reader's attention on the miracle (Mk 6:44; Mt 14:21). Thus, the multiplication is told as a miracle story, and the climax is reached in the announcement that five thousand had been fed. In John's account, the climax of the story is not the miracle but the negative response of the Jews (6:14-15). To make sure that the focus of his story was on the negative response of the Jews, John wisely moved back to the middle of his account the large number of those fed by the miraculous bread.

(b') The multitude is filled (6:11-13).

6:11 took . . . had given thanks . . . distributed them. As in the synoptic accounts, the telling of the story has been influenced by the celebration of the original Eucharist by Jesus, at which he "took" the bread, "gave thanks," and "gave" it to his apostles to eat (cf. Mk 14:22; Mt 26:26; Lk 22:19; 1 Cor 11:24). The words served John's theological purpose well. They alerted the readers to the Eucharistic symbolism of the miracle and at the same time laid the groundwork for the great discourse on the Eucharist that would follow in 6:31-58. His omission of the words "he broke them" (cf. Mt 14:19; 15:36; Mk 6:41; 8:6) is probably to be explained in view of his later reference to the paschal lamb, "Not a bone of him shall be broken," in relation to Jesus' body escaping the crurifragium (cf. 19:36). For John, Jesus is the Lamb of God (1:29, 36) whose legs were not broken on the cross in order that this scripture might be fulfilled.

Another difference between John and the Synoptics is the fact that in John the disciples take no part in distributing the loaves. In the Synoptics, the disciples, like deacons at the Eucharistic celebration, tend to the distribution of the loaves (Mk 6:41; 8:6; Mt 14:19; 15:36; Lk 9:16). The omission may be inadvertent. It is more likely, however, that John wants to stress the theological fact that it is Jesus and Jesus alone who gives the true bread of life (cf. 6:52-58), just as he alone gives the water "welling up to eternal life" (4:14), "gives life to whom he will" (5:21), and is alone "the gate," so that whoever enters by him "will be saved" (10:9). John's interest is focused entirely on Jesus as the sole and immediate source of eternal life.

6:12 Gather up the fragments. In a chapter that is filled with symbolism and Johannine twists, it is difficult not to see some symbolism in the gathering up of the fragments. One thinks of the following texts: "This is the will of him who sent me, that I should lose nothing of all that he has given me" (6:39; this may even constitute a loose parallel of 6:12); ". . . Jesus should die for the nation, and not for the nation only, but to gather into one the children of God who are scattered abroad" (11:52); "I have guarded them, and none of them is lost" (17:12); "This was to fulfill the word which he had spoken, 'Of those whom thou gavest me I lost not one' " (18:9). John's influence and the ecclesial aspect of his symbolism are evident in the Eucharistic prayer of the *Didache* (ix, 4): "As this broken bread was scattered on the mountains and was gathered up and so became one, so may thy Church be gathered from the ends of the earth into thy kingdom."

The words "that nothing may be lost" might better be translated, in accordance with the Johannine symbolism, "so that nothing will perish (*apolētai*)"—the same verb used in 6:39; 17:12; 18:9. The Synoptics say nothing about Jesus commanding the gathering up of the fragments. It is only the Johannine Jesus who is concerned lest anything be lost!

6:13 twelve baskets. Lindars, for one,[5] sees no symbolism in the number "twelve," but the symbolism of gathering up the "fragments" (v 12) and the overall symbolism of the exodus that pervades the whole context of 6:1-15, 6:16-21, and 6:31-58 make it entirely likely that the number twelve is symbolic of the new twelve tribes of Israel—the Christian Church.

(a′) Misinterpreted by the multitude, Jesus flees again to the hills (6:14-15).

6:14 When the people saw the sign. The words are almost ominous in John's vocabulary of phrases. Wherever they are used, they are used in a context of little or no or inadequate faith (cf. 2:23; 4:45, 48; 6:2, 26, 30; 7:3-5; 9:41; 11:18; 12:37-43; 20:24-29). They form a fitting preamble to the climax of the story according to John. The Galilean Jews have seen Jesus' miracle-sign, but instead of believing in him, they get swept away with enthusiasm for a Messiah, declare Jesus to be the promised prophet like Moses of Dt 18:15, and try to compel him to become a power-politics king. Thus, just as John had used the cure of the paralytic in 5:1-9 to serve as the occasion for the Jerusalem Jews' rejection of Jesus (5:10-18, 30-47), so here he uses the miracle of the loaves to serve as the occasion for the Galilean Jews' grossly inadequate response to Jesus. In the light of what follows in 6:59-67, where Jesus' disciples, except for the Twelve, leave him after his Eucharistic discourse, the gross reponse of 6:14-15 is only the first step in the ultimate rejection of Jesus by the Jews of Galilee.

6:15 again to the hills. With Jesus' return to the hills, which forms an inclusion-conclusion with the mention of the hills in 6:3, the circle is closed and the account of the multiplication of the loaves is finished. The aftertaste, however, remains, and it is the same as the aftertaste of sequence 9 (5:1-47): Jesus has been rejected by all the Jews—the Jews of Jerusalem and the Jews of Galilee. He must now turn to those who accept him—the Twelve. Hoskyns, as usual, catches and expresses admirably the full import of the whole passage:

> To have assumed that the promise of the prophets is fulfilled, and the desire of the Jews and, indeed, of all men satisfied, by a rearrangement of human affairs undertaken by the force of human initiative, was the fundamental and persistent misunderstanding of the Galilean crowd; for, having experienced the power of Jesus to heal the sick and to provide food for the hungry, they proposed *to take him by force* and *make him king* (v. 14). This misunderstanding is unbelief (vv. 27-29, 36); and Jesus *withdrew into the mountain himself alone* (v. 15), and afterwards, in a long discourse, exposed the rejection of God (vv. 38-40) that is involved in such behavior and in the ideas that made it possible (vv. 27-31).[6]

Themes

The function of 6:1-15 is substantially the same as that of sequence 9 (5:1-47). Jesus has manifested himself to the Jews of Galilee. They have seen his miracles but have not believed. Instead, they have tried to force him to become king.[7] Jesus' flight to the hills is his way of showing that he rejects such an unbelieving reception. John has thus concluded part II (4:4–6:15) of his Gospel with two sequences depicting the unbelief of the Jews. In contrast with the believing reception of Jesus by the Samaritan woman in sequence 6 (4:4-38), he shows the unbelieving reception of Jesus by the Galilean

Jews (6:1-15). In contrast with the believing reception of Jesus by the Samaritans in sequence 7 (4:39-45), he shows the unbelieving reception of Jesus by the Jerusalem Jews in sequence 9 (5:1-47).

Thus, the concentric themes of witness and response dominate in sequence 10 (6:1-15), just as they did in sequence 9 (5:1-47). The replacement theme is implicit in the new Sinai mountain, in the Eucharistic overtones of the loaves, and in the replacement of the Jewish Passover by the Christian Passover.

The negative response of the Galilean Jews at the end of part II (4:4–6:15) paves the way for part III (6:16-21), where the evangelist will portray Jesus on the waters of the lake, like Yahweh on the waters of the Red Sea, bringing his own people safely to the far shore. To Jewish Christians, the episode, in the context of the Passover feast, will have the ring of a new exodus and a new people of God.

Chiastic parallels with sequence 6 (4:4-38)

The sixth sequence (the Samaritan woman) and the tenth sequence (the multiplication of the loaves) of John's Gospel parallel each other chiastically in the same manner as the first sequence (John the Baptist) and the fifth sequence (John's final witness to Jesus) paralleled each other. The parallels are numerous and can be viewed best by arrangement in parallel columns.

Sequence 10	*Sequence 6*
6:3: Jesus . . . **sat** down (*ekathēto*) with his disciples.	4:6: Jesus, wearied from his journey, **sat** (*ekathezeto*) down beside the well.
6:5b: How are we to **buy bread** (*agorasōmen*), so that these people may eat?	4:8: His disciples had gone away into the city to **buy food** (*agorasōsin*).
6:5b: **How** (*pothen*) are we to buy bread?	4:11b: **Where** (*pothen*) do you get that living water?
6:9: There is a lad here who has **five** barley loaves . . . (cf. 6:13).	4:18: You have had **five** husbands.
6:10: The men sat down, in number about **five** thousand . . . 6:14b: This is indeed the **prophet** who is to come into the world!	4:19: I perceive that you are a **prophet.**
6:5b How are we to buy bread, so that these people may **eat** (*phagōsin*)?	4:31: Rabbi, **eat** (*phage*). 4:32: I have food to **eat** (*phagein*) of which you do not know.
6:3: Jesus then went up into the **hills** (*eis to oros*). 6:15: . . . Jesus withdrew again to the **hills** (*eis to oros*) by himself.	4:20: Our fathers worshiped on this **mountain** (*en tō orei*) . . .

6:15: Perceiving then that they were about to come and take him by force to make him **king** (*basilea*) . . .

4:25: I know that **Messiah** (*Christos*) is coming . . . 4:29b: Can this be **the Christ** (*Christos*)?

In addition to the verbal parallels cited above, there is the thematic parallel of the water that springs up to life eternal and the bread from heaven (the Eucharist), which "if any one eats . . . he will live for ever" (6:51). The parallel of 4:14: ("But whoever drinks of the water that I shall give him will never thirst") with 6:35: ("I am the bread of life; he who comes to me shall not hunger, and he who believes in me shall never thirst") sums up perfectly the parallelism of the two sequences.

Part III

THE NEW EXODUS
6:16-21

Sequence 11 is numerically and dramatically the central sequence of the whole Gospel. It is the hinge upon which the Gospel turns. It is flanked on the one side by sequences 1 to 10 and on the other side by sequences 12 to 21. It is precisely in the structural center of the Gospel and is parallel to no other sequence. It is, therefore, the chiastic center and turning point of the Gospel as a whole.

It may be objected that sequence 11 occurs too near the beginning of the Gospel to be the turning point. In quantitative terms this is true. The ten sequences following 6:16-21 are at least twice the length of the ten sequences preceding. In addition, the denouement of the Gospel—the passion, death, and resurrection—occurs far along on the descending side of the hinge. How then can we speak of sequence 11 as the hinge of the whole Gospel? Quite simply because it is as much the turning point of the Gospel as the crossing of the Red Sea is the turning point of the Pentateuch. A turning point in any literary piece with a dramatic structure occurs where the rising action begins to descend toward the denouement.[1] In dramas, novels, and movies, the turning point is sometimes prior to, sometimes precisely in the center of, and sometimes following the quantitative center, materially or temporally considered.

In John's Gospel, the dramatic action begins with Jesus' manifestation of himself to his people. It rises with a series of stories recounting first a positive response to Jesus (the disciples in 2:11; the Samaritan woman and the townspeople in 4:4-45; the royal official in 4:46-54) and then a negative response (the Jews of Jerusalem in 5:1-47; the Jews of Galilee in 6:1-15). The rejection by his own people constitutes a major crisis in Jesus' life and mission. As the prologue put it, "He came to his own home, and his own people received him not" (1:11). Jesus is at the turning point of his career among his own people. He must do something.

What Jesus does at the turning point of his career in John's Gospel is the same as what he does at the turning point of his career in each of the synoptic Gospels—he turns away from those who have rejected him and turns

107

to those who have accepted him. In Matthew's Gospel, the turning point is in chs 10–13. In chs 11–12, the Jews reject Jesus, and Jesus rejects the Jews. In ch 13, Jesus turns to his apostles. In Mark's Gospel, following Jesus' disputes with the Pharisees after his two multiplications of the loaves (6:30–8:10ff) and immediately after Peter's acceptance of him as Messiah (Mk 8:27-30), Jesus turns to his disciples and begins the series of instructions on discipleship that forms the core of Mark's Gospel and leads to the denouement of the passion, death, and resurrection. In Luke's Gospel, the turning point is the same. It occurs when Jesus turns his face toward Jerusalem and death (9:51ff) and in the course of his journey distinguishes between those who reject him and those who accept him.[2]

In a manner far more artistic than that of the Synoptics, the genius of John is evident in his choosing as his turning point the storm at sea and the walking on the waters. It is the one episode that would most certainly evoke in his readers the remembrance of the great turning point in Israel's earlier history—the Passover in Egypt, the exodus, the passage through the sea, the eating of the manna in the desert, and the constitution of Israel as the people of God (cf. Ex 12–24).

To enhance the evocation of the exodus event, John has flanked the walking on the sea on the one side with the multiplication of loaves episode (6:1-15), which takes place in the wilderness near the time of the Passover and on a mountain (evoking Sinai) with a gift of bread that is almost literally from heaven through a miraculous multiplication by Jesus. On the other side, he has flanked the walking on the sea with the great Eucharistic discourse (6:22-71), which similarly takes place near the Passover, explicitly mentions Israel's ancestors, the figure of Moses, and the gift of bread (manna) from heaven. In short, John has evoked memories of the old exodus to create as the turning point of his Gospel a new exodus and a new people of God![3]

Sequence 11

THE NEW EXODUS—JESUS WALKS
ON THE SEA

6:16-21

Parallel structure

(a) The disciples depart from **one side of the sea** (6:16-17a).
(b) The disciples are **alone** on the sea (6:17b).
(c) The wind blows and the sea rises (6:18).
(b′) **Jesus joins the apostles** and declares, "It is I" (6:19-20).
(a′) The disciples arrive on the **other side of the sea** (6:21).

Text

(a)   6:16 When evening came, **his disciples** went down to the sea, ¹⁷got **into a boat,** and **started across the sea to Capernaum.**

(b)   ¹⁷ᵇIt was now dark, and **Jesus had not yet come to them.**

(c)   ¹⁸The sea rose because a strong wind was blowing.

(b′)   ¹⁹When they had rowed about three or four miles, they saw **Jesus** walking on the sea and drawing near to the boat. **They** were frightened, ²⁰but **he** said to **them, "It is I; do not be afraid."**

(a′)   ²¹Then **they** were glad to take **him into the boat,** and immediately **the boat was at the land to which they were going.**

Parallelism is achieved in (a) and (a′) by the repetition of the verb *egeneto* in 6:16, when evening "came," and in 6:21b, "was" at the land. John also balances the phrases "down to the sea" (*epi tēn thalassan*) in 6:16 and "at the land" (*epi tēs gēs*) in 6:21b. This parallelism is antithetic. It amounts to saying "on the one side and on the other." In addition, John uses the phrase "into the boat" in v 17 of (a) and v 21 of (a′). In (b) and (b′), parallelism is achieved by the antithetic parallelism of absence in (b)—the apostles are alone because "Jesus had not yet come to them" (6:17b)—versus presence in (b′)—Jesus "comes" to them walking on the waters (6:19).

Commentary

(a) The disciples depart from one side of the sea (6:16-17a).

6:16 When evening came. As Brown points out, the episode of the walking on the waters in the synoptic Gospels (Mk 6:46-52; Mt 14:23-33) is intimately bound up with the episode of the multiplication of loaves that precedes it.⁴ In John, however, 6:14-15 closes off the multiplication episode from what follows and gives the walking on the sea greater independence as a separate narrative. The walking on the waters serves in John, therefore, as a transition (it happens at night) between the multiplication of the loaves on the one day and the explanation of the loaves as the Eucharist on the next day (6:22-71). Standing as an independent narrative, the episode serves John's purpose well. It allows him to place greater emphasis on the sea scene as a new exodus event. Significantly, the crossing of the sea and Jesus' walking upon the waters take place *at night*—the same time as the original passage through the sea at the time of the first exodus (cf. Ex 14:19-25).

(b) The disciples are alone on the sea (6:17b).

6:17b Jesus had not yet come to them. Some consider these words the work of a redactor, but they are almost certainly Johannine, since they serve to set off (b) from (b′). In the former, Jesus is *not with them;* in the latter (v 19), he is *with them on the sea.*

(c) The wind blows and the sea rises (6:18).

6:18 because a strong wind was blowing. In the synoptic Gospels, Jesus calms the sea, and the emphasis is on the twofold miracle—the calming of the sea and the walking on the water. John says nothing about the calming of the sea, in all probability because his primary intention is to emphasize the exodus aspect of the event—the passage through the sea and the theophanic words of Jesus: "It is I." His emphasis here, as in the previous episode, is quite different from the emphasis on the miracles as found in the Synoptics. John presupposes miraculous events. It simply suits his purpose better to emphasize the theophany of Jesus and the exodus aspect of the whole episode.

(b′) Jesus joins the apostles and declares, "It is I" (6:19-20).

6:20 It is I. Jesus uses for himself the name God had given himself in Ex 3:14. The Galilean Jews had acclaimed Jesus as "the prophet" (6:14-15) and had wanted to seize him and force him to be their king. Here John, without at all denying the validity of the titles prophet and king, has Jesus identify and interpret himself as infinitely more than prophet and king. In the Passover ambient of the whole episode, Jesus' walking on the waters and declaring "It is I" evokes remembrance of the passage through the sea in Ex 14 and recalls to the reader's mind such poetic interpretations of that event as Ps 77:19, which says of Yahweh, "Thy way was through the sea, thy path through the great waters"; and Ps 29:3, which speaks of "the voice of the Lord . . . upon the waters." Esthetically speaking, it is this emphasis on the divinity of Jesus more than anything else that explains John's downgrading of the miraculous that is so prominent in the synoptic accounts of the episode.

(a') The disciples arrive on the other side of the sea (6:21).

6:21a they were glad to take him into the boat. The words are peculiar to John's account. Mk 6:51 says, "he got into the boat with them." Mt 14:32 says, "they [Jesus and Peter] got into the boat." It is perhaps too much to read this line as a positive response to Jesus in contradistinction to the negative response of the Jerusalem Jews in 5:17-47 and the Galilean Jews in 6:14-15, but it finds good support in 6:68-71, where the apostles respond positively to Jesus after negative responses from the Jews in general and even from many of Jesus' disciples. It is fitting also in a new exodus account that the new Israel should show its willingness to accept its redeemer.

6:21b the boat was at the land. Nothing is said about how the boat got to land, simply that it got there. The miraculous is perhaps implied but, as throughout, it is not emphasized. The journey that had begun on the one shore (v 16: *epi tēn thalassan*) ends up on the other shore (*epi tēs gēs*). It is a perfect inclusion-conclusion. At the same time, it is another recall of the original exodus event. It was Yahweh who had brought the Israelites through the sea to liberate them from slavery and make them his people.[5]

Themes

In sequence 11, more is implicit than explicit. It is difficult, as a consequence, to capture the themes without seeming to read into the account more than it contains. The theme of replacement is the dominant theme. It is, however, almost entirely implicit. Only when the reader recognizes the episode as the turning point of the Gospel and as the dramatization of a new exodus constituting a new people of God does it dawn upon him or her that responsive Israel (the disciples and Christians in general) is about to replace unresponsive Israel (the synagogue) as the true Israel of God—the Christian Church.

The concentric theme of response is barely recognizable in the words "they were glad to take him into the boat" (6:21a) and is clarified in the following sequence when many of Jesus' disciples leave him and only the Twelve remain (6:68-70).

The theme of witness is unambiguous in the miracle of walking on the water and in the theophanic words of Jesus, "It is I; do not be afraid" (6:20). The words "It is I" (*egō eimi*) recall Ex 3:14; Dt 32:39; Is 41:4; 43:10, 25; 48:12 and constitute a typical Johannine testimony to the divinity of Jesus.

Part IV

FRUITLESS APPEALS TO THE JEWS
6:22–12:11

In part IV the Johannine Jesus, in a series of highly theological dialogues and discourses, refutes the charges brought against him and the Christian Church by the synagogue leaders and makes a last passionate appeal to the Jews to believe in him. The twelfth (6:22-71) and sixteenth (10:40–12:11) sequences take place just before the feast of the Passover, the thirteenth (7:1–8:59) and fourteenth (9:1–10:21) at the feast of Tabernacles, and the fifteenth (10:22-39) at the feast of the Dedication.

Parallel structure of part IV

(a) *Sequence 12 (6:22-71):*   I will **raise him up** on the last day.
(b) *Sequence 13 (7:1–8:59):*   **At the feast** of Tabernacles
(c) *Sequence 14 (9:1–10:21):*   The blind man and the good shepherd
(b′) *Sequence 15 (10:22-39):*   **At the feast** of the Dedication
(a′) *Sequence 16 (10:40–12:11):*   I am the **resurrection** and the life.

Parallelism is achieved in (a) and (a′) by means of the theme of the resurrection and eternal life. In the Eucharistic discourse (a), Jesus repeats a number of times that he is God's bread which comes down from heaven to give life to the world and that whoever "eats my flesh and drinks my blood has eternal life, and I will raise him up at the last day." In (a′), Jesus tells Martha, "I am the resurrection and the life" and then raises Lazarus from the dead. In (b) and (b′), the evangelist creates parallelism by balancing Jesus' defense of his divinity at the feast of Tabernacles (chs 7–8) with the defense of his divinity at the feast of the Dedication (10:22-39). The center (c) in 9:1–10:21 is used by the evangelist to contrast Jesus, the good shepherd, with the synagogue leaders, the hireling shepherds.

Sequence 12

THE TRUE BREAD GIVES LIFE EVERLASTING
6:22-71

Parallel structure

(a) The crowd comes to **Capernaum** looking for Jesus (6:22-24).
(b) Jesus is the **true bread** from heaven (6:25-40).
(c) The Jews protest Jesus' claim that he came down from heaven (6:41-42).
(b') Jesus insists he is the **true bread** and this bread is his flesh (6:43-58).
(a') Many reject Jesus' teaching and leave him; only the Twelve remain at **Capernaum** (6:59-71).

Text

(a)   6:22 On the next day the people who remained on the other side of the sea saw that there had been only one boat there, and that Jesus had not entered the boat with his **disciples,** but that his **disciples had gone away** alone. ²³However, boats from Tiberias came near the place where they ate the bread after the **Lord** had given thanks. ²⁴So when the people saw that Jesus was not there, nor his **disciples,** they themselves got into the boats and went to **Capernaum,** seeking Jesus.

(b)   ²⁵When they found him on the other side of the sea, they said to him, "Rabbi, when did you come here?" ²⁶Jesus answered them, **"Truly, truly, I say to you,** you seek me, not because you saw signs, but because you ate your fill of the loaves. ²⁷Do not labor for the food which perishes, but for **the food which endures to eternal life,** which the Son of man will give to you; for on him has God the Father set his seal." ²⁸Then they said to him, "What must we do, to be doing the works of God?" ²⁹Jesus answered them, "This is the work of God, that you **believe** in him whom he has sent." ³⁰So they said to him, "Then what sign do you do, that we may see, and **believe** you? What work do you perform? ³¹Our **fathers ate the manna in the wilderness;** as it is written, 'He gave them **bread from heaven** to eat.' " ³²Jesus then said to them, **"Truly, truly, I say to you,** it was not Moses who gave you the **bread from heaven;** my Father gives you the **true bread from heaven.** ³³For the bread of God is that **which comes down from heaven,** and gives life to the world." ³⁴They said to him, "Lord, give us this bread always." ³⁵Jesus said to them, **"I am the bread of life; he who comes to me** shall not hunger, and he who **believes** in me shall never thirst. ³⁶But I said to you that you have seen me and yet do not **believe.** ³⁷All that the Father gives me **will come to me;** and **him who comes to me** I will not cast out. ³⁸For

114

I **have come down from heaven,** not to do my own will, but the will of him **who sent me;** [39]and this is the will of him **who sent me,** that I should lose nothing of all that he has given me, but **raise it up at the last day.** [40]For this is the will of my Father, that **every one who sees the Son and believes in him should have eternal life; and I will raise him up at the last day.**''

(c)   [41]The Jews then murmured at him, because he said, ''I am the bread which came down from heaven.'' [42]They said, ''Is not this Jesus, the son of Joseph, whose father and mother we know? How does he now say, 'I have come down from heaven'?''

(b′)   [43]Jesus answered them, ''Do not murmur among yourselves. [44]No one can **come to me** unless the Father **who sent me** draws him; and **I will raise him up at the last day.** [45]It is written in the prophets, 'And they shall all be taught by God.' Every one who has heard and learned from the Father **comes to me.** [46]Not that any one has seen the Father except him who is from God; he has seen the Father. [47]**Truly, truly, I say to you, he who believes has eternal life.** [48]**I am the bread of life.** [49]Your **fathers ate the manna in the wilderness,** and they died. [50]**This is the bread which comes down from heaven,** that a man may eat of it and not die. [51]**I am the living bread which came down from heaven;** if any one eats of this bread, he **will live for ever;** and the bread which I shall give for the life of the world is my flesh.''

[52]The Jews then disputed among themselves, saying, ''How can this man give us his flesh to eat?'' [53]So Jesus said to them, **''Truly, truly, I say to you,** unless you eat the flesh of the Son of man and drink his blood, you have no life in you; [54]**he who eats my flesh and drinks my blood has eternal life, and I will raise him up at the last day.** [55]For my flesh is food indeed, and my blood is drink indeed. [56]He who eats my flesh and drinks my blood abides in me, and I in him. [57]As the living Father sent me, and I live because of the Father, so he who eats me will live because of me. [58]This is **the bread which came down from heaven,** not such as the **fathers ate** and died; he who eats this bread **will live for ever.''**

(a′)   [59]This he said in the synagogue, as he taught at **Capernaum.** [60]Many of his **disciples,** when they heard it, said, ''This is a hard saying; who can listen to it?'' [61]But Jesus, knowing in himself that his **disciples** murmured at it, said to them, ''Do you take offense at this? [62]Then what if you were to see the Son of man ascending where he was before? [63]It is the spirit that gives life, the flesh is of no avail; the words that I have spoken to you are spirit and life. [64]But there are some of you that do not believe.'' For Jesus knew from the first who those were that did not believe, and who it was that should betray him. [65]And he said, ''This is why I told you that no one can come to me unless it is granted him by the Father.''

[66]After this many of his **disciples drew back** and no longer went about with him. [67]Jesus said to the twelve, ''Will you also **go away?''** [68]Simon Peter answered him, **''Lord,** to whom shall we go? You have the words of eternal life; [69]and we have believed, and have come to know, that you are the Holy One of God.'' [70]Jesus answered them, ''Did I not choose you, the twelve, and one of you is a devil?'' [71]He spoke of Judas the son of Simon Iscariot, for he, one of the twelve, was to betray him.

The evangelist parallels (a) with (a′) by coming back in (a′) to the same personages and the same place mentioned in (a): Jesus, the disciples, and

Capernaum. In (b) and (b'), the parallelism is more complex. It consists in repeating both key words and key ideas. At the beginning of (b) in v 31, the Jews say, "Our fathers ate the manna in the wilderness"; at the end of (b') in v 58, Jesus declares, ". . . not such as the fathers ate and died; he who eats this bread will live for ever." In v 33 of (b), Jesus declares, "For the bread of God is that which comes down from heaven, and gives life to the world"; in v 51 of (b'), Jesus declares, "I am the living bread which came down from heaven; if any one eats of this bread, he will live for ever; and the bread which I shall give for the life of the world is my flesh." At the end of (b) in vv 39-40, Jesus speaks of raising up at the last day those whom the Father has given him; at the beginning of (b'), Jesus declares, "No one can come to me unless the Father who sent him draws him; and I will raise him up at the last day" (v 44). Finally, in both (b) and (b'), the evangelist forms concatenations of the key words "bread," "eat," and "Father," with the word "bread" in vv 31, 32, 33, 34, 35 of (b) paralleled by the word "bread" in vv 48, 50, 51, 52, 58 of (b'); the word "eat" in vv 26, 31 of (b) paralleled by the word "eat" in vv 49, 50, 51, 52, 53, 54, 56, 57, 58 of (b'); and the word "Father" in vv 27, 32, 37, 40 of (b) paralleled by the word "Father" in vv 44, 45, 46, 57 of (b'). The reader who compares (b) and (b') will find many other parallels.

The center (c) marks the Jews' negative response to Jesus' claim to be the true bread of life by emphasizing their insistence that they know his earthly parentage and that as a consequence he cannot have come down from heaven from the Father.

In (b'), Jesus counters the Jews' objection by challenging them to eat his flesh and drink his blood. This leads to the climax (a') of the whole episode and to the Jews' definitive rejection of Jesus' claim that he is the true bread that has come down from heaven from the Father. The Jewish attitude toward Jesus, which was hardening in (c), has become thoroughly hardened in (a').

The hardening of the Jews' attitude in (a') is important for the movement of the Gospel because the evangelist is careful to recount at the same time the positive attitude of the twelve apostles (vv 67-70). Here in John's Gospel, as at the center of Matthew's Gospel (Mt 13:36ff) and at the center of Mark's Gospel (Mk 8:31ff), Jesus moves away from the Jews who have rejected him and turns to the twelve who have accepted him.

In the remaining sequences of part IV of the Gospel, John will show Jesus in hiding from the Jews and in mortal danger because of their plots to put him to death. The animosity that John first indicated in 5:18 ("This was why the Jews sought all the more to kill him, because . . .") is continued in the sequences that follow with frequent repetition of such key words as "arrest," "fear," "hate," "kill" (cf. 7:1, 6-8, 13, 20, 25, 30, 32, 44; 8:20, 28, 37, 59; 9:1ff; 10:11, 15, 17-18, 31, 39; 11:46-53; 12:4, 7, 23, 32, 37-50).

The complex but clear parallelism of (b) and (b') has special significance in view of the debate concerning the authenticity of the section on the Eucharist in 6:51-58. Since the time of Bultmann, 6:51-58 has been considered the interpolation of an ecclesiastical redactor who added it to the Gospel in its final stage of redaction. He is believed by some to have taken the material from the Eucharistic liturgy of the Johannine Church (and, according to some critics, to have displaced it from its more natural position at the beginning of the Last Supper discourse in ch 13) and to have patterned it on the original "bread of life" discourse section in 6:32-50.

The critics argue that if 6:51-58 is eliminated, the concluding section of the chapter (6:59-71) follows without a break in sense from 6:50. In this case it is presupposed that the ecclesiastical redactor and interpolator of 6:51-58, by paralleling his discourse section with the discourse section in 6:32-50, which insists on the necessity of believing in Jesus, intended to make it clear that the gift of life is effected through a *believing* reception of the Eucharist.

Despite the arguments of the critics who hold for the interpolation of 6:51-58 and despite the apparent reasonableness of their explanations, the parallel structure of 6:22-71 indicates clearly that 6:51-58 was an authentic and integral part of the sequence from the beginning. It is certainly a part of 6:43-59, which is the (b') section of the sequence. It clearly looks back to (b) in 6:25-40. At the same time, it does precisely what the (b') section is supposed to do—it advances the action toward the climactic inclusion (a'). Thus, far from being either a duplicate discourse or the clumsy interpolation of an ecclesiastical redactor, the whole section is both authentic and original. Hoskyns, in a passing remark concerning the good shepherd parable in relation to the death of Jesus, catches perfectly the relationship between 6:51ff and 6:1-15: "In similar fashion," he says, "the significance of the feeding of the 5000 is not exhausted until the bread is expounded as the flesh Jesus will give for the life of the world, and the feeding which provides life is declared to be the eating of his body and the drinking of his blood (vi. 51ff)."[1]

Commentary

Sequence 12 begins with the Galilean Jews doubting Jesus and asking for a sign (6:25-30). Later they murmur when he declares that he is the bread that came down from heaven (6:41-43). In the end they give up following him (6:60-66).

In addition to the parallelism of parts, there are five major clues to the interpretation of Jesus' Eucharistic discourse. First, the discovery of P. Borgen that the discourse follows the format of the midrashic homily.[2] Second, A. Guilding's discovery that the discourse contains many allusions to the readings used in the synagogue during the Passover celebration.[3] Third, the similar sequence of events in Mk 8:1ff. Fourth, the great similarity in format between 6:22-58 and 4:4-38. Fifth, the great probability that what John is doing in the discourse is refuting the synagogue Jews, who protest against and refuse to believe in a crucified Messiah who, Christians claim, has given himself to them in the Eucharist as a remembrance of his death and resurrection.

First, Borgen sees the discourse as patterned upon the format of a midrashic homily. In a midrashic homily, the sequence went as follows: (a) citation of the text; (b) paraphrase of the text; (c) an interpretation of each word of the citation; (d) a reference to the prophets. If the discourse is read as follows, it will be seen to follow this pattern almost exactly.

a) *Citation of the text*

v 31: He gave them bread from heaven to eat.

b) *Paraphrase*

v 32: . . . it was not Moses who gave you the bread from heaven; my Father gives you the true bread from heaven.

c) *Exegesis of each word:*
   1) he gave
   2) them

v 32: My Father gives you . . .

v 35b: He who comes to me shall not hunger . . .

v 37b: and him who comes to me I will not cast out.

vv 39-40: and this is the will of him who sent me, that I should lose nothing of all that he has given me, but raise it up at the last day. For this is the will óf my Father, that every one who sees the Son and believes in him should have eternal life; and I will raise him up at the last day.

   3) bread from heaven

v 35: I am the bread of life (cf. vv 41, 51, 58).

   4) to eat

vv 49-51: Your fathers ate . . . This is the bread which comes down from heaven, that a man may eat . . . If any one eats . . .

v 52b: How can this man give us his flesh to eat?

v 53: . . . unless you eat . . .

v 54: . . . he who eats my flesh . . .

v 57b: . . . so he who eats me . . .

v 58: This is the bread which came down from heaven, not such as

the fathers ate and died; he who
eats this bread will live for ever.

d) *Citation from the prophets*   v 45: It is written . . . "And they
shall all be taught by God."

Borgen's theory, though not universally accepted, has the great value of bringing out clearly the continuity and integrity of the discourse as a whole. It argues cogently against those who see two parallel but different discourses in 6:31-58, the original in 6:31-50 and the second, the interpolation of a so-called ecclesiastical redactor, in 6:51-58. Since the bread from heaven that is eaten is the Eucharist (cf. 6:51-58, which all admit to be Eucharistic), Borgen rightly concludes that the discourse as a whole deals primarily with the Eucharist and only secondarily with Jesus as revelation.

Second, Guilding's discovery that the discourse contains allusions to the readings used in the synagogue during the Passover celebration fortifies Borgen's theory that what we have in 6:31-58 is a midrashic homily and at the same time helps to explain a number of otherwise strange words in the homily. Guilding theorizes that parts of 6:22-71 center on readings used in the synagogue for the six weeks around Passover, in particular those readings taken from Gn 1–8 (chs 2–3); Ex 11–16 (ch 16); Nm 6–14 (ch 11).

The discourse echoes the synagogue reading from Ex 16 (the chapter dealing with manna from heaven) as well as the readings from Gn 2 (compare Gn 2:17: "But of the tree of the knowledge of good and evil you shall not *eat,* for in the day that you *eat* of it you shall *die,"* with Jn 6:49-50: "Your fathers *ate* the manna in the wilderness, and they *died.* This is the bread which comes down from heaven, that a man may *eat* of it and not *die."* Gn 3:24 compares well with Jn 6:37: ". . . and him who comes to me I will not cast out"; and Gn 3:22 with Jn 6:51: ". . . if any one eats of this bread, he will live for ever." Brown gives other readings and parallels and concludes: "These parallels are impressive, and it seems legitimate to maintain that John vi reflects a medley of themes drawn from the synagogue readings at Passover time."[4]

Third, the similar sequence of events in Mk 8:1ff, where Jesus feeds the multitude (8:1-9), crosses the sea (8:10), refuses the request of the Pharisees for a sign (8:11-13), warns his disciples to be on guard against the yeast (unbelief) of the Pharisees (8:14-15), and concludes by rebuking his disciples for not understanding the miracle of the loaves in 6:34-52 and 8:1-9 (8:16-21), indicates that John's interpretation of the loaves as the Eucharist is no different than the interpretation of Mark. Q. Quesnell has made a very good case for proving that what the disciples did not understand in Mk 6:34-44 and 8:1-9 (the second Markan version of the loaves miracle) was the meaning of the loaves as the Eucharistic remembrance of Jesus' passion and death.[5] If Quesnell is correct, then not only is the sequence the same in Jn 6:31-58 but also the interpretation of the loaves as the Eucharist. In John the sequence runs: (1) the loaves miracle (6:1-15); (2) the crossing (6:16-21); (3) the request for a sign (6:30); (4) the misunderstanding about the bread, which is cleared up by John through Jesus' discourse on the bread as the Eucharist (6:31-58).

This would not prove John's dependence on Mark, though it suggests it. What it proves is that each evangelist took the same traditional material about the loaves, the crossing, and the request for a sign and used it *theologically* to inculcate both the importance of the Eucharist and the meaning of the Eucharist as the sacrament and remembrance of Jesus' death. Where Mark in his usual mysterious and cryptic manner only hints at the real meaning of the loaves (cf. Mk 6:52 and 8:14-21), John in his more forthright manner declares for all to hear that the Eucharist, symbolized by the loaves, is indeed the sacrament of the body and blood of the crucified Jesus.

Fourth, the similarity in format between 6:22-58 and 4:4-38 suggests that the two sequences contain different concentric presentations of the central Johannine teaching that Jesus is the source and giver of eternal life to all who believe in him. Unlike ch 4, in which Jesus speaks about himself as the one who gives the water of eternal life but does not identify himself with the water, in 6:31ff Jesus speaks about giving the bread of life and then explicitly identifies himself with the bread that is Eucharistic bread. What is more clear, as a result, in Jn 6:31-58 is that the belief that saves is a belief in Jesus crucified, since the Eucharistic bread is the memorial of Jesus' death. The following table shows the similarity of the two concentric-circle presentations.

Jn 6:25ff	*Jn 4:4ff*
Question (v 25): Rabbi, when did you come here?	*Question* (v 9): How is it that you, a Jew, ask a drink of me, a woman of Samaria?
Answer (v 27): Do not labor for the food which perishes.	*Answer* (v 13): Every one who drinks of this water will thirst again.
Question (vv 30-31): Then what sign do you do, that we may see, and believe you? Our **fathers** ate the manna in the wilderness. . . .	*Question* (vv 11-12): Where do you get that living water? Are you greater than our **father** Jacob, who gave us the well?
Answer (vv 32-33): It was not Moses who gave you the bread from heaven; my Father gives you the true bread from heaven. For the bread of God is that which comes down from heaven, and gives **life** to the world.	*Answer* (v 14): . . . the water that I shall give him will become in him a spring of water welling up to eternal **life.**
Reaction (v 34): Lord, **give** us this bread always.	*Reaction* (v 15): Sir, **give** me this water, that I may not thirst, nor come here to draw.

Fifth, what John is doing in 6:31-58 is refuting the synagogue Jews, who not only refuse to believe in a crucified Messiah who is remembered in the Eucharist but refuse outright to accept the Eucharist. This is another of John's great refutations of his Jewish adversaries at the end of the first century. In chs 7-8, he will refute their objections against Jesus' messiahship and divinity. In 9:1-10:21, he will refute their objections against Jesus' miracles. In 10:22-39, he will again refute their objections against Jesus' divinity. The contrast between "your fathers" and Christians is clear in 6:49. As Brown puts it: "This is one of the instances of 'your' indicating the deep cleavage that exists between Church and Synagogue at the time when the evangelist is writing; see 'your law' in viii 17, and 'your father Abraham' in viii 56.''[6]

Parallels such as 6:32 with 6:55 and 6:39 with 6:57 make eminent sense when the whole discourse is seen as centered on the Eucharist and the synagogue's refusal to accept such an outrageous sacrament and what it implied—the passion and death of the Messiah. The same thought is central to 2:19-22; 3:14-17; 8:28; 12:31-34 and is indeed central to the whole Gospel, which deals so often with Jesus' hour and Jesus' glorification, both of which clearly refer to the passion. A final argument for the centrality of the Eucharist in the discourse is the parallelism of 6:25-40 with 6:44-58. In brief, in view of John's appeal to the Jews on the fence at the end of the first century and his refutation of the synagogue leaders' charges against Christianity, the whole of the discourse in 6:22-71 looks clearly to be John's refutation of the synagogue's charge that Christians worshiped a crucified Messiah and remembered him in the sacrament of the Eucharist.

(a) The crowd comes to Capernaum looking for Jesus (6:22-24).

6:22   the other side of the sea. Literally "across the lake." Since the crowd finds Jesus in Capernaum, this location favors a place on the east side of the lake for the multiplication of the loaves. However, it does not seem that John is greatly interested in geography. His interest is primarily theological, and by emphasizing that the crowd has been left behind and that only Jesus and the Twelve have crossed the sea together, he further highlights his symbolism of a new exodus and a new crossing of the sea. **The people . . . saw.** The crowd of five thousand (6:10) is treated as if it had one mind and thought and acted as a unity. This is surely permissible dramatic license on John's part. His purpose is to link the dialogue and discourse in 6:25ff with the multiplication of the loaves on the previous day. To accomplish this, he had to get the crowd to Capernaum.

6:23   boats from Tiberias. The boats may be historical, but they are also convenient. The mention of Tiberias here in sequence 12 supplies a parallel with the mention of Tiberias (6:1) in sequence 10 (6:1-15), which is the chiastic parallel of sequence 12 (6:22-71).

6:24 to Capernaum. In the Markan account, Jesus crosses the sea and arrives at Gennesaret (Mk 6:53). The same is true in Mt 14:34. In the second account in Mark and Matthew, however, Jesus arrives at Dalmanutha (Mk 8:10; Mt 15:39). There is no way to explain these geographical discrepancies, and least of all to explain why John has Jesus arrive at a completely different place. One may suggest that John located the Eucharistic discourse at Capernaum because he found it the fitting locale for the Jews' rejection of Jesus, which is so prominent in 6:60-66. It was of Capernaum that Jesus had said: "And you, Capernaum . . . . If the mighty works done in you had been done in Sodom, it would have remained until this day. But I tell you that it shall be more tolerable on the day of judgment for the land of Sodom than for you" (Mt 11:23).

(b) Jesus is the true bread from heaven (6:25-40).

6:26 Jesus answered them. Presumably the crowd came looking for Jesus because they had seen the loaves sign (6:14). Jesus' answer, therefore, deals with the way the crowd had seen the sign. They had not seen it in a believing but in a self-interested way. This was already a matter of record from their attempt to make Jesus king (6:14-15). John, therefore, has Jesus repeat this reference to their faithless seeing in order to set the stage for the dialogue about faith and about working for "food which endures to eternal life."[7] This imperishable food, as John will explain in 6:51-58, is the Eucharist.

6:28 What must we do, to be doing the works of God? Literally: "What must we do to work (*ergazōmetha*) the works (*ta erga*) of God?" The literal translation brings out the key theological play on words John uses when he speaks of work. His theology centers on the concept of the work that is done by the Father, the work that is done by the Son, and the work that is done by human beings. The work of the Father is to send and give the Son for the salvation of the world (cf. 3:16-18 and Jesus' statement in 4:34: "My food is to do the will of him who sent me, and to accomplish his work." See also 17:4: "I glorified thee on earth, having accomplished the work which thou gavest me to do"; and 19:30: "It is finished," where the "it" refers to the work of the Father that Jesus completed on the cross).

6:29-30 This is the work of God. Jesus' answer defines the work of human beings as the work of faith: "This is the work (*ergon*) of God, that you believe in him whom he has sent." Jesus' declaration sets the stage for the rest of the chapter. The people will ask him for a sign and they will ask him, "What *work do you perform* (*ti ergadzē*)?" The only sign he gives them is literally the sign of the cross, since the rest of the discourse deals with the bread from heaven that is Jesus himself in the Eucharist, the sign and remembrance of his death. This sign also explains Jesus' work, which is doing the will of him who sent him and accomplishing his work (4:34). Jesus' work is to die on the cross as the Lamb of God who takes away the sin of the world—a work commemorated most perfectly in the Eucharist.

It is interesting to observe that when Jesus refuses the request of the Pharisees and Sadducees for a sign in Mt 16:1-4, his reply is substantially the same as here in Jn 6: "An evil and adulterous generation seeks for a sign, but no sign shall be given to it except the sign of Jonah." The sign of Jonah that Jesus gives is his three days in the tomb (which presupposes his death on the cross) and his subsequent resurrection. Both the sign of Jonah and the Eucharist are signs of the crucifixion and death of Jesus.

The Jews' asking for a sign only twenty-four hours after witnessing the multiplication of the loaves (6:14) and after Jesus himself referred to their having seen signs (6:26) has posed a problem for exegetes. Some suggest a different crowd; others suggest individuals who had not seen the sign on the previous day. John's purpose, however, in the transitional passage in 6:22-24 was to show that the crowd which had seen the loaves miracle was the same crowd that sought and found Jesus in Capernaum. Still others suggest that the crowd was asking for a special sign expected from the Messiah, who, as a prophet like Moses, would do what Moses had done, namely, provide a new manna-from-heaven miracle. There are a number of references to such an expectation in rabbinic sources, making this a possible explanation of the problem.[8]

We suggest a literary explanation. The question the crowd asks is not an actual historical question put to Jesus but the question John has the crowd put to him in order to set the stage for the discourse that follows. The same kind of literary question is asked by Mary in Luke's Gospel: "How can this be, since I have no husband?" (Lk 1:34),[9] and by John the Baptist in Matthew's Gospel: "Are you he who is to come, or shall we look for another?" (Mt 11:3).[10]

6:31 He gave them bread from heaven to eat. The text upon which Jesus will deliver his Eucharistic homily is supplied by his questioners. It is not found in these exact words anywhere in the Old Testament but is a conflation of Ex 16:4-5, Ps 78:24, and Neh 9:15.

6:32-33 it was not Moses. Following the midrashic pattern for a homily, Jesus' discourse begins with a paraphrase of the text for the homily given in 6:31. It will continue with a word-for-word explanation of the text. Here we have the paraphrase. Jesus makes it clear that the true giver of both the ancient manna and the true bread from heaven that is himself is the Father and not Moses. The contrast between the verbs "gave," referring to the old manna in the desert, and "gives," referring to Jesus, the real heavenly bread that comes down from heaven, updates the text and makes it immediately relevant to the audience. This true bread from heaven is different from the old manna because it gives life to the world.

6:34 Lord, give us this bread always. Like the Samaritan woman in 4:15, the crowd misunderstands, thinking, as the Samaritan woman did about not having to go for water anymore, that this bread would save them the trouble of baking their daily bread. It is the typical Johannine misunderstanding technique used first in 2:19-20, used brilliantly in the Nicodemus dialogue (3:4), and then used regularly throughout the Gospel (cf. 6:26, 34, 41-42; 8:39, 52, 57; 11:11-15, 23-26; 13:7-9, 36-38; 14:4-5, 8-9).

6:35a I am the bread of life. Jesus has explained the first words of the text, "He gave"; now he explains the words "bread from heaven." Unlike the manna that the fathers ate in the desert and died, Jesus is the true bread (the Eucharist). Those who eat the true bread live (cf. 6:48-58).

6:35b-40 he who comes to me. With these words, Jesus explains the "them" of "He gave them bread from heaven to eat." To come to Jesus is the equivalent of believing in him. **All that the Father gives me** (v 37) continues in the same vein, since John regularly refers to those who believe in Jesus as those whom the Father gives him and protects (cf. 10:28f; 17:12; 18:9). **Everyone who sees the Son** (v 40): Jesus is still explaining the "them" of the homily text. The expression "sees the Son and believes in him," in view of the Johannine reference to scripture in 19:37 ("They shall *look upon* him whom they have pierced," from Zech 12:10), suggests that John's thought here takes in the crucified Jesus commemorated in the Eucharist, even though the verb in 6:40 (*theōrōn*) differs from the verb in 19:37 (*opsontai*).

(c) The Jews protest Jesus' claim that he came down from heaven (6:41-42).

6:41 murmured at him. The remark conjures up the exodus aura of the whole sequence, since the Old Testament frequently speaks of the Israelites "murmuring" in protest during the long years of the exodus (cf. Ex 16:2, 7ff and Ps 78:17-20, 40-43, 56-58).

6:42 Is not this Jesus? The Jews' misunderstanding of Jesus' real origin—the usual Johannine misunderstanding technique—bridges the first half of the discourse (6:31-40) and the second (6:43-58), and also prepares the way for the second half of the discourse, in which Jesus explains how he has come down from heaven as the one sent by the Father and as the bread that will enable men and women to eat and live forever.

(b′) Jesus insists he is the true bread and this bread is his flesh (6:43-58).

6:44 No one can come to me. Section (b′) takes up where section (b) left off in v 40—interpreting the "them" of the homily text ("He gave *them* bread from heaven to eat") as those whom the Father draws (*helkysē*) to Jesus. Significantly, in relation to the Eucharistic tenor of the discourse, the same verb is used when Jesus speaks of himself on the cross drawing all men to himself: "And I, when I am lifted up from the earth, will draw (*helkysō*) all men to myself" (12:32). "He said this," as John goes on to say, "to show by what death he was to die" (12:33).

6:45-48 It is written in the prophets. Jesus continues his midrashic interpretation of the "them" as those to whom the Father (not Moses, as explained in v 32) "gives bread from heaven to eat." The citation from the prophets, according to Borgen, is a typical element of the rabbinic homily. The citation here appears to be from Is 54:13, with dependence on the new covenant prophecy of Jer 31:31-34. Those "taught" by God believe, and what they believe is the truth of what Jesus states in v 48: "I am the bread of life."

6:49 Your fathers ate. From v 49 to v 58, Jesus gives the midrashic interpretation of the word "eat" in the text "He gave them bread from heaven to eat." The homily on the text had been occasioned by the Jews' statement in v 31: "Our fathers ate the manna in the wilderness." Jesus will now explain the differences between the ancestors who "ate" manna in the desert and the believers in him who "eat the flesh of the Son of man and drink his blood." Implicit in the word "your" of "your fathers" is the opposition between the Jewish synagogue and the Christian synagogue at the end of the first century. This opposition will come to a climax in the inclusion-conclusion of the sequence, when many of those who hear Jesus draw back and refuse to go about with him (v 66).

6:50-51 This is the bread. The great difference between the old bread from heaven and the bread that is Jesus' flesh and blood is that the ancestors who ate the manna in the desert died, while those who eat Jesus' flesh and drink his blood have life eternal and will be raised up on the last day.

6:52 The Jews then disputed among themselves. The Jews' quarreling emphasizes the tremendous import of what Jesus (and Christians at the end of the first century) claimed for the Eucharist. The quarreling and the question "How can this man give us his flesh to eat?" function as a literary misunderstanding (the usual Johannine technique, though far more subtle in this case than in most others) that allows Jesus to explain in even clearer terms the tremendous claim being made for the Eucharist.

6:53-55 Truly, truly, I say to you. Jesus does not explain the how of the Jews' question "How can this man give us his flesh to eat?" Rather, he repeats emphatically the truth of what he had said in v 51: "The bread which I shall give for the life of the world is my flesh."

6:56-57 abides (*menei*) in me. In v 27, Jesus told the Jews, "Do not labor for the food which perishes, but for the food which endures (*menei*) to eternal life." As with so many of the parallels between vv 24-40 (b) and vv 44-58 (b′), e.g., "fathers" (v 30 and v 49); "Father" (vv 27, 32, 37-40 and vv 44, 46, 57); "I will raise him up on the last day" (vv 39, 40 and vv 44, 54), the parallel between "endures" in v 27 and "abides" in v 56 serves to reinforce the same meaning for the verb in each case. The meaning is clearer in v 56 and is similar to the meaning of the verb in 15:4-5, where John uses the verb *menein* ("abides") for the indwelling of the Father and the Son in the Christian. Here that indwelling is attributed to the Eucharist (see also 17:11, 21-23).[11]

6:58   This is the bread. The reference to the bread that came down from heaven and the fathers who ate and died forms a parallel with vv 30-33 and an inclusion-conclusion for the whole midrashic homily. At the same time, it repeats in an updated, newly interpreted form the text upon which the homily was based: "He gave them bread from heaven to eat" (v 31).

Unlike many commentators,[12] we have interpreted the discourse on the bread as Eucharistic from beginning to end.[13] In addition to the arguments given in our commentary for interpreting vv 51-58 as authentic and as an integral part of the structural parallel to vv 24-40 rather than as the interpolation of a later ecclesiastical redactor, there is another, and to us, very persuasive argument. It is the argument from the author's format. We have shown that the author regularly structures his thought in a fivefold parallel format. He uses this parallel format for the Gospel as a whole, for each of the twenty-one sequences, sometimes for sections within sequences, as in 5:1-47, which has three sections (vv 1-18; 19-30; 31-47), and sometimes even, as here, within a part of his sequence. Thus, even though 6:43-58 forms the (b´) section of the whole sequence, the author has, from force of habit perhaps, written it in his usual fivefold parallel form. Reading the text as follows shows how impossible it is to separate vv 44-50, the (a) section of 6:43-58, from vv 54-58, the (a´) section; and v 51, the (b) section, from v 53 the (b´) section.

Parallel structure of 6:43-58[14]

(a)   6:43 Jesus answered them, "Do not murmur among yourselves. [44]No one can come to me unless the **Father** who sent me draws him; and **I will raise him up at the last day.** [45]It is written in the prophets, 'And they shall all be taught by God.' Every one who has heard and learned from the **Father** comes to me. [46]Not that any one has seen the **Father** except him who is from God; he has seen the *Father.* [47]Truly, truly, I say to you, he who believes has **eternal life.** [48]I am the bread of life. [49]**Your fathers** ate the manna in the wilderness, and they **died.** [50]**This is the bread which comes down from heaven, that a man may eat of it and not die.**

(b)   [51]I am the **living** bread which came down from heaven; if any one **eats** of this bread, he will **live for ever;** and the bread which I shall give for the **life** of the world is my **flesh.**"

(c)   [52]The Jews then disputed among themselves, saying, "How can this man give us his flesh to eat?"[15]

(b´)   [53]So Jesus said to them, "Truly, truly, I say to you, unless you **eat** the **flesh** of the Son of man and drink his blood, **you have no life in you;**

(a´)   [54]he who **eats** my flesh and drinks my blood **has eternal life,** and **I will raise him up at the last day.** [55]For my flesh is food indeed, and my blood is drink indeed. [56]He who **eats** my flesh and drinks my blood abides in me, and I in him. [57]As the living **Father** sent me, and I live because of the **Father,**

so he who **eats** me will live because of me. ⁵⁸**This is the bread which came down from heaven, not such as the fathers ate and died; he who eats this bread will live for ever.**

It would seem obvious from the verbal and conceptual parallels and from the parallel structure of 6:43-58 that the whole section should be construed as a unit. If this is accepted, there can be no question of eliminating 6:51-58 as a later interpolation, and one must rather interpret the whole unit as Eucharistic. As Hoskyns puts it:

> To eat of His Flesh and to drink of His Blood is as necessary for salvation as to believe in Him who alone has seen the Father (v 47). The former is the inevitable corollary of the latter. Then follows a further repetition of the provocative words, but substituting *munch* for *eat*. This rather vulgar word . . . makes the Saying more provocative still. No room is left for any "spiritualizing" interpretation. The eating and drinking of the Flesh and Blood of the Son of man involve a real physical eating and drinking, although the Flesh and Blood are altogether misconceived if they be thought of, as the Jews are determined to think of them, as the mere material of the human Body of Jesus, instead of being rigorously defined in terms of the significance wrought out and manifested in His sacrificial death. The apparent contradiction implied in the insistence that there must be a real physical eating and drinking of what is grievously misunderstood if it is interpreted purely physically is resolved and explained only if the conscious reference to the Eucharist is perceived . . . . As the Father communicates life to the Son, so the Son communicates life to those who feed on him, and will bestow on them immortality. It is now abundantly clear that the incarnate Son of God, the Son of man, is the Bread who came down from heaven, and the manna is the type of the Son and of the Eucharistic Feast: but only the type.[16]

(a′) Many reject Jesus' teaching and leave him; only the Twelve remain (6:59-71).

6:59   at Capernaum. In the introduction (6:22-24), the crowd sought Jesus and found him in Capernaum (6:24). John's second reference to Capernaum signals the beginning of his inclusion-conclusion. In section (a′), the *dramatis personae* (the crowd, the disciples, and Jesus) will be the same as in section (a). What has happened in between—the Eucharistic homily—explains the dramatic change between the introduction and the inclusion-conclusion. In the former (a), the crowds came (*ēlthen*) to Capernaum looking for Jesus. In the latter (a′), they have found and heard Jesus in Capernaum and they leave him (*apēlthon eis ta opisō*).

6:60   Many of his disciples. Not only the crowd but even some of his disciples find Jesus' teaching hard to accept. Brown says concerning these disciples that John may be thinking here "of apostates in the late first century (1 John ii 19)."[17] The apostates mentioned in the Johannine letters appear to have been Gnostic Christians. For them, the doctrine of the Eucharist, like the doctrine of the incarnation, would have been particularly repugnant. Gnostic and Docetist Christians scorned the flesh and tried to explain both the incarnation and the Eucharist in non-material, spiritual terms.[18]

6:61 Do you take offense at this? Literally: Does it scandalize you? A scandal is something that makes one stumble or fall—in this case, something that makes the hearers fall into the sin of disbelief in Jesus because of his words about the Eucharist.

6:62 Son of man ascending. The question presupposes what Jesus has said about the Eucharist and scandal. Fully expressed, the question would be: "If you find my teaching concerning the Eucharist too incredible to believe, what would your reaction be if you were to see the Son of man ascending where he was before?"

Here as elsewhere, John associates Jesus' ascension with his death, which in turn is associated with and commemorated by the Eucharist. In John's Gospel, as Hoskyns observes, "The Incarnation, Death, and Resurrection of the Christ are the necessary prolegomena, not only to eating His Flesh and drinking His Blood, but also to understanding what this means."[19] The relationship between ascension and death is typically Johannine. In 3:13-14, Jesus says: "No one has ascended into heaven but he who descended from heaven, the Son of man. And as Moses lifted up the serpent in the wilderness, so must the Son of man be lifted up . . . ." In 8:28, he says, "When you have lifted up the Son of man, then you will know that I am he." And in 12:32-34, he says, " '. . . and I, when I am lifted up from the earth, will draw all men to myself. He said this to show by what death he was to die.' " That Jesus is speaking here about the Eucharist, which commemorates his death, gains added support from the double reference to Judas, who "was to betray him" (6:64 and 71).

Some interpreters understand the question as a reference to what Jesus said about "coming down from heaven" in vv 33-38, making the question mean: "If you find my teaching concerning my descent from heaven too difficult to believe, what would your reaction be if you were to see the Son of man ascend to where he was before?" This interpretation presupposes that 6:51-58 constitutes an interpolation by a later ecclesiastical redactor. If that were so (though we think not, as we have tried to show by demonstrating that 6:51-58 is the necessary conclusion of the homily and that 6:44-58 is the parallel of 6:25-40, a conclusion that eliminates the so-called ecclesiastical redactor), then the only "hard" teaching referred to would be Jesus' teaching about coming down from heaven. The immediate context, however, is the teaching of Jesus about the Eucharist in 6:51-58. This is a teaching far more difficult to accept—so difficult indeed that it is no longer just the Jews who murmur in protest but even Jesus' disciples!

6:63 It is the spirit that gives life. The contrast between spirit and flesh is typically Semitic. The spirit signifies the power of God; the flesh signifies the weakness of man. The thought and the situation are similar to that of Mt 16:16-17, where Peter declares, "You are the Christ, the Son of the living God," and Jesus replies, "Blessed are you, Simon Bar-Jona! For flesh and blood has not revealed this to you, but my Father who is in heaven." The incredible thing Peter believes through the revelation of the Father is the divinity of Jesus. The incredible thing Jesus speaks about in 6:51-58 and the disciples find hard to accept is the Eucharist. It is only the spirit that gives the power to believe. The flesh—man's weakness unaided by the spirit— is useless. In a similar vein and in words that mean the same thing, Jesus will say in v 65, "This is why I told you that no one can come to me [i.e., believe] unless it is granted him by the Father." Earlier Jesus had said to Nicodemus concerning baptism and faith: "That which is born of the flesh is flesh, and that which is born of the Spirit is spirit" (3:6). For John, no one can believe unless the Father gives the power to believe.[21]

6:64 But there are some of you that do not believe. With the supernatural knowledge characteristic of the Johannine Jesus, Jesus' statement fore-shadows the ensuing unbelief and departure of the Jews and some of his disciples and the ultimate betrayal by Judas. The reference to Judas, repeated in 6:71, serves to keep the reader's attention on Jesus' death, which is commemorated by the Eucharist.

6:65 no one can come to me. John's Gospel regularly asserts that faith is a gift. It is the gist of what Jesus says to Nicodemus (3:3-8), to the Samaritan woman (4:10-14), to the Jews in the bread of life discourse (6:35-50), to the Jews at the feast of the Dedication (10:27-29), and to the apostles in the discourse at the Last Supper (17:6, 9, 12, 24). But not all accept the gift of faith. Here in 6:59-71, many do not accept and believe Jesus' teaching about the Eucharist and the death, resurrection, and ascension that is implicit in the Eucharist. To the many who do not accept, John will contrast the twelve minus one who do accept him (6:68-71).

6:66 drew back. Literally: went away back. The many disciples may represent Jews who had begun to follow Jesus. More likely, they represent those Christians at the end of the first century who, because of Gnostic or Docetist tendencies, refused to accept the Eucharist and all it implied for the reality of the incarnation, death, and resurrection of Jesus. One thinks immediately of 2 Jn 7: "For many deceivers have gone out into the world, men who will not acknowledge the coming of Jesus Christ in the flesh," and 1 Jn 2:19: "They went out from us, but they were not of us; for if they had been of us, they would have continued with us; but they went out, that it might be plain that they all are not of us." Similar sentiments are expressed in 1 Jn 4:1-6; 5:5-8.

6:68a to whom shall we go? In v 65, Jesus had said: ". . . no one can come to me unless it is granted him by the Father." Peter, speaking for the Twelve (mentioned here for the first time in John's Gospel), equivalently asserts that to him and the Twelve (minus Judas) the Father has given the gift of faith to believe in Jesus. Jesus himself, in the Last Supper discourse, will say the same thing: "I am praying for them [the Twelve]; I am not praying for the world but for those whom thou hast given me" (17:9; cf. 17:24). The whole episode, but especially vv 67-69, resembles the Petrine confession in Mk 8:27-30 and Mt 16:17-19 and is doubtless the Johannine version of that critical incident.[22]

6:68b   words of eternal life. The words refer back to what Jesus had said in the whole discourse from 6:31-58, but especially to 6:47-58, where Jesus had begun by saying, "Truly, truly, I say to you, he who believes has *eternal life*" (6:47), and then went on to state, "He who eats my flesh and drinks my blood has *eternal life*" (6:54). True believers are those who believe that Jesus has come in the flesh and has given his flesh in the Eucharist.

6:69a   and we have believed. The "we" is emphatic and contrasts the Twelve (minus Judas) who believe with the "many" (*polloi*) in vv 60 and 66 who refuse to believe. One thinks of Jesus' declaration "Many are called but few are chosen." In the context of the Gospel, in which John repeatedly condemns the Jews for not believing and carries on a continual refutation of Jewish charges against Christianity (cf. 5:1-47; 7-8; 9-10; 11:1-54; 15:1-25; 18:28-19:16), the contrast here may well be that between the few Jews who believed Jesus and became Christians and the many who rejected Jesus and decided to remain in the synagogue.

Nothing is said about *what* the Twelve have come to believe. The whole context of the Gospel, with its insistence on such great truths as the divinity and pre-existence of Jesus, which the Jews refuse to accept, and the immediate context, in which Jesus speaks of the Eucharist (6:47-58), which the Jews and even many of Jesus' disciples refuse to believe (6:60-66), suggests that what the Twelve have come to believe is the truth Jesus enunciated in declaring, "He who eats my flesh and drinks my blood has eternal life" (6:54). One cannot believe in the Eucharist without believing at the same time in the incarnation, passion, death, resurrection, and ascension of Jesus.

Paul, in his first letter to the Corinthians, written c. 55 A.D., some thirty years before John wrote his Gospel, had asserted substantially the same thing as Jesus did in 6:47-58: " 'This is my body which is for you. Do this in remembrance of me.' . . . For as often as you eat this bread and drink the cup, you proclaim the Lord's death until he comes" (1 Cor 11:24-26). By the time John wrote his Gospel, belief in the Eucharist might well have become a subject of debate between Christians and Jews. 6:59-71 reflects such a debate and indicates how critical it had become.

6:69b   the Holy One of God (*ho hagios tou theou*). One would have expected Peter to say, as in Mt 16:16, "You are the Christ, the Son of the living God." The title "Holy One" seems strange, but it is peculiarly Johannine. In 10:36, Jesus tells the Jews that he is the one "whom the Father consecrated (*hēgiasen,* from *hagiazō,* "to make holy" or "consecrate"). The context of 10:36 is Jesus speaking to the Jews at the feast of the Dedication, which involved the consecration of the altar of the restored temple in Maccabean times (cf. 1 Mc 4). In 17:19, Jesus says of his disciples, "And for their sake, I consecrate (*hagiazō*) myself." The context of Jesus' statement here is clearly his approaching death. In view of the fact that John goes on in 6:70-71 to speak of Jesus' death in his reference to Judas as the one who "was to betray him," it is extremely probable that John understands Peter's use of the title "the Holy One of God" to mean the one God has destined as a victim for sacrifice. This would fit with the whole context of the Eucharistic discourse, with the two references to Judas' betraying him in vv 65 and 71, and with the Baptist's title for Jesus, "the Lamb of God, who takes away the sin of the world" (1:29, 36). It would be further, though indirectly, supported by John's reference to Jesus as the sacrificial lamb in 19:36.[23]

6:70-71   Judas . . . was to betray him. The inclusion-conclusion ends with an ominous reminder of Jesus' approaching death. The theme of Judas' betrayal will be taken up again in 12:4 (a chiastic parallel to 6:65, 71-72), 13:2, 11, 21-31; 17:12; 18:3. For John, Judas "represents the Satanic influence in the Gospel story."[24]

We have left to the end John's parallel structure for 6:59-71. As in so many other places (and notably 6:43-58) where John writes at length, he falls almost unconsciously into his characteristic parallel structure. In 6:59-71, this structure serves to heighten the contrasts between the many who do not believe and the twelve who do. It serves also to heighten the theme of Jesus' death, which is so important for understanding the whole discourse as a discourse about the Eucharist and for understanding the refusal of the many to believe in 6:66 because, as they said, "This is a hard saying" (6:60).

Parallel structure of 6:59-71

(a) **Many (*polloi*) do not accept Jesus' teaching: one will betray him** (*paradōsōn auton*)—(6:59-64).

(b) Jesus says: **"No one can come** to me (*elthein pros me*) unless it is granted by the Father" (6:65).

(c) Many leave Jesus (6:66).

(b′) Peter says: **"To whom shall we go** (*pros tina apeleusometha* [the future of *elthein*])"—(6:67-69).

(a′) **One** (*heis*) of the Twelve **will betray him** (*paradidonai auton*)—(6:70-71).

Text

(a)   6:59 This he said in the synagogue, as he taught at Capernaum. [60]**Many of his disciples,** when they heard it, said, "This is a hard saying; who can listen to it?" [61]But Jesus, knowing in himself that his disciples murmured at it, said to them, "Do you take offense at this? [62]Then what if you were to see the Son of man ascending where he was before? [63]It is the spirit that gives life, the flesh is of no avail; the words that I have spoken to you are spirit and life. [64]But there are some of you that do not believe." For Jesus knew from the first who those were that did not believe, and **who it was that would betray him.**

(b)   ⁶⁵And he said, "This is why I told you that **no one can come to me** unless it is granted him by the Father."

(c)   ⁶⁶After this many of his disciples drew back and no longer went about with him.

(b′)   ⁶⁷Jesus said to the twelve, "Will you also go away?" ⁶⁸Simon Peter answered him, "Lord, to whom **shall we go?** You have the words of eternal life; ⁶⁹and we have believed, and have come to know, that you are the Holy One of God."

(a′)   ⁷⁰Jesus answered them, "Did I not choose you, the twelve, and **one** of you is a devil?" ⁷¹He spoke of Judas the son of Simon Iscariot, for he, **one of the twelve, was to betray him.**

Themes

The major themes—witness, response, and replacement—recur regularly throughout 6:22-71. Jesus witnesses to himself as the bread of life (6:35, 48, 51, 58); as the one who raises up on the last day all who believe in him (6:40, 44, 54); as the one who is from God and has seen the Father (6:46); as the one who gives his flesh for the life of the world (6:51, 54, 57).

The negative response of the Galilean Jews is implicit in Jesus' charge, "you seek me . . . because you ate your fill of the loaves" (6:26). It becomes explicit in the center section (6:41-42), when the Jews murmur and declare, "Is this not Jesus, the son of Joseph, whose father and mother we know? How does he now say, 'I have come down from heaven'?" It continues in 6:52-53, when the Jews quarrel among themselves and say, "How can this man give us his flesh to eat?" It becomes definitive in 6:60-66, when many of his disciples remark, "This is a hard saying; who can listen to it?" (6:60), and John declares, "After this many of his disciples drew back and no longer went about with him" (6:66).

In contrast to the Jews' negative response and the response of the disciples who left him, the positive response of the Twelve is poignantly expressed by Peter in his unforgettable reply to Jesus' question "Will you also go away?"—"Lord, to whom shall we go? You have the words of eternal life; and we have believed, and have come to know, that you are the Holy One of God" (6:68-69).

The theme of replacement is explicit in Jesus' replacement of the manna in the desert with his own flesh and blood given for the life of the world (6:48-58). It is implicit in the context of the whole sequence, which deals with a new Passover, a new exodus, a new Moses, and a new Eucharistic bread from heaven.

The dominant theme of the sequence is the theme of response. It is introduced by the Jews' question: "What must we do, to be doing the works of God?'' and Jesus' response: "This is the work of God, that you believe in him whom he has sent" (6:28-29). The key word is "work." Whereas 5:16-18 emphasized the dual work of Father and Son—a work of giving life—6:22-71 continues this theme but emphasizes the other side of the coin, namely, the human work of "believing in the one he has sent" (6:29), entering into union with him through the Eucharist (6:51), and thus living in union with the Father and the Son (6:56-57). The substance of the chapter is similar to that of ch 4 (the living water) and ch 3 (rebirth from above), and amounts to another concentric-circle presentation of the basic Johannine message.

The advance in thought is effected by a concentration on what constitutes human work (6:29) in response to God's and Jesus' work. Where people respond by believing, the dual work of the Father and the Son comes to fruition; where it does not—and in this sequence it does not—the negative factor of judgment enters. The whole account shows the Jews not doing the work of believing and as a consequence bringing judgment upon themselves (6:41, 60-66).

The sequence shows also the distinction between the Jews who will not accept Jesus and the twelve who do. For John, the Twelve represent the Christian Church—the true Israel of God. The Jews who do not accept Jesus represent the Israel of the flesh; they have cut themselves off from the true Israel by refusing to believe in him who has brought about a new Passover and a new exodus for the people of God and, as of old, feeds them with bread from heaven that is his own body and blood in the sacrament of the Eucharist.

Chiastic parallels with sequence 10 (6:1-15)

In the Gospel as a whole, sequence 10 parallels sequence 12, just as sequence 1 (1:19-51) parallels sequence 21 (20:19-21:25), sequence 2 (2:1-12) parallels sequence 20 (20:1-18), etc. The hinge upon which the whole Gospel turns is sequence 11—the little episode about Jesus on the waters saying, "It is I; do not be afraid" (6:16-21). After sequence 11, every succeeding sequence looks back upon its counterpart in the first half of the Gospel.

The parallels between sequence 12 and sequence 10 are numerous and, if one takes into consideration the exodus setting of both sequences, rich and penetratingly meaningful. To begin with, there are the parallels of time and place. The loaves miracle takes place on one side of the lake (6:1), the explanation of the meaning of the loaves on the other side (6:22-25). In each sequence the time is the same: it is near the feast of the Passover. In each there is a reference to signs (6:2, 14 and 6:26, 30). In each the central topic is bread in the wilderness, and in each the bread is Eucharistic bread (6:11 and 6:31-58).

In sequence 10, the crowd acclaims Jesus as the "prophet who is to come into the world" (6:14), the prophet Moses had predicted God would raise up "like" him (Dt 18:15-18). In sequence 12, Moses is spoken about (6:32) and is eclipsed by Jesus, the prophet "like" Moses who has now come to fulfil the prediction of Moses and perform signs greater than those performed by Moses.

In sequence 10, the description of the multiplication of the loaves has linguistic overtones of the Eucharistic liturgy (6:11). In sequence 12, the discourse on the Eucharist (6:31-58) balances with, and supplies the commentary for, the Eucharistic overtones of the loaves account in 6:1-15. Hoskyns, in a passing remark concerning the relationship between the good shepherd parable in ch 10 and the death of Jesus, catches perfectly the relationship between 6:1-15 and 6:22-71. "In similar fashion," he says, "the significance of the feeding of the five thousand is not exhausted until the bread is expounded as the flesh Jesus will give for the life of the world, and the feeding which provides life is declared to be the eating of his body and the drinking of his blood (vi 51ff)."[25]

Sequence 13

JESUS AT THE FEAST OF TABERNACLES
7:1–8:59

Sequence 13 has an extremely elaborate *abcb'a'* structure. In addition it has *abcb'a'* structures in (a) and (a'). Here we indicate the parallelism of the sequence as a whole. In the commentary, we will deal with the parallel structures of the (a) section (7:1-36) and the (a') section (8:21-59).

Parallel structure

(a) **Jesus comes out of hiding** from the **Jews seeking to kill him** (7:1-36).
(b) Living **water** and the **Spirit** (7:37-44)
(c) The Jewish leaders fail to arrest Jesus (7:45-52).
(b') The **light** of the world and the **Father** (8:12-20)
(a') **Jesus again hides himself** from the **Jews seeking to kill him** (8:21-59).

Text

(a)   7:1 After this Jesus went about in Galilee; he would not go about in Judea, because the Jews **sought to kill him.** ²Now the Jews' feast of Tabernacles was at hand. ³So his brothers said to him, "Leave here and go to Judea, that your disciples may see the **works** you are doing. ⁴For no man works **in secret** if he seeks to be known openly. If you do these things, show yourself to **the world.**" ⁵For even his brothers **did not believe** in him. ⁶Jesus said to them, **"My time has not yet come,** but your time is always here. ⁷**The world** cannot hate you, but it hates me because I testify of it that its **works** are evil. ⁸Go to the feast yourselves; I am not going up to this feast, for **my time has not yet fully come."** ⁹So saying, he remained in Galilee.

¹⁰But after his brothers had gone up to the feast, then he also went up, not publicly but **in private.** ¹¹The Jews **were looking for him** at the feast, and saying, "Where is he?" ¹²And there was much muttering about him among the people. While some said, "He is a good man," others said, "No, he is leading the people astray." ¹³Yet for fear of the Jews no one spoke openly of him.

¹⁴About the middle of the feast Jesus **went up into the temple and taught.** ¹⁵The Jews marveled at it, saying, "How is it that this man has learning, when he has never studied?" ¹⁶So Jesus answered them, "My **teaching** is not mine, but **his who sent me;** ¹⁷if any man's will is to do his will, he shall know whether the **teaching** is from God or whether I am speaking on **my own authority.** ¹⁸He who speaks on his **own authority** seeks his own **glory;**

but he who seeks the **glory** of **him who sent** him is **true,** and in him there is no falsehood. ¹⁹Did not Moses give you the law? Yet none of you keeps the law. **Why do you seek to kill me?**" ²⁰The people answered, "You have a **demon!** Who is **seeking to kill you?**" ²¹Jesus answered them, "I did one deed, and you all marvel at it. ²²Moses gave you circumcision (not that it is from Moses, but from the fathers), and you circumcise a man upon the sabbath. ²³If on the sabbath a man receives circumcision, so that the law of Moses may not be broken, are you angry with me because on the sabbath I made a man's whole body well? ²⁴Do not **judge** by appearances, but **judge** with right **judgment.**"

²⁵Some of the people of Jerusalem therefore said, "Is not this the man whom **they seek to kill?** ²⁶And here he is, speaking openly, and they say nothing to him! Can it be that the authorities really know that this is the Christ? ²⁷Yet we know where this man comes from; and when the Christ appears, no one will know where he comes from." ²⁸So Jesus proclaimed, as he **taught in the temple,** "You know me, and you know where I come from? But I have not come of my own accord; **he who sent me is true,** and **him you do not know.** ²⁹I **know him,** for I come from him, and **he sent me.**" ³⁰So they **sought** to arrest him; but no one laid hands on him, because **his hour had not yet come.** ³¹Yet **many of the people believed in him;** they said, "When the Christ appears, will he do more signs than this man has done?"

³²The Pharisees heard the crowd thus muttering about him, and the chief priests and Pharisees sent officers to arrest him. ³³Jesus then said, "I shall be with you a little longer, and then **I go to him who sent me;** ³⁴**you will seek me** and you will not find me; **where I am you cannot come.**" ³⁵The Jews said to one another, "Where does this man intend **to go** that we shall not find him? Does he intend **to go** to the Dispersion among the Greeks and teach the Greeks? ³⁶What does he mean by saying, '**You will seek me** and you will not find me,' and, '**Where I am you cannot come**'?"

(b)   ³⁷On the last day of the feast, the great day, **Jesus stood up and proclaimed,** "If any one thirst, let him come to me and drink. ³⁸**He who believes in me,** as the scripture has said, 'Out of his heart shall flow rivers of living water.'" ³⁹Now this he said about the Spirit, which those who believed in him were to receive; for as yet the Spirit had not been given, because Jesus was not yet glorified. ⁴⁰When they heard these words, some of the people said, "This is really the prophet." ⁴¹Others said, "This is the Christ." But some said, "Is the Christ to **come** from Galilee? ⁴²Has not the scripture said that the Christ is descended from David, and **comes** from Bethlehem, the village where David was?" ⁴³So there was a division among the people over him. ⁴⁴**Some of them wanted to arrest him, but no one laid hands on him.**

(c)   ⁴⁵The officers then went back to the chief priests and Pharisees, who said to them, "Why did you not bring him?" ⁴⁶The officers answered, "No man ever spoke like this man!" ⁴⁷The Pharisees answered them, "Are you led astray, you also? ⁴⁸Have any of the authorities or of the Pharisees believed in him? ⁴⁹But this crowd, who do not know the law, are accursed." ⁵⁰Nicodemus, who had gone to him before, and who was one of them, said to them, ⁵¹"Does our law judge a man without first giving him a hearing and learning what he does?" ⁵²They replied, "Are you from Galilee too? Search and you will see that no prophet is to rise from Galilee."

(b')   8:12 **Again Jesus spoke to them,** saying, "I am the light of the world; **he who follows me** will not walk in darkness, but will have the light of life." [13]The Pharisees then said to him, "You are bearing witness to yourself; your testimony is not true." [14]Jesus answered, "Even if I do bear witness to myself, my testimony is true, for I know whence I have **come** and whither I am going, but you do not know whence I **come** or whither I am going. [15]You judge according to the flesh, I judge no one. [16]Yet even if I do judge, my judgment is true, for it is not I alone that judge, but I and he who sent me. [17]In your law it is written that the testimony of two men is true; [18]I bear witness to myself, and the Father who sent me bears witness to me." [19]They said to him therefore, "Where is your Father?" Jesus answered, "You know neither me nor my Father; if you knew me, you would know my Father also." [20]These words he spoke in the treasury, as he taught in the temple; but **no one arrested him,** because his hour had not yet come.

(a')   [21]Again he said to them, **"I go away, and you will seek me** and die in your sin; **where I am going, you cannot come."** [22]Then said the Jews, "Will he kill himself, since he says, **'Where I am going, you cannot come'?"** [23]He said to them, "You are from below, I am from above; you are of this **world,** I am not of this **world.** [24]I told you that you would die in your sins, for you will die in your sins **unless you believe** that I am he." [25]They said to him, "Who are you?" Jesus said to them, "Even what I have told you from the beginning. [26]I have much to say about you and much to **judge; but he who sent me is true,** and I declare to the **world** what I have heard from him." [27]They did not understand that he spoke to them of the Father. [28]So Jesus said, **"When you have lifted up the Son of man, then you will know that I am he,** and that I do nothing **on my own authority** but speak thus as the Father **taught** me. [29]And **he who sent me** is with me; he has not left me alone, for I always do what is pleasing to him." [30]As he spoke thus, **many believed in him.**

[31]Jesus then said to the Jews who had **believed** in him, "If you continue in my word, you are truly my disciples, [32]and you will know the truth, and the truth will make you free." [33]They answered him, "We are descendants of Abraham, and have never been in bondage to any one. How is it that you say, 'You will be made free'?"

[34]Jesus answered them, "Truly, truly, I say to you, every one who commits sin is a slave to sin. [35]The slave does not continue in the house for ever; the son continues for ever. [36]So if the Son makes you free, you will be free indeed. [37]I know that you are descendants of Abraham; yet **you seek to kill me,** because my word finds no place in you. [38]I speak of what I have seen with my Father, and you do what you have heard from your father."

[39]They answered him, "Abraham is our father." Jesus said to them, "If you were Abraham's children, **you would do what Abraham did,** [40]but now **you seek to kill me,** a man who has told you the truth which I heard from God; this is not what Abraham did. [41]You do what your father did." They said to him, "We were not born of fornication; we have one Father, even God." [42]Jesus said to them, "If God were your Father, you would love me, for I proceeded and came forth from God; I came not of my own accord, but **he sent me.** [43]Why do you not understand what I say? It is because you cannot bear to hear my word. [44]You are of your father **the devil,** and your will is to do your father's desires. He was a murderer from the beginning, and has nothing to do with the truth, because there is no truth in him. When

he lies, he speaks according to his own nature, for he is a liar and the father of lies. ⁴⁵But, because I tell the truth, you do not believe me. ⁴⁶Which of you convicts me of sin? If I tell the truth, why do you not believe me? ⁴⁷He who is of God hears the words of God; the reason why you do not hear them is that you are not of God.''

⁴⁸The Jews answered him, ''Are we not right in saying that you are a Samaritan and have **a demon?**'' ⁴⁹Jesus answered, ''I have not **a demon;** but I honor my Father, and you dishonor me. ⁵⁰Yet **I do not seek my own glory;** there is One who seeks it and he will be **the judge.** ⁵¹Truly, truly, I say to you, if any one keeps my word, he will never see death.'' ⁵²The Jews said to him, ''Now we know that you have **a demon.** Abraham died, as did the prophets; and you say, 'If any one keeps my word, he will never taste death.' ⁵³Are you greater than our father Abraham, who died? And the prophets died! Who do you claim to be?'' ⁵⁴Jesus answered, ''If I **glorify** myself, my **glory** is nothing; it is my Father who **glorifies** me, of whom you say that he is your God. ⁵⁵But you have not known him; **I know him.** If I said, I do not **know him,** I should be a liar like you; but **I do know him** and I keep his word. ⁵⁶Your father Abraham rejoiced that he was to see my day; he saw it and was glad.'' ⁵⁷The Jews then said to him, ''You are not yet fifty years old, and have you seen Abraham?'' ⁵⁸Jesus said to them, ''Truly, truly, I say to you, before Abraham was, I am.'' ⁵⁹So they took up stones to throw at him; but Jesus **hid himself,** and **went out of the temple.**

John creates parallelism between sections (a) and (a') in a number of ways. He repeats similar phrases, e.g., the Jews ''were seeking to kill'' Jesus (cp. 7:1, 11, 19, 20 with 8:37, 40, 59); Jesus ''went up into the temple'' (7:14) and Jesus ''went out of the temple'' (8:59); ''in secret'' (*en kryptō*) in 7:4 and 11 and ''hid himself'' (*ekrybē*) in 8:59; ''you have a demon'' (*daimonion echeis*) in 7:20 and 8:48, 49, 52; to ''know'' the Father (cp. 7:28 with 8:55); ''he who sent me'' (cp. 7:28, 33 with 8:26, 29); ''many believed in him'' (cp. 7:31 and 8:30); and ''I am going away'' (cp. 7:33, 35 with 8:21). In addition, he has verbal parallels: ''works'' (cp. 7:3 and 8:39) and ''the world'' (cp. 7:4, 7 with 8:23, 26, 41).

Finally, there are two important conceptual parallels. In 7:6, 8, 30, Jesus in different ways expresses the thought that his hour has not yet arrived to manifest himself to the world. In 8:28, he explains that ''when you have lifted up the Son of man, then you will know that I am he . . . .'' The implied concept is that people will know who Jesus truly is (and we must remember that the central subject of the whole dialogue is Jesus' identity as divine Son sent by the Father) only when he has been ''lifted up.'' Then his hour will have arrived! The other conceptual parallel is more simple. The sequence opens in the (a) section (7:1-11) with Jesus not going about in Judea ''because the Jews sought to kill him.'' It ends with the Jews seeking to kill him by stoning and Jesus hiding himself and departing from the temple (8:59). Thus, the whole sequence begins with Jesus coming out of hiding by going up to the feast of Tabernacles in Jerusalem and going back into hiding when he is once again (at a time when his hour has not yet arrived) threatened with death by the Jews who seek to kill him. It forms a perfect inclusion-conclusion and both frames the whole sequence and assures its unity.

In (b) and (b'), John creates parallelism by having Jesus begin each section with a solemn declaration (cp. 7:37 with 8:12) that contains a promise for him "who believes in me" (7:38) and him "who follows me" (8:12b). Each ends with a reference to the Jews' failing to arrest Jesus (cp. 7:44 with 8:20).

In the center (c), John has the police officers, the Pharisees, the chief priests, and Nicodemus on a separate stage, thus clearly setting off from each other sections (b) and (b').

Commentary

Sequence 13 is long and involved. It takes place over the full eight days of the feast of Tabernacles, and it appears to lack unity. In addition, it is not easy to ascertain the author's overall purpose in sustaining so long and so involved a polemical dialogue. We must therefore deal first with the unity and purpose of the sequence.

To begin with, John establishes the unity of the sequence in four ways. First, he has all the action take place before and during the feast of Tabernacles. The action begins with Jesus' brethren urging him to go up to the feast (7:1-11). Second, John explicitly states that Jesus' debates with the Jews took place on the middle (7:14) and on the last day of the feast (7:37). Third, John establishes unity of subject matter. Jesus witnesses to himself as teacher from God, as Messiah, and as "I am," i.e., the one who is "God's equal." The Jewish leaders consistently oppose these claims. Fourth, John frames the whole sequence with an inclusion-conclusion. It opens with Jesus in hiding because the Jews seek to kill him (7:1, 4, 10). It closes with Jesus hiding himself from the Jews because they want to kill him by stoning (8:58). In short, the unity of the sequence is much greater than one might think from a cursory reading.

John's overall purpose in sustaining so long and so involved a polemical dialogue is more difficult to ascertain. There are two clues, however. To begin with, there is the complete unity of subject matter, which is Jesus' witness to himself as teacher from God, Messiah, source of living water, light of the world, pre-existent and only Son of the Father.

The unity of subject matter is the principal clue and contains the second clue in an implicit manner. All the subject matter in one way or another deals with Jesus' and the Johannine community's claim that Jesus is the pre-existent Son of God and therefore divine. At the end of the first century, when John was writing his Gospel, the most serious charge the synagogue could bring against Christians, and the most difficult charge for Christians to refute, was the charge that Christians were guilty of ditheism—worshiping two Gods—God the Father and Jesus, God the Son.

John's overall purpose in chs 7–8 is to refute this charge. He had already begun to refute the charge of ditheism in sequence 9 (5:1-47), the chiastic parallel of sequence 13, and he will continue to refute it in sequence 15 (10:22-39), the other chiastic parallel of sequence 13 in part IV of the Gospel (6:22–12:11). Here he refutes it at length. It is his hidden agenda throughout the whole of the long and involved sequence.

We have used the words "hidden agenda" because although ditheism is the charge John refutes, he nowhere uses the word himself or even allows his opponents to use it. It is both too far from the truth and too close to the truth. The Father is God and Jesus is God, but there are not two Gods. In later centuries, Christian theologians deal philosophically with the problem of three Persons in one God and use philosophical concepts and terminology to "solve" it. John was not so fortunate. He had to deal with it in his own way. Sequence 13 represents his refutation of the charge of ditheism. It should be and has been associated with his other implicit refutations of ditheism in the prologue (1:1-18), in sequence 9 (5:1-47), and in sequence 15 (10:22-39). It is his greatest single theological achievement!

In interpreting Jn 7–8, the reader should attend carefully to the parallel structure of the sequence as a whole and in addition should advert to the following Johannine literary techniques. First, the use of different stages for the dramatic action. Jesus is always on front stage. On an intermediate stage, John dramatizes the different responses of the people in the crowd to Jesus (cf. 7:11-14, 25-27, 31-32, 35-36, 40-44; 8:22). On a back stage, in the police barracks, John dramatizes the futile attempts of the Jewish leaders to have Jesus arrested (7:32, 45-52). Second, the use of oracular statements to introduce a theme and highlight the debate (cf. 7:16-17, 28, 33, 37-38; 8:12, 19, 28, 31-32, 51). Third, the use of references to the feast or to the rites of the feast (cf. 7:8, 37-38; 8:12). Fourth, the use of a "roving reporter," who seemingly wanders in and out of the crowd on the intermediate stage and records what different individuals are saying for and against Jesus and his claims (cf. 7:11-15, 25-27, 31-32, 35-36, 40-44; 8:22). Fifth, John's use of irony. He has individuals say what is true or false according to their lights but is the opposite of the truth believed by John and his community (cf. 7:15, 27, 41b-42). Sixth, the typical and much used Johannine misunderstanding technique (cf. 7:15, 27, 35-36; 8:31-33, 52-53, 57).

(a) Jesus comes out of hiding from the Jews seeking to kill him (7:1-36).

In the (a) section of the great debate with the Jews that runs from 7:1–8:59, John has so much to say that he breaks it down into his usual *abcb'a'* format. The reader will find it much easier to follow the debate if he or she adverts to this format.

Parallel structure of 7:1-36

(aa) **Where** is Jesus going? (7:1-11)

(bb) **Muttering** among the people (7:12-13)
(cc) Jesus in the temple at the middle of the feast (7:14-30)
(b′b′) **Muttering** among the Pharisees (7:31-32)
(a′a′) **Where** is Jesus going? (7:33-36)

Text

(aa)   7:1 After this Jesus went about in Galilee; he would not go about in Judea, because the Jews **sought** to kill him. ²Now the Jews' feast of Tabernacles was at hand. ³So his brothers said to him, "Leave here and **go** to Judea, that your disciples may see the works you are doing. ⁴For no man works in secret if he **seeks** to be known openly. If you do these things, show yourself to the world." ⁵For even his brothers did not believe in him. ⁶Jesus said to them, "My time has not yet come, but your time is always here. ⁷The world cannot hate you, but it hates me because I testify of it that its works are evil. ⁸**Go** to the feast yourselves; I am not **going** up to this feast, for my time has not yet fully come." ⁹So saying, he remained in Galilee. ¹⁰But after his brothers had **gone** up to the feast, then he also went up, not publicly but in private. ¹¹The Jews **were looking** for him at the feast, and saying, **"Where** is he?"¹

(bb)   ¹²And there was much **muttering about him** among **the people.** While **some said,** "He is a good man," **others said,** "No, he is leading **the people** astray." ¹³Yet for fear of the Jews no one spoke openly of him.

(cc)   ¹⁴About the middle of the feast Jesus went up into the temple and taught. ¹⁵The Jews marveled at it, saying, "How is it that this man has learning, when he has never studied?" ¹⁶So Jesus answered them, "My teaching is not mine, but his who sent me; ¹⁷if any man's will is to do his will, he shall know whether the teaching is from God or whether I am speaking on my own authority. ¹⁸He who speaks on his own authority seeks his own glory; but he who seeks the glory of him who sent him is true, and in him there is no falsehood. ¹⁹Did not Moses give you the law? Yet none of you keeps the law. Why do you seek to kill me?" ²⁰The people answered, "You have a demon! Who is seeking to kill you?" ²¹Jesus answered them, "I did one deed, and you all marvel at it. ²²Moses gave you circumcision (not that it is from Moses, but from the fathers), and you circumcise a man upon the sabbath. ²³If on the sabbath a man receives circumcision, so that the law of Moses may not be broken, are you angry with me because on the sabbath I made a man's whole body well? ²⁴Do not judge by appearances, but judge with right judgment."

²⁵Some of the people of Jerusalem therefore said, "Is not this the man whom they seek to kill? ²⁶And here he is, speaking openly, and they say nothing to him! Can it be that the authorities really know that this is the Christ? ²⁷Yet we know where this man comes from; and when the Christ appears, no one will know where he comes from." ²⁸So Jesus proclaimed, as he taught in the temple, "You know me, and you know where I come from? But I have not come of my own accord; he who sent me is true, and him you do not know. ²⁹I know him, for I come from him, and he sent me." ³⁰So they sought to arrest him; but no one laid hands on him, because his hour had not yet come.²

(b′b′)   ³¹Yet many of **the people** believed in him; **they said,** "When the Christ appears, will he do more signs than this man has done?" ³²The Pharisees heard the crowd thus **muttering about him,** and the chief priests and Pharisees sent officers to arrest him.

(a′a′) [33]Jesus then said, "I shall be with you a little longer, and then **I go** to him who sent me; [34]**you will seek me** and you will not find me; **where** I am you cannot come." [35]The Jews said to one another, "**Where** does this man intend to **go** that we shall not find him? Does he intend to **go** to the Dispersion among the Greeks and teach the Greeks? [36]What does he mean by saying, '**You will seek** me and you will not find me,' and, '**Where** I am you cannot come'?"

Parallelism in (aa) and (a′a′) is achieved by concentrating on Jesus' movements. In section (aa), one asks: Why does he not go about in Judea? Will he go up to the feast? Where is he (the people's question)? These ideas dominate section (aa). In section (a′a′), Jesus declares to the Jews that he is going away (7:33). The Jews then ask one another where he is going (7:35-36). The parallels are more conceptual than verbal, but there are several verbal parallels in the repetition of the words "go" (cp. 7:3 with 7:33); "seek" (cp. 7:1, 4 with 7:34, 36); and "where" (cp. 7:11 with 7:35, 36). In (bb) and (b′b′) the "muttering" of the crowd (7:12) balances with the "muttering" of the Pharisees (7:32).

(aa) Where is Jesus going? (7:1-11)

7:1a　After this. The reference is a very loose connection with the events of 6:60-66, where Jesus was deserted at Capernaum by many of his disciples following the hard truths of the Eucharistic discourse. The events of 6:22-71 took place around Passover. The events of chs 7–8 take place at the feast of Tabernacles, some seven weeks later.

7:1b　he would not go about in Judea. The reference to the Jews' seeking to kill him gives the reason for Jesus' decision and harks back to 5:18a, where the Jews first began to look for an opportunity to kill Jesus when they realized he was making himself "equal to God" (5:18b).[3] The Greek in 5:18 and 7:1 is identical: *ezētoun auton hoi Ioudaioi apokteinai.* The sequence as a whole will end as it began, with the Jews trying to kill Jesus (8:59).

7:3　his brothers said to him. The relatives of Jesus, as in Mk 3:20-35, do not believe in Jesus. Their suggestion that he go to Judea so that his disciples *there* might see his works is based on the events following Jesus' Eucharistic discourse, when many of Jesus' Galilean disciples deserted him (6:60-66).

7:4　show yourself to the world. The cynical suggestion implies that working miracles in rustic Galilee is a waste of time. If Jesus wants a following, he should work his miracles in Jerusalem, where the world can see and appreciate him. What is more, it is the time for the feast of Tabernacles, a time when Jerusalem will be filled with spectators who have heard about Jesus and are now waiting and wondering about him (cf. 7:12-13, 15, 31-32).

7:6a My time has not yet come. In John's Gospel, "the time" (*ho kairos*) and "the hour" (*hē hōra*) are the time of Jesus' passion, death, and exaltation (cf. 2:4; 3:14; 7:6, 30, 44; 8:20, 28; 10:17-18, 39; 12:23, 27, 31-36; 13:1, 31). By this remark the stage is set for the play on words in 7:8, where Jesus says, "I am not going up to this feast, for my time (*kairos*) has not yet fully come." The implication, which John's Christian readers and even those Jews who were tending toward accepting Jesus would catch, is that Jesus' hour for going up, i.e., "going up" on the cross, will not take place at this feast (cf. 3:13; 6:62; 20:17).

7:6b your time is always here. Jesus' relatives do not have an appointed hour to die as he does. Therefore, a "going up" to Jerusalem means nothing to them except a religious pilgrimage.

7:7 The world cannot hate you. Since Jesus' relatives do not believe in him (v 5), they are for all practical purposes on the side of the world, along with the Jewish leaders who do not believe in Jesus. "World" here is equivalent to the Jewish leaders and their like who are looking for a chance to kill Jesus, the author of life (cf. 7:1, 11, etc.). In John's Gospel, the world frequently represents the forces of evil, particularly the synagogue leaders, arrayed against Jesus and the Church (cf. 8:23; 14:9, 22, 31; 15:18-19; 16:8, 11; 17:6, 14-16, 23).

7:10 he also went up, not publicly but in private. Jesus goes up to Jerusalem when he wants to. He acts with complete freedom and independence (cf. 2:4ff; 10:17-18). No human being dictates his actions. The repetition of "in private" (*en kryptō*), which has already been used in 7:4, serves to form the first part of an inclusion-conclusion with 8:59, where Jesus goes into hiding (*ekrybē*). The sequence as a whole begins and ends with Jesus in hiding from the Jews.

(bb) Muttering among the people (7:12-13)

7:12-13 much muttering about him. The crowd's debate about Jesus probably reflects the opinions of the ordinary synagogue Jews at the time the Gospel was written. The distinction drawn here and elsewhere (7:31-32, 45-52) between the ordinary Jews and the Jewish leaders is clear in v 13, where those who debate about Jesus do not dare to talk openly "for fear of the Jews," i.e., the synagogue leaders. John's technique of putting on record the crowd's opinions about Jesus is the equivalent of our modern roving reporter who solicits opinions in the crowd and reports them selectively on television. It is a technique closely associated with the technique of using Nicodemus to symbolize those leaders in the synagogue who cannot make up their minds about leaving the synagogue and committing themselves to Jesus and the Christian Church (cf. 3:1ff; 7:45-52; 12:42-43; 19:38-39).

(cc) Jesus in the temple at the middle of the feast (7:14-30)

7:15-16 How is it that this man has learning? The question of "origins"

dominates the whole of sequence 13 and its chiastic parallels in 5:1-47 and
10:22-39. What is the origin of Jesus' teaching? What is the origin of Jesus
himself? The question is occasioned by Jesus' teaching in the temple and
by the fact that Jesus was never known to have been an accredited student
in any rabbinic school. The question elicits from Jesus a statement that asserts
his close relation to the Father: "My teaching (*didachē*) is not mine, but his
who sent me." How very close this relationship is will be the main subject
of the bitter debate between Jesus and the Jews in 8:21-59.

7:17-19 if any man's will is to do his will. The disposition necessary for
the acceptance of Jesus' teaching as teaching from the Father is quite simply
the disposition to do God's will. Those who do God's will are capable of
recognizing that Jesus is not bent on his own glorification (v 18). Since the
Jews do not keep the law of Moses, as is evident from the fact that they
are seeking to kill Jesus (v 19), it is proof enough that they do not have this
right disposition.

7:20a You have a demon! The accusation, reminiscent of Mk 3:22, will
be repeated several times in section (a') of this sequence (cf. 8:48b and 49a,
52b).

7:20b Who is seeking to kill you? Jesus' answer (v 21) to this question
points the reader back to 5:1-18, where Jesus cured a paralytic on a sabbath
and justified his action by saying, "My Father is working still, and I am working" (5:17). The Jews rightly interpreted this statement as a claim of equality with God and consequently determined to kill Jesus (5:18). Jesus' answer
refutes resoundingly the denial implicit in the Jews' question "Who is seeking to kill you?"

7:21-24 I did one deed. Most commentators see this statement, and the
subsequent argumentation from the Mosaic law justifying what Jesus had
done, as a reference back to the cure of the paralytic in 5:1-9. Since Jesus
speaks as if the cure had taken place recently, many commentators presume
that ch 7 originally followed ch 5 and that ch 6, as a consequence, is out
of place. There might be justification for this position if John were writing
according to the laws of strict narrative. According to the laws of parallelism,
however, ch 7 is precisely where it ought to be, and the reference back to
5:1-9 serves as a typical parallel re-enforcing the chiastic parallelism of chs
7-8 (sequence 13) with ch 5 (sequence 9). For John's readers, the cure took
place recently enough—only two sequences back!

7:25-26 Some of the people . . . said. John again uses his roving-reporter
technique to canvass the opinions of the crowd about Jesus. This time the
technique is used to elicit opinions about Jesus as Messiah and about his
geographical origin. Both opinions provide a springboard for the next section of Jesus' debate with the Jews about his origin.

7:27 when the Christ appears, no one will know where he comes from.
There was a belief to this effect among the Jews, probably based upon

speculation about the mysterious origin of the Son of man of Dn 7:13. Here the Jews make this an objection against Jesus as Messiah, since they know his origin from Nazareth. But that is only the lesser half of the truth about his origin. His ultimate origin is indeed unknown and mysterious. His ultimate origin is from the Father!

7:28 You know me, and you know where I come from? The question implies both agreement and disagreement. Jesus agrees with what the crowd claims to know about his origins, namely, that he comes from Nazareth. But he does not agree with them in their belief that Nazareth answers the question about his origin. The truth is that Nazareth is only his geographical origin; his ultimate origin is from the Father who sent him (v 28b).

7:29-30 I know him, for I come from him. Jesus' statement of origin from the Father infuriates the people, who subsequently try to seize him, presumably to put him to death as the Jewish leaders wanted (cf. 5:18; 7:1, 11, 19-20). In typical Johannine fashion, John states that "no one laid hands on him, because his hour had not yet come." Jesus alone decides when he will die.

(b'b') Muttering among the Pharisees (7:31-32)

7:31-32 Yet many of the people believed in him. Again, the distinction is made between the ordinary Jews and the leaders. Because some of the ordinary Jews begin to believe in Jesus (cf. 8:30, where the same remark is made), the Jewish leaders (v 32) send temple officers to arrest him. Implied is what will be stated later, namely, that one reason why the Jewish leaders plotted to kill Jesus was because many ordinary Jews were believing in him and leaving the synagogue (cf. 10:42; 11:45-54; 12:11). The situation certainly fits the circumstances of the Johannine Church at the end of the first century (cf. 9:22-23; 16:1-4). According to the Synoptics, it is at least implied that the Jewish leaders plotted to kill Jesus because many Jews were coming to believe in him (cf. Mt 26:4-5; Mk 11:7-10, 18; 14:1-2; Lk 19:47-48; 22:1-2).

(a'a') Where is Jesus going? (7:33-36)

7:33 a little longer. The end of the introduction (7:33-36) looks back to the beginning (7:1-11). There the Jews were looking for Jesus to kill him (7:1). John made it clear that they would not succeed until Jesus himself, who had declared that on the occasion of *this* feast he would not "go up" (i.e., ascend the cross and, via the cross, go to the Father), determined that his time (*kairos*) had arrived. Here Jesus speaks mysteriously about his death and his going to the Father. The key words "you will seek me" are repeated at the beginning and at the end (7:34 and 36), as they were repeated at the beginning and the end of the first section of the introduction of the sequence (7:1 and 11). What Jesus says in speaking about "a little longer" is that he knows the plot to kill him will fail because some time must still intervene before his death (cf. 12:35). The Jews have no control over the time of his death.

7:34a you will seek me and you will not find me. Presumably Jesus is talking about the time of judgment, when it will be too late for the Jews who did not believe in him when they had the opportunity. The words contain an implicit warning for John's contemporaries similar to the warning in 12:35-36.

7:34b where I am you cannot come. The saying is expressed ambiguously so that John can utilize his misunderstanding technique. The Jews understand the saying geographically (the Diaspora). Jesus means his death and his return to the Father.

7:35 Where does this man intend to go? The Jews think that Jesus means he will leave Palestine and go to the Jews of the Diaspora or perhaps even go and teach the Greeks, i.e., either proselyte Greeks, known as God-fearers (*phoboumenoi*), or outright pagans. John is probably indulging in irony, since the truth is the opposite of what the Jews are thinking. They think that teaching the pagans is out of the question, but, as John's Christian readers well know, Jesus, through the Church, will indeed go to teach the pagans.

(b) Living water and the Spirit (7:37-44)

John neatly balances his (b) section (7:37-44) and his (b') section (8:12-20), with the former treating of Jesus and the Spirit, and the latter treating of Jesus and the Father. In each there will be a debate. In the former, there will be a debate about Jesus' messianic credentials; in the latter, a debate about the relationship of Jesus to the Father. The (c) section (7:45-52) is distinguished from the (b) and the (b') sections by its subject matter—the Jewish leaders' frustration at their inability to have Jesus arrested. In the (b) section, Jesus will play on the water theme of the feast of Tabernacles. In the (b') section, he will play on another theme of the feast—the lighting of the women's court of the temple.

7:37-38 If any one thirst, let him come to me and drink. The implicit warning of vv 33-36 is supplemented here with an explicit invitation to believe in Jesus. One of the rites of the feast of Tabernacles was to fill golden ewers with water from the pool of Siloam and pour the water on the altar while prayers for rain were recited. Jesus' statement implies a play on this water rite. In the (b') section (8:12-20), he will make a similar play on words in relation to the rite of illuminating the women's court during the feast when he says, "I am the *light* of the world" (cf. 8:12). The invitation "Let him come to me and drink" supplements the warning of vv 33-36, where Jesus spoke of the "little longer" that he would be with the Jews, implicitly inviting them to make the most of the time available to come to a decision about believing in him.[4]

7:38   as the scripture has said. Commentators cannot discover where the Old Testament contains this quotation. It is probably a midrashic comment either on the "wells of salvation" mentioned in Is 12:3 or on the "waters" mentioned in Is 55:1.[5] The quotation itself provides further difficulties, since the identity of the "his" in "Out of his heart shall flow rivers of living water" is not at all clear.[6] According to the NAB reading, the "his" would be Jesus himself, and the sense would be similar to the sense of 4:10ff, where Jesus is the source of living water for the Samaritan woman, just as he is the living bread and the source of life in 6:31-58. The NAB translation is fortified but not confirmed by the water that pours from Jesus' side when the soldier pierces his body on the cross (cf. 19:34).

7:39a   Now this he said about the Spirit. John's theological comment reminds the reader of what Jesus will make clear in his farewell discourse, namely, that the Spirit-Paraclete cannot come until Jesus himself has been glorified by his going to the Father (cf. 14:16-18, 25-26; 16:7-16).

7:39b   as yet the Spirit had not been given. The meaning is not that the Spirit does not exist but that he has not yet been sent. As Jesus says in 16:7, "I tell you the truth: it is to your advantage that I go away, for if I do not go away, the Counselor will not come to you; but if I go, I will send him to you."[7] **Those who believed in him** would include the apostles (16:33) and those who came to believe in Jesus through the apostles (17:20; 20:29). **Because Jesus was not yet glorified.** The reference is to Jesus' passion, death, and return to the Father. Jesus is glorified through his passion and death (13:1, 31). Only after he has been glorified does he send the Spirit (16:7).

7:40-41a   some of the people. Jesus' claim to be able to supply the Spirit to those who believed in him (vv 37-39) provides the basis upon which some in the crowd say, "This is really the prophet," and others, "This is the Christ." The background for the prophet title could be expectations based on the promise of a prophet like Moses in Dt 18:18 or Mal 3:1. The background for the Christ title could be Is 11:1ff. It is impossible to be more precise.

7:41b-42   But some said. The objection is another example of Johannine irony. The objectors think that Jesus was born in Galilee, because he was known to be a native of Nazareth. As John and his readers know, however, Jesus' geographical origin is from Bethlehem, and, far more important, his ultimate origin is from the Father (cf. 7:28). The dispute and the irony, while trivializing geographical origins, serve to emphasize the subject central to all of chs 7-8, namely, Jesus' origin from God.

7:44   wanted to arrest him. The inability of anyone, whether the Jewish leaders, Jerusalem Jews, or simply factions within the crowd, to arrest Jesus before his time is a regular theme of sequence 13 and indeed of the whole Gospel (cf. 7:30, 32, 44, 45-52; 8:20, 59; 10:39; 11:53-57). It is central to the scene that follows in 7:45-52.

(c) The Jewish leaders fail to arrest Jesus (7:45-52).

The account of the inept officers, the frustrated Pharisees, and the nervous but courageous Nicodemus provides an almost comic interlude between the increasing intensity of the debate between Jesus and the Jews in the (a) section (7:1-36) and the (b) and the (a′) sections (8:21-59). As so often in John, the chiastic center is concerned with the machinations of Jesus' enemies. It requires little comment in this case.

7:45 The officers then went back. They had been sent out at the middle of the feast (7:32), and it is now the last (seventh or eighth) day of the feast (7:37)! Either John wishes to stress the ineptness of the officers, or, more probably, temporal indications are of little account in narratives constructed according to the principles of parallelism. John's account of the cleansing of the temple in 2:13-25 is a parade example of such callous lack of concern for temporal indications in this kind of parallel narrative.

7:48 authorities. The Pharisees' remark about none of the authorities believing is ironic to some extent, since they do not know that Nicodemus, a member of the Sanhedrin, has been to see Jesus (3:1ff) and is at least tending toward becoming a believer (cf. 7:50 and 19:34).

7:50-51 Nicodemus. Nicodemus' defense of Jesus is on legal grounds. According to Dt 17:6, the Pharisees should first listen to Jesus' defense before arresting him. Here, however, as in 9:1-38, the Pharisees will neither listen nor see.

7:52 Are you from Galilee too? The Pharisees' only retort is sarcastic. They presume that Nicodemus is defending Jesus for nationalistic reasons. Since the prophet Jonah was known to have come from Galilee, their testy rejoinder about no prophets from Galilee is obviously wrong, showing that they are blind even to the scriptures.

(b′) The light of the world and the Father (8:12-20)

After the interlude in 7:45-52, Jesus continues speaking in the vein of 7:37-44, the (b) section, only this time instead of speaking about himself as the source of living water (7:38), he speaks about himself as the light of the world and the source of the light of life. Both sections (b) and (b′) begin with oracular sayings (7:37 and 8:12), continue with a debate (between different people in the crowd in 7:40-42 and between Jesus and the Pharisees in 8:13-19), and end with a remark about the Jews' inability to arrest Jesus (7:44 and 8:20). Where the (b) section dealt with Jesus and the Spirit, the (b′) section deals with Jesus and the Father, thus leading the reader back to the central subject of the whole sequence—the divine origin and identity of Jesus—and to the Trinitarian relationships between Jesus and the Spirit and Jesus and the Father.

8:12 the light of the world. As a person sees physically by the light of the sun, so he or she sees spiritually by the light of God's revelation.[8] As the light of the world, Jesus claims that he is the source of revelation for all people. It follows that whoever possesses Jesus' revelation walks in the light and not in the darkness, because such a person possesses the light-revelation that shows him/her the way to walk (i.e., behave morally according to God's will) in order to gain eternal life. That person has, in a word, the light that shows him/her the way to life. Implicit in these words is Jesus' claim to ultimate authority as teacher of God's will. The expression "light of the world" suggests that Jesus is making a play on words by alluding to another (cf. 7:37-38) of the rites of the feast of Tabernacles—the rite of nightly illumination of the court of the women. Implied is Jesus' replacement of the authority of the Mosaic law (cf. Mt 5:21-48).

8:13 your testimony is not true. According to Dt 19:15, the testimony of one person is not sufficient. It is on this basis that the Pharisees attempt to rebut the astounding claim of Jesus to be the light of the world, i.e., the ultimate authority for the revelation of God's will. Legally, according to Dt 17:6 and Nm 35:30, several witnesses were required to convict a person of a capital crime.

8:14 my testimony is true. There is an apparent contradiction here with 5:31, where Jesus said, "If I bear witness to myself, my testimony is not true." The contradiction is only apparent, however, because in 5:31 Jesus was speaking in reply to a question of law according to which the testimony of a single witness was not valid. Here Jesus shows that the source of his testimony is based upon credentials far beyond those of a merely human witness. The Father, moreover, stands behind Jesus as a second witness (8:16-18). Thus, even according to the law of Dt 17:6 and Nm 35:30, Jesus can claim that he is not alone as a witness.

8:15 I judge no one. There might seem to be a contradiction here with 5:27, where Jesus says, "The Father has given him [the Son] authority to execute judgment," but in Johannine terms there is really no contradiction, since each person actually judges himself or herself according to whether he or she believes or does not believe in Jesus (cf. 3:17-21). Moreover, in the immediate context, there is a contrast between Jesus and the Pharisees. The Pharisees "judge according to the flesh"; Jesus judges no one according to appearances. Either way, instead of a contradiction, there is complete Johannine consistency.

8:17 In your law. The stress on "your law" instead of "in the law" or "in our law" makes excellent polemical sense at the end of the first century, when the Gospel was written and when Christianity was separated from Judaism. It does not make good sense at the time of Jesus. It should be noted that this reference to the scriptures forms a parallel with the two references to the scriptures in the (b) section (7:38, 42).

8:18 the Father who sent me. The Father is another witness along with Jesus. Thus, even on the legal grounds demanded by Dt 17:6 and Nm 35:30, Jesus' testimony is valid.

8:19   Where is your Father? While it is obvious to anyone who has read John's Gospel up to this point who Jesus means when he speaks of his Father, the Pharisees are represented here as misunderstanding Jesus. Their question implies that they expect Jesus to point out his Father, as if he were a visible being. The use of misunderstanding here, as in the case of Nicodemus' misunderstanding of Jesus' words about being born anew (3:5ff), sets the stage for further and deeper theological teaching. In this instance, it sets the stage for the climax of Jesus' discussion with the Pharisees—a discussion that deals with Jesus' origin from God (8:21-23, 42), equality with God (8:24-30), and pre-existence (8:56-58).

8:20   no one arrested him. The (b′) section (8:12-20) ends the same way as the (b) section (7:37-44) did. The Jews cannot arrest Jesus because his hour, the hour of his death, is determined not by humans but by God.

(a′) Jesus again hides himself from the Jews seeking to kill him (8:21-59).

The (a′) section of sequence 13 provides a reinforcement of, and a climax to, all that was more mysteriously hinted at in the (a) section (7:1-36). Like section (a), this section is written in parallel format.

Parallel structure of 8:21-59

> (aa) Then you will know that **I am** he (8:21-30).
> (bb) **Abraham** (8:31-41a)
> (cc) You are of your father the devil (8:41b-47).
> (b′b′) **Abraham** (8:48-56)
> (a′a′) Before Abraham was, **I am** (8:57-59).

Text

(aa)   8:21 Again he said to them, "I go away, and you will seek me and die in your sin; where I am going, you cannot come." ²²**Then said the Jews,** "Will he kill himself, since he says, 'Where I am going, you cannot come.'?" ²³He said to them, "You are from below, I am from above; you are of this world, I am not of this world. ²⁴I told you that you would die in your sins, for you will die in your sins unless you believe that **I am he.**" ²⁵They said to him, **"Who are you?"** Jesus said to them, "Even what I have told you from **the beginning.** ²⁶I have much to say about you and much to judge; but he who sent me is true, and I declare to the world what I have heard from him." ²⁷They did not understand that he spoke to them of **the Father.** ²⁸So Jesus said, "When you have lifted up the Son of man, then you will know that **I am he,** and that I do nothing on my own authority but speak thus as **the Father** taught me. ²⁹And he who sent me is with me; he has not left me alone, for I always do what is pleasing to him." ³⁰As he spoke thus, many believed in him.

(bb)   ³¹Jesus then said to the Jews who had believed in him, **"If you continue in my word,** you are truly my disciples, ³²and you will know the truth, and the truth will make you free." ³³They answered him, "We are **descendants**

of Abraham, and have never been in bondage to any one. How is it that you say, 'You will be made free'?"

³⁴Jesus answered them, **"Truly, truly, I say to you,** every one who commits sin is a slave to sin. ³⁵The slave does not continue in the house for ever; the son continues for ever. ³⁶So if the Son makes you free, you will be free indeed. ³⁷I know that you are **descendants of Abraham;** yet you seek to kill me, because **my word** finds no place in you. ³⁸I speak of what I have seen with **my Father,** and you do what you have heard from **your father."**

³⁹They answered him, **"Abraham is our father."** Jesus said to them, "If you were **Abraham's children,** you would do what **Abraham** did, ⁴⁰but now you seek to kill me, a man who has told you the truth which I heard from God; this is not what **Abraham** did. ⁴¹ᵃYou do what **your father** did."

(cc) ⁴¹ᵇThey said to him, "We were not born of fornication; we have one Father, even God." ⁴²Jesus said to them, "If God were your Father, you would love me, for I proceeded and came forth from God; I came not of my own accord, but he sent me. ⁴³Why do you not understand what I say? It is because you cannot bear to hear my word. ⁴⁴You are of your father the devil, and your will is to do your father's desires. He was a murderer from the beginning, and has nothing to do with the truth, because there is no truth in him. When he lies, he speaks according to his own nature, for he is a liar and the father of lies. ⁴⁵But, because I tell the truth, you do not believe me. ⁴⁶Which of you convicts me of sin? If I tell the truth, why do you not believe me? ⁴⁷He who is of God hears the words of God; the reason why you do not hear them is that you are not of God."

(b'b') ⁴⁸The Jews answered him, "Are we not right in saying that you are a Samaritan and have a demon?" ⁴⁹Jesus answered, "I have not a demon; but I honor **my Father,** and you dishonor me. ⁵⁰Yet I do not seek my own glory; there is One who seeks it and he will be the judge. ⁵¹**Truly, truly, I say to you, if any one keeps my word,** he will never see death." ⁵²The Jews said to him, "Now we know that you have a demon. **Abraham** died, as did the prophets; and you say, **'If any one keeps my word,** he will never taste death.' ⁵³Are you greater than **our father Abraham,** who died? And the prophets died! Who do you claim to be?" ⁵⁴Jesus answered, "If I glorify myself, my glory is nothing; it is **my Father** who glorifies me, of whom you say that he is your God. ⁵⁵But you have not known him; I know him. If I said, I do not know him, I should be a liar like you; but I do know him and I keep his **word.** ⁵⁶**Your father Abraham** rejoiced that he was to see my day; he saw it and was glad."

(a'a') ⁵⁷**The Jews then said** to him, "You are not yet fifty years old, and have you seen Abraham?" ⁵⁸Jesus said to them, "Truly, truly, I say to you, **before Abraham was, I am."** ⁵⁹So they took up stones to throw at him; but Jesus hid himself, and went out of the temple.

John creates parallelism between (aa) and (a'a') by repeating in each the solemn words "I am." In (bb) and (b'b'), he creates parallelism by repeating the name Abraham six times in (bb) and three times in (b'b'). In addition, he parallels "If you continue in *my word*" in 8:31 with "if any one keeps *my word*" in 8:51. In the (cc) section, as so often in the Gospel, Jesus condemns the Jews as children of the devil. Underlying the whole section is the question of origin. Jesus is the Son of God, the Jews are children of the devil.

(aa) Then you will know that I am he (8:21-30).

8:21-22 I go away. These words repeat the last words of section (a) and thus signal the reader that John is about to return to the themes of section (a) and conclude what he had begun to say there. In 7:33-36, as here, the Jews misunderstand Jesus. There they thought he might be going off to teach the Greeks; here they think he means to kill himself. Ironically, his words do speak of his death, but not by his own hand.

8:23 You are from below. Jesus' explanation of why the Jews cannot follow where he is going is that he and they belong to different worlds. Instead of killing himself—the Jews' misunderstanding of his words—the truth is that Jesus will lay down his life voluntarily (10:17-18), precisely because *he* belongs to that world which always does the will of the Father and *they* belong to that world which refuses to do the will of the Father. In 7:7, the parallel to this text, Jesus had said: "The world cannot hate you[his brethren], but it hates me because I testify of it that its works are evil." The evil in 7:7 and 8:23 is the same—refusal to believe in Jesus. The contrast between the two worlds had already been expressed in the contrast between the light and the darkness in 3:19-21. It will figure again in 15:18-25, where Jesus speaks about the hatred of the world for his disciples and himself, a passage in which the two opposing worlds are the world of his disciples and the world of the synagogue.

8:24 die in your sins. The warning concerning belief in Jesus is made more precise. They will die in their sins unless they believe that Jesus is "I am." The "I am" is the divine name. This is the Johannine sense of the text, and it is meant to introduce the conclusion of the debate between John's community and the synagogue concerning the identity of Jesus.

8:25 Who are you? Typically, John has the Jews misunderstand Jesus' mysterious words "I am," providing Jesus with another opportunity to speak even more mysteriously about his identity. **What I have told you from the beginning.**[9] Ever since his discussion with Nicodemus (3:1ff), Jesus had been telling the Jews in one way or another who he was: the one from above, the one sent by the Father, the source of living water and living bread, the light of the world, the one who bears the divine name.

8:26-27 he who sent me is true. Jesus' reference to the truthful one who sent him occasions another misunderstanding on the part of the Jews and allows John to introduce in sharp focus the Father and, what is more important for the debate with the synagogue Jews, the filial relationship of Jesus with the Father.

8:28-29 When you have lifted up the Son of man. "Lifting up" in Johannine terminology refers to the crucifixion of Jesus (cf. 3:14; 12:32). This is one of those places where John can be understood only in the context of the audience for whom he wrote his Gospel. Since the understanding of Jesus' words requires an understanding of the Johannine theology of the passion and glorification of Jesus, the only way to interpret these words, and especially the audience designated as the "you" who "will know," is to understand them as addressed to synagogue Jews like Nicodemus who have been taught the Johannine theology and are hesitating about accepting it. When they understand and accept the passion and death of Jesus, which is the lifting up of the Son of man, they will realize that Jesus is who he says he is—"I am"—and that he does nothing by himself but only according to the will of the one who sent him—the Father.

8:30 many believed in him. The reason given for the many believing in Jesus is because "he spoke thus." Perhaps the reason is because Jesus has emphasized his dependence on the Father. Whatever the meaning, it is clear from what follows (8:31ff) that those who believed in him believed only temporarily, since their belief turns to homicidal hatred (8:59) when they grasp the full meaning of Jesus' claims to divinity and pre-existence. It should be noted that 8:21-30 ends on a positive note, while 8:57-59 ends on a negative note. This may be an example of antithetic parallelism used by John to create parallelism between section (aa) and section (a′a′).

(bb) Abraham (8:31-41a)

8:31a to the Jews who had believed in him. The reference is to those who believed in him according to 8:30. Because of the Jews' virulent refusal of belief in 8:31-59, the RSV and some authors read a pluperfect here (*pepisteukotas*) and translate: those who "*had* believed."[10] The change makes sense but is not necessary. As early as 2:23-25, John had indicated that not all belief in Jesus was necessarily adequate belief (cf. also 4:48; 6:14-15; 6:60-66, where even some of Jesus' disciples leave him when faced with the harsh truth of the Eucharist).

8:31b If you continue in my word. The "word" (*logos*) designates Jesus' revelation and is a key word, along with "Abraham," for establishing parallelism between vv 31-41 and vv 51-58 (cf. its recurrence in vv 31, 37 and 51, 52, 55).

8:32-34 the truth will make you free. The "truth" is Jesus' revelation (cf. 8:51). The Jews misunderstand, and as usual this gives Jesus the opportunity to explain. The freedom he speaks about is freedom from sin, not political freedom or even that religious freedom the Jews boasted about as subjects of the law of Moses who served not human beings but God.

8:35-36 The slave . . . the son. In this one-line parable, there is a contrast between the slave and the son. Jesus is the Son of the Father and has a place and a power with and through the Father that no one else can claim. The little parable reinforces Jesus' claim that the truth, i.e., his revelation, can effect freedom from sin (8:34). It explains as well v 36: "So if the Son makes you free, you will be free indeed."

8:37a I know that you are descendants of Abraham. Jesus' admission of the Jews' carnal relationship to Abraham sets the scene for the discussion that follows concerning paternity. The unimportance of a carnal relationship to Abraham versus a relationship based on the same faith in God as Abraham had in the past had already been adverted to in the synoptic Gospels (cf. Mt 3:9: "Do not presume to say to yourselves, 'We have Abraham as our father' . . .").

8:37b you seek to kill me. The words recur almost like a refrain linking the inclusion (8:21-59) with the introduction (7:1-36) of the whole sequence (cf. 7:1, 11, 19, 25; and 8:37b, 40, 59).

8:38 I speak of what I have seen with my Father. The declaration anticipates Jesus' later accusation against the Jews that their true father is not Abraham but the devil (8:44).

8:39-41a Abraham is our father. Jesus refutes this claim by pointing out that Abraham heard the truth and believed it; the Jews have heard the truth and refused to believe. They cannot therefore be true children of Abraham. The fact that they are trying to kill Jesus, who reveals God's truth, proves that their parentage lies elsewhere. The question of parentage or paternity will take up the whole of section (cc).[11]

(cc) You are of your father the devil (8:41b-47).

8:41b We were not born of fornication. Jesus implied in vv 40-41a that the Jews were not children of Abraham but rather the offspring of adultery, in the Hosean sense of the word, and therefore had a different father than God. Such an implication means that the Jews are illegitimate children of someone other than Abraham. Their statement in v 41b may be taken as a simple denial of this charge, inasmuch as the Jews, through the Mosaic covenant, claimed to be God's children (cf. Ex 4:22 and Is 63:16). If the accent, however, is put on the "we," the Jews' rejoinder may well be an accusation that Jesus is of illegitimate birth. The accusation was not uncommon among Jewish adversaries of Christianity in the early centuries. The following words, "we have one Father, even God," set the stage for the most bitter exchange in John's Gospel.

Jesus' charge that the Jews are children of the devil can be understood only in the context of the theological hatred that was building up at the end of the first century between the Johannine community and those synagogue Jews who were opposing with every argument and even with persecution the overtures of other Jews to enter the Christian community (cf. 12:37-43; 15:18-16:4; Mt 10:34-39; 23:13-39).[12]

8:42-43 If God were your Father. The proof that God is not the Father of the Jews is that they do not love Jesus, who came from God and was sent by God, and refuse to understand and accept his word, i.e., his message of revelation.

8:44a **Yóu are of your father the devil.** The accusation is consistent with such less harsh but similarly dualistic statements as: "You are from below, I am from above. You are of this world, I am not of this world" (8:23); "If you were blind, you would have no guilt; but now that you say, 'We see,' your guilt remains" (9:41); and the whole of 12:37-40 and 15:18-16:4. The Jews seek to bring about the death of Jesus. This is the work of the devil, as John will point out later (cf. 12:31; 13:2; 14:30; 16:11; 17:15).

8:44b **He was a murderer from the beginning.** The characterization of the devil as a murderer and liar is probably an allusion to the stories of Gn 2-3, where Jewish tradition had interpreted the serpent's lies as the cause of Adam and Eve's fall, and also to Gn 4, where the devil's influence was seen in Cain's murder of his brother Abel (cf. Wis 2:24; 5:24).

8:45 **because I tell the truth.** The contrast between Jesus and the devil, the father of the Jews who seek to kill Jesus, is the contrast between truth and lies. It is like the contrast between light and darkness in 3:17-21. The lying is something deeper than an occasional falsehood. It is a perversion of the truth and has to do with the obstinate refusal to accept Jesus. This perverse aspect of lying is expressed well in 1 Jn 2:22: "Who is the liar but he who denies that Jesus is the Christ? This is the antichrist, he who denies the Father and the Son." The Jews' perversion of the truth is not so much that they do not believe Jesus but that they do not believe him *because* he speaks the truth. It is the perversion of those who love the darkness (3:19-21), who are blind because they can see but will not see (9:41).

8:47 **you are not of God.** Jesus categorically denies the Jews' claim in vv 41b-42 that God is their Father.

(b′b′) Abraham (8:48-56)

8:48 **you are a Samaritan and have a demon.** The accusation repeats 7:20 of the introduction (7:1-36) and forms one of the many parallels between the introduction and the inclusion (8:21-59) of the whole Tabernacles sequence.

8:50 **I do not seek my own glory.** The statement forms another parallel with the introduction (7:1-36), where Jesus in 7:18 stated, "He who speaks on his own authority seeks his own glory."

8:51-53 **if any one keeps my word.** The "word" is Jesus' message of revelation (cf. the parallels in 8:31, 37). In (bb) and (b′b′), parallelism is achieved by the repetition of the words "Abraham" and "word" (*logos* and its synonym *didachē*). Jesus' declaration "he will never see death" (51b) is, as usual, misunderstood by the Jews, who take it to mean physical death (vv 52-53).

8:54-55 **Jesus answered, "If I glorify myself . . . ."** The statement repeats the glory theme of 8:49-50 and goes on to repeat the theme of the word or message of the Father—"I keep his *word.*" Here, however, keeping the word of the Father more properly refers to Jesus' doing the will of the Father on the basis of the proverb "Like father, like son." This the Jews cannot claim, since, unlike Jesus, they do not keep the Father's word and thereby prove that their paternity is not of God.

8:56   Abraham rejoiced that he was to see my day. It is not explained how Abraham saw Jesus' day—whether by vision, as Isaiah did, (cf. 12:41) or because Jesus existed contemporally with Abraham. The statement implies that Abraham, like Moses in 5:46, was a forerunner and witness to Jesus. The Jews as usual misunderstand (v 57). This time, however, their misunderstanding cuts ironically close to the truth.

(a′ a′) Before Abraham was, I am (8:57-59).

8:57   The Jews then said. The objection presupposes the impossibility that Jesus, who is not yet even fifty years old, existed in the time of Abraham.

8:58   before Abraham was, I am. The "I am" claim of divinity and pre-existence points the reader back to section (aa) of the inclusion (8:21-30), where Jesus twice referred to himself as "I am" (8:24, 28). The statement implies equality with God. It parallels 5:18, where Jesus said, "The Father works and I work," and the Jews accused him of blasphemy for claiming equality with God. Here the situation is the same.

8:59a   they took up stones. Lv 24:17 commanded that anyone who "blasphemes the Name, shall be put to death." The Jews' attempt to stone Jesus indicates that they understand fully the portentous meaning of his words "Before Abraham was, I am."

8:59b   Jesus hid himself. These words recall the introduction, where Jesus went secretly (*en kryptō,* meaning "secretly" or "in hiding") to the feast, forming a perfect inclusion-conclusion for the whole of the long sequence (cf. 7:10).

Themes

In a manner similar to its chiastic parallels (5:1-47 and 10:22-39), sequence 13 (chs 7–8) concentrates on the theme of witness. Jesus witnesses to himself in a number of ways: (1) to the origin of his teaching, which is from the one who sent him (7:16-18); (2) to himself as the source of "living water" (7:37-39); (3) as the "light of the world" (8:12); (4) as the one who is "I am" (7:23-29); (5) as the one who existed before Abraham (7:49-58). Finally, in witness to himself, he again refers (7:21-23) to his cure of the paralytic in 5:1-9, just as he had in 5:16-18, 36.

The response theme, like the witness theme, is similar to the response theme in 5:1-47. There the Jews wanted to kill Jesus because he claimed to be equal to God (5:18). In 7:1 and 7:19-25, Jesus speaks again about the Jews' wanting to kill him because of his cure of the paralytic (cp. 7:10-25 with 5:18). Throughout the sequence, the Jewish leaders are looking for a way to arrest him (7:30-32, 44-52; 8:20). At the end, they pick up rocks to stone him (8:59), and he is forced to go into hiding, as he had at the beginning of the sequence (7:1, 10).

In brief, by emphasizing the increasingly negative response of the Jews, John expounds the opposition between Jesus, the light of the world, and the Jews, the forces of darkness, who are of this world and as a consequence refuse to come to the light and believe in Jesus. The heightening of the opposition should be noted: (1) In 2:13-22, the Jews oppose Jesus because he drove the moneychangers out of the temple and said he would destroy the temple—the Jews' interpretation of his words. (2) In 5:17-19, the Jews oppose Jesus because he works like the Father on the sabbath and thus makes himself God's equal. (3) In 7:7, the hatred of this world (the Jews—cp. 15:18-25) is foreshadowed. (4) In 7:16-19, John scores the Jews' opposition to the Father, the source of Jesus' teaching; in 7:28-29, their refusal to know the Father who sent Jesus; in 8:13-19, their refusal to accept the witness of the Father. (5) Finally, in 8:31-58, the Jews will not acknowledge Jesus because they are children of the devil, not true children of Abraham, and they want to put Jesus to death by stoning (8:58).

The replacement theme is implicit in the replacement of the Jewish feast of Tabernacles by Jesus, who is God "tabernacled" among us ("The Word became flesh and dwelt [Greek *eskēnōsen;* Latin: *tabernaculavit*] among us"). Replacement is implicit also in Jesus' replacement of the rites of the feast of Tabernacles, e.g., in relation to the rite of the water libations, Jesus says, "If any one thirst, let him come to me" (7:37-38); in relation to the illumination of the women's court, Jesus says, "I am the light of the world" (8:12).

Chiastic parallels with sequence 9 (5:1-47)

Parallelism between sequences 13 and 9 is primarily conceptual, but there are also verbal parallels. The conceptual parallels have to do with the divine identity of Jesus. In 5:18, the Jews accuse Jesus of making himself *"equal with God."* In 8:24, Jesus tells the Jews, "You will die in your sins unless you believe that *I am he."* In 8:28, Jesus says, "When you have lifted up the Son of man, then you will know that *I am he."* Finally, in 8:58, Jesus declares, "Before Abraham was, *I am."* In each sequence, Jesus is present in Jerusalem at the feast. In each, there is reference to Jesus' cure of a paralytic (cp. 5:5-16 with 7:21-24). In each, there recurs the ominous words "the Jews sought to kill him" (cp. 5:18 with 7:1, 19, 20, 25; 8:37, 40).

The attentive reader will find many more verbal parallels. But it is the conceptual parallels that are important. In both of these chiastically balanced sequences, John deals with and refutes the synagogue's accusation that Christians are ditheists—they worship two Gods, Yahweh and Jesus. John's refutation of this accusation in sequences 9 and 13 was as important for his community then as it is for Christians today.

Sequence 14

THE MAN BORN BLIND AND
THE GOOD SHEPHERD

9:1–10:21

Sequence 14 has two sections, each dealing with the motif of seeing (the man born blind) versus not seeing (the Pharisees). Section A (9:1-38) recounts the cure of the man born blind and the Pharisees' total lack of concern for him. Section B (9:39–10:21) deals with Jesus' castigation of the Pharisees as false shepherds who have no care for the flock.

Section A (9:1-38): The man born blind

Parallel structure

> (a) **Jesus** gives **sight** to the **man born blind** (9:1-7).
> (b) The **Pharisees reject** the man's **testimony** (9:8-17).
> (c) The Pharisees reject the parents' testimony (9:18-23).
> (b′) The **Pharisees again reject** the man's **testimony** (9:24-34).
> (a′) **Jesus** gives **spiritual sight** to the **man born blind** (9:35-38).

Text

(a)   9:1 As he passed by, he saw **a man blind from his birth.** ²And his disciples asked him, "Rabbi, who sinned, this man or his parents, that he was born blind?" ³**Jesus** answered, "It was not that this man sinned, or his parents, but that the works of God might be made manifest in him. ⁴We must work the works of him who sent me, while it is day; night comes, when no one can work. ⁵As long as I am in the world, I am the light of the world." ⁶As he said this, he spat on the ground and made clay of the spittle and anointed the man's eyes with the clay, ⁷saying to him, "Go, wash in the pool of Siloam" (which means Sent). So he went and washed and came back **seeing.**

(b)   ⁸The neighbors and those who had seen him before as a beggar, said, "Is not this the man who used to sit and beg?" ⁹Some said, "It is he"; others said, "No, but he is like him." He said, "I am the man." ¹⁰They said to him, **"Then how were your eyes opened?"** ¹¹He answered, "The man called Jesus made clay and anointed my eyes and said to me, 'Go to Siloam and wash'; so I went and washed and **received my sight."** ¹²They said to him, "Where is he?" He said, "I do not know."

¹³They brought to the Pharisees **the man who had formerly been blind.** ¹⁴Now it was a sabbath day when Jesus made the clay and opened his eyes. ¹⁵The Pharisees **again asked him how he had received his sight.** And he said to them, "He put clay on my eyes, and I washed, and **I see.**" ¹⁶Some of the Pharisees said, "**This man is not from God,** for he does not keep the sabbath." But others said, "How can a man who is **a sinner** do such signs?" There was a division among them. ¹⁷So they again said to the blind man, "What do you say about him, since **he has opened your eyes?**" He said, "He is a prophet."

(c)   ¹⁸The Jews did not believe that he had been blind and had received his sight, until they called the parents of the man who had received his sight, ¹⁹and asked them, "Is this your son, who you say was born blind? How then does he now see?" ²⁰His parents answered, "We know that this is our son, and that he was born blind; ²¹but how he now sees we do not know, nor do we know who opened his eyes. Ask him; he is of age, he will speak for himself." ²²His parents said this because they feared the Jews, for the Jews had already agreed that if any one should confess him to be Christ, he was to be put out of the synagogue. ²³Therefore his parents said, "He is of age, ask him."

(b′)   ²⁴So for the **second time** they called **the man who had been blind,** and said to him, "Give God the praise; we know that this man is **a sinner.**" ²⁵He answered, "Whether he is **a sinner,** I do not know; one thing I know, that though **I was blind, now I see.**" ²⁶They said to him, "**What did he do to you? How did he open your eyes?**" ²⁷He answered them, "I have told you already, and you would not listen. Why do you want to hear it again? Do you too want to become his disciples?" ²⁸And they reviled him, saying, "You are his disciple, but we are disciples of Moses. ²⁹We know that God has spoken to Moses, but as for this man, we do not know where he comes from." ³⁰The man answered, "Why, this is a marvel! You do not know where he comes from, and yet **he opened my eyes.** ³¹We know that God does not listen to **sinners,** but if any one is a worshiper of God and does his will, God listens to him. ³²Never since the world began has it been heard that any one **opened the eyes of a man born blind.** ³³**If this man were not from God,** he could do nothing." ³⁴They answered him, "You were born in utter sin, and would you teach us?" And they cast him out.

(a′)   ³⁵**Jesus** heard that they had cast him out, and having found him he said, "Do you **believe** in the Son of man?" ³⁶He answered, "And who is he, sir, that I may **believe** in him?" ³⁷**Jesus** said to him, "You have **seen** him, and it is he who speaks to you." ³⁸He said, "Lord, **I believe**": and he worshiped him.

In (a) and (a′), John creates a parallelism of personages—Jesus and the man born blind—and parallelism of ideas—the physical opening of the eyes in (a) and the spiritual opening of the eyes in (a′). Both scenes take place on a stage separate from the main stage, where the Pharisees interrogate the blind man and his parents. Parallelism in (b) and (b′) is created by the repetition of the blind man's testimony with nine verbal parallels.

John's dramatic artistry in sequence 14 has been admired by all. A closer look at his staging technique, however, makes the reader even more aware of his artistry. There is, to begin with, a back stage, with Jesus and the man born blind in (a) and (a'). Then there are the man born blind and his neighbors on an intermediate stage at the beginning of (b), followed by three scenes on center stage: the first with the Pharisees interrogating the man born blind; the second with the Pharisees interrogating the man's parents; and the third with the Pharisees again interrogating the man born blind. On all stages John follows the rule of two, and the economy of his dialogue is exquisite.

Commentary

(a) Jesus gives sight to the man born blind (9:1-7).

9:1 blind from his birth. There are a number of stories in the Synoptics about the healing of the blind,[1] but none is really the same as the story in Jn 9. The story closest to Jn 9 is Mark's account about a blind man who is healed with the use of spittle (Mk 8:22-26). But as Brown says: "The most striking and important features in John are not found in the Synoptic scenes, for example: blind from birth; use of mud; healing through the water of Siloam; interrogation about the miracle; questioning of parents . . . . In general, then, it seems that probability favors the theory that behind ch ix lies a primitive story of healing preserved only in the Johannine tradition (so also Dodd, *Tradition,* 181-199)."[2]

Whatever the source of the story, the evangelist has gone far beyond the actual events in the telling of the miracle. As Barrett understands it, ". . . the form of the present narrative is dictated primarily by the main theme of the trial of the man, and of Jesus through the man, and of the *Jews through Jesus.*"[3] This is certainly the main thrust of the narrative, but Hoskyns' insights go significantly further:

> The opposition of the Jews to Christianity had its counterpart in the opposition of the Jews to Jesus. In broad outlines his life was reflected in the history of the community of his disciples. The controversy with the Jews was both the expression of this, and the proof that those who believed in Him were indeed inspired by his spirit. The miracles He had once worked were repeated in the miracles of conversion. Blind men saw the truth, lame men were set free to walk in the commandments of God, and the dead were raised to a new life. Thus by a natural and unconscious symbolism the traditional narratives of His miraculous actions were related in such a way as to identify the converts with those who had originally been healed, and the later opponents of Christianity, with the original opponents of Jesus. The earlier narratives tended to become more and more clearly symbolical of the later experiences of the Christians, the original history providing the framework within which reference was made to contemporary history, and the materials out of which narratives and discourses could be constructed. The story of the blind man is not, therefore, the outcome of a desire to give concrete embodiment to the idea of Jesus as the light of the world,

but is, rather, the result of a very complicated and complete fusion into one narrative of the experience of conversion to Christianity, of the controversy with the Jews which was caused by the success of the Christian mission, and of the traditional accounts of the healing of blind men by Jesus."[4]

9:2   who sinned, this man or his parents? Although refuted in substance by the theology of the book of Job and later on by the teaching of the rabbis, it was nevertheless a popular belief that all punishments were in some way the consequences of sin.

9:3   that the works of God might be made manifest in him. Since Jesus accomplishes the work (*ergon*) of the Father (4:34) and shares the Father's miraculous power (14:10), what he is about to do will manifest not only his own but the Father's miraculous power. John is using here the dramatist's technique of foreshadowing. What is foreshadowed primarily is the physical and spiritual cure of the man born blind. In the context of the sequence as a whole, however, it is possible that under the category of "God's work" the evangelist means to include as well the blinding of the Pharisees, not because they are unable to see, but because they willfully refuse to see what God, through Jesus, has done. In 11:4, John uses his foreshadowing technique in a very similar manner. The foreshadowing technique may also explain the disciples' otherwise strange question in 9:2: "Rabbi, who sinned, this man or his parents, that he was born blind?" The answer in all likelihood dictated the question, since the question provides Jesus with the opportunity to make his foreshadowing declaration concerning the miracle as a manifestation of God's "work."

9:4   while it is day. Jesus associates his disciples with himself here, as he does in 4:35-38 and 11:7-16. Doing "while it is day; night comes, when no one can work" is probably a proverbial saying which, in this context as in 4:35-38, emphasizes the importance of the work of Jesus sent by the Father and the disciples sent by Jesus (cf. 13:15-17, 20; 17:18).

9:5   I am the light of the world. In view of what is about to happen—the restoration of physical and spiritual sight to the man born blind and the statement, "We must work the *works* of him who sent me"—Jesus' reference to himself as "the light of the world" (cf. 8:12 and Is 49:6) should be taken not so much as a metaphysical description of his person, i.e., as the source of God's revealed truth, but rather as a description of his effect on men. He is the light inasmuch as he brings about judgment between the good and the wicked, saving the good and punishing the wicked (cf. 3:17-21; 5:20-29). Judgment, positive and negative, in this sequence pertains respectively to the man born blind and the Pharisees (cf. 9:39–10:21). As the "light of the world," Jesus brings about a separation between those who love the "darkness rather than the light" (3:19) and those who come "into the light" (3:21).

9:6   spat . . . made clay . . . and anointed. Mark (7:33; 8:23) mentions Jesus' using spittle, and the practice may have something to do with the primitive belief that spittle had medicinal value.[5]

9:7   the pool of Siloam. A pool at the south end of the Tyropoean valley constructed to receive the water, via a tunnel dug in the time of King Hezekiah, from the Gihon spring. Isaiah (8:6) uses it to symbolize the help of God. Here it probably symbolizes Jesus himself, as the author indicates by his popular etymology of the word: "which means sent," alluding to Jesus as the one sent by the Father.[6]

(b) The Pharisees reject the man's testimony (9:8-17).

9:8-12   The neighbors. John is out to condemn the obdurate refusal of the Pharisees at the end of the first century to accept the clear evidence of Jesus' miraculous cures. The cure of the man born blind is a case in point. The evidence is irrefutable. His neighbors recognized him as the man born blind. The man himself testified both to his blindness and to the one who cured him. In 9:20-22, the man's parents will testify to the fact that he was born blind.

9:13-17   to the Pharisees. The least obvious but most effective literary technique that John uses is his masterful presentation of the Pharisees' stubborn refusal to even consider the miracle Jesus has performed. They begin by ignoring the miracle and concentrating on the fact that Jesus had put mud on the eyes of the blind man *on the sabbath* (9:16). They then dismiss the man's testimony (9:13-17) and question his parents. Their questions do not deal directly with the miracle but with whether the man had really been blind from birth (9:18-23).

When they question the man again in 9:24-34, they begin by saying: "Give God the praise, *we know* that this man is a sinner." The statement that Jesus is a sinner implies that by this time the Pharisees have become irrevocably hardened in their stubborn refusal to recognize the working of a miracle by Jesus. Recognition of the technique is important because the author's presentation of the Pharisees' attitude gives a good indication of his purpose in the composition of the whole sequence. As we shall see below, there is a difference of opinion concerning the author's purpose in 9:1-38.

(c) The Pharisees reject the parents' testimony (9:18-23).

9:22-23   His parents said this. The parents' cautious answer is attributed to their fear of being "put out of the synagogue." This reference to excommunication (cf. 12:42; 16:2) is anachronistic as regards the time of Jesus but perfectly in place at the end of the first century, following the ban against Christians enacted by the synod of Jamnia (c. 85). Jews who wanted to become Christians were excommunicated from the synagogue, abandoned by friends and relatives, and actively persecuted (cf. Mt 10:16-25, 34-39).

Along with 12:42 and 16:2, this passage, more than any other in the Gospel, helps to establish the date of the Gospel as sometime after the year 85 A.D.[7]

(b′) The Pharisees again reject the man's testimony (9:24-34).

9:24 we know that this man is a sinner. The hardening of the Pharisees becomes solidified with this categorical declaration. In 9:16a, some Pharisees had asserted, "This man is not from God, for he does not keep the sabbath." Other Pharisees, however, had demurred (9:16b). From this point on, only the man born blind defends Jesus. That the arguments of the man born blind are in reality the arguments of the Johannine community against the synagogue at the end of the first century seems more than likely. Brown describes the hostile situation as follows:

> Here we pass from the arguments of Jesus' ministry to the apologetics of Church and Synagogue in the era of spreading Christianity, and the evangelist shows us the prolongation into his own time of the debate over Jesus that had already begun to rage when Jesus was alive. In vss. 28-33 we have in capsule form the violent polemic between the disciples of Moses and the disciples of Jesus in the late 1st century. The same mentality is at work here that prompted the anachronistic designation of the authorities of Jesus' time as "the Jews," for the "we" that is heard on the lips of the Pharisees is really the voice of their logical descendants, that is, the Jews at the end of the 1st century who have once and for all rejected the claims of Jesus of Nazareth and who regard his followers as heretics. The "we" on the lips of the former blind man is the voice of the Christian apologists who think of the Jews as malevolently blinding themselves to the obvious truth implied in Jesus' miracles.[8]

(a′) Jesus gives spiritual sight to the man born blind (9:35-38).

9:35a having found him. The inclusion, as usual, turns the reader's mind back to the introduction. Once again, Jesus and the man born blind are on the stage by themselves. Only now Jesus seeks the man to give him the gift of spiritual sight.

9:35b Do you believe in the Son of man? In the Greek, the pronoun is emphatic (*sy pisteueis?*), giving the sense: "Do *you* (unlike the willfully blind Pharisees) believe in the Son of man?"

9:38 Lord, I believe. The man responds with a perfect expression of Christian faith and worship. The story is now completed. It has contrasted Jesus' salvific concern for the man born blind with the callous unconcern of the Pharisees. The Pharisees ignore the miracle, intimidate the parents, turn a deaf ear to all testimony, and eject the man born blind from their presence. In section B (9:39-10:21), Jesus will address himself to the Pharisees and, in the discourse on the good and bad shepherds, will sum up the lessons to be learned from the contrasting attitudes of himself and the Pharisees toward the man born blind.

Themes

The story deals with the themes of witness and response to Jesus. Of the two, the second is primary. This has been expressed by Dodd as "the effect of the light in judgment."[9] According to Dodd, the dominant theme is the contrast between the man born blind, who sees physically and spiritually because he accepts Jesus, and the Pharisees, who refuse to believe Jesus even though they can see physically and have the evidence before their eyes that Jesus has cured the blind man. In their blindness, the Pharisees are represented as judging themselves!

The best proof that Dodd is correct would seem to be the evangelist's dramatic technique of portraying the Pharisees as persons who obstinately refuse to even look at the evidence that is so clearly put before their eyes. The story, in other words, is told precisely to emphasize the blindness of those who can see but will not see. It is the theme of 3:19-20: "And this is the judgment, that the light has come into the world, and men loved darkness rather than light, because their deeds were evil. For every one who does evil hates the light, and does not come to the light, lest his deeds should be exposed."

The triumph of the light over darkness, which many consider the primary theme of 9:1-38, has much to be said for it.[10] Jesus does speak of himself as "the light of the world" (9:5), and the blind man does see through the intervention of Jesus, the light of the world. Indeed, he sees both physically and spiritually. Nonetheless, the account of the miracle is restricted to seven verses (9:1-7), whereas the account of the obstinacy and blindness of the Pharisees takes up the major part of the story. In addition, the judgment that the Pharisees call upon themselves in 9:1-38 is made explicit by Jesus in the discourse that follows in 9:39–10:21. The discourse on the good shepherd, as all agree, is intimately associated with the story of the blind man in 9:1-38, and the discourse condemns the Pharisees as thieves, robbers, hirelings, and false shepherds.

The story is told precisely to emphasize the blindness of those who can see but will not see. The most important dramatic technique, therefore, that the evangelist uses is his skillful presentation of the Pharisees' stubborn refusal to even consider the miracle Jesus has performed. They begin by ignoring the miracle and concentrating on the fact that Jesus put mud on the eyes of the man born blind *on the sabbath* (9:16)! They then dismiss the man's testimony and question his parents. Their questions again do not deal directly with the miracle but with whether the man had really been blind from birth (9:18-23).

When they question the man for the second time (9:24-34), they begin by saying, "Give God the praise; *we know* that this man is a sinner." The statement that Jesus is a sinner implies that by this time the Pharisees have become irrevocably hardened in their stubborn refusal to recognize the miracle wrought by Jesus. Recognition of this dramatic technique is important because, more than anything else in the sequence, it points to the author's purpose as "the effect of the light in judgment" rather than "the triumph of the light over darkness."

The baptismal theme

There are several reasons for believing that the evangelist has told the story of the blind man in such a way as to make it a paradigm both of conversion and of the sacrament of baptism.[11] To begin with, it is known that Jn 9 was read on the day of the great scrutiny before baptism in the early Church, as testified to by the early lectionaries.[12] Also, it is well known that anointing with spittle became part of the baptismal rites early on.

In addition to the testimony of the liturgy, there is the sacramental level of the account itself. The man is healed only when he goes to the pool of Siloam and washes, thus showing the healing power of water. Siloam itself is explained by the author as meaning "sent" (9:7), allowing the reader to recall that Jesus is "the one who has been sent" by the Father for the salvation of the world. In addition, it is noteworthy that Siloam and its waters are used by Isaiah to symbolize the help of God (Is 8:6).

Finally, the emphasis on the fact that the man was *born* blind may very well be by design to indicate, as in ch 3, that true life—birth from above, which comes through "water and the Spirit" (3:5)—can come only from above, and that all men by physical birth have only a natural life and need to be "born anew" through baptism before they can enter into God's kingdom.[13]

Chiastic parallelism with sequence 8 (4:46-54)

Balance between the sequences 8 and 14 is achieved by means of both synonymous and antithetic parallelism. In 4:46-52, the royal official believes on the word of Jesus alone, and well before he learns that his son has been cured. In 9:1-38, just the opposite happens. The Pharisees have the evidence for the cure of the blind man thrust continually before their eyes; nevertheless, they adamantly and willfully refuse to admit the cure of the man born blind. They are, in a word, determined not to believe in Jesus. In 4:46-54, there is believing without seeing; in 9:1-38, there is seeing without believing. In both sequences there is the parallelism of the royal official who believes and the man born blind who believes. Finally, both sequences deal with miracles.

Section B (9:39–10:21): Jesus condemns the Pharisees as false shepherds.

Parallel structure

    (a) **Jesus accuses** the Pharisees of blindness (9:39-41).
    (b) The parable of the **door** and **the shepherd** (10:1-5)

(c) The Pharisees do not understand the parable (10:6).
(b′) Explanation of the **door** and **the shepherd** (10:7-18)
(a′) The **Jews accuse** Jesus of having a demon (10:19-21).

Text

(a)   9:39 Jesus said, "For judgment I came into this world, that those who do not see may see, and that those who see may become **blind.**" ⁴⁰**Some** of the Pharisees near him **heard** this, and they said to him, "Are we also **blind?**" ⁴¹Jesus said to them, "If you were **blind,** you would have no guilt; but now that you say, 'We see,' your guilt remains.

(b)   10:1 "**Truly, truly, I say to you,** he who does not enter the **sheepfold** by the **door** but climbs in by another way, that man is a **thief and a robber;** ²but he who enters by the **door** is **the shepherd of the sheep.** ³To him the gatekeeper opens; the **sheep hear his voice,** and he calls his own **sheep** by name and leads them out. ⁴When he has brought out all his own, he goes before them, and the **sheep** follow him, for they **know** his voice. ⁵A stranger they will not follow, but they will flee from him, for they do not **know** the voice of strangers."

(c)   ⁶This figure Jesus used with them, but they did not understand what he was saying to them.

(b′)   ⁷So Jesus again said to them, "**Truly, truly, I say to you,** I am the **door** of the **sheep.** ⁸All who came before me are **thieves and robbers;** but the **sheep did not heed them.** ⁹I am the **door;** if any one enters by me, he will be saved, and will go in and out and find pasture. ¹⁰The **thief** comes only to steal and kill and destroy; I came that they may have life, and have it abundantly. ¹¹I am **the good shepherd.** The **good shepherd** lays down his life for the **sheep.** ¹²He who is a hireling and not a **shepherd,** whose own the **sheep** are not, sees the wolf coming and leaves the **sheep** and flees; and the wolf snatches them and scatters them. ¹³He flees because he is a hireling and cares nothing for the **sheep.** ¹⁴I am the **good shepherd;** I **know** my own and my own **know** me, ¹⁵as the Father **knows** me and I **know** the Father; and I lay down my life for the **sheep.** ¹⁶And I have other **sheep,** that are not of this **fold;** I must bring them also, and **they will heed my voice.** So there shall be one flock, one **shepherd.** ¹⁷For this reason the Father loves me, because I lay down my life, that I may take it again. ¹⁸No one takes it from me, but I lay it down of my own accord. I have power to lay it down, and I have power to take it again; this charge I have received from my Father."

(a′)   ¹⁹There was again a division among the Jews because of these words. ²⁰**Many** of them said, "He has a demon, and he is mad; why **listen** to him?" ²¹**Others** said, "These are not the sayings of one who has a demon. Can a demon open the eyes of the **blind?**"

John creates parallelism in (a) and (a′) by the repetition of the word "blind" (*typhlos*) in 9:39, 40, 41 and 10:21; "hears" (*ēkousan*) in 9:40 and 10:20 (*akouete*). There is also the antithetic parallelism created by Jesus' accusing the Pharisees of blindness in 9:39-41 and the Jews' accusing Jesus of having a demon in 10:20. Finally, Jesus says in (a), "For judgment I came into this world, that those who do not see may see, and that those who see may become blind" (9:30). In (a'), John says there is a division among the Jews (10:19). Some refuse to see and accuse Jesus of having a demon, while others indicate their willingness to see by maintaining, "These are not the sayings of one who has a demon. Can a demon open the eyes of the blind?"

The center (c) bridges (b) and (b') by explaining that the Jews did not understand Jesus' parable in (b), thus paving the way for his explanation in (b') of himself as the "door" and as the "good shepherd."

In (b) and (b'), there is almost exact repetition of words and concepts. Each begins with the same words: "Truly, truly, I say to you" (10:1 and 10:7). Each repeats the words "thieves and robbers" (10:1 and 10:8). Each repeats the word "sheepfold" (10:1 and 10:16) and "heed the voice" (10:4 and 10:16). In (b), Jesus tells the parable of the door and the shepherd; in (b'), he explains how he is the door (10:7-10) and the good shepherd (10:11-18), whose sheep know him, hear his voice, and follow him (cp. 10:3-5 with 10:14-16).

Commentary

In 9:1-38, the evangelist contrasted Jesus' concern for the blind man with the Pharisees' unconcern. This was done in view of the discourse in 9:39–10:21, in which Jesus spells out this contrast by showing himself as the good shepherd and the Pharisees as bad shepherds, thieves, robbers, and hirelings who have no concern for the sheep.[14] The discourse proper (10:1-18) is introduced by Jesus' scathing denunciation of the Pharisees as willfully blind (9:39-41) and is concluded by the Jews' vitriolic denunciation of Jesus as possessed and mad (10:19-21).

(a) Jesus accuses the Pharisees of blindness (9:39-41).

9:39 For judgment I came into this world. The words announce the theme of the discourse that follows in 10:1-18, in which Jesus gives his judgment on the Pharisees as thieves, robbers, hirelings, and false shepherds. In 9:1-38, the Pharisees had judged themselves by their willful refusal to believe in Jesus, the light of the world. Their self-judgment is perfectly consistent with John's description of judgment in 3:19-21 and 12:46-48, where those who love the darkness refuse to come into the light.

9:41 If you were blind. The Pharisees, by their obstinate refusal to accept the testimony concerning Jesus' cure of the man born blind in 9:1-38 and by their prejudged insistence that Jesus "is not from God" (9:16) and "is a sinner" (9:24), have demonstrated publicly, not their inability to see, but their stubborn refusal to see.

(b) The parable of the door and the shepherd (10:1-5)

10:1a Truly, truly I say to you. The identical words are repeated in 10:7, the beginning of (b'). The "you" of 10:1 is addressed to the Pharisees of

9:39-41. As Barrett points out: "No break is indicated by John between chs. 9 and 10; but the present passage is rather a comment upon ch. 9 than a continuation of it. A signal instance of the failure of hireling shepherds has been given; instead of properly caring for the blind man the Pharisees have cast him out (9:34). Jesus, on the other hand, as the good shepherd, found him (9:35, *euron auton*) and so brought him into the true fold."[15]

10:1b-5 he who does not enter . . . by the door. The sheepfold was the enclosure in which shepherds kept their flocks for safety overnight. A gatekeeper guarded the flocks. In the morning, he would admit to the enclosure the shepherds, who would then call their sheep, each by name, as a master calls his dog. The sheep, recognizing their shepherd's voice, would follow him out of the enclosure and be led to pasture, their shepherd walking before them. This little parable, based upon customs every native of the Middle East would recognize, is aimed at the Pharisees. They are the ones who cannot enter through the door because the gatekeeper would not admit them and because the sheep would not recognize their unfamiliar voices. The only way for them to get at the sheep would be the way of thieves and robbers—over the wall.

(c) The Pharisees do not understand the parable (10:6).

10:6 This figure. John's word for "figure" is *paroimia*. It is peculiar to John (cf. 16:25, 29) and does not occur in the Synoptics, who prefer the word "parable" (*parabolē*). Nevertheless, the two words are practically identical and are used in the Septuagint to translate the same Hebrew word (*mashal*). In this case, John represents the Pharisees as not understanding that they themselves are the thieves and robbers of the parable in order to allow Jesus the opportunity to explain the parable more at length in 10:7-18 (b').

(b') Explanation of the door and the shepherd (10:7-18)

10:7 I am the door. Here Jesus begins an allegorical explanation of the terms of the parable in 10:1-5. He identifies himself as the door through which the sheep enter the sheepfold and find safety. The Johannine meaning is that Jesus is the door and the way to life; through him alone can men and women come to the Father and receive that fullness of life which the Father offers. Only those who believe in the Son can come to the Father (3:16-18). Jesus says substantially the same when he declares, "I am the *way,* and the truth, and the life; no one comes to the Father, but by me" (14:6).

10:8 All who came before me. Within the context of the parable, which speaks of thieves and robbers who climb into the sheepfold "by another way" (10:1), the thieves and robbers would be the Pharisees, at whom the parable is aimed. The remark may also be aimed at other messianic claimants. Since

Jesus alone is the true shepherd, it follows that the sheep would not "heed" these false shepherds (v 8b and cp. v 5).

10:10-14 to steal and kill and destroy. The thieves' depredations sometimes resulted in death for the sheep. The good shepherd, on the contrary (vv 11-18), reverses the roles: he himself dies in order to bring about life for his sheep.

10:12 a hireling. The hired hand, for obvious reasons, would not have the same concern for the sheep as the owner. Most likely Jesus refers here to the Pharisees, just as he does in the rest of 9:39–10:21.[16]

10:16 I have other sheep. The theme of the other sheep and the one flock and the one shepherd prepares the way for the universalist statements of 11:52 and 12:20-22 and fits with the declaration of John the Baptist, "Behold, the Lamb of God, who takes away the sin of the world" (1:29), and the declaration of Jesus to Nicodemus, "For God so loved the world that he gave his only Son . . . ." That the other sheep are the Gentiles is the almost unanimous opinion of commentators.[17] A supporting argument for the other sheep as Gentiles can be drawn from the parallelism of this sequence with sequence 8 (4:46-54), which deals with the conversion of the royal official and his whole household. It is interesting that in speaking about the conversion of the royal official's household (4:53), John uses the same expression used in Acts to describe the conversion of groups of pagans: "He himself believed, and all his household" (cf. Acts 16:15, 31; 18:8; also 10:2 and 11:14).

10:16b one flock, one shepherd. John is thinking of the unity of Jews and Gentiles in the one Church. For the one shepherd, cf. Ez 34:23.

10:16-18 the Father loves me, because I lay down my life. This is John's refutation of the Jewish charge that Jesus' death was like that of any common criminal. On the contrary, he was doing the work of the Father, who "so loved the world that he gave his only Son." The Son dies only when he determines that his hour has come. What is more, the Son not only dies when he wills to die but he takes up his life again. The allusion to the resurrection here is similar to the allusion to the resurrection in 2:17ff. The theme of dying for the sheep, which anticipates the passion and resurrection, will be taken up again when Jesus appoints Peter vicar-shepherd of the sheep and reminds him that he, like Jesus, will have to die for the sheep (21:15-19).

(a′) The Jews accuse Jesus of having a demon (10:19-21).

10:19 a division among the Jews. In 9:39, Jesus had said: "For judgment I came into this world" (*eis krima,* meaning "for judgment," in the Johannine sense that Jesus' presence forces men to judge themselves according as they believe or do not believe in Jesus). In the inclusion, the Jews are divided and judge themselves. Some refuse to believe and accuse Jesus of having a demon (v 20); others show signs of at least incipient faith inasmuch as they defend Jesus and declare, "Can a demon open the eyes of the blind?"

(v 21). The statement, which refers back to the cure of the man born blind in 9:1-38, resembles the blind man's retort to the Pharisees in 9:32-33: "Never since the world began has it been heard that any one opened the eyes of a man born blind. If this man were not from God, he could do nothing."

10:20 why listen to him? (*ti auton akouete*). In 9:40, John mentioned how "some of the Pharisees near him *heard* this" (*ēkousan . . . tauta*). The repetition of the same verb (*akouō*) here in 10:20 reminds the reader that those who had at least listened to (heard) Jesus before his discourse now refused even to listen. Jesus' words "For judgment I came into this world, that those who do not see may see, and those who see may become blind" (9:39) have now been verified in the Jews' divided response to this discourse.

10:21 open the eyes of the blind. The reference to the man born blind returns the reader's mind to 9:39-41 and to the story of the blind man in 9:1-38 and provides a perfect inclusion-conclusion for the whole of sequence 14 (9:1–10:21).

Themes

The themes of witness and response dominate section B (9:39–10:21) in the same way they dominated section A (9:1-38). In 9:39–10:21, Jesus witnesses to himself as "the door" of salvation, as "the good shepherd," and as the one who will lay down his life for the sheep. The response of the Jews is divided but is more on the negative than the positive side.

Chiastic parallels with sequence 8 (4:46-54)

Parallels between the shepherd parable and the conversion of the royal official and his household are slight but significant. In 10:16, Jesus says: "And I have other sheep, that are not of this fold; I must bring them also, and they will heed my voice." Almost all commentators consider these "other sheep" to be Gentiles like the royal official and his household. In addition, one might point out that the royal official is similar, in the way he listens to Jesus, to the sheep that hear and recognize the voice of their shepherd (cf. 10:16b).

Sequence 15

JESUS AT THE FEAST OF THE DEDICATION

10:22-39

Parallel structure

- (a) The **Jews menace Jesus** (10:22-24).
- (b) Jesus declares: "**I and the Father are one**" (10:25-30).
- (c) The Jews take up stones to stone Jesus (10:31).
- (b') Jesus declares: "**The Father is in me and I am in the Father**" (10:32-38).
- (a') The **Jews** try to **arrest Jesus** (10:39).

Text

(a) 10:22 It was the feast of the Dedication at Jerusalem; ²³it was winter, and Jesus was walking in the temple, in the portico of Solomon. ²⁴So the Jews **gathered round him** and said to him, "How long will you keep us in suspense? If you are the Christ, tell us plainly."

(b) ²⁵Jesus answered them, "I told you, and **you do not believe. The works that I do in my Father's name,** they bear witness to me; ²⁶but **you do not believe,** because you do not belong to my sheep. ²⁷My sheep hear my voice, and I know them, and they follow me; ²⁸and I give them eternal life, and they shall never perish, and no one shall snatch them out of my hand. ²⁹**My Father,** who has given them to me, is greater than all, and no one is able to snatch them out of the Father's hand. ³⁰**I and the Father are one.**"

(c) ³¹The Jews took up stones again to stone him.

(b') ³²Jesus answered them, "**I have shown you many good works from the Father;** for which of these do you stone me?" ³³The Jews answered him, "We stone you for no good work but for blasphemy; because **you, being a man, make yourself God.**" ³⁴Jesus answered them, "Is it not written in your law, 'I said, you are gods'? ³⁵If he called them gods to whom the word of God came (and scripture cannot be broken), ³⁶do you say of him whom the Father consecrated and sent into the world, 'You are blaspheming,' because I said, 'I am the Son of God'? ³⁷**If I am not doing the works of my Father,** then do not **believe** me; ³⁸but if I do them, even though **you do not believe** me, **believe the works,** that you may know and understand that **the Father is in me and I am in the Father.**"

(a') ³⁹Again they **tried to arrest him,** but he escaped from their hands.

John creates parallelism in (a) and (a') by paralleling the Jews' hostility toward Jesus in 10:24 with their attempt to arrest him in 10:39.

In (b) and (b'), Jesus repeats his invitation to the Jews to believe in him because of the works he has done in his Father's name. In each the same words recur: "believe" (10:25-26 and 10:37-38); "works" (10:25 and 10:32-33); "Father" (10:25, 29, 30 and 10:32, 36, 37, 38). In (b), Jesus declares, "I and the Father are one" (10:30). In (b'), the Jews say, "You, being a man, make yourself God" (10:33), and Jesus replies, "The Father is in me and I am in the Father" (10:38).

In (c), the Jews understand Jesus' claim to divinity in the words "I and the Father are one" (10:30) and want to stone him. Their reaction prompts Jesus in (b') to give a fuller explanation of his claim to divinity.

Commentary

(a) The Jews menace Jesus (10:22-24).

10:22 the feast of the Dedication. Otherwise known as Hanukkah, the feast was first celebrated on or about December 25, 164 B.C., when the temple was reconsecrated after its desecration by the Syrian king Antiochus Epiphanes. From 168 to 165 B.C., he had enshrined in the temple a bust of Jupiter Capitolinus and turned the temple into a place of pagan worship. In 2 Mc 1:9, Hanukkah is called "the Tabernacles of the month Chislev." The two feasts were similar (cf. 1 Mc 4:36-52; 2 Mc 1:9, 18; 10:1-8), and the similarity is not insignificant for the interpretation of 10:22-39.

In sequence 13 (chs 7–8), at the feast of Tabernacles, Jesus had defended his origin from, and unity with, the Father. Here again, in the sequence that is the chiastic parallel of chs 7–8 and at the feast that was called "the Tabernacles of the month Chislev," Jesus defends his divinity by declaring, "I and the Father are one" (10:38). In substance, 10:22-39 defends again the claim of the prologue that "the Word became flesh and dwelt (tabernacled) among us."

10:24 If you are the Christ. The vehemence of the question and John's use of the words "the Jews" (so frequently used for the enemies of Jesus) suggest that John means his readers to see Jesus in a menacing situation. This is borne out by the Jews' threat to stone Jesus (10:31) and their attempt to arrest him (10:39). The question and Jesus' reply in 10:25ff are reminiscent of the high priest's interrogation of Jesus at the trial before the Sanhedrin in Mk 14:61: "Are you the Christ, the Son of the Blessed?" John answers both these questions in 10:22-39.

(b) Jesus declares: "I and the Father are one" (10:25-30).

10:25a I told you, and you do not believe. In chs 7–8 (cf. 7:25-31, 40-43) and in 10:11-16, Jesus had at least implicitly asserted his messiahship. Here in 10:25-30, he reasserts it. In 10:32-38, he will reassert his divinity, first asserted in 5:17-47 and chs 7–8.

10:25b   The works that I do . . . bear witness. The works are Jesus' miracles, which the Jews have steadfastly ignored, particularly his cure of the paralytic (5:1-18; 7:21-24) and his cure of the blind man (9:1-38). Jesus' appeal to the witness of his works resembles his appeal in 5:36: "But the testimony which I have is greater than that of John; for the works which the Father has granted me to accomplish, these very works which I am do-ing, bear me witness that the Father has sent me."

10:26   you do not believe, because you do not belong to my sheep. The reprise of the sheep theme from 10:1-21 is at first surprising. It suggests that John has forgotten the three months that have passed between the feast of Tabernacles (the occasion of Jesus' words in 10:1-21) and the feast of the Dedication (the occasion of Jesus' words in 10:22-39).

John, however, has not forgotten. He is simply reflecting once again on Ez 34, where Ezekiel spoke in parabolic terms about Yahweh as the good shepherd and about David as the one shepherd-king (cf. Ez 34:11-24). As A. Guilding has pointed out, the reading from Ez 34 was common to the feast of Tabernacles and to the feast of the Dedication. It was used on the sabbath nearest the feast of the Dedication, probably because the Jews con-sidered the Dedication a sort of second Tabernacles. As 2 Mc 10:6 says: "And they celebrated it for eight days with rejoicing, in the manner of the feast of booths [Tabernacles] . . . ." The reading from Ez 34 bridged the two similar feasts. John, in repeating the sheep theme, is doing nothing more than repeating the themes of the reading common to both.

It should be noted that in 10:22-39 the first section (10:22-30) opens with the question "Is Jesus the Messiah?" which corresponds to Ez 34:24-25, and closes with the question "Is Jesus claiming to be the Son of God?" (10:31-39), which corresponds to the implication of Ez 34:11-23 that Yahweh is Israel's good shepherd. The double theme—Jesus is Messiah and Son of God—would imply, according to Ez 34, that Jesus is the good shepherd of Ez 34:11ff and also the "one David" of Ez 34:24-25.

10:27   My sheep hear my voice. The contrast between the Jews who refuse to believe and those who do believe—the sheep who "hear my voice," "follow me," and are given "eternal life"—forms an antithetic parallel with sequence 7 (4:39-45), which is the chiastic counterpart of 10:22-39 in the Gospel as a whole. In 4:39-45, the Samaritans "hear" Jesus as sheep that hear and recognize their shepherd's voice, "follow" him, and acclaim him "the Savior of the world."

10:28-29   no one shall snatch them out of my hand. The security of the sheep is vouched for in a twofold way: no one can snatch them from the hand of Jesus, and no one can snatch them from the hand of the Father. The sense of these words is clear. The same cannot be said for v 29: **"My**

Father . . . is greater than all." In the Greek, it is not clear whether it is the Father who "is greater than all" or "what he has given" Jesus that is "greater than all." The words could be meant to confirm the fact that no one can "snatch them out of [Jesus'] hand" or to confirm that no one can snatch them from the hand of the Father. Since the latter needs no confirmation, it seems more likely that the words are meant to confirm the fact that no one can snatch them from the hand of Jesus. In this case the reference would be to the authority-power that the Father has given to Jesus (cf. 3:27, 35; 5:19-30; 13:3; 17:2).

10:30 I and the Father are one. Some have suggested that the unity spoken of here is only a moral unity, i.e., the Father and the Son are of one mind and will about the security of the sheep. The context, however, and the parallelism of 10:30 with 10:38, along with the parallelism of the whole sequence with its chiastic counterpart in sequence 13 (chs 7–8), argue more cogently for an ontological oneness. This is confirmed by the Jews' reaction in 10:31 and 10:33.

(c) The Jews take up stones to stone Jesus (10:31).

10:31 took up stones. The Jews' reaction implies that they have understood Jesus to be claiming equality with the Father—a claim they would logically consider blasphemy and therefore worthy of death. This is clear in 10:33.

(b′) Jesus declares: "The Father is in me and I am in the Father" (10:32-38).

10:32 many good works. As usual, parallels with (b) follow immediately upon the center (c). Here the parallel is with 10:25: "the works that I do in my Father's name."

10:33 you, being a man, make yourself God. The Jews' protest re-echoes Jesus' declaration in (b), "I and the Father are one" (10:30), and confirms its ontological rather than moral sense. The words have, in addition, a touch of Johannine irony. As many commentators have pointed out, John's Christian readers would react to this statement by replying, "On the contrary, he who is God has made himself man."

10:34 you are gods. Jesus' argument is an *a fortiori* argument, i.e., an argument from the lesser to the greater. If judges can be called gods, as they are in Ps 82:6, because they are given a power over life and death (a power that theoretically belongs only to God himself), then all the more can Jesus be truly called God, since he is the one whom the Father has "consecrated and sent into the world."

10:36 consecrated. In the context of the feast of the Dedication, the word "consecrated" (*hēgiasen*) suggests that Jesus is the new temple that will replace the temple in Jerusalem. Jesus had intimated as much in 2:19: "Destroy this temple [meaning his body], and in three days I will raise it up." The feast of the Dedication recalled not only the consecration of the temple that had been desecrated by Antiochus Epiphanes in 168–165 B.C., but all the consecrations of the temple from the time of the temple of Solomon (c. 940 B.C.) to the time of the temple of Zerubbabel (c. 519 B.C.). John is renewing the Christian claim that Jesus is the new tabernacle (cf. 1:14) and the new temple (cf. 2:21 and 4:21-24).

Support for this interpretation is found in several other places in the Gospel. In 6:69, Peter had spoken of Jesus as the "Holy One of God" (*ho hagios tou theou*). In 17:19, Jesus himself says, ". . . for their [the apostles'] sake I consecrate (*hagiazō*) myself." In his passion account, John emphasizes the holiness of Jesus as sacrificial victim by having Jesus, like Isaac (Gn 22), carry the wood (of the cross) for his own sacrifice (19:17); by adverting to Jesus' tunic without seam, the garment traditionally worn only by the high priest (19:23); and by emphasizing, through his use of a text associated with the paschal lamb, that Jesus is the sacrificial lamb of God of the new Passover (19:31, 36).

10:37-38 If I am not doing the works of my Father. The argument for faith in Jesus because of his works was first made in 10:25. It is paralleled here, but with a difference. Even if the Jews will not believe Jesus, let them believe because of the works he has performed. If they will put faith in these works as the works of the Father, then perhaps they will come to the further belief that the one who performed them is in Jesus, and Jesus in him.

10:38b the Father is in me and I am in the Father. Jesus' declaration sums up the whole argumentation for his divinity. The argumentation began with his words "I and the Father are one" (10:30), advanced with the Jews' threat to stone Jesus because, as they said, "You, being a man, make yourself God" (10:33), and concluded with Jesus' *a fortiori* argument that if the law (Ps 82:6) could call men gods, then all the more could he Jesus call himself "the Son of God," since he was the one whom "the Father consecrated and sent into the world" (10:36).

(a') The Jews try to arrest Jesus (10:39).

10:39 tried to arrest him. The sequence ends as it began in the introduction (10:22-24) with the Jews menacing Jesus. As usual, and as throughout the Gospel, they cannot succeed. They will succeed, as the reader well knows by now, only when Jesus' hour has arrived.

Themes

The theme of witness dominates 10:22-39, just as it dominates its chiastic counterpart (7:1–8:59). Jesus witnesses to his messiahship in 10:25-30 and to his filial relation to the Father in 10:30 and 10:34-38. There are few stronger statements in the Gospel than "I and the Father are one" (10:30) and "the Father is in me and I am in the Father" (10:38).

As in 7:1–8:59, the Jews' response is negative. In both sequences they threaten Jesus with stoning (10:31 and 8:59) on grounds of blasphemy—a clear indication that they thoroughly understood Jesus' claim to divinity.

Chiastic parallels with sequence 13 (7:1–8:59)

In part IV of the Gospel (6:22–12:11), sequence 15 forms the chiastic counterpart to sequence 13. In each there is conflict and animosity. In each it is for the same reason—Jesus' claim to be equal to the Father, to be "I am," to "be" before Abraham was. In each the feast deals with God's tabernacling among men. In each Jesus is threatened with stoning. And in each the subject of Jesus' messiahship is debated.

Chiastic parallels with sequence 7 (4:39-45)

In the Gospel as a whole, sequence 15 forms the chiastic counterpart to sequence 7. In sequence 7, the Samaritans, like sheep that recognize their shepherd's voice, hear Jesus and come to him. It is a response and an acceptance that contrasts by antithetic parallelism with the Jews' rejection of Jesus in 10:33-39 and with Jesus' statement to the Jews: ". . . you do not believe because you do not belong to my sheep" (10:26). In addition, the Samaritans' avowal that Jesus is "the Savior of the world" (4:42) is borne out in 10:27-29, where Jesus declares that he gives his sheep eternal life, that they shall never perish, and that no one is able to snatch them out of his hand.

Sequence 16

JESUS IS THE RESURRECTION AND THE LIFE
10:40–12:11

Parallel structure

(a) At Bethany beyond Jordan **many believe in Jesus** (10:40-42).

(b) **At Bethany near Jerusalem** Jesus raises Lazarus four days **buried** (11:1-44).

(c) The Jewish leaders plot to kill Jesus (11:45-57).

(b′) **At Bethany near Jerusalem** Mary anoints Jesus for **burial** (12:1-8).

(a′) At Bethany near Jerusalem **many believe in Jesus** (12:9-11).

Text

(a)   10:40 He went away again across the Jordan to the place where John at first baptized, and **there** he remained. ⁴¹And **many came** to him; and they said, "John did no sign, but everything that John said about this man was true." ⁴²And **many believed in him** there.

(b)   11:1 Now a certain man was ill, **Lazarus of Bethany,** the village of **Mary** and her sister **Martha.** ²It was Mary who **anointed the Lord with ointment and wiped his feet with her hair,** whose brother Lazarus was ill. ³So the sisters sent to him, saying, "Lord, he whom you love is ill." ⁴But when Jesus heard it he said, "This illness is not unto death; it is for the glory of God, so that the Son of God may be glorified by means of it."

⁵Now Jesus loved **Martha** and **her sister** and **Lazarus.** ⁶So when he heard that he was ill, he stayed two days longer in the place where he was. ⁷Then after this he said to the **disciples,** "Let us go into Judea again." ⁸The **disciples** said to him, "Rabbi, the Jews were but now seeking to stone you, and are you going there again?" ⁹Jesus answered, "Are there not twelve hours in the day? If any one walks in the day, he does not stumble, because he sees the light of this world. ¹⁰But if any one walks in the night, he stumbles, because the light is not in him. ¹¹Thus he spoke, and then he said to them, "Our friend Lazarus has fallen asleep, but I go to awake him out of sleep." ¹²The disciples said to him, "Lord, if he has fallen asleep, he will recover." ¹³Now Jesus had spoken of his **death,** but they thought that he meant taking rest in sleep. ¹⁴Then Jesus told them plainly, "Lazarus is **dead;** ¹⁵and for your sake I am glad that I was not there, so that you may believe. But let us go to him." ¹⁶Thomas, called the Twin, said to his fellow **disciples,** "Let us also go, that we may **die** with him."

¹⁷Now when Jesus came, he found that Lazarus had already **been in the tomb** four days. ¹⁸Bethany was near Jerusalem, about two miles off, ¹⁹and

177

many of the Jews had come to Martha and **Mary** to console them concerning their brother. [20]When Martha heard that Jesus was coming, she went and met him, while **Mary** sat in the house. [21]Martha said to Jesus, "Lord, if you had been here, my brother would not have **died.** [22]And even now I know that whatever you ask from God, God will give you." [23]Jesus said to her, "Your brother will **rise** again." [24]Martha said to him, "I know that he will **rise** again in the resurrection at the last day." [25]Jesus said to her, "I am the resurrection and the life; he who believes in me, though he **die,** yet shall he live, [26]and whoever lives and believes in me shall never **die.** Do you believe this?" [27]She said to him, "Yes, Lord; I believe that you are the Christ, the Son of God, he who is coming into the world."

[28]When she had said this, she went and called her sister **Mary,** saying quietly, "The Teacher is here and is calling for you." [29]And when she heard it, she rose quickly and went to him. [30]Now Jesus had not yet come to the village, but was still in the place where Martha had met him. [31]When the Jews who were with her in the house, consoling her, saw **Mary** rise quickly and go out, they followed her, supposing that she was going to the tomb to weep there. [32]Then **Mary,** when she came where Jesus was and saw him, fell at his feet, saying to him, "Lord, if you had been here, my brother would not have **died.**" [33]When Jesus saw her weeping, and the Jews who came with her also weeping, he was deeply moved in spirit and troubled; [34]and he said, "**Where have you laid him?**" They said to him, "Lord, come and see." [35]Jesus wept. [36]So the Jews said, "See how he loved him!" [37]But some of them said, "Could not he who opened the eyes of the blind man have kept this man from **dying?**"

[38]Then Jesus, deeply moved again, came to the tomb; it was a cave, and a stone lay upon it. [39]Jesus said, "Take away the stone." Martha, the sister of the dead man, said to him, "Lord, by this time there will be an odor, for he has been **dead** four days." [40]Jesus said to her, "Did I not tell you that if you would believe you would see the glory of God?" [41]So they took away the stone. And Jesus lifted up his eyes and said, "Father, I thank thee that thou hast heard me. [42]I knew that thou hearest me always, but I have said this on account of the people standing by, that they may believe that thou didst send me." [43]When he had said this, he cried with a loud voice, "**Lazarus,** come out." [44]The **dead** man came out, his hands and feet bound with bandages, and his face wrapped with a cloth. Jesus said to them, "Unbind him, and let him go."

(c)   [45]Many of the Jews therefore, who had come with Mary and had seen what he did, believed in him; [46]but some of them went to the Pharisees and told them what Jesus had done. [47]So the chief priests and the Pharisees gathered the council, and said, "What are we to do? For this man performs many signs. [48]If we let him go on thus, every one will believe in him, and the Romans will come and destroy both our holy place and our nation." [49]But one of them, Caiaphas, who was high priest that year, said to them, "You know nothing at all; [50]you do not understand that it is expedient for you that one man should die for the people, and that the whole nation should not perish." [51]He did not say this of his own accord, but being high priest that year he prophesied that Jesus should die for the nation, [52]and not for the nation only, but to gather into one the children of God who are scattered abroad. [53]So from that day on they took counsel how to put him to death.

⁵⁴Jesus therefore no longer went about openly among the Jews, but went from there to the country near the wilderness, to a town called Ephraim; and there he stayed with the disciples.
⁵⁵Now the Passover of the Jews was at hand, and many went up from the country to Jerusalem before the Passover, to purify themselves. ⁵⁶They were looking for Jesus and saying to one another as they stood in the temple, "What do you think? That he will not come to the feast?" ⁵⁷Now the chief priests and the Pharisees had given orders that if any one knew where he was, he should let them know, so that they might arrest him.

(b′)   12:1 Six days before the Passover, Jesus came to **Bethany,** where **Lazarus** was, whom Jesus had **raised** from the **dead.** ²There they made him a supper; **Martha** served, and **Lazarus** was one of those at table with him. ³**Mary** took a pound of costly **ointment** of pure nard and **anointed the feet of Jesus and wiped his feet with her hair;** and the house was filled with the fragrance of the ointment. ⁴But Judas Iscariot, one of his **disciples** (he who was to betray him), said, ⁵"Why was this ointment not sold for three hundred denarii and given to the poor?" ⁶This he said, not that he cared for the poor but because he was a thief, and as he had the money box he used to take what was put into it. ⁷Jesus said, "Let her alone, let her keep it for the day of my **burial.** ⁸The poor you always have with you, but you do not always have me."

(a′)   ⁹When the great crowd of the Jews learned that he was **there, they came,** not only on account of Jesus but also to see Lazarus, whom he had raised from the dead. ¹⁰So the chief priests planned to put Lazarus also to death, ¹¹because on account of him **many** of the Jews were going away and **believing in Jesus.**

John achieves his parallel structure in (a) and (a′) by repeating in each the comment that "many believed in him" (cp. 10:42 with 12:11) and by locating both events in places with the name Bethany—the Bethany beyond Jordan, where John baptized, and the Bethany near Jerusalem, where Mary, Martha, and Lazarus lived (cp. 10:40 with 12:11).

In (b) and (b′), he parallels the same people—Jesus, Lazarus, Martha, and Mary—and makes a cross-reference in 11:2 to the account of the anointing in 12:3. Also, both deal with burial: the burial of Lazarus in (b), the burial of Jesus in (b′), where Jesus says, "Let her keep it for the day of my burial" (12:7).

In (c), the action rises when the leaders of the Jews meet to plot Jesus' death. They argue, "If we let him go on thus, every one *will believe in him*" (11:48). The movement of the sequence flows from the fact that "many believe in Jesus," a remark first made in the introduction (10:42), repeated twice in (c) in 11:45, 48, and once again in the inclusion (12:11). It is because so many believe in Jesus that the leaders of the Jews plot the death of Jesus.[1]

The unity of the whole sequence is assured by the inclusion formed by the reference to the two Bethanys in the introduction and the inclusion. Continuity is achieved by the repetition of the remark that "many believed in him." The function of the sequence is established by the nexus between the miracle Jesus performed and the faith of the Jews who believe in him—a faith that incites the leaders of the Jews to plot his death. The sequence is a fitting climax to part IV of the Gospel and forms a perfect inclusion-conclusion with 6:22-71, the opening sequence of part IV (6:22–12:11).

Commentary

(a) At Bethany beyond Jordan many believe in Jesus (10:40-42).

10:40   where John at first baptized. According to 1:28, John had been baptizing in Bethany beyond Jordan. The introduction thus establishes Jesus' presence in Bethany beyond Jordan, prepares the way for his delay in coming to Bethany near Jerusalem (11:6-15), and forms the first part of the inclusion-conclusion made up by the repetition in 10:40-42 and 12:9-11 of the common place (Bethany) and the comment that "many believed in him" (10:42 and 12:11).

Since the previous sequence (10:22-39) had Jesus in Jerusalem at the feast of the Dedication, there can be no question but that 10:40-42 begins a new sequence, which is continued in 11:1ff, where Jesus is still in Bethany beyond Jordan until he comes to Bethany near Jerusalem, and which ends in 12:10-11, where the chief priests make plans to kill Lazarus. The mention of Lazarus in 12:9-11 and the chief priests' motivation for killing him "because on account of him many of the Jews were going away and believing in Jesus" clearly links the material in 11:45–12:11 with everything from 10:40 on.

10:42   And many believed in him there. While functioning as an excellent introduction to everything in the whole of sequence 16, 10:40-42 does something more. It sounds a strange note—a note that has not been heard in the Gospel up to this time; it tells the reader for the first time that *"many* believed in him" (cf. also 11:45-48; 12:11).

The new note inclines some commentators to believe that the evangelist has here incorporated material from a different source.[2] The suggestion may be correct, but it fails to take into account a central motif of the whole sequence and indeed of the whole Gospel. In 10:40–12:11, it is precisely the fact that many Jews were coming to believe in Jesus that leads the chief priests to plot Jesus' death. The futile plans to arrest Jesus earlier in the Gospel (cf. chs 7–8 *passim*) now take on a determination hitherto lacking. What leads to such determination is precisely that now, finally, *"many* of the Jews were going away and believing in Jesus" (12:11).

Earlier in the Gospel, most of the Jews had not believed in Jesus. There had been divisions among the people (cf. 7:25-27, 31-32, 40-41, 48-49; 8:30-31; 10:19-21). Some rejected him, others were inclined to accept and believe in him. Ultimately, most will reject him. But in 10:40–12:11, John is establishing the motivation for the chief priests' plot to have Jesus put to death. The fact that "many" were coming to believe in him, therefore, fits perfectly with the movement of the Gospel as a whole and does not require a new and different source to account for the strange phenomenon of "many" believing in Jesus. When it is recalled that the evangelist is in all probability mirroring the sentiments of the Jews of his own time in the divisions among the people and in the animosity of the Jewish leaders toward those who wanted to accept Jesus and abandon the synagogue (cf. 9:22 and 16:2), the motif of the "many" believing in him and the opposition of the chief priests becomes much more understandable.

(b) At Bethany near Jerusalem, Jesus raises Lazarus four days buried (11:1-44).

The function of the Lazarus story, as most commentators agree, is to set the stage for the Jewish leaders' decision to have Jesus put to death. In sequence 16, therefore, the miracle story (11:1-44) leads up to the priests' plot (11:45-57). Under such circumstances, the evangelist needed to focus full attention on the miracle itself. The reader can appreciate this aspect of the story by contrasting it with the way Jesus' miracles are recounted in 5:2-9 and 9:1-7.

In 5:2-9, the cure of the paralytic is told in eight short verses. It is then used as a springboard for the disagreement between Jesus and the Jews about the sabbath and for the subsequent long discourse of Jesus in 5:19-47. In ch 9, the cure of the blind man is described in the first seven verses. The cure is then used, first, as a foil to highlight the blindness of the Pharisees and their refusal to even consider the miraculous cure of the blind man and, second, as a backdrop for the discourse against the Pharisees in the shepherd discourse of 9:39–10:21. The function of the miracles in chs 5 and 9 is not to draw attention to Jesus' miraculous power to heal but to serve as springboards for Jesus' judgmental discourses against the leaders of the Jews.

In the Lazarus story, the miracle is recounted for quite the opposite reason. It is the miracle itself that claims center stage. It takes place at the end of the whole narrative (11:43-44). Everything about Jesus' delay in coming to Bethany, about his discussion with Martha and Mary, and about his very gradual approach to the tomb serves to lead up to the climactic moment of the miracle. Unlike the stories in chs 5 and 9, the function of the Lazarus story is to throw a spotlight on the miracle. Its function is to focus attention on the power of Jesus to raise the dead and give eternal life. It is for that reason that the evangelist purposely locates Jesus in Bethany across Jordan—a good two days' journey from there to this Bethany near Jerusalem where Lazarus lies sick and dying (10:40-42). Even if he wanted to, Jesus could not be there on time (11:6-10).

To emphasize the certainty of the death of Lazarus, the disciples are made to misunderstand Jesus' words about Lazarus sleeping (11:11-15). The misunderstanding allows Jesus to explain in no uncertain terms that Lazarus was not sleeping but dead (11:14-15). Lest there be any doubt at all, John states that when Jesus arrived at Bethany, "he found that Lazarus had already

been in the tomb four days'' (11:17), and that friends had already come out
to Bethany to console Martha and Mary on the loss of their brother (11:19).

Confirmation for the emphasis on the miracle in the telling of the story
is found not only in the way the story is told but in the parallel structure
the evangelist has given it. Actually, the whole story follows the typical Johannine *abcb'a'* structure. Significantly, the center deals with Jesus' power to
raise the dead and give eternal life (11:23-27), and the inclusion shows him
demonstrating his power by raising Lazarus from the dead (11:33-44). Thus,
both the center (11:23-27) and the inclusion (11:40-44) focus attention on
the miracle.

Parallel structure of 11:1-44

(aa) Jesus **comes** from Bethany to Bethany (11:1-19).
(bb) Martha **comes out to meet Jesus** (11:20-22).
(cc) Jesus declares: ''I am the resurrection and the life'' (11:23-27).
(b'b') Mary **comes out to meet Jesus** (11:28-32).
(a'a') Lazarus **comes** out of the tomb (11:33-44).

Text

(aa)   11:1 Now a certain man was ill, **Lazarus** of Bethany, the village of Mary
and her sister Martha. ²It was Mary who anointed **the Lord** with ointment
and wiped his feet with her hair, whose brother **Lazarus** was ill. ³So the
sisters sent to him, saying, **''Lord,** he **whom you love** is ill.'' ⁴But when Jesus
heard it he said, ''This illness is not unto **death;** it is for **the glory of God,**
so that the Son of God may be glorified by means of it.''

⁵Now Jesus **loved** Martha and her sister and **Lazarus.** ⁶So when he heard
that he was ill, he stayed two days longer in the place where he was. ⁷Then
after this he said to the disciples, ''Let us go into Judea again.'' ⁸The disciples
said to him, ''Rabbi, **the Jews** were but now seeking to **stone** you, and are
you going there again?'' ⁹Jesus answered, ''Are there not twelve hours in
the day? If any one walks in the day, he does not stumble, because he sees
the light of this world. ¹⁰But if any one walks in the night, he stumbles,
because the light is not in him.'' ¹¹Thus he spoke, and then he said to them,
''Our friend **Lazarus** has fallen asleep, but I go to awake him out of sleep.''
¹²The disciples said to him, **''Lord,** if he has fallen asleep, he will recover.''
¹³Now Jesus had spoken of his **death,** but they thought that he meant taking rest in sleep. ¹⁴Then Jesus told them plainly, **''Lazarus** is **dead;** ¹⁵and
for your sake I am glad that I was not there, so that you may believe. But
let us go to him.'' ¹⁶Thomas, called the Twin, said to his fellow disciples,
''Let us also go, that we may **die** with him.''

¹⁷Now when Jesus came, he found that **Lazarus** had already been in the
tomb four days. ¹⁸Bethany was near Jerusalem, about two miles off, ¹⁹and
many of **the Jews** had come to Martha and Mary to console them concerning their brother.

(bb)   ²⁰**When Martha heard** that Jesus was coming, she went and **met him,**
while Mary sat in the house. ²¹Martha said to Jesus, **''Lord, if you had been
here, my brother would not have died.** ²²And even now I know that whatever
you ask from God, God will give you.''

(cc) ²³Jesus said to her, "Your brother will rise again." ²⁴Martha said to him, "I know that he will rise again in the resurrection at the last day." ²⁵Jesus said to her, "I am the resurrection and the life; he who believes in me, though he die, yet shall he live, ²⁶and whoever lives and believes in me shall never die. Do you believe this?" ²⁷She said to him, "Yes, Lord; I believe that you are the Christ, the Son of God, he who is coming into the world."

(b'b') ²⁸When she had said this, she went and called her sister Mary, saying quietly, "The Teacher is here and is calling for you." ²⁹And **when she heard** it, she rose quickly and went to him. ³⁰Now Jesus had not yet come to the village, but was still in the place where **Martha had met him.** ³¹When the Jews who were with her in the house, consoling her, saw Mary rise quickly and go out, they followed her, supposing that she was going to the tomb to weep there. ³²Then Mary, when she came where Jesus was and saw him, fell at his feet, saying to him, **"Lord, if you had been here, my brother would not have died."**

(a'a') ³³When Jesus saw her weeping, and **the Jews** who came with her also weeping, he was deeply moved in spirit and troubled; ³⁴and he said, "Where have you laid him?" They said to him, **"Lord,** come and see." ³⁵Jesus wept. ³⁶So **the Jews** said, **"See how he loved him!"** ³⁷But some of them said, "Could not he who opened the eyes of the blind man have kept this man from **dying?"**
³⁸Then Jesus, deeply moved again, came to the **tomb;** it was a cave, and a **stone** lay upon it. ³⁹Jesus said, "Take away the **stone.**" Martha, the sister of the **dead** man, said to him, "Lord, by this time there will be an odor, for he has been **dead four days."** ⁴⁰Jesus said to her, "Did I not tell you that if you would believe you would see **the glory of God?"** ⁴¹So they took away the **stone.** And Jesus lifted up his eyes and said, "Father, I thank thee that thou hast heard me. ⁴²I knew that thou hearest me always, but I have said this on account of the people standing by, that they may believe that thou didst send me." ⁴³When he had said this, he cried with a loud voice, **"Lazarus,** come out." ⁴⁴The **dead** man came out, his hands and feet bound with bandages, and his face wrapped with a cloth. Jesus said to them, "Unbind him, and let him go."

Parallelism is achieved in (aa) and (a'a') in a number of ways. To begin with, Lazarus is the center of attention—in (aa) everything centers on his death; in (a'a'), everything centers on his resurrection. In (aa), it is remarked that Jesus loved Lazarus (11:3, 5, 11); in (a'a'), the Jews remark, "See how he loved him" (11:36). In (aa), Jesus says that Lazarus' sickness is "for the glory of God" (11:4); in (a'a'), Jesus declares, "Did I not tell you that if you would believe you would see the glory of God?" (11:40). In (aa), it is said that Lazarus had been in the tomb four days (11:14); in (a'a') the word "tomb" recurs (11:39), and Martha tells Jesus, "Lord, he has been dead four days" (11:39). Finally, it is not insignificant that the Jews who came out to comfort Martha and Mary figure prominently in (aa) and (a'a'). In 11:19, it is remarked that "many of the Jews had come to Martha and Mary to console them." In 11:33-37, these same Jews are back on the stage. Their presence is not insignificant. Many of them come to believe in Jesus because he raised Lazarus. It is precisely because so many of them believe in Jesus that the chief priests plot Jesus' death (11:45-53; 12:10-11).

In (bb), Martha goes out to meet Jesus. In (b'b'), Mary goes out to meet Jesus (11:29), just as Martha had gone out (11:20). Mary says, "Lord, if you had been here, my brother would not have died" (11:32), repeating word for word what Martha had earlier said to Jesus (11:21).

The center (cc) focuses the reader's attention on Jesus' words "I am the resurrection and the life" and provides the pivot around which the whole narrative turns. In what preceded, emphasis had been on Lazarus' death. In what follows, emphasis will be on Jesus, "the resurrection and the life," raising Lazarus and returning him to life.

(aa) Jesus comes from Bethany to Bethany (11:1-19).

11:1 Lazarus of Bethany. The geographical note is significant. John wishes to distinguish the Bethany near Jerusalem from the Bethany beyond Jordan (10:40 and cf. 1:28). Jesus will remain in Bethany beyond Jordan for two more days (11:6); only then will he move on to Bethany near Jerusalem (11:15-16). By that time, there is no doubt that Lazarus is dead, not just sick.

11:2 Mary who anointed the Lord with ointment. The evangelist throws in this parenthetical remark about Mary to create a parallel with the anointing of Jesus' body for burial in 12:1-9 (cf. 12:3). Thus, 11:1-44, which is the (b) section of sequence 16, is made to look ahead to 12:1-9, which is the (b') section.

11:4 This illness is not unto death. Jesus' statement, which is also a prediction, is a highly charged theological foreshadowing text. It is also the key text of the whole sequence. The foreshadowing prepares the reader to understand that Lazarus' sickness will result in God's glory inasmuch as through Lazarus' death the Son of God will be glorified. This statement prepares the reader to understand that Lazarus' death/resurrection is to be the occasion for Jesus' death. But since it is through his death that Jesus returns to the Father, it is through his death that he is glorified. Thus, Lazarus' sickness will end (result) not in death either for Lazarus or for Jesus; rather "it is for the glory of God, so that the Son of God may be glorified by means of it." As we shall see, it is because Jesus raises Lazarus that the Sanhedrin plots his death (11:45-52). Ultimately, therefore, Lazarus' sickness leads to, and results in, Jesus' death and glorification.

11:6 stayed two days longer. As indicated in 11:4, the Johannine Jesus knows exactly what will happen as a result of Lazarus' death and resurrection. Since the miracle is to trigger the chief priests' decision to put Jesus to death and thereby reveal God's glory to the world, it is essential that there be no doubt that Lazarus was indeed dead. Jesus' two-day delay in Bethany beyond Jordan is not a sign of callous disregard for Lazarus' welfare, but a Johannine literary touch to assure the reader that the Lazarus who is to be raised was indubitably dead.

11:8 but now seeking to stone you. The reference is to the previous sequence (10:22-39), when the Jews had picked up rocks to stone Jesus for blasphemy at the feast of the Dedication in Jerusalem (cf. 10:31-33).

11:9-10 twelve hours in the day. The saying is to assure the disciples that as long as Jesus' day (time) on earth has not arrived at the hour of his death, the Jews of Judea cannot possibly harm him. This has been said in many different ways throughout the Gospel (cf. 2:4; 7:6, 30, 44; 8:20, 59; 10:39; 13:1, 31-32).

11:11-15 Our friend Lazarus has fallen asleep. Jesus uses the word "asleep" to mean death. The disciples are made to misunderstand, as if Lazarus were only sleeping. This allows Jesus, in typical Johannine style (cf. Nicodemus' gross misunderstanding in 3:5ff and the Samaritan woman's misunderstanding in 4:15), to correct their misunderstanding and make it perfectly clear that Lazarus is dead. The misunderstanding technique here serves the same literary purpose as Jesus' two-day delay in Bethany beyond Jordan (11:6).

11:16 Let us also go, that we may die with him. Thomas at this point in Jesus' life does not really know the full meaning of what he is saying. Christian readers at the end of the first century, however, would recognize his words as a Johannine invitation to take up the cross and follow Jesus to death—an invitation put more clearly in 13:1-17, 34-38 and 15:12-13.

11:17 in the tomb four days. The mention of four days in the tomb, which will be repeated in 11:39 to form a parallel with 11:17, is meant to extinguish any last doubt that the Lazarus whom Jesus will raise is dead. The statement serves the same literary purpose as 11:6 and 11:11-15.

11:19 many of the Jews had come to Martha and Mary to console them. John will not let his readers forget these many Jewish friends of Martha and Mary. And for a good reason. It is because many of them witness the miracle and believe in Jesus that the Sanhedrin will decide to have Jesus put to death (cf. 11:45-51 and 12:9-11). John completes his introduction (11:1-19) with the mention of these many Jews. They will figure again significantly in 11:33-44 (especially 11:33, 35-37), which forms an inclusion with the introduction to the story in 11:1-19.

(bb) Martha comes out to meet Jesus (11:20-22).

11:20 while Mary sat in the house. In conformity with the rule of two, John has Mary remain in the house while Martha goes out alone to meet Jesus. Mary will get her turn in the (b'b') section (11:28-32).

11:21-22 Lord, if you had been here. Mary will repeat the identical words in 11:32. The words testify to Jesus' power to heal and to Martha's confidence that whatever Jesus asks from God, God will do. Her confidence is borne out in the raising of her brother from the tomb.

(cc) Jesus declares: "I am the resurrection and the life" (11:23-27).

11:23-24 Your brother will rise again. Jesus' words have more than one meaning, as the ensuing conversation and events will show. Martha misunderstands, taking them to mean that Lazarus will rise "in the resurrection at the last day." She thereby expresses the common belief of Pharisaic Judaism in a general resurrection at the last judgment (cf. Acts 23:8). She thus misses the main meaning of Jesus' words. Jesus means that Lazarus will rise shortly (cf. 11:44). But as Jesus' ensuing remarks show, there is even more to it than that. The best commentary on these words is given by Jesus himself in 5:21-30.

11:25-26 I am the resurrection and the life. The best commentary on everything that Jesus says in 11:25-26 is given, as we have just said, by Jesus himself in 5:21-30. Jesus speaks not only of resurrection at the last day but of that resurrection to life which takes place in any person who believes in him. Jesus speaks here, as he did in 5:21-30, of both realized and final eschatology. He speaks, therefore, of two resurrections. The first is spiritual and is brought about by belief in him; the second is physical and is brought about on the last day. Barrett expresses the thought well: "The pattern of the life of all Christians is determined by the movement from death to life experienced by Lazarus. Christians have already risen with Christ (Rom 6:4f; Col 2:12; 3:1). This movement, to be completed only at the last day, has already taken place in regard to sin; the resurrection of Lazarus therefore is an acted parable of Christian conversion and life."[3]

11:27 the Christ, the Son of God. Martha, like the disciples in 1:35-51 and the Samaritan woman in 4:6-32, heaps up titles testifying to Christian belief in Jesus at the end of the first century. Expression of belief in Jesus is precisely what John was looking for from all his readers when he wrote his Gospel (cf. 20:31).

(b'b') Mary comes out to meet Jesus (11:28-32).

11:29-32 And when she heard it. Mary, like Martha (11:20), when she hears that Jesus is present, goes immediately to meet him. Again, in perfect parallelism with Martha, she repeats what Martha had said: "Lord, if you had been here, my brother would not have died" (cp. 11:32 with 11:21).

(a'a') Lazarus comes out of the tomb (11:33-44).

11:33 he was deeply moved. The Greek verb used here implies some form of anger or indignation. The problem is to explain what causes this anger. Is it the weeping of Mary and the Jews? Is it the anger of the Lord of life in the presence of death? Or is Jesus angry and troubled, almost as in the agony in the garden as described by the Synoptics, because he realizes that his raising of Lazarus is going to bring about his own death on the cross (cf. 11:4; 11:45-52)? No certain answer is possible. The major commentators are in complete disarray.[4]

In the context of Jesus' statement in 11:4 that this sickness would be the means of bringing about his own death, it seems not improbable that Jesus' emotion here is mixed. There is that deep sorrow always felt at the death of a beloved friend. There is also a certain anger that it should be through the restoring of life that his own life should be taken away. Since John does not tell the story of Jesus' agony in the garden in his passion account, it is perhaps not unfitting that he should express the substance of the agony at this time and in this place (cf. 13:21, where Jesus is troubled because he realizes that Judas is about to betray him).

11:38   a cave, and a stone lay upon it. The stone was to keep out animals. It was sometimes on top, sometimes at the side, depending on whether it was a vertical shaft tomb or a cave with an opening on the horizontal.

11:39   he has been dead four days. Paralleling the statement in the introduction that "Lazarus had already been in the tomb four days" (11:17), Martha's remark supplies the final literary touch to the indubitably miraculous nature of his resurrection.

11:40   the glory of God. Since Jesus had nowhere in the story spoken to Martha about seeing the glory of God, except very indirectly in 11:25-27, one must suppose that John is referring here to the words of Jesus in 11:4, which form a parallel with these words in the inclusion.

11:41-42   Father, I thank thee. Jesus' prayer is "on account of the people," in the sense that it makes clear what had already been said by Jesus in 5:19-30, especially 5:19: "The Son can do nothing of his own accord, but only what he sees the Father doing." In addition, it is a prayer for the crowd. Jesus prays that the crowd will believe through the miracle that the Father has sent him. This implicit reference back to 5:19-30 prepares the reader for what follows.

11:43   cried with a loud voice. In 5:28 Jesus had said: ". . . the hour is coming when all who are in the tombs will hear his voice [the voice of the Son of man] and come forth." When Lazarus hears Jesus' voice, he comes forth! His resurrection, therefore, is the pattern for all who believe, who will someday hear that same voice and "come out."⁵ It is perhaps not without interest to note how this motif of "coming out" has run through the whole story. Jesus comes out of Bethany across Jordan (11:15). The Jewish friends of Martha, Mary, and Lazarus come out from Jerusalem to comfort Martha and Mary (11:19). Martha comes out of the house to meet Jesus (11:20). Mary comes out of the house to meet Jesus (11:29). Lastly, Lazarus comes out of the tomb (11:44). In a story climaxed by Lazarus' coming out of the tomb, such an emphasis on "coming out" provides an exquisite literary touch.

(c) The Jewish leaders plot to kill Jesus (11:45-57).

The unity of the material in 11:45-57 is not obvious at first sight. John, however, has imposed unity upon his material by associating everything with the priests' plot. It is because Jesus raised Lazarus that many Jews believe in him and some others report to the Pharisees what he has done (11:45-46). It is because many believe in Jesus that the Sanhedrin plots Jesus' death (11:47-53). It is because of the Jews' plot that Jesus withdraws for safety to Ephraim (11:54). Finally, the episode recalls what people in Jerusalem were saying about Jesus just before the Passover (11:55-56) and concludes with another reference to the priest's plot: "The chief priests and the Pharisees had given orders that if any one knew where he was, he should let them know, so that they might arrest him" (11:57).

11:45-48 Many of the Jews. The fact that many Jews believe in Jesus because of Lazarus is critical for the interpretation of the whole sequence. It is because many Jews believe that the Sanhedrin decides to put Jesus to death (11:47-53). It is for this reason that they say, "If we let him go on thus, every one will believe in him" (11:48). It is because "many Jews were going away and believing in Jesus" that the Sanhedrin plots to kill Lazarus as well as Jesus (12:11). It is the Lazarus miracle, as Jesus had foretold (11:4), that would lead to his own death and glorification.

11:50 expedient for you that one man should die for the people. For John's Christian readers at the end of the first century, there is immense irony in what Caiaphas says. Caiaphas thinks that doing away with Jesus will save the Jewish nation and stave off destruction of both temple and nation by the Romans. He thinks politically and thinks wrong. In 70 A.D., the Romans destroyed the temple and dispersed the Jews. Jesus' death does not save the nation and the temple's destruction by the Roman armies. It does, however, save from eternal destruction all those Jews who believe in him. By his death, "the Lamb of God, who takes away the sin of the world" takes away the sin of the Jews as well.

11:51-52 and not for the nation only. What Caiaphas unwittingly predicted came true not only for the Jewish nation but for all the dispersed children of God. Jesus' death, contrary to the expectations of Caiaphas, would affect not only the Jewish nation but all humankind. That John is thinking of all humankind and not just the Jews of the dispersion has already been discussed (see the comment on 10:16). It is through the Church that all the children of God are to be brought into the one sheepfold of Jesus (cf. 17:21), but it is the death of Jesus that makes them children of God.

11:54 no longer went about openly. It is for fear of the Jewish leaders that Jesus stays in Ephraim, a town some twenty miles north of Jerusalem. Jesus stays there until the Passover of his death. Then he returns to Jerusalem (12:1-9). In 12:23, he will declare concerning this Passover: "The hour has come for the Son of man to be glorified."

11:57 had given orders. It was because of the Sanhedrin's orders to arrest Jesus that the Jews who had come up for the celebration of the Passover (11:55) were on the lookout for Jesus, wondering whether he would come to the feast or not (11:56).

(b') At Bethany near Jerusalem Mary anoints Jesus for burial (12:1-8).

12:1 Six days before the Passover. John has the anointing before Jesus'
entry into Jerusalem (12:12-19); the Synoptics have it after (cf. Mt 26 and
Mk 14). It may be that John places it before in order to end his Gospel with
a final seven days and thus complement the initial seven days with which
he began his Gospel (1:19–2:1). Whether his chronological scheme is more
historical than that of the Synoptics is problematic. If the final seven days
are in some way meant to signify a new week of creation beginning with the
passion of Jesus, then they serve a theological purpose and we can draw from
them no real chronological information. This is possible. It would fit with
the anointing for "burial," which also serves a theological purpose by
highlighting the significance of the "hour" that is the hour of Jesus' death
(12:23-24; 12:32-35; 13:2).

Bethany. The (b') section brings Jesus back to Bethany near Jerusalem,
where he had been in the (b) section (11:19-44). Martha, Mary, and Lazarus
are present again. This time, however, the scene is set, not outside the town,
but in the house of Jesus' beloved friends.

12:3 anointed the feet of Jesus. John uses the anointing story to point
to the death of Jesus (cf. 12:7). Mark (14:3-9) and Matthew (26:6-13) use
it in the same way.[6] Otherwise, there are two major differences. In Mark
and Matthew, the anointing is on the head; in John, it is on the feet. In Mark
and Matthew, the anointing takes place after Jesus' entry into Jerusalem and
just prior to the passion (two days before, according to Mk 14:1); in John
it precedes the entry and takes place at least six days before the passion (12:1).

The simplest solution to John's placement of the story is that he needed
a parallel for the Bethany story of 11:1-44 and used the anointing story as
his parallel by situating it in the house of Martha, Mary, and Lazarus in
Bethany. The best confirmation of this solution, besides the clearly parallel
personages and place in both episodes, is John's parenthetical comment in
11:2: "It was Mary who anointed the Lord with ointment and wiped his feet
with her hair, whose brother Lazarus was ill." The remark is meant to cross-
reference the two episodes, thereby alerting the reader to their parallelism.[7]
The anointing of the feet (from Lk 7:38) rather than the head, as in the
Synoptics, may be because John is familiar with the Lukan story, but not
with the Markan and Matthean story. More likely, he preferred the feet to
the head because in anointing for burial the whole body was anointed. Since
anointing of the head was a common practice at banquets, its significance
for the burial would not have been so evident. Thus, John changes the anointing from the head to the feet for theological reasons.

12:4 Judas Iscariot. In Mk 14:3-5 and Mt 26:8-9, the complaints attributed here to Judas are attributed to some of the disciples. No particular
disciple is named. Commentators give several reasons for John's singling out
Judas by name.[8] What is perhaps the more likely explanation is that John

wished to establish a parallel with sequence 12 (6:22-70), the chiastic parallel of sequence 16 (10:40–12:11). In 6:64, 70-71, Jesus twice refers to Judas as the one who is going to betray him. In both 6:71 and 12:4, John uses almost identical words: "he who was to betray him" (6:64: *houtos gar emellen paradidonai auton;* 12:4: *ho mellon auton paradidonai*). **He was a thief.** Only John so stigmatizes Judas.

(a′) At Bethany near Jerusalem many believe in Jesus (12:9-11).

12:9 the great crowd of the Jews. The remark keeps the reader alerted to the fact that it is because so many come to believe in Jesus because of Lazarus that the Sanhedrin plots the death of Jesus (cf. 11:4, 45-53). The remark introduces the inclusion to the whole sequence by recurring to the theme of the "many" (the great crowd) and by repeating the word "there" (*ekei*), i.e., in Bethany near Jerusalem, the same word used in 10:41 to specify that Jesus remained (there), i.e., in Bethany by Jordan.

12:11 many of the Jews were going away and believing in Jesus. Since these Jews are said to believe in Jesus "on account of" Lazarus, it may be presumed they are the Jews who were at Bethany when Lazarus was raised. The sequence ends, thus, somewhat as it began. It began in Bethany beyond Jordan, where many came to believe in Jesus. It ends in Bethany near Jerusalem, with many Jews coming to believe in him. The place-name Bethany is not mentioned explicitly in 10:40-42 or in 12:10-11, but in each it is clearly implicit. It thus provides a subtle inclusion to the whole of sequence 16 (10:40–12:11).

Themes

The themes of witness and response dominate the sequence. The raising of Lazarus bears witness that Jesus can indeed raise up the dead, not only on the last day, but even in the present (cf. 5:21-28). The heaping up of titles by Martha also bears witness. She addresses Jesus as "Lord" and then goes on to say, "I believe that you are the *Christ, the Son of God, he who is coming into the world*" (11:27). These are all important Christological titles and remind the reader of the similar heaping up of titles by the Samaritan woman in 4:4-38 and by the disciples in 1:35-51. In 11:25-26, Jesus bears witness to himself by declaring, "I am the resurrection and the life."

The theme of response runs throughout and gives the sequence its movement and its continuity. To the positive response of the Jews beyond Jordan (10:42) and of the Jews at Bethany near Jerusalem (11:17-32, 45, 48; 12:10-11), there is contrasted the negative response of the Jewish leaders. They plot to kill Jesus precisely because so many of the people have come to believe in him (11:45-53). As in the story of the paralytic's cure (5:1-18) and in the story of the blind man's cure (9:1-38), the leaders of the Jews obstinately refuse to accept the witness provided by Jesus' miracles. They have eyes to see, but they will not see.

It is very likely that John's description of the Jewish leaders' plot to kill Jesus (11:47-52) and Lazarus (12:9-11) because "many of the Jews were going away and believing in Jesus" on account of Lazarus (12:11) belongs, along with 9:22ff and 15:26ff, to the late first-century Christian polemic against the leaders of the Jews who were making it so difficult for believing Jews to leave the synagogue and cross over to the Christian Church. The polemic, if we are to judge by the Gospels of John and Matthew, was typical of the late first-century struggle between the Church and the synagogue.

Chiastic parallels with sequence 12 (6:22-71)

Just as in part I (1:19–4:3), the introductory sequence (1:19-51) about John the Baptist formed a grand inclusion with sequence 5 (3:22–4:3), also about John the Baptist; and just as in part II (4:4–6:15), the introductory sequence about the Samaritan woman (4:4-38) near Mount Gerizim formed a grand inclusion with sequence 10 (6:1-5), which showed Jesus on a mountain, so in part IV (6:22–12:11), the introductory sequence (6:22-71) forms a grand inclusion with sequence 16 (10:40–12:11).

The grand inclusion is formed by the repetition in each sequence of such themes as: (1) eternal life and raising up on the last day (6:27, 39, 40, 44, 47, 51, 54, 58 and 11:25-26, 43-44); (2) the "many coming to Jesus" in the twelfth sequence but not believing in him (6:22-71 *passim*) and the "many coming to Jesus" in the sixteenth sequence (10:40; 12:11) and believing in him; (3) the passion of Jesus implicit in the symbolism of the Eucharist in 6:44-58, 64, 71 and explicit in 11:45-57 and 12:7-8; (4) Judas in 6:64, 70-71 and 12:4-6.

In addition to the repetition of the above themes in each sequence, John has re-echoed in 10:40–12:11 many things he said in 6:22-71. The following are notable:

1) the time is the same: in 6:4 John says, "The Passover was at hand" (*ēn de eggys to Pascha*), and in 6:22 he places the Eucharistic discourse on "the next day." In 11:55, following the raising of Lazarus and the priests' plot to put Jesus to death, John says, "The Passover of the Jews was at hand" (*ēn de eggys to Pascha*).

2) In both sequences, John draws attention to Jesus' mighty works. In 6:26 Jesus says, ". . . you seek me, not because you saw signs" (*eidete sēmeia*); in 6:30 the Jews ask, "What sign do you do?" (*ti oun poieis sy sēmeion*). In 10:41 the Jews who believe in Jesus say, "John did no sign" (*sēmeion epoiēsen ouden*); in 11:45 John says that many of the Jews who had seen what Jesus did (*theasamenoi ho epoiēsen*) believed in him. Finally, in 11:47 the Jewish leaders are in a quandary because, as they say, "What are we to do? For this man performs many signs" (*polla poiei sēmeia*).

3) In both sequences, one individual is singled out with the numeral one (*heis*) in relation to Jesus' death. In 6:70 Jesus says, "Did I not choose you,

the twelve, and one (*heis*) of you is a devil?'' In 11:49 one of the leaders of the Jews, Caiaphas, is singled out with the numeral one (*heis*): "But one of them, Caiaphas, who was high priest that year . . . .''

4) In both sequences, Jews come looking for Jesus. In 6:24 the Jews come to Capernaum looking for Jesus (*zētountes ton Iēsoun*). In 11:56 the Jews come to Jerusalem looking for Jesus (*ezētoun ton Iēsoun*).

5) In both sequences, there are references to the "many" (*polloi*) who either believe in Jesus (in the last sequence) or do not believe in Jesus (in the first sequence). Thus, in 6:66 John says, "Many (*polloi*) of his disciples drew back and no longer went about with him.'' In 10:41 he says: "Many (*polloi*) believed in him there.'' It is noteworthy in relation to the word "many" that in both sequences there is a contrast between the many and the few. In 6:22-71 "many" refuse to believe and leave Jesus, while the few, the Twelve, remain and Peter says, "To whom shall we go?'' In 10:40–12:11 many believe in Jesus—many in Bethany beyond Jordan (10:40-42) and many in Jerusalem (11:45, 48; 12:10-11)—while only a few (11:46-54), principally the leaders of the Jews, do not believe in him.

6) In both sequences, there are mysterious allusions to the destiny of Jesus as a sacrificial victim. In 11:50-51, Caiaphas, the high priest, says, "You do not understand that it is expedient for you that one man should die for the people.'' In 6:59-71, in the context of speaking about the many who do not believe in Jesus because of what he said about the Eucharist, there are two references to Judas as Jesus' betrayer (6:64, 70-71); one reference to Jesus as "the Son of man ascending" (6:62), which in Johannine terms signifies the cross; one reference to Jesus as "God's holy one," with the implication, via 10:36, where Jesus speaks of himself as "he whom the Father consecrated," that Jesus is the Lamb of God who is to be sacrificed for the sin of the world (cf. 1:29) and about whose death on the cross the evangelist can call in witness the text from Scripture about the paschal lamb: "break none of his bones" (19:36).

7) Finally, there is the subtle re-echoing in the Apostle Thomas' words in 11:16, "Let us also go, that we may die with him," of Peter's words in 6:68-69, "Lord, to whom shall we go? . . . we have come to know that you are the Holy One of God" (i.e., the one consecrated for death as a sacrificial victim).

We may conclude from the repetition in 10:40–12:11 of so many of the themes found in 6:22-71 and from the re-echoing of so many of the same words, expressions, and ideas that sequence 16 makes a recognizable inclusion-conclusion for the whole of part IV (6:22–12:11) of John's Gospel.

Chiastic parallels with sequence 6 (4:4-38)

Just as sequence 1 (1:19-51) parallels chiastically with sequence 21 (20:19–21:25) and sequence 2 with sequence 20 and so on, so sequence 6 (the

Samaritan woman) parallels chiastically with sequence 16 (the Martha, Mary, and Lazarus story). The parallels, as with the parallels between sequence 2 (Mary, the woman at Cana) and sequence 20 (Mary, the woman at the tomb), are few in number but significant.

In both stories, Jesus arrives from afar. In 4:4ff, he arrives from Galilee. In 10:40ff, he arrives from Bethany beyond Jordan. In both stories, Jesus is outside of the town. In 4:8, his disciples go off to the town to buy provisions, and later the Samaritans come out from the town to meet Jesus (4:30). In 11:30, it is expressly stated: "Jesus had not yet come to the village [Bethany]. . . ."

In both stories, women are the central characters. These two balanced sequences, along with sequence 2 and sequence 20, are the only extensive stories about women in the whole of John's Gospel. In both stories, the women speak about Jesus as the Christ. In 4:25, the Samaritan woman says, "I know that Messiah is coming." In 4:29, she wonders, "Can this be the Christ?" In 11:27, Martha says, "I believe that you are the Christ, the Son of God, he who is coming into the world."

In both stories, something is said about the temple of Jerusalem. In 4:20, the Samaritan woman says, "You say that in Jerusalem is the place (*ho topos*) where men ought to worship." In 11:48, the Pharisees fear that the "Romans will come and destroy our holy place (*ton topon*)."

In both stories, the disciples are concerned about Jesus. In 4:31, they are concerned that he should eat. In 11:8, they are concerned for his safety when he determines to go back to Judea. In both stories, people associated with the women come out to meet Jesus and believe in him. In 4:30, townspeople of the Samaritan woman "set out (*exēlthon*) from the town to meet him" because of what the woman said about him. In 12:9, "when the great crowd of the Jews learned that he was there, they came (*ēlthon*), not only on account of Jesus but also to see Lazarus." As John goes on to mention in 12:11, ". . . many of the Jews were going away and believing in Jesus" on account of Lazarus.

In both stories, there is a strong emphasis on "eternal life." In 4:9-15, Jesus' whole discussion with the woman deals with the water of "eternal life," and Jesus specifically says, ". . . the water that I shall give him will become in him a spring of water welling up to eternal life" (4:14). In 11:25, Jesus says, "I am the resurrection and the life; he who believes in me, though he die, yet shall he live, and whoever lives and believes in me shall never die."

Finally, it is hardly insignificant that in 4:4-38 Jesus is concerned for Samaritans who did not belong to Israel and might well be characterized as "dispersed people of God." In 11:51-52, it is said of Jesus that he "should die for the nation, and not for the nation only [the Jewish nation], but to gather into one the children of God who are scattered abroad," precisely what Jesus does in his ministry to the Samaritans.

Part V

THE HOUR OF GLORY
12:12–21:25

Part V deals with Jesus' hour. It begins with the arrival of his hour (12:12-50). It goes on to expound in the Last Supper discourse (13–17), in the passion (18–19), the resurrection (20:1-18), and the post-resurrection appearances (20:19–21:25) the profound significance of that hour for all people. The structure of part V shows the unity and the inner relationships of all the material in 12:12–21:25.

Parallel structure of part V

(a) *Sequence 17 (12:12-50):* The arrival of Jesus' hour. Jesus **comes** to Jerusalem. The Greeks come to Jesus. **Seeing and not believing. The purpose of the signs. Universal salvation.**

(b) *Sequence 18 (13–17):* Jesus' farewell discourse to his **disciples** about his **absence** "for a little while," followed by his **presence** "in a little while."

(c) *Sequence 19 (18–19):* The passion, death, and burial of the king.

(b′) *Sequence 20 (20:1-18):* Mary and the **disciples** at the tomb. **Absence** and **presence** of Jesus.

(a′) *Sequence 21 (20:19–21:25):* The blessedness of those who **"do not see but believe." The purpose of the signs.** The apostles' and Peter's commissioning **for the salvation of the world.** The discussion about Jesus' **second coming.**

The most obvious of the many parallels between (a) and (a′) are: (1) the discussion about signs in 12:37-43 and 20:30-31; (2) the theme of seeing and believing and not seeing and believing in 12:20-22, 37-43 and 20:24-29.

Less obvious parallels are: (1) Jesus' *coming* to Jerusalem in 12:12-19 and Jesus' discussion with Peter about his *second coming* in 21:20-23; (2) the theme of universal salvation, so central to (a) with its references to the great crowds, the coming of the Greeks (Gentiles), the Pharisees' complaint that "the world has gone after him" (12:19), and Jesus' declaration, "And

195

I, when I am lifted up from earth, will draw all men to myself" (12:32), and so almost equally central to (a'), with its commissioning of the apostles and Peter and its story about the great catch of fish, symbolizing the salvation of all nations (21:17); (3) the perfect parallelism between the parenthetical comment about Jesus' death in 12:33, "He said this to show by what death he was to die," and the comment about Peter's death in 21:19, "This he said to show by what death he was to glorify God."

The parallelism between (b) and (b') is simple but perhaps not too obvious. In (b), Jesus' supper discourse deals with the gap that will occur in the lives of his disciples when he dies. He speaks about his "going away" and in "a little while" returning. The theme is absence and presence. In (b'), the "little while" is over and Jesus is present again, but only for a short time (21:18). The theme of absence and presence is tersely put in the words of Mary, "They have taken the Lord out of the tomb, and we do not know where they have laid him" (20:2 and 13), and in the words of Jesus, "Do not hold me, for I have not yet ascended to the Father" (20:17).

The center (c) has five sections: (aa) 18:1-12: the arrest; (bb) 18:13-27: the trial before Caiaphas; (cc) 18:28–19:16: the trial before Pilate; (b'b') 19:17-30: the passion and death; (a'a') 19:31-42: the burial. Quite aptly and in thoroughly Johannine manner, section (cc) deals with the trial before Pilate, in which Jesus is shown to be the true king of the world, whose kingdom nevertheless is "not of this world" (18:36). Thus the theme introduced at the beginning of part V in (a), the account of Jesus' entrance into Jerusalem, characterized by his disavowal of a kingdom of this world (12:12-19), is resolved with absolute clarity in the turning point (cc) of part V as a whole.

Sequence 17

THE ARRIVAL OF JESUS' HOUR

12:12-50

Parallel structure

(a) The crowds greet Jesus **as a nationalistic Messiah** (12:12-19).

(b) The Greeks **want** to see Jesus (12:20-22).

(c) Jesus declares the "hour" has arrived for the salvation of the world (12:23-36).

(b') The Jews **refuse** to see, even though Jesus has done so many signs before them (12:37-43).

(a') Jesus **comes as God's emissary,** sent by the Father to save the world (12:44-50).

Text

(a) 12:12 The next day a great crowd who **had come** to the feast heard that Jesus was **coming** to Jerusalem. [13]So they took branches of palm trees and went out to meet him, **crying,** "Hosanna! Blessed is he who **comes** in the name of the Lord, even the King of Israel!" [14]And Jesus found a young ass and sat upon it; as it is written, [15]"Fear not, daughter of Zion; behold, your king is **coming,** sitting on an ass's colt!" [16]His disciples did not understand this at first; but when Jesus was glorified, then they remembered that this had been written of him and had been done to him. [17]The crowd that had been with him when he called Lazarus out of the tomb and raised him from the dead bore witness. [18]The reason why the crowd went to meet him was that they heard he had done this sign. [19]The Pharisees then said to one another, "You see that you can do nothing; look, the **world** has gone after him."

(b) [20]Now among those who went up to worship at the feast were some Greeks. [21]So these came to Philip, who was from Bethsaida in Galilee, and said to him, "Sir, **we wish to see Jesus.**" [22]Philip went and told Andrew; Andrew went with Philip and they told Jesus.

(c) [23]And Jesus answered them, "The hour has come for the Son of man to be glorified. [24]Truly, truly, I say to you, unless a grain of wheat falls into the earth and dies, it remains alone; but if it dies, it bears much fruit. [25]He who loves his life loses it, and he who hates his life in this world will keep it for eternal life. [26]If any one serves me, he must follow me; and where I am, there shall my servant be also; if any one serves me, the Father will honor him.

[27]"Now is my soul troubled. And what shall I say? 'Father, save me from this hour'? No, for this purpose I have come to this hour. [28]Father, glorify thy name." Then a voice came from heaven, "I have glorified it, and I will glorify it again." [29]The crowd standing by heard it and said that it had thundered. Others said, "An angel has spoken to him." [30]Jesus answered, "This voice has come for your sake, not for mine. [31]Now is the judgment of this world, now shall the ruler of this world be cast out; [32]and I, when I am lifted up from the earth, will draw all men to myself." [33]He said this to show by what death he was to die. [34]The crowd answered him, "We have heard from the law that the Christ remains for ever. How can you say that the Son of man must be lifted up? Who is this Son of man?" [35]Jesus said to them, "The light is with you for a little longer. Walk while you have the light, lest the darkness overtake you; he who walks in the darkness does not know where he goes. [36]While you have the light, believe in the light, that you may become sons of light." When Jesus had said this, he departed and hid himself from them.

(b′) [37]Though he had done so many signs before them, yet they did not believe in him; [38]it was that the word spoken by the prophet Isaiah might be fulfilled: "Lord, who has believed our report, and to whom has the arm of the Lord been revealed?" [39]Therefore they could not believe. For Isaiah again said, [40]"He has blinded their eyes and hardened their heart, lest they should **see** with their eyes and perceive with their heart, and turn for me to heal them." [41]Isaiah said this because he **saw** his glory and spoke of him. [42]Nevertheless many even of the authorities believed in him, but for fear of the Pharisees they did not confess it, lest they should be put out of the synagogue: [43]for they loved the praise of men more than the praise of God.

(a′) [44]And Jesus **cried** out and said, "He who believes in me, believes not in me but in him who sent me. [45]And he who sees me sees him who sent me. [46]**I have come** as light into the **world,** that whoever believes in me may not remain in darkness. [47]If any one hears my sayings and does not keep them, I do not judge him; for **I did not come** to judge the **world** but to save the **world.** [48]He who rejects me and does not receive my sayings has a judge; the word that I have spoken will be his judge on the last day. [49]For I have not spoken on my own authority; the Father who sent me has himself given me commandment what to say and what to speak. [50]And I know that his commandment is eternal life. What I say, therefore, I say as the Father has bidden me."

Parallelism in (a) and (a′) is achieved by means of the inclusion-conclusion formed by Jesus' protesting the crowds' interpretation of him as a nationalistic messiah "who comes in the name of the Lord" in (a) and by his insistence in (a′) that he comes as God's emissary, sent by the Father to save the world. Also, the crowd "cries out" in 12:13; Jesus "cries out" in 12:44, and in each section the word "world" is repeated (cf. 12:19 and 12:46-47).

In (b) and (b′), the evangelist creates antithetic parallelism by contrasting the Greeks who *want to see* Jesus (the Johannine "see" meaning "believe") with the Jews who *refuse to see,* even though Jesus "had done so many signs before them."

The center (c) flows from the crowd's hailing Jesus as a nationalistic messiah and from the Pharisees' complaint that "the world has gone after him," followed by the coming of the Greeks to see Jesus. The coming of the Greeks triggers Jesus' declaration that "the hour has come for the Son of man to be glorified" (12:23ff). Jesus then explains his hour as the hour when he is "lifted up from the earth" and "draws all men" to himself (12:32), thus effectively and clearly denying that he is the kind of nationalistic messiah expected by the crowds.

Sequence 17 (12:12-50) introduces and sets the theme for the whole of part V (12:12-21:25), which deals with the hour of Jesus' passion, death, resurrection, and glorification. Sequence 18 (chs 13-17) elaborates on the significance of the hour for the life of the apostles and the Church. Sequence 19 (chs 18-19) deals with the hour itself: the passion and death of Jesus. Sequence 20 (20:1-18) gives John's account of the resurrection. And sequence 21 (20:19-21:25) repeats in different ways the themes of sequence 17 (12:12-50), namely, the significance of the signs, seeing and believing and not seeing and believing, universal salvation, and Jesus' second coming—all themes flowing from the critical significance of the coming of Jesus' hour.

Commentary

(a) The crowds greet Jesus as a nationalistic Messiah (12:12-19).

12:12-13 a great crowd . . . went out to meet him. Like the Galilean Jews after the multiplication of the loaves (6:14-15), the Palm Sunday crowd wants to make Jesus a nationalistic Messiah. This is John's interpretation of the event. He indicates it by having the crowd take the initiative and perhaps by his reference to the palms, which are mentioned in the account of the crowds greeting Simon Maccabeus in 1 Mc 13:51.

12:13b comes in the name of the Lord. Jesus is truly God's emissary (12:44-50), but the crowd is thinking of him as a nationalistic Messiah.

12:14 And Jesus found a young ass and sat upon it. Jesus reacts to the crowd's initiative by riding upon an ass, with the obvious intention of fulfilling the prophecy of Zech 9:9ff, which foretold, not a conquering, political Messiah, but a humble Messiah. By entering Jerusalem in this way, Jesus protests against the Jews' misunderstanding of him as a political Messiah. As Hoskyns says: "The author does not draw out the implications of the action of Jesus, because the discourse which follows (vv 23-36) makes sufficiently clear the distinction between the messiahship of Jesus and the royal Messiah whom the Jews supposed they were welcoming into the city. He is content merely to note that the disciples did not understand until later, after the glorification of Jesus, either the significance of His action or the precise nature of the misunderstanding of the crowd."[1]

In the Synoptics (Mk 11; Mt 21; Lk 19), Jesus prepares for his entry by sending disciples to fetch the ass, and the cheers of the crowd *follow* his entry. In John, the cheers *occasion* Jesus' finding the ass, thus indicating that Jesus used the prophecy of Zech 9:9ff to *protest* the crowd's manner of acting.

12:16 disciples did not understand. John's interpretative comment that "his disciples did not understand this at first; but when Jesus was glorified, then they remembered that this had been written of him and had been done to him" highlights his intention of interpreting Jesus' action according to the Zechariah prophecy in contrast to the way the crowd greeted Jesus.

In confirmation of this interpretation, it can be pointed out that in 6:14-15, in similar circumstances, Jesus had protested against the nationalistic enthusiasm of the crowd by fleeing alone to the hills (6:15). Similarly, when Jesus answers Pilate's question "So you are a king?" he gives a thoroughly unambiguous explanation of the non-nationalistic nature of his messianic kingdom and title (18:33-37). Finally, it should be noted that John's presentation of Jesus as a non-nationalistic Messiah in 12:12-19 is considerably enhanced by the content of the three passages that follow: 12:20-22; 12:23-28; 12:32-35.

First, the coming of the Greeks in 12:20-22 is an implicit commentary on Zech 9:9ff, which goes on to say that the king entering Jerusalem on a donkey "shall command *peace to the nations* [*Gentiles*]; his dominion shall be from sea to sea. Jesus' statement in 12:32, "And I, when I am lifted up from the earth, will draw all men to myself," would seem to further corroborate this interpretation of Jesus' action by associating the two elements mentioned, namely, the humble entry and the coming of the Greeks (Gentiles) to Jesus.

Second, Jesus' discourse on his approaching passion, death, and glorification in 12:23-36 further explains the kind of messianic king he intends to be—a crucified king, which is hardly the kind of Messiah the Jews envision.

Third, the Jews' misunderstanding in 12:34 indicates that they are finally beginning to understand the kind of Messiah Jesus intends to be, and their very misunderstanding allows Jesus to explain further the fact that the time of his death is near (12:35-36).

(b) The Greeks want to see Jesus (12:20-22).

12:20-22 some Greeks. Since they have come to the feast to worship, they are not gentile pagans but gentile God-fearers, i.e., Gentiles attracted to the worship of Israel (cf. Acts 12:2, 22, 34; 13:16, 26; Lk 7:2-10). Their coming to see Jesus connects with the entry story in 12:12-19 in two ways. First, their coming follows up the unexpressed but implicitly understood continuation of the Zechariah prophecy about the coming of the Gentiles to Jerusalem in the time of the Messiah (cf. Zech 9:13ff). Second, it ratifies the ironic and frustration-filled judgment of the Pharisees that "the world has gone after him" (12:19).

In the light of the Zechariah prophecy about the Gentiles' coming to Jerusalem in messianic times, the Greeks' wanting to see Jesus is in all likelihood to be interpreted as a Johannine seeing, i.e., believing. The evangelist thus sets up a contrast between the Gentiles who want to see and believe Jesus and the crowds who do not because, as John says, "Though he had done so many signs before them, yet they did not believe in him" (12:37ff). The contrast creates an antithetic parallelism between the (b) section (12:20-22) and the (b') section (12:37-43).

The fact that Jesus does not even speak to the Greeks perhaps best explains the evangelist's purely symbolic purpose in incorporating this otherwise strange and abruptly dismissed incident. Early in the Gospel the evangelist had John the Baptist point to Jesus as "the Lamb of God, who takes away the sin of the world" (1:29) and had Jesus declare that "God so loved the world that he gave his only Son" (3:16). In his references to the harvest (4:34-38), to the Samaritans' calling Jesus "the Savior of the world" (4:42), and to teaching the Greeks (8:35), the evangelist had already anticipated Jesus' mission to the world, his gathering of the other sheep into the one fold (10:16), and his ingathering through his death of all the scattered children of God (11:52).

The fulfillment of the prophecy of Zech 9:9-14 is thus used by the evangelist to focus the reader's attention on Jesus' climactic announcement that "the hour has come for the Son of man to be glorified" (12:23). It is the hour of the passion that brings about the salvation of the Gentiles, who are the "other sheep," the scattered children of God. The coming of the Greeks serves, as a consequence, to set the stage for the discourse on the hour, the crucifixion, and discipleship that Jesus gives in 12:23-36.

(c) Jesus declares the "hour" has arrived for the salvation of the world (12:23-36).

This section, with its accent on a suffering and dying Messiah, clarifies the Johannine account of Jesus' entry into Jerusalem in 12:12-19. Hoskyns rightly understands it as an explanation of Jesus' protest against the crowd's welcoming him into Jerusalem as a political Messiah. He says: "The action of Jesus [in 12:12-19] is occasioned by the nature of the welcome, and is a protest against it, explained in the discourse that follows (12:23-36)"[2] In 12:23-33, Jesus explains that, far from being a political Messiah, he will be a suffering and dying Messiah. He will be like the grain of wheat that must die before it can produce fruit (v 24). And once he has been "lifted up from the earth," he will draw all to himself, indicating by this statement "by what death he was to die" (vv 32-33). The crowd's objection in v 34 to a dying Messiah is perfectly in line with the mistaken interpretation of Jesus' messiahship manifested by them in their enthusiastic welcome of Jesus to Jerusalem in 12:12-19.

While Hoskyns' insightful comment contains the central clue to the interpretation of this otherwise puzzling little discourse, John himself gives us a clue to its interpretation by composing it in his typical parallelism. If it is read as follows, with attention to the parallels in bold print, it becomes significantly clearer.

Parallel structure of 12:23-36

(aa)   The hour has come for **the Son of man** to be **glorified,** i.e., to be **lifted up** on the cross (12:23-24).

(bb)   He who hates his life **in this world** will keep it for eternal life (12:25-26).

(cc)   Save me from this hour? But it was for this that I came to this hour. Father, glorify your name (12:27-30).

(b'b') Now is the judgment **of this world,** now shall the ruler **of this world** be cast out (12:31).

(a'a') How can you claim that **the Son of man** must be **lifted up?** (12:32-36).

Text

(aa)   12:23 And Jesus answered them, **"The hour has come for the Son of man to be glorified.** ²⁴Truly, truly, I say to you, unless a grain of wheat falls into the earth and **dies,** it remains alone; but if it **dies, it bears much fruit.**

(bb)   ²⁵He who loves his life loses it, and he who hates his life **in this world** will keep it for eternal life. ²⁶If any one serves me, he must follow me; and where I am, there shall my servant be also; if any one serves me, the Father will honor him.

(cc)   ²⁷"Now is my soul troubled. And what shall I say? 'Father, save me from this hour'? No, for this purpose I have come to this hour. ²⁸Father, glorify thy name." Then a voice came from heaven, "I have glorified it, and I will glorify it again." ²⁹The crowd standing by heard it and said that it had thundered. Others said, "An angel has spoken to him." ³⁰Jesus answered, "This voice has come for your sake, not for mine.

(b'b')   ³¹"Now is the judgment of **this world,** now shall the ruler of **this world** be cast out;

(a'a')   ³²"and I, **when I am lifted up from the earth, will draw all men to myself."** ³³He said this to show by what **death** he was to **die.** ³⁴The crowd answered him, "We have heard from the law that the Christ remains for ever. How can you say that **the Son of man must be lifted up?** Who is this Son of man?" ³⁵Jesus said to them, "The light is with you for a little longer. Walk while you have the light, lest the darkness overtake you; he who walks in the darkness does not know where he goes. ³⁶While you have the light, believe in the light, that you may become sons of light."

John creates parallelism between (aa) and (a'a') by dealing in each with the passion and death of Jesus and by repeating in each the words "die" and "death." In (bb) and (b'b'), he repeats the word "world" and emphasizes the concept of judgment. The center (cc) deals with Jesus' prayer and the voice from heaven.

12:23 The hour has come. The hour is the time of Jesus' death, resurrection, and glorification. It introduces the theme that will dominate the whole of part V (12:12–21:25).[3] In the earlier parts of the Gospel, the reader was told that Jesus' hour had not yet come (cf. 2:5; 7:6, 30; 8:20). Now it has arrived, and its association with Jesus' death and glorification is clarified in what follows in 12:24, 32 and in all that follows from ch 13 through ch 21 (cf. especially 13:1, 31).

That the hour has definitively arrived is confirmed by the triple repetition of "now" (*nyn*) in vv 27 and 31. The hour is the hour when the temple of Jesus' body will, like the "grain of wheat that falls into the earth and dies" in 12:24, be "destroyed and raised up" as Jesus predicted in 2:13-22. It is the hour of the Messiah, when the true nature of Jesus as the suffering Messiah is revealed (cf. 12:12-19). It is the hour when the good shepherd lays down his life for his sheep (cp. 12:23-27 with 19:17-18). It is the hour when the bread of life (6:31-58) falls into the ground, dies, and yields a rich harvest (12:23-24). It is the hour when he who is the resurrection and the life (11:25) will be lifted up from the earth and will draw all to himself (12:32, and compare with the theme of universal salvation in 3:13-16; 10:15-16; 11:49-51).

12:24 grain of wheat. The little parable of the wheat is clarified by its parallel in vv 32-33, where Jesus speaks about his death. It illustrates both the necessity and the fruitfulness of Jesus' death, so that as a consequence he will "draw all men" to himself (12:32).

12:25-26 He who hates his life in this world will keep it for eternal life. As in Mk 8:34-36, this saying refers to the hatred, persecution, and death that Christians suffered for their faith. It is particularly pertinent in view of the situation of the Johannine community in the nineties and in view of what so many Christians had suffered in the intervening years (cf. 16:1-2, 32-33; 21:18-19). The brief reference to missionary activity in v 26 will be expanded in 13:12-18; 15:5-8, 18-21; 17:18-19; 20:21-22; 21:1-11, 15-19. In several of these passages, John, like Mark, associates following Jesus with suffering and death. The association is particularly clear in 13:12-17 and 21:15-19.

12:27 Now is my soul troubled. This little scene has rightly been called John's version of Jesus' agony in the garden. The language is different—in John it is associated with the key word "hour"—but in each case the end is the same: Jesus declares firmly that he will accept his passion and death and thereby do the will of the Father (cf. Mk 14:32-36; Mt 26:36-46; Lk 22:40-46).

12:28b   Then a voice came from heaven. In the Synoptics, the voice from heaven approving Jesus is found in the accounts of Jesus' baptism and transfiguration. Where John got this story is difficult to determine. As Schnackenburg says: ". . . it is probable that in the references to the heavenly voice and the angel the evangelist is using motifs from the traditions available to him. Mythological though they may sound, the evangelist brings out the real meaning: Jesus comes to terms with the 'hour' by looking to his Father, who gives him assurance of his glorification."[4]

12:28c   I have glorified it. This reference to the past glorification of Jesus would embrace all the signs performed by Jesus (cf. 2:11; 11:4).

12:30   This voice. Jesus' explanation of the phenomenon of the voice being for the sake of the crowd is similar to his explaining the signs as means whereby those who love the light can come to the light (cf. 2:11; 5:36; 11:42; 12:37; 20:30-31). How the crowd could have interpreted the voice as approval of Jesus is difficult to understand. Brown asks: ". . . does its obvious synchronization with Jesus' preaching signify for the crowd that God approves of Jesus?"[5]

12:31   judgment . . . of this world. The effect of Jesus' hour on humanity, even though cumulatively carried out over the course of history, is the destruction of the forces of evil, personified here as "the ruler of this world."

12:32   lifted up from the earth. With this reference to his death, based on Is 53:13 and similar to the sayings about his death in 3:14-15 and 8:28, Jesus returns to the theme of the seed that "must die" in order to produce much fruit (12:24) and applies it to his own death, as a result of which he "will draw all men" to himself. The "lifted up," as the parenthetical comment declares, is a reference to the kind of death Jesus will die—death by being "lifted up" on the cross (cf. the parallel to this statement in 21:19).

12:34   The crowd answered him. The objection, probably based on Ps 89:37, which speaks about the seed of David "remaining forever," accords with the crowd's superficial expectations on Palm Sunday (12:12-19). The crowds are looking for a conquering, political Messiah, not a crucified Messiah. Almost certainly John is doing here what he has done so often throughout his Gospel, namely, refuting the arguments of his synagogue opponents in the nineties. In this case, they would have argued that a crucified Messiah is no Messiah at all!

12:35-36a   Jesus said to them. Jesus ignores the objection. He had already dealt with it in his Palm Sunday protest (12:12-19) and in his parable of the seed (12:24, 31-32). Instead, he appeals to the crowd once more to come to the light while there is time. The appeal, like the crowd's objection, deals with the situation in the nineties. For John, judgment depends on one's decision for or against Jesus, and that decision is made during the short span of each person's lifetime.

12:36b   hid himself. Since Jesus has already accepted his hour, it is unlikely that he goes into hiding out of fear of the Jews, as he did in 8:59; 10:40-42; and 11:54. More likely, as Brown says: "To illustrate dramatically the theme of the passing of the light, Jesus now hides himself."[6]

(b′) The Jews refuse to see, even though Jesus has done so many signs before them (12:37-43).

This section, in which the Jews *refuse* to see Jesus, parallels by antithetic parallelism the (b) section (12:20-22), in which the Greeks are shown *wanting* to see, i.e., believe, in Jesus. The contrast is striking and constitutes John's judgment on his own people's historical response to Jesus both in the time of Jesus and in his own time. Paul dealt with the problem of the Jews' rejection of Jesus throughout Rom 1–11, but especially in chs 9–11. Mark dealt with the problem by means of his parable theory (Mk 4:1-34). Matthew dealt with it by means of a continual polemic against the Pharisees and by his revision of Mark's parable discourse (Mk 4) into a discourse (Mt 13) that represents Jesus as turning away from the old Israel to form a new Israel. Luke picks up the parable theory of Mark (Mk 4) in 8:4-18, recounts the opposition of the Jews to the early Church and to Paul in Acts (*passim*), and puts into Paul's mouth a speech that is remarkably similar to Jn 12:37-43 (Acts 28:25-28). John offers no real explanation of the phenomenon beyond declaring that it was already predicted by the scriptures in Is 53 and Is 6:9-10.

John's judgment on the Jews is important as a key to the audience to whom he directed his Gospel at the end of the first century. If we are correct in interpreting 12:35-36 as a warning to John's contemporaries rather than as the historical words of Jesus, then the warning there, in combination with the warning of 12:42-43 that follows, is a direct appeal to those of John's contemporaries who were hesitating between staying with the synagogue and going over to Christianity. The references in 12:42 to the many who believed in him, even among the leading men, but did not admit it, and to the reasons for not admitting it, namely, "for fear of the Pharisees . . . lest they should be put out of the synagogue" (12:42), as well as the charge "for they loved the praise of men more than the praise of God," would seem to indicate that John is addressing Jews who were on the fence between Judaism and Christianity (cf. 3:1ff; 5:44; 7:48-52; 19:39). If this interpretation is correct, then John's discourse here may be construed as a direct appeal to these hesitant Jews at the time he wrote his Gospel.

12:37   Though he had done so many signs. John incorporates into his Gospel only a limited number of the signs worked by Jesus, but he knows and his audience knows that Jesus worked many other signs. As he says at the end of the Gospel, "There are also many other things which Jesus did; were every one of them to be written, I suppose that the world itself could not contain the books that would be written'' (21:25). Despite these signs, the Jews, taken as a collectivity in the past and in the present, have refused to believe. How explain this phenomenon—especially in view of the uncited but obviously well-known acceptance of Jesus by the Gentiles (cf. 12:20-22; 21:1-11)? In 12:38-43, John gives a theological analysis of the problem, trying to explain the Jews' unbelief in scriptural terms.

12:38   the word spoken by the prophet Isaiah. John appropriates the text of Is 53 to highlight the Jews' refusal to accept Jesus: "Lord, who has believed our report . . . ?'' Such an incredible refusal requires an explanation. In the original Servant song of Is 52:13–53:12, the words are attributed positively to the gentile kings and express their awed but believing incredulity in face of the Servant's extraordinary career. John, however, refers the words in a negative sense to the Jews of the past and the present.

12:39-40   Therefore they could not believe. John quotes Is 6:9-10 to explain the Jews' refusal to believe, insinuating that their refusal was already known by Isaiah and foreordained by God as part of his divine plan. That this refusal is not a matter of predestination of individuals is evident, first, from John's paradoxical assertion in 12:42 that "many even of the authorities believed in him'' and, second, from his consistent appeals throughout the Gospel to his Jewish compatriots to believe in Jesus (cf. 5:31-47; 6:28-29; 6:52-58; 8:28-32; 10:37-38; 12:35-36).

12:41   because he saw his glory. In Is 6:1-3, what Isaiah sees is the glory of Yahweh. John says he saw the glory of Jesus, connecting the glory of Yahweh with the glory that Jesus shared with Yahweh since the foundation of the world (cf. 17:5 and John's *Logos* theology in 1:1-18). Since this glory had always belonged to Jesus (cf. 1:15; 2:11; 11:4, 40) and was manifested in his signs, John conceives Isaiah as having seen it somewhat in the same manner that he conceives Abraham as having seen Jesus' day (8:56). Because Isaiah saw all this, he also saw the Jewish response of unbelief and said, as a consequence, the words "He has blinded their eyes . . .'' (Jn 12:40; Is 6:9-10).

12:42-43   many even of the authorities. This statement seems to qualify v 37, showing that the Jews' refusal to believe in Jesus was not something foreseen because predestined, but foreseen as a historical but contingent event. For John, each individual freely decides whether to accept or deny Jesus. That many Jews accepted him, even though many more did not, rules out any element of predestination in Johannine theology. The remark about the Pharisees and fear of being expelled from the synagogue reflects the situation of the Johannine community in the nineties and continues John's polemic against those synagogue leaders who were making it so difficult for Jews to become Christians (cf. chs 7–9, *passim,* but especially 9:22; also 15:18-25; 16:1-3). In v 43, John would appear to be talking about people like Nicodemus and Joseph of Arimathea.

(a′) Jesus comes as God's emissary, sent by the Father to save the world (12:44-50).

This section, for those who presuppose that John's Gospel follows the strict laws of narrative rather than the laws of parallelism, appears to be the interpolation of an editor, since the earlier evangelist had (supposedly) closed Jesus' public preaching with his words in 12:36: "When Jesus said this, he departed and hid himself from them."[7]

According to the laws of parallelism, however, this section is not only not an interpolation but is demanded as an inclusion-conclusion to 12:12-19, the story of Jesus' entry into Jerusalem. In 12:12-19, the crowds cried out: "Hosanna! Blessed is he *who comes in the name of the Lord,* even the King of Israel!" (12:13). Jesus protests such a nationalistic interpretation of his coming by entering Jerusalem on a donkey and thus fulfilling Zechariah's prediction concerning the humble nature of the Messiah (12:14-16). He goes even further in his protest in 12:23-36 by speaking about his death on the cross (cf. 12:24, 32-33).[8] Finally, in 12:44-50, Jesus cries out that he indeed "comes in the name of the Lord," but as God's emissary sent by the Father to save the world.

The parallels of 12:44-50 with 12:12-19 can hardly be accidental. The crowds in 12:13 "cry out" (*ekraugazon* = imperfect of *ekraugazō*), and Jesus in 12:44 "cries out" (*ekraxen* = aorist of *krazō*). The crowds in 12:13 cry "Hosanna" (Hebrew = *"Save, I pray"*). Jesus in 12:47 says, "I did not come to judge the world but to *save* the world." Most significantly, Jesus' words in 12:44-50 define *how* he "comes in the name of the Lord," namely, not as the political Messiah the crowds wanted but as the one sent by the Father as his emissary to save the world.

In short, John has positioned 12:44-50 where it is because of the laws of parallelism. It forms an inclusion-conclusion to the story of the misunderstood entry in 12:12-19. It also helps to provide chiastic parallelism with sequence 5 (3:22–4:3), which parallels 12:12-50 in the Gospel as a whole. Contrary, therefore, to those who consider 12:44-50 to be the interpolation of an editor, the passage is positioned precisely where it should be in order to ensure parallelism with the introduction to sequence 17 in 12:12-19 and with its chiastic parallel in the Gospel as a whole (3:22–4:3).

12:44-45 He who believes in me. As so often in John's Gospel, people are called upon to believe in Jesus as the Father's emissary (cf. 3:12-17, 31-36; 5:36b-37, 43; 6:44; 7:16-18, 28-29; 8:26, 29, 42; 10:36-38; 13:20; 14:24; and especially 16:29 and 17:8).

12:46-48 I have come. These verses constitute a last appeal to the Jews and reflect in that appeal one of John's purposes in writing his Gospel, namely, to appeal to his Jewish compatriots to hear and believe in Jesus.

12:49-50 For I have not spoken on my own. These last words repeat in another form what was said in 12:44 and in so many other places in the

Gospel: Jesus is God's emissary, and obedience to his message means eternal life. He is not, as the Jews wanted to understand him when he entered Jerusalem on Palm Sunday (12:12-19), a nationalistic Messiah!

Themes

The themes of witness and response dominate sequence 17. Jesus corrects the crowd's false witness to him as a political Messiah by entering Jerusalem humbly on a donkey (12:12-19). He then clarifies the kind of Messiah he is—a Messiah who will die on the cross (12:23-36)—and this witness is corroborated by the voice from heaven (12:28-30). Finally, in 12:44-50, he testifies to himself as God's emissary and to his word as the word he received from the Father. The theme of response occurs in two places: positively, in 12:20-22; negatively, in 12:37-43.

Chiastic parallels with sequence 5 (3:22–4:3)

Parallels between sequence 17 and sequence 5 are primarily conceptual. Both deal with the nature and origin of Jesus' ministry as the ministry of one sent and empowered by the Father as the Father's emissary to the world for the salvation of the world.

Verbal parallels are few but significant. In 3:34, the Baptist says, "For he *whom God has sent utters* the words of God . . . ." In 12:49, Jesus declares, "For I have not *spoken* on my own authority; *the Father who sent me* has himself given me commandment what to *say* and what to *speak.*" In 3:26, John's disciples say of Jesus, ". . . here he is baptizing, and all are going to him." In 12:19, the Pharisees complain, ". . . *the world has gone after him.*" In 3:36, the Baptist says, "He who *believes* in the Son has *eternal life.*" In 12:44-50, Jesus speaks about belief in himself and about the commandment he has received from the Father and declares, "He who *believes* in me, believes not in me but in him who sent me" (12:44), and concludes with the words "And I know that his commandment is *eternal life*" (12:50). In both sequences, what is central is the concept of Jesus as a Messiah who has come, not as a power-politics Messiah, but as a Messiah sent by God to bring eternal life.

Sequence 18

JESUS' FAREWELL DISCOURSE
13:1–17:26

The farewell discourse deals with the gap created in the life of the Church by the absence of Jesus. It declares that the gap will be filled by the presence of the Paraclete-Counselor and by Jesus' gifts of peace, joy, and consolation. It calls upon Christians to be united with Jesus and the Father in a mutual indwelling love unto death. This is the clue and the glue that holds the whole long discourse together.

The discourse is intensely theological and ecclesiological. It is directed to the apostles and their successors, whose mission is to continue the work of Jesus in the world. In this context, what is said about the apostles is also said about their successors. The discourse thus takes on the added aspect of instructions on the nature of discipleship and on the use of authority in the Church. As a result, the discourse has much in common with the instructions on discipleship in the synoptic Gospels (cf. Mk 8:31–10:52; Mt 5–7; 10; 13; 18; 23–25; Lk 9:51–19:44).

The major commentaries have much to say about the sources and the formation of the farewell discourse.[1] But whatever the sources used by the evangelist, the parallel structure of the discourse as a whole makes it clear that the discourse as it stands was composed as a unity by the author. When read according to the laws of parallelism, it is not necessary to postulate either independent discourses or successive redactors. What appear to be independent and repetitive discourses successively joined together turn out to be, when viewed through the focus of parallelism, only parallel sections of the one discourse. The focus of parallel structure reveals the artistry of the evangelist. Any other focus distorts the unity of the discourse and subjects the evangelist to the charge of repetitiveness, confusion, and complete failure to integrate his material.

There are three clues to the interpretation of the discourse. The first is to read it according to the laws of parallelism; the second, to realize that it deals with the gap created by the departure of Jesus; the third, to read it as a farewell discourse. Only the third requires some explanation.

The farewell discourse as a literary form is well known from many examples in the Old Testament, e.g., Jacob's farewell discourse to his twelve sons (Gn 47:29–49:33); Joshua's (Jos 22-24); David's (1 Chr 28-29); Moses' (Dt as a whole). In the New Testament there are Paul's farewell address at Miletus (Acts 20:17-38) and the eschatological discourses attributed to Jesus in Mk 13; Mt 24; Lk 21.

The literary form has several characteristics. First, a great man on the eve of his death gathers his followers to instruct them for the future and to encourage them to persevere. Second, the instruction emphasizes what the disciples are to do to continue the work of the master. The master urges them to keep his commandments and follow his advice, reminds them of what he has done for them, and encourages them to preserve unity in the face of persecution and temptation. Third, the speaker looks into the future and speaks about the fate of his followers, calling down blessings upon them and maledictions upon their enemies. Fourth, the great man speaks about a successor who will take his place and help his followers to fulfill his work.

The discourse in Jn 13–17 fits this literary form perfectly. It is given on the eve of Jesus' departure to the Father. His followers are apprehensive and fearful. Jesus consoles, encourages, and instructs them. He promises peace, joy, consolation, and the sending of a successor—the Counselor-Paraclete. He urges them to abide by his commandments, especially the commandment of love unto death. He promises that as long as they remain in him, they will produce much fruit. At the end he prays for them and for all who will come to believe in him through their preaching of his word. The discourse, as a result, deals with the immediate and the distant future—the approaching death of Jesus and the life of the Church up to and beyond the time of the evangelist.

The discourse as a whole has five sections, each approximately the same length, arranged in John's usual *abcb'a'* parallel structure. In addition, each section has a similar parallel structure. Because of the length of the discourse, the longest in the New Testament, it will be advisable to look first at the parallel structure of the discourse as a whole and then at each section.

Parallel structure of the discourse as a whole

Section A (13:1-32): The footwashing and Judas the traitor. Jesus speaks about the arrival of **his hour,** about **love** unto the end, about **the mission of the apostles,** and about **his glorification.**

Section B (13:33–14:31): Jesus speaks about **his going away, the Counselor,** his love commandment, dwelling places in heaven, **asking in his name,** and **his gift of peace.**

Section C (15:1-25): The true vine and the false vine. During the time of the gap, the disciples must remain in Jesus as the branch remains in the vine. Despite the hatred and persecution of the world, the disciples will produce much fruit as long as they remain in Jesus.

Section B' (15:26–16:33):   Jesus speaks about **his going away, the Counselor, asking in his name,** and **his gift of peace.**

Section A' (17:1-26):   Jesus prays for the Church. He speaks about the arrival of **his hour, his glorification,** the mission of the **apostles,** and the **love** that he prays may be in those who believe in him.

Section A (13:1-32): The footwashing and Judas the traitor. Jesus speaks about the arrival of his hour, about love unto the end, about the mission of the apostles, and about his glorification.

Parallel structure

(a) The **hour** has arrived (13:1).
(b) All are **clean** except **one** (13:2-11).
(c) The footwashing is an example for the apostles (13:12-17).
(b') Jesus singles out the **one** who is not **clean** (13:18-27).
(a') Judas' departure sets in motion the **hour** of Jesus' death and glorification (13:28-32).

Text

(a)   13:1 Now before **the feast** of the Passover, when Jesus **knew** that **his hour had come** to depart out of this world to the Father, having loved his own who were in the world, he loved them to the end.

(b)   ²And during supper, when **the devil** had already put it into the heart of **Judas Iscariot, Simon's son,** to **betray** him, ³Jesus, knowing that the Father had given all things into his hands, and that he had come from God and was going to God, ⁴rose from supper, laid aside his garments, and girded himself with a towel. ⁵Then he poured water into a basin, and began to wash **the disciples'** feet, and to wipe them with the towel with which he was girded. ⁶He came to **Simon Peter;** and Peter said to him, **"Lord,** do you wash my feet?" ⁷Jesus answered him, "What I am doing you do not know now, but afterward you will understand." ⁸Peter said to him, "You shall never wash my feet." Jesus answered him, "If I do not wash you, you have no part in me." ⁹**Simon Peter** said to him, **"Lord,** not my feet only but also my hands and my head!" ¹⁰Jesus said to him, "He who has bathed does not need to wash, except for his feet, but he is clean all over; and you are clean, **but not all of you."** ¹¹For he knew who was to **betray** him; that was why he said, **"You are not all clean."**

(c)   ¹²When he had washed their feet, and taken his garments, and resumed his place, he said to them, "Do you know what I have done to you? ¹³You call me Teacher and Lord; and you are right, for so I am. ¹⁴If I then, your Lord and Teacher, have washed your feet, you also ought to wash one another's feet. ¹⁵For I have given you an example, that you also should do as I have done to you. ¹⁶Truly, truly, I say to you, a servant is not greater than his master; nor is he who is sent greater than he who sent him. ¹⁷If you know these things, blessed are you if you do them.

(b′)   ¹⁸**"I am not speaking of you all;** I know whom I have chosen; it is that
the scripture may be fulfilled, 'He who ate my bread has lifted his heel against
me.' ¹⁹I tell you this now, before it takes place, that when it does take place
you may believe that I am he. ²⁰Truly, truly, I say to you, he who receives
any one whom I send receives me; and he who receives me receives him who
sent me."

   ²¹When Jesus had thus spoken, he was troubled in spirit, and testified,
"Truly, truly, I say to you, one of you will **betray** me." ²²**The disciples** looked
at one another, uncertain of whom he spoke. ²³One of his **disciples,** whom
Jesus loved, was lying close to the breast of Jesus; ²⁴so **Simon Peter** beckoned
to him and said, "Tell us who it is of whom he speaks." ²⁵So lying thus,
close to the breast of Jesus, he said to him, **"Lord,** who is it?" ²⁶Jesus
answered, "It is he to whom I shall give this morsel when I have dipped
it." So when he had dipped the morsel, he gave it to **Judas, the son of Simon
Iscariot.** ²⁷Then after the morsel, **Satan** entered into him. Jesus said to him,
"What you are going to do, do quickly."

(a′)   ²⁸Now no one at the table **knew** why he said this to him. ²⁹Some thought
that, because Judas had the money box, Jesus was telling him, "Buy what
we need for **the feast";** or, that he should give something to the poor. ³⁰So,
after receiving the morsel, he immediately went out; and it was night. ³¹When
he had gone out, Jesus said, **"Now** is the Son of man glorified, and in him
God is glorified; ³²if God is glorified in him, God will also glorify him in
himself, and glorify him **at once.**

John creates parallel in (a) and (a′) by the words "feast" (cp. 13:1 with
13:29) and "knew" (cp. 13:1 and 13:28), and by emphasizing in each the
arrival of Jesus' "hour" (cp. 13:1 with 13:31-32). In (b) and (b′), he parallels
the names Judas and Simon Peter and the concept "you are not all clean."
The (c) section deals with the lesson the apostles are to learn from the
footwashing.

Commentary

(a) The hour has arrived (13:1).

The movement of section A (13:1-32) as a whole is governed by the activity of Judas. He is mentioned explicitly in every part except the introduction (cf. vv 11, 13, 21, 30, 31) and at least implicitly in the introduction inasmuch as Jesus realizes that his hour has come to pass from this world
because he knows that Judas is about to betray him (cf. 13:1 and cp. with
13:18-32).

13:1a knew that his hour had come. Foreknowledge of events is
characteristic of the Johannine Jesus. The foreknowledge here is of Judas'
imminent betrayal and the passion and death which that betrayal will
precipitate. It is because Jesus knows that Judas is about to betray him that
he determines to demonstrate by the symbolic footwashing how much he loves
his apostles.

13:1b he loved them to the end. The statement signifies primarily the
depth of Jesus' love, but the chronological aspect of the expression "to the

end" (*eis telos*) can hardly be absent, since the whole section deals with the hour of Jesus' death as an imminent event.

(b) All are clean except one (13:2-11).

13:2-9 during supper. The footwashing seems at first sight to be simply a parable in action demonstrating the import of Jesus' words about serving in the synoptic Gospels: "For the Son of man also came not to be served but to serve, and to give his life as a ransom for many" (Mk 10:45). A closer scrutiny of the text, however, shows that the evangelist intends the foot-washing to be symbolic of Jesus' death. The reference to Judas' betrayal in v 2 points to the imminent death of Jesus. The statement that Jesus acted this way because he knew "he had come from God and was *going* to God" (v 3) also points to his death.

The clearest indication that the evangelist means the footwashing to symbolize Jesus' death is found in Peter's misunderstanding of what Jesus is doing. Peter thinks that Jesus is performing a simple act of humble service such as a slave might perform. He refuses, therefore, to let Jesus wash him. Peter's misunderstanding is confirmed by Jesus' words: "What I am doing you do not know *now*, but *afterward* you will understand" (v 7). "Later," when Jesus has died, Peter will understand correctly what Jesus was symbolizing by the footwashing.

Equally clear is the import of Jesus' statement that the footwashing is so essential that without it Peter will not be able to have a "part" with Jesus. "If I do not wash you, you have no part in me" (v 8). It is through Jesus' death that the disciples will receive the heritage of eternal life with Jesus (cf. 14:1-3; 21:18-19). As Brown puts it:

> In demeaning himself to wash his disciples' feet Jesus is acting out before-hand his humiliation in death, even as Mary acted out beforehand the anoint-ing of his body for burial (xii 1-8). The footwashing is an action of service for others, symbolic of the service he will render in laying down his life for others; that is why Jesus can claim that the footwashing is necessary if the disciples are to share in his heritage (8) and that it will render the disciples clean (10). Naturally the disciples would not understand this symbolism until after "the hour" was over (7).[2]

13:11 he knew who was to betray him. Section (b) is framed by two references to Judas (vv 2 and 11). The reference to the devil in v 2 will be paralleled in section (b') by a reference to Satan (v 27), and the statement "You are not all clean" in v 11 will be paralleled in v 18 by the words "I am not speaking of you all."

Two questions are frequently asked about the footwashing. First, did John intend it to symbolize baptism? Second, did it really happen, i.e., is it historical? Evidence for baptismal symbolism in the footwashing is found in John's use of the verb "to wash" (*louein*), which is used regularly in the

New Testament to refer to baptism (cf. Acts 22:16; 1 Cor 6:11; Eph 5:26; Ti 3:5). Jesus' statement "He who has bathed does not need to wash, except for his feet, but he is clean all over" would seem to point to baptism, since the statement is predicated upon Peter's enthusiastic request that Jesus wash not only his feet but his hands and his head also (13:9-10). The implication is that Peter has misunderstood Jesus by thinking that more washing will increase his lot with Jesus. Jesus' statement, on the contrary, implies that *only* the footwashing is essential because it symbolizes his death and the share his disciples have with him through death-baptism.[3]

Two supporting arguments for baptismal symbolism can be found in Mk 10:32-45 and in the chiastic parallelism of sequence 18 (chs 13–17) with sequence 4 (3:1-21). Mk 10:32-45 associates the idea of Jesus' death and the idea of baptism in a context that is similar to the context of 13:1-32. Mark speaks clearly about the necessity of baptism, in the sense of dying with Jesus, and also of the necessity of following Jesus' example of "serving" others. In Jn 3:5, Jesus says: ". . . unless one is born of *water* and the Spirit, he cannot enter the kingdom of God." Many commentators consider the word "water" to be the interpolation of an ecclesiastical redactor. The chiastic parallelism of 13:1-10 with 3:5, however, suggests that the word "water" in 3:5 comes from the evangelist himself and was in the Gospel from the beginning.

The question of historicity is more difficult. The Synoptics do not mention the footwashing. Some commentators, therefore, consider it a purely symbolic story composed by John and based upon either Lk 22:27 or Mk 10:38-45. This is possible. However, Dodd and others make a good case for the historicity of the main events in John's Gospel.[4] Luke's statement (Lk 22:27) may be a résumé of the Johannine event. And the fact that in Mk 11:12-14 and 9:36-37 Jesus acts out parables similar to those of Jeremiah (Jer 18) and Ezekiel (Ez 4) enhances considerably the possibility that the footwashing is actually an acted-out parable.

(c) The footwashing is an example for the apostles (13:12-17).

13:12 Do you know what I have done to you? Like Peter (vv 6-10), the apostles would not have understood until after the resurrection that by the footwashing Jesus was symbolically acting out beforehand his death and thereby his "love unto the end." The readers of the Gospel, however, would appreciate fully the symbolism and understand what Jesus meant by speaking of the footwashing as an example for the apostles.

13:15 I have given you an example. In speaking of an example, Jesus advances the action by applying the lesson of the footwashing to the apostles. The little instruction on discipleship given here is consequently strongly ecclesial inasmuch as it calls upon the apostles (and all Christians) to love one another "unto the end" as Jesus did. As Jesus says, ". . . you also should do as I have done to you." His words are similar to the instruction on discipleship in Mk 8:31ff, which begins, ". . . the Son of man must suffer many things . . . be rejected . . . , be killed . . ." and continues with the solemn declaration: "If any man would come after me, let him deny himself and take up his cross and follow me."

(b') Jesus singles out the one who is not clean (13:18-27).

13:18 I am not speaking of you all. Subsection (b') looks back to Jesus' words in 13:11: "For he knew who was to betray him; that was why he said, *'You are not all clean.'*" Jesus reveals now the knowledge the evangelist referred to in 13:1 when he said, "Jesus *knew* that his hour had come to depart out of this world . . . ." The implicit references to Judas here in vv 18-19 continue the motif that provides the unity for the whole section. It is Judas' imminent betrayal that will initiate the passion and the manifestation of Jesus' glory (cf. 13:1, 31-32).

13:20 he who receives me receives him who sent me. These words repeat almost word for word (Mt 10:40) what Jesus says to the apostles at the end of the long missionary mandate in Mt 10. They enhance considerably, therefore, the *ecclesial* content of the farewell discourse in John.

13:21 one of you will betray me. That Jesus is speaking about Judas is clear from 13:26-30. The purpose of the dialogue between Peter and the disciple whom Jesus loved is to set the stage for the farewell discourse, which begins properly at 13:33. It does so by showing Jesus' foreknowledge of what Judas was about to do and by showing Judas departing into the night to betray Jesus.

13:27 Satan entered into him. The words form an almost perfect parallel with the words of (b): "when the devil had already put it into the heart of Judas Iscariot" (13:2).

(a') Judas' departure sets in motion the hour of Jesus' death and glorification (13:28-32).

13:28 no one at the table knew why he said this to him. The remark refers to Jesus' words in 13:27, "What you are going to do, do quickly," and focuses the reader's attention on the treacherous act of Judas that will initiate Jesus' hour. Section (a) began with the words "Jesus knew that his hour had come" (13:1); here in section (a'), John shows how well Jesus knew what Judas had in mind.

13:29 Buy what we need for the feast. The reference to the feast (*heortēn*) recalls the beginning of section A, where the evangelist began with the words "Now before the feast (*heortēs*) of the Passover . . ." (13:1). The apostles, as John had already pointed out in 2:22, understood none of these things until Jesus "was raised from the dead." Their surmises here concerning what Jesus said to Judas indicate their complete ignorance of Judas' traitorous intent.

13:30 he immediately went out; and it was night. "It was night" may be a simple chronological comment. More likely John means it to evoke all the memories associated in the Gospel with darkness and light. In sequence 4 (3:1-21), John spoke of Nicodemus coming to Jesus "by night" and of those who loved the darkness and hated the light. Jesus himself had said, "I am the light of the world" (8:12), and had frequently spoken about his time on earth as the time of light before the darkness comes (cf. 11:9; 12:35-36, 46).

13:31-32 Now is the Son of man glorified. Judas' departure into the night to betray Jesus elicits the declaration that the hour has *now* indeed come. For John, the betrayal is the event that initiates the passion. In all that happens to him from this point on, Jesus is in perfect accord with the will of his Father. Such an accord demonstrates his complete union with the Father, and this union is his glory. Jesus can therefore say, *"Now* is the Son of man *glorified."* With these words section A ends, and the time has come for the farewell discourse to begin. From this time on, the apostles will have to learn to cope with the gap that will be created in their lives by Jesus' departure to the Father. There follows, therefore, Jesus' consoling farewell discourse. Properly speaking, section A (13:1-32) is not a part of the farewell discourse but serves as its introduction.

Section B (13:33–14:31): Jesus speaks about his going away, the Counselor, his love commandment, dwelling places in heaven, asking in his name, and his gift of peace.

Properly speaking, the farewell discourse begins at 13:33 with Jesus' words "Little children." The words are addressed to the apostles, but in the ecclesiological context of the whole discourse and in John's mind and intention, the discourse is meant as Jesus' last testament given from heaven and intended for Christians of all times. The ambivalence of many of the statements can be resolved if the reader puts himself or herself in spirit in the midst of the Johannine community at the end of the first century and realizes that some of the statements reflect the past and others reflect the time of the evangelist and his readers. As Dodd says: "The whole series of discourses, including dialogues, monologues, and the prayer in which it culminates, is conceived as taking place within the moment of fulfillment. It is true that the dramatic setting is that of the 'night in which he was betrayed,' with the crucifixion in prospect. Yet in a real sense it is the risen and glorified Christ who speaks."[5]

Parallel structure

(a) Jesus speaks about his **going away,** about **his love commandment,** and about **dwelling places** in heaven (13:33–14:4).

(b) Jesus speaks of himself as "the way, and the truth, and the **life,** and says, **"I am in the Father . . ."** (14:5-14).

(c) Jesus will ask the Father, and he will give another Counselor (14:15-17).

(b′) Jesus says, "You see me as one who has **life** . . . . On that day you will know that **I am in my Father** . . ." (14:18-20).

(a′) Jesus speaks about **his love commandment**, about him and the Father making a **dwelling place** with him who loves, and about his **going away** (14:21-31).

Text

(a)   13:33 Little children, yet a little while I am with you. You will seek me; and as I said to the Jews so now I say to you, 'Where **I am going** you cannot **come**.' ³⁴A new **commandment** I give to you, that you **love** one another; even as I have **loved** you, that you also **love** one another. ³⁵By this all men will know that you are my disciples, if you have **love** for one another."

³⁶**Simon Peter said to him, "Lord, where are you going?" Jesus answered,** "**Where I am going** you cannot follow me now; but you shall follow afterward." ³⁷Peter said to him, "**Lord,** why cannot I follow you now? I will lay down my life for you." ³⁸Jesus answered, "Will you lay down your life for me? Truly, truly, I say to you, the cock will not crow, till you have denied me three times.

14:1 "**Let not your hearts be troubled;** believe in God, believe also in me. ²In my Father's house are many **rooms;** if it were not so, would I have told you that **I go** to prepare a place for you? ³And **when I go** and prepare a place for you, **I will come** again and will take you to myself, that where I am you may be also. ⁴And you know the way where **I am going**."

(b)   ⁵Thomas said to him, "Lord, we do not know where you are going; how can we know the way?" ⁶Jesus said to him, "I am the way, and the truth, and the **life;** no one **comes to the Father,** but by me. ⁷If you had known me, you would have **known** my Father also; henceforth you **know** him and have **seen** him."

⁸Philip said to him, "Lord, show us the Father, and we shall be satisfied." ⁹Jesus said to him, "Have I been with you so long, and yet you do not know me, Philip? He who has **seen** me has **seen** the Father; how can you say, 'Show us the Father'? ¹⁰Do you not believe that **I am in the Father** and the Father in me? The words that I say to you I do not speak on my own authority; but the Father who dwells in me does his works. ¹¹Believe me that **I am in the Father** and the Father in me; or else believe me for the sake of the works themselves.

¹²"Truly, truly, I say to you, he who believes in me will also do the works that I do; and greater works than these will he do, because I go to the Father. ¹³Whatever you ask in my name, I will do it, that the Father may be glorified in the Son; ¹⁴if you ask anything in my name, I will do it.

(c)   ¹⁵"If you love me, you will keep my commandments. ¹⁶And I will pray the Father, and he will give you another Counselor, to be with you for ever, ¹⁷even the Spirit of truth, whom the world cannot receive, because it neither sees him nor knows him; you know him, for he dwells with you, and will be in you.

(b′)   ¹⁸"I will not leave you desolate; I will **come** to you. ¹⁹Yet a little while, and the world will **see me** no more, but you will **see me;** because I **live,** you will **live** also. [20]In that day you will **know** that **I am in my Father,** and you in me, and I in you.

(a')   [21]"He who has my **commandments** and keeps them, he it is who **loves** me; and he who **loves** me will be **loved** by my Father, and I will **love** him and manifest myself to him." [22]**Judas (not Iscariot) said to him,** "Lord, how is it that you will manifest yourself to us, and not to the world?" [23]**Jesus answered** him, "If a man **loves** me, he will keep my word, and my Father will **love** him, and we will **come to him** and make our **home** with him. [24]He who does not **love** me does not keep my words; and the word which you hear is not mine but the Father's who sent me.

[25]"These things I have spoken to you, while I am still with you. [26]But the Counselor, the Holy Spirit, whom the Father will send in my name, he will teach you all things, and bring to your remembrance all that I have said to you. [27]Peace I leave with you; my peace I give to you; not as the world gives do I give to you. **Let not your hearts be troubled,** neither let them be afraid. [28]You heard me say to you, '**I go away,** and **I will come to you.**' If you **loved** me, you would have rejoiced, because **I go** to the Father; for the Father is greater than I. [29]And now I have told you before it takes place, so that when it does take place, you may believe. [30]I will no longer talk much with you, for the ruler of this world is **coming.** He has no power over me; [31]but I do as the Father has commanded me, so that the world may know that I **love** the Father. Rise, **let us go** hence."

Parallelism is created in (a) and (a') by repetition of the words "going away," "commandment(s)," "rooms," "loved," and "let not your hearts be troubled." In (b) and (b'), John creates parallelism by repeating the words "I am in the Father." Section (c) deals with the Counselor.

Commentary

(a) Jesus speaks about his going away, about his love commandment, and about dwelling places in heaven (13:33–14:4).

13:33 Little children. This endearing form of address is used seven times in 1 Jn, once in a slightly different form in Mk 10:24, but only here in John's Gospel. It is particularly apt for a Passover meal, at which the father of the family explains the significance and symbolism of the meal in relation to the exodus, the going out of captivity in Egypt to the freedom of the promised land. The "little while" the disciples will seek but not find Jesus is different from the little while Jesus spoke about to the Jews (cf. 7:33 and 8:21). The words are to prepare the disciples for Jesus' departure, but, unlike the Jews, they will see Jesus again. They cannot follow him now, but they will follow and be with him later.

13:34 A new commandment. Jesus' announcement that he is going away, i.e., that he is about to die and go to the Father, is followed by his giving of the new commandment—a sequence of ideas that seems abrupt until one recollects that the same sequence had already been dealt with in the symbolic footwashing, which was introduced with the words ". . . when Jesus knew that his hour had come to depart out of this world to the Father, having loved his own who were in the world, he loved them to the end. And during supper . . . ." (13:1-2). In the new commandment, Jesus repeats more explicitly what he meant when he followed the footwashing with the words "For I have given you an *example,* that you also should do as I have done to you" (13:15).[6] In substance, what Jesus says amounts to this: "Such as my love has been for you (i.e., love unto the end, even to death), so must your love be for one another." The meaning is even more clearly expressed in 15:12, where Jesus follows the love command, "This is my commandment, that you love one another *as I have loved you,"* with the words "Greater love has no man than this, that a man lay down his life for his friends" (15:13).

The new commandment is new not only in content—it is love unto death, whereas the old love command of Lv 19:18, "You shall love your neighbor as yourself," apparently never demanded so extreme a love—but new as the commandment of the new covenant foretold by Jeremiah (Jer 31:31ff). In Johannine theology, it is not so much love for all as for the covenanted brethren, who have been born from on high through the death of Jesus and through having been "begotten of water and Spirit" (3:5). Such a love unto death will, of course, bring the brethren into perfect conformity with Jesus, so that Jesus can say, "By this all men will know that you are my disciples, if you have love for one another" (13:35). The effect of this unity in love on the world is expressed in 17:23: "I in them and thou in me, that they may become perfectly one, so that the world may know that thou hast sent me and hast loved them even as thou hast loved me."

13:36 Simon Peter said to him. The dialogue with Peter constitutes a subtle commentary on the love commandment. For his readers, who know well Peter's denial of Jesus, John's little dialogue is tinged with pathos and irony. With irony, because the Peter who says "Lord, why cannot I follow you now? I will lay down my life for you" (v 37) will, within twenty-four hours, deny Jesus three times. With pathos, because what Peter does not do *now,* namely, show his love for Jesus unto the end, he will do later when, as an old man, he will be crucified during Nero's persecution (cf. 21:18-20).

John's use of the misunderstanding technique is here used with extraordinary subtlety. When Jesus says, "Where I am going you cannot follow me *now . . . ,"* he means that he is going to his death imminently. Peter, if he had understood how close the agony and death were, would perhaps not have been so brash as to say, "Lord, why cannot I follow you now? I will lay down my life for you." Jesus' question "Will you lay down your life for me?" (v 38) is not a denial of what Peter actually would eventually do (cf. 21:18-19), but a wry Johannine observation on how easy it is to talk the love commandment and how difficult it is to live it. Jesus' apparent denial of the apostles' belief in him in 16:31ff should be interpreted in the same way. The two episodes (13:36-38 and 16:29-33), the one in section B and the other in section B′, are very sophisticated parallels.

14:2 In my Father's house are many rooms. In 14:1-4, Jesus consoles his apostles by promising to provide dwelling places with him in heaven, a promise that is meant to comfort them and encourage them to take up their mission to the world after Jesus' departure to the Father (cf. the parallel in 14:23).

14:3b I will come again. These words are best interpreted as a reference to the parousia, or second coming, as in Paul and the Synoptics, rather than as a reference to the Counselor who will be mentioned later as a further source of help and consolation (cf. 14:15-18, 25-27).

(b) Jesus speaks of himself as "the way, and the truth, and the life, and says "I am in the Father . . ." (14:5-14).

14:5 Thomas said to him, ". . . how can we know the way?" Just as the first exchange between Jesus and Peter (13:36-38) hinged on Peter's misunderstanding of Jesus' words "Where I am going, you cannot follow me now," so his second exchange with Thomas (14:5ff), his third exchange with Philip (14:8ff), and his fourth exchange with Judas (14:22ff) follow upon misunderstandings. In each case the misunderstanding allows Jesus to explain the deeper meaning of his double-meaning original statement.

Jesus' double-meaning declaration in 14:4, "And you know the way where I am going," leads Thomas to think that Jesus is speaking about a road or a direction. His reply that he does not know the way allows Jesus to explain the deeper meaning of his words. He means that since Thomas knows *him,* he knows the way. He explains then why he is the way. He is the "way, and the truth, and the life," and therefore anyone who comes to the Father comes through Jesus. As Barrett says: ". . . the way which he himself is now about to take is the road which his followers must also tread. He himself goes to the Father by way of crucifixion and resurrection; in future he is the means by which Christians die and rise."[7]

There are many theories about the relationship of the words "way," "truth," and "life," but since the ensuing dialogue deals primarily with the "way," it seems best to interpret this as the primary term, and "truth" and "life" as qualifiers. Equivalently, Jesus says, "I am the true *way* to life." Jesus' way to the Father is through the cross. It is the true way because Jesus is the truth, i.e., the source of revelation. It is the way to life because Jesus is the source of eternal life.

The best commentary on these words are Jesus' statements in 14:6b: "No one comes to the Father, but by me," and 10:9: "I am the door; if any one enters by me, he will be saved, and will go in and out and find pasture." Jesus is the way to eternal life because, as he said in 10:10, "I came that they may have life, and have it abundantly." The inner logic that governs everything from 13:33 on is concerned with Jesus' going away to the Father. Since the apostles are to follow him, they must know the way. But since Jesus' way to the Father is through the cross, so the apostles' way must be the way of Jesus.

14:8 Philip said to him. Philip's request is based upon his misunderstanding of Jesus' words in 14:7: "If you had known me, you would have known my Father also," just as Thomas' misunderstanding in 14:5 was based upon Jesus' words in 14:4.

14:8-9 Philip said to him, "Lord, show us the Father." Philip's misunderstanding of Jesus' words in 14:7 gives Jesus the opportunity in vv 9-10 to explain the unity of Father and Son that makes seeing the Son the same as seeing the Father. Possibly Philip was thinking of a theophany such as those seen by Moses and Elijah, but more likely his request is simply John's way of setting the stage for Jesus' explanation of his union with the Father.

14:10 Do you not believe that I am in the Father . . . ? In seeing Jesus, Philip and the others see the Father. The unity emphasized here is a unity in words and works (v 10b). It is at the very least the union of agent and sender as expressed in the rabbinic principle: "An agent is like the one who sent him." As such, the agent represents the sender and is looked upon as one with the sender. A similar thought is expressed in 10:37-38: "If I am not doing the *works* of my Father, then do not believe me; but if I do them, even though you do not believe me, believe the *works,* that you may know and understand that *the Father is in me* and I am in the Father." While a unity in nature between Son and Father is not emphasized, it is certainly implicit (cf. 1:1; 5:16-18; 8:58; 10:30, 38; 20:28-30).

14:11 or else believe me for the sake of the works themselves. Jesus adds to his personal call to belief (v 11a) a call to believe in his works. One who understands his works as signs will see what the signs reveal, namely, that the signs-works are the mutual work of the united Father and Son.

14:12 and greater works than these will he do. According to ch 17, Jesus accomplishes his work in an effective sense when he brings his apostles to believe that he has been sent by the Father (cf. 17:6-8). The work that the apostles will accomplish is to bring others to believe as they believe (cf. 17:18-23). By the time John wrote his Gospel at the end of the first century, many thousands had come to believe in Jesus; thus Jesus can say of an apostle who believes in him and brings others to believe in him, "And greater works than these will he do." In brief, Jesus is speaking here of the work of the apostles and the Church in bringing about the realization of the reign of God in the world—a reign that is effectively realized as more and more individuals come to believe in Jesus (cf. 15:5, where Jesus speaks of those in union with him bearing "much fruit").

14:13-14 Whatever you ask in my name. The prayer theme encapsulated in these words is traditional (cf. Mt 7:7-8; 18:19; 21:22; Mk 11:24; Lk 11:9).

In John, the theme is repeated in 15:7, 16; 16:23-24. In its present context, as Brown points out, ". . . the theme of asking 'in my name' in 14:13-14 continues and develops the indwelling motif of 10-11: because the Christian is in union with Jesus and Jesus is in union with the Father, there can be no doubt that the Christian's requests will be granted."[8]

(c) Jesus will ask the Father, and he will give another Counselor (14:15-17).

14:15-17 another Counselor. Up to this point, Jesus has consoled his apostles by telling them that he is going to prepare a place for them (14:23) and by promising to do for them whatever they ask in his name (14:13-14). The sending of the Counselor is meant as a further source of consolation and help. The meaning of "Counselor" in John's Gospel is best understood by synthesizing what is said about the Counselor in 14:1-17, 26; 15:26-27; 16:11-14. According to these texts, the Counselor has the following characteristics: (a) he comes only when Jesus departs; (b) he remains with and instructs the disciples; (c) he is a spokesman for them in time of trial; (d) he is a witness to Jesus and continues Jesus' work as Joshua continued the work of Moses; (e) he is like Jesus in that he will come as Jesus will come, is known by the disciples as Jesus is known by the disciples, is opposed to the world in the same way Jesus is opposed to the world, and is *another* Counselor in the sense that Jesus himself is a Counselor. In brief, the Counselor is everything Jesus is and by his coming will fill the gap caused by Jesus' departure to the Father.[9]

(b') Jesus says, "You see me as one who has life. . . . On that day you will know that I am in my Father . . ." (14:18-20).

This part of section B picks up, but does not develop, two ideas expressed in 14:5-14: first, the theme of life (cf. 14:6); second, the theme of the indwelling (cf. 14:9-11).[10]

14:18 I will not leave you desolate; I will come to you. The Greek text reads, "I will not leave you *orphans,"* and "orphans" makes excellent sense in the context of Jesus' opening words in 13:33: "Little children. . . ." Dying rabbis spoke in a similar fashion to their mournful disciples. The promise "I will come to you," when taken in conjunction with what is said in 14:19a, refers primarily to the resurrection appearances of Jesus rather than to the parousia. It probably also refers to Jesus' abiding indwelling presence in his disciples.

14:19a the world will see me no more, but you will see me. The fact that the world will not see Jesus rules out a reference to the parousia in 14:18 and also here. Theoretically, all will see Jesus at the parousia. The promise that the disciples "will see" Jesus will be fulfilled in the resurrection (chs 20–21) and in another way in the indwelling.

14:19b   because I live, you will live also. Spoken from the vantage point of the resurrection, Jesus reminds his disciples in another way of what he had said in 14:6: "I am the way, and the truth, and the *life*"—i.e., I am the true way to eternal life. The theme of life through Jesus had already been expressed in 3:14-15; 6:39-40, 51-58; 11:23-26. The life referred to here is not specified as future resurrection life or present realized eschatological life. In either case, it is associated through the words "you will see me" (14:19a) with Jesus' resurrection.

14:20   In that day you will know that I am in my Father. But for the addition of the words "and you in me," Jesus repeats what he said in 14:10-11. The "you in me" is fittingly added in view of the promise in 14:19a: "Because I live, you will live also." The heart of the indwelling consists in a sharing with Jesus of his resurrection life in union with the Father (cf. 17:21-24).

(a′) Jesus speaks about his love commandment, about him and the Father making a dwelling place with him who loves, and about his going away (14:21-31).

14:21   He who has my commandments and keeps them.[11] The inclusion-conclusion of section B begins with the realistic observation that only the person who keeps, i.e., observes, Jesus' commandments is the one who truly loves him. It will end with a similarly realistic observation in 14:31, when Jesus says of himself, ". . . but I *do* as the Father has commanded me, so that the world may know that I love the Father."

14:22   Lord, how is it that you will manifest yourself to us, and not to the world? Judas, like Peter (13:37), Thomas (14:7), and Philip (14:8), has misunderstood Jesus. In this case, the misunderstood words are "manifest myself" in 14:21. Jesus is speaking about a manifestation through indwelling. Judas is thinking of the manifestation of Jesus at his second coming and cannot understand, therefore, why Jesus would manifest himself to his disciples only and not also to the whole world. This gives Jesus the opportunity to further explain the indwelling, which he does in vv 23-24.

14:23   If a man loves me, he will keep my word. Jesus continues the theme of realistic love already broached in v 21. Keeping Jesus' words is the equivalent in biblical terms of *doing* what he has commanded. After announcing his new commandment of love in 13:34-35, Jesus went on to speak of going to prepare rooms (*monai*) for his disciples in his Father's heavenly house; the context of "going away" and "preparing rooms" looked entirely to the future. Here in v 23, the process is subtly changed from future to realized eschatology. Jesus says, ". . . we *will come to him* and make *our home (monēn) with him.*" He is speaking about the indwelling.

14:24   He who does not love me does not keep my words. Jesus' words are the equivalent of his commandment of love. His word, i.e., his love commandment, comes from his Father (cf. 3:16 and 4:34 for implicit referrals of the love command to the Father).

14:26   The Counselor . . . will teach you all things. Jesus' insistence on the love command has run throughout section B (cf. 13:34-35; 14:15, 21, 23, 24). How difficult it was to really understand and live the love command had been brought out indirectly through Peter's misunderstanding of the foot-washing (13:6-10) and his brash declaration "Lord, why cannot I follow you now? I will lay down my life for you" (13:37). Here Jesus promises that the Counselor will teach them the meaning of all things. In the context, "all things" would certainly refer to the love commandment. In a more general sense, "all things" would refer to Jesus' overall teaching. After the resurrection and the coming of the Counselor (cf. 20:22-23), many things that Jesus said and did would become clear in a way they had never been during the days of his mortal life (cf. Jn 2:21-22; 12:16; Lk 24:25-28, 44-45).

14:27   Peace I leave with you. Peace is not merely the absence of war or psychological tension, but the peace that goes with the indwelling, a peace equivalent to salvation, to all the things a person could desire. It is a peace that embraces the light, truth, joy, and eternal life mentioned elsewhere in the Gospel. It is the covenant peace of Ez 37:26, "I will make a covenant of peace with them," and is equivalently the central gift of the new covenant, a gift of realized eschatology, since the Christian who possesses this gift already possesses eternal life even during this life (cf. Jn 11:25-26).

14:28a   You heard me say to you, "I go away." These words return the reader's mind to the beginning of section B (cf. 13:33c, 36; 14:2-3) and signal the end of the first part of the farewell discourse.

14:28b   If you loved me, you would have rejoiced. It is not that they do not love him but that they do not understand that his going away, even though it is through death, is his going away to the Father who will glorify him. It is for this reason that they would and should rejoice.

14:28c   for the Father is greater than I. The statement has nothing directly to do with ontological relations. It is best understood in the biblical sense that the sender is greater than the one sent. Its logic is the same as that of 13:16: "Truly, truly, I say to you, a servant is not greater than his master; nor is he who is sent greater than he who sent him." When Jesus has completed the work for which he was sent, he will return to the Father and be as he was before, and for this reason the disciples should rejoice.

14:30   the ruler of this world is coming. Jesus uses the customary mythological terminology of his contemporaries in referring to the devil as the ruler of this world. Actually, the more immediate reference would be to Judas, into whom Satan had entered (cf. 13:2, 27) and whose arrival in the garden to betray Jesus was imminent (cf. 18:1ff).

14:31   I do as the Father has commanded me. By freely accepting his passion and death, Jesus fulfills the will of the Father (cf. 4:34; 17:5; 19:30) and thus demonstrates to the world his love for the Father. In 17:22-23, a similarly realistic test of the Church's love and unity will be stipulated as the means whereby the world will know that the Father sent Jesus and loves the Church as he loved Jesus.

14:31b Rise, let us go hence. These words seem to signal the end of the farewell address, and many commentators use them to argue that what follows in chs 15-17 must be the work of a later redactor. This may be so, since 14:31b leads so smoothly into the opening of the passion account in 18:1ff. However, the least that can be said for such a redactor is that he was not the least bit concerned with narrative continuity, since he could easily have eliminated these words.

A better explanation is that the author, who composed his Gospel according to the laws of parallelism, was not concerned with narrative continuity here any more than elsewhere in his Gospel. In 12:36, the evangelist stated, "When Jesus had said this, he departed and hid himself from them." Without the least embarrassment, however, the same evangelist has Jesus continue speaking in 12:44-50. Similarly, in 2:13-25, at the very beginning of Jesus' ministry, the evangelist has Jesus cleanse the temple. There seems to be little doubt that the evangelist and his readers knew that this event took place toward the end of Jesus' life. For those who read the Gospel according to the laws of narrative, the narrative is clearly out of place; for those who read it according to the laws of gradational, introverted parallelism, it is just as clearly in place, i.e., in chiastic parallelism with the passion story in sequence 19, the chiastic parallel of sequence 3.

Section C (15:1-25): The true vine and the false vine

The structure of 15:1-25 is difficult to determine. Without explicitly breaking it down in an *abcb'a'* pattern, Brown nevertheless divides the text into five parts—(a) 1-6; (b) 7-10; (c) 11; (b') 12-17; (a') 18-25—and says: "It is always difficult to be sure that the discovery of such an elaborate chiastic structure does not reflect more of the ingenuity of the investigator than of the intention of the Johannine writer. . . . Nevertheless, here there are too many correspondences to be coincidental."[12] Gerhard structures the section as follows: (a) 1-8; (b) 9-12; (c) 13; (b') 14-17; (a') 18-25, but in this case Brown's structure seems superior to Gerhard's.

Parallel structure

> (a) The **true** vine, i.e., the true Israel (15:1-6)
> (b) This is **my commandment,** that you **love** one another (15:7-10).
> (c) These things I have spoken to you, that my joy may be in you (15:11).
> (b') This **I command you,** to **love** one another (15:12-17).
> (a') The **false** vine, i.e., the synagogue (15:18-25)

Text

(a)   15:1 "I am **the true vine,** and **my Father** is the vinedresser. [2]Every branch of mine that bears no fruit, he takes away, and every branch that does bear fruit **he prunes,** that it may bear more fruit. [3]You are already made clean by **the word** which I have spoken to you. [4]Abide in me, and I in you. As the branch cannot bear fruit by itself, unless it abides in **the vine,** neither can you, unless you abide in me. [5]I am **the vine,** you are the branches. He who abides in me, and I in him, he it is that bears much fruit, for apart from me you can do nothing. [6]If a man does not abide in me, he is cast forth as a branch and withers; and the branches are gathered, thrown into the fire and burned.

(b)   [7]"If you **abide** in me, and my words **abide** in you, **ask whatever you will,** and it shall be done for you. [8]By this **my Father** is glorified, that you **bear much fruit,** and so prove to be my disciples. [9]As the Father has **loved** me, so have I **loved** you; **abide** in my **love.** [10]If you keep **my commandments,** you will **abide** in my **love,** just as I have kept my Father's **commandments** and **abide** in his **love.**

(c)   [11]"These things I have spoken to you, that my joy may be in you, and that your joy may be full.

(b′)   [12]"This is **my commandment,** that you **love** one another as I have **loved** you. [13]Greater **love** has no man than this, that a man lay down his life for his friends. [14]You are my friends if you do what I **command** you. [15]No longer do I call you servants, for the servant does not know what his master is doing; but I have called you friends, for all that I have heard from **my Father** I have made known to you. [16]You did not choose me, but I chose you and appointed you that you should go and **bear fruit** and that your **fruit** should **abide;** so that **whatever you ask** the Father in my name, he may give it to you. [17]This I command you, to **love** one another.

(a′)   [18]"If **the world** hates you, know that it has hated me before it hated you. [19]If you were of **the world, the world** would love its own; but because you are not of **the world,** but I chose you out of **the world,** therefore **the world** hates you. [20]Remember **the word** that I said to you, 'A servant is not greater than his master.' If **they** persecuted me, **they** will **persecute** you; if **they** kept **my word, they** will keep yours also. [21]But all this **they** will do to you on my account, because **they** do not know him who sent me. [22]If I had not come and spoken to them, **they** would not have sin; but now **they** have no excuse for their sin. [23]He who hates me hates **my Father** also. [24]If I had not done **among them** the works which no one else did, **they** would not have sin; but now **they** have seen and hated both me and **my Father.** [25]It is to fulfil **the word** that is written in **their** law, **'They** hated me without a cause.'

John creates antithetic parallelism in (a) and (a′) by contrasting the true vine, the Church, in (a) with the false vine, the synagogue, which persecutes the Church in (a′). In (b) and (b′), John creates parallelism by repeating in each the love command and the promise that anything the disciples ask in Jesus' name they will receive (cf. vv 7 and 16). The center (c) deals with the joy of the disciples and supplies the hinge, which is flanked on either side by Jesus' words about the love command.

John creates conceptual parallelism by contrasting the true vine in (a) with the world, which here represents the synagogue, the false Israel, in (a'); and by paralleling the concept of pruning in v 2 of (a) with persecution in vv 20-21 of (a'). In each there recurs the verbal parallel, "the word" (cf. vv 3, 20-25).

In (b) and (b'), he repeats the verbal parallels "whatever you ask," "bear fruit," "commandments," "love as I have loved you." In the center, he speaks about joy.

Commentary

(a) The true vine, i.e., the true Israel (15:1-6)

15:1 I am the true vine. In the Old Testament, Israel is symbolized both by the vineyard (cf. Is 5:1-7; 27:2-6; Jer 12:10) and by the vine (cf. Ez 15:1-6; 17:5-10; Ps 80:9, 13). In the New Testament, the Synoptics carry over this symbolism to the distinction between the Church, the true Israel, and the synagogue, the false Israel (cf. Mt 20:1-16; 21:33-43; Mk 12:1-12; Lk 20:9-19). Here, therefore, the key word is "true." The true Israel consists of those united with Jesus, the vine, and with the Father, the vinedresser, as opposed to the false Israel, *the world,* which hates both Jesus and the Father (cf. 15:22-25). The antithetic parallelism of vv 1-6 (a) with vv 18-25 (a') supports a strong interpretation of the word "true" as opposed to "false."[13]

15:2 Every branch. Both in the Old (Is 5:4) and in the New Testament (Mt 21:43), an element central to the allegory of the vineyard is the bearing of fruit (the theme of response). Here the Father's intention is that those united with Jesus should bear fruit. How they will do so is explained in vv 4-6, 7-10, and 12-17, where Jesus speaks about abiding in him and loving "as I have loved you" (v 12) and where he defines that love as "no greater love than this, that a man lay down his life for his friends" (v 13).

15:3 You are already made clean by the word. "Made clean" is a reference back to the footwashing in 13:4-11 (especially vv 10-11), symbolic of Jesus' death and also of baptism, a sharing in Jesus' death that enables the disciples to be reborn through water and the Spirit (cf. 3:5). That this is accomplished "by the word," i.e., Jesus' teaching, is based upon what is presupposed in the whole of the farewell discourse, namely, that the apostles have believed Jesus' "word" (message) that he was sent by the Father (cf. 16:29-32; 17:6-8).

15:4-5 Abide in me. This allegorical motif based on the union of vine and branches is expressed most succinctly in the words "apart from me you can do nothing" (cf. Jn 1:3; 21:4-6; and 2 Cor 3:5). The word "abide" (*menein*) occurs ten times in vv 4-10 and recalls the similar use of the verb in the Eucharistic discourse of 6:32-58 (cf. 6:56). This abiding in Jesus produces "much fruit" (v 5) because it is an abiding in Jesus' sacrificial love unto death (cf. vv 7-10).

15:6 If a man does not abide in me. Jesus and those in union with him constitute the true Israel. Those who elect not to abide in him constitute the false Israel. In the context of 15:1-25, those who elect not to abide in Jesus are described in vv 18-25 (a'). They are those who persecute both Jesus and his apostles, who refuse to accept either the word or the works of Jesus (v 19), and who have hated Jesus and his Father, thereby fulfilling the word "written in *their* law, 'They hated me without a cause' " (vv 23-25).

The antithetic parallelism of v 6 (a) with vv 18-25 (a') suggests strongly that Jesus is speaking of the false Israel, the synagogue, in both places. It may be objected that the branches mentioned in v 6 were once united to Jesus the vine and that this would not be true of the synagogue. But the overall allegory deals with the vine as the true Israel. Until Jesus came, the synagogue represented the true Israel. It was in refusing to accept Jesus that they separated themselves from the true Israel, the vine.

(b) This is my commandment, that you love one another (15:7-10).

15:7a If you abide in me. Verses 7-17, as Brown says, "unfold the implications of the indwelling that was the theme of the *mashal* in 1-6."[14] The indwelling is constituted by a union with Jesus and the Father and is manifested in the same way that the Father manifested his love for the world, namely, by giving to death his only Son (cf. 3:16), and in the same way that the Son manifested his love "unto the end" (cf. 13:1), namely, by laying down his life for those he loved. In essence, Jesus says here what he said in 13:34-35: "A new commandment I give to you, that you love one another; *even as I have loved you,* that you also love one another. *By this* all men will know that you are *my disciples,* if you have love for one another."

15:7b-8   ask whatever you will. Whoever asks to grow in that sacrificial love that constitutes the indwelling is assured that the request will be granted precisely because it is through such love that the Father is glorified and the recipients bear much fruit. The thought here is similar to those other words on discipleship in 12:24: ". . . unless a grain of wheat falls into the earth and dies, it remains alone; but *if it dies,* it *bears much fruit."* There, Jesus was speaking directly about his own imminent death; here, he speaks about his followers who prove they are his disciples by doing for others what Jesus has done for all. In vv 16-17, the parallel of vv 7-8, the same is said in another way and, in 17:20-23, in still another way.

15:9-10   As the Father has loved me. These two verses provide a perfect summary of John's basic theology: the Father loves the Son, the Son loves his apostles, his apostles and disciples love one another—thus the circle is completed and all abide in a mutual indwelling love, flowing from the Father through the Son and manifested in Christians' love unto death for one another (cf. 3:16; 4:34).

(c) These things I have spoken to you, that my joy may be in you (15:11).

15:11a These things. Presumably "these things" are what Jesus has said about the abiding, fruit-bearing union of vine and branches. Fruit-bearing is only another way of speaking about the salvific work of Jesus expressed most succinctly in 3:16: "For God so loved the world that he gave his only Son, that whoever believes in him *should not perish but have eternal life.*" From such fruit-bearing there arises the mutual joy of Father, Son, and disciples.

15:11b joy. Abiding in Jesus' and the Father's love and bearing fruit is the source of Jesus' joy and also the joy of the disciples (cf. 13:12-17). Brown notes "how often in the gospel joy is associated with the saving work of Jesus" (cf. 3:29, the joy of the Baptist; 4:36, the joy of the sower and the reaper; 8:56, the joy of Abraham; 14:28, the joy of the apostles because Jesus goes to the Father).[15]

(b′) This I command you, to love one another (15:12-17).

15:12-13 my commandment. "My commandment" parallels "my commandments" in v 10 inasmuch as the love commandment is the summary and heart of all that Jesus commands (cf. 13:34). It is defined as a commandment of love unto death for others in v 13: ". . . that a man lay down his life for his friends." Thus, it is not simply an emotional love but a demonstrative love (cf. 1 Jn 3:16: *"By this we know love,* that he laid down his life for us; and we ought to lay down our lives for the brethren"; and Rom 5:8: "But God *shows* his love for us in that while we were yet sinners, Christ died for us").

15:14-15 friends. Friends, in Johannine terminology, are those who live by the love commandment as defined in v 13. As the parallel in v 10 puts it, "If you keep my commandments, you will abide in my love." The emphasis is on doing rather than on knowing. In v 16, there is a further explanation of what it is that makes one a friend of Jesus.

15:15 servants. Servants do what they are commanded because they are servants. Friends are different. A friend *knows* what the master or mistress is doing and commanding because the master or mistress confides in him/her. As Hoskyns says: "The initiative belonged to and remained with the Son. He selected the few, and initiated them into the mystery of His death, in order that they might go forth, and declare the truth to the world (vi. 70; Luke vi. 13)."[16] Friends know that Jesus' love unto death is a manifestation of the Father's love for them and for the world. This is what is new about Jesus' love and what is equally true about his love command. Love unto the end is like the Father's love for the world manifested by Jesus in his death.

15:16 You did not choose me. In the context of the farewell discourse, these words are directed to the apostles but have in view all Christians. The apostles are the first of Jesus' friends, sent by him in a special way (cf. 6:70; 13:12-18; 17:18-20; see also Mt 28:18-20; Lk 10:3). At the same time, the apostles are to be models of what all Christians should be. **You should go and bear fruit.** The apostles continue the salvific mission of Jesus, and therefore whatever they ask the Father in Jesus' name the Father will grant. The Father will respond to their requests because they do the work for which the Father "gave" his only Son (cf. 3:16; 4:34). As Hoskyns so well expresses it, ". . . prayer for the extension of the Church is the one petition proper to Christians."[17]

(a') The false vine, i.e., the synagogue (15:18-25)

15:18a If the world hates you. The nature of the Church has been defined by its union in self-sacrificing love with Jesus and the Father. That, in short, is the meaning of the allegory of the vine, the vinedresser, and the branches in vv 1-5 and the meaning of the discourse on the love commandment in vv 7-10 and 11-17. As the Church is defined by love, so the world is defined by hatred. The gist of vv 18-25 has already been expressed in another way in the discourse to Nicodemus (cf. 3:17-21), where Jesus speaks of the world loving the darkness and hating the light (cf. 1 Jn 3:11-15, where the world is similarly described).

15:18b know that it has hated me before it hated you. With these words, there begins the identification of the world as the synagogue. It is not so much the world in general that has hated Jesus in John's Gospel, but the synagogue (cf. 3:19-20; 7:7; 8:23-26; 16:1-3). According to 3:16, God so loved the world that he gave his only Son. But there are those in the world who will not accept God's only Son, and foremost among these are those of the synagogue who oppose, hate, and persecute the Church as they opposed, hated, and persecuted Jesus. They are that segment of the world that loves the darkness and hates the light, and consequently refuses to accept either Jesus or those whom he has sent (cf. 3:1-20).[18]

15:19 If you were of the world. In Johannine categories, there are no in-betweens—one either accepts Jesus or one does not, either loves the light and hates the darkness or hates the light and loves the darkness. Those who accept Jesus can no longer belong to the world, which by definition does not accept Jesus. Thus, here and in other places in the Gospel (cf. 3:18-20; 7:7; 17:6, 9, 14-16, 25; 18:36), the world is not coterminous with all human beings as in 3:16-17; 17:18, 21, 23; 18:37, but only with that part of humanity, exemplified in a particularly characteristic way by the synagogue enemies of Jesus and the Church, who adamantly refuse to come to the light and accept Jesus as the one sent by the Father. The Jews "belong to this world" (8:23).

15:20 Remember the word that I said to you, 'A servant . . . .' The reference is to 13:16 and is similar to Mt 10:24-25: "A disciple is not above his teacher, nor a servant above his master . . . . If they have called the master of the house Beelzebul, how much more will they malign those of his household." In both Matthew and John (v 20b), the "they," i.e., the persecutors, refers to the Church's synagogue enemies at the end of the first century. **If they kept my word** (v 20c) does not mean they actually kept Jesus' word, but rather "to the extent that they kept my word (which they did not keep at all), they will keep yours also."

15:21-24 because they do not know him who sent me. The charges against the Jews in these verses sum up what has been said many times in the Gospel (cf. 3:2; 5:36-40; 7:28-29; 8:19, 24, 42-43; 9:39-41; 10:25-26; 11:10-11; 12:37-50; 16:8-11; 17:25).

15:25 It is to fulfil the word that is written in their law. The reference is to either Ps 69:5 (also quoted in Jn 2:19 and 19:28-30) or to Ps 35:19. The critical words, however, are "in their law." These words show clearly that the people of the "world" envisioned in vv 18-25 are not just people in general but the people of the "law," i.e., the synagogue, who here are condemned out of their own scriptures.

One cannot close a commentary on 15:1-25 without recalling the great Eucharistic discourse in 6:22-71. Those who rejected Jesus in 6:22ff (6:41, 52, 60, 66, 70, 71), i.e., the Jews, the unbelieving disciples, and Judas, re-appear here as the branches that have been cast off. Just as they refused to eat Jesus' flesh and drink his blood and thus "abide in him," so here they are those who will not "abide" in the vine. Just as the Father was the one who gave the true bread from heaven in ch 6 (cf. 6:27, 32), so here the Father is the one who gives the true vine. Just as Jesus said, "I am the true bread" (cf. 6:32, 35, 41, 48, 51), so here he says, "I am the true vine." In each case, the word "true" (*alēthinē*) is the same. The imagery of the vine at the Last Supper suggests the Eucharist, and the emphasis on abiding in Jesus suggests the same.

Section B' (15:26–16:33): Jesus speaks about his going away, the Counselor, asking in his name, and his gift of peace.

Commentators agree that the dominant themes of section B (13:33–14:31), namely, the Counselor, Jesus' going away, asking in Jesus' name, and his gift of peace, recur in section B'. The recurrence is usually explained as the work of an editor or redactor who interpolated the material in 15:26–16:33 into the Gospel in a later edition of an earlier Johannine work. Recognition of the chiastic parallelism governing the five sections of the discourse, however, makes it far more probable that all five sections belonged to the original Gospel and formed a unity from the beginning.[19]

Parallel structure

(a) **The time** of persecution **is coming** (15:26–16:4).

(b) I am **going to him who sent me** (16:5-15).
(c) A little while, and you will see me no more (16:16-22).
(b′) I am leaving the world and **going to the Father** (16:23-30).
(a′) **The time** of persecution **is coming** (16:31-33).

Text

(a)   15:26 But when the Counselor comes, whom I shall send to you from **the Father,** even the Spirit of truth, who proceeds from **the Father,** he will bear witness to me; ²⁷and you also are witnesses, because you have been with me from the beginning. 16:1 **I have said all this to you** to keep you from falling away. ²They **will put you out of the synagogues;** indeed, **the hour is coming** when whoever **kills you** will think he is offering service to God. ³And they will do this because they have not known **the Father,** nor me. ⁴**But I have said these things to you,** that **when their hour comes** you may remember that I told you of them.

(b)   ⁵"But now **I am going** to him who sent me; **yet none of you asks me, 'Where are you going?'** ⁶But because I have said these things to you, sorrow has filled your hearts. ⁷Nevertheless I tell you the truth: it is to your advantage that **I go away,** for **if I do not go away,** the Counselor will not come to you; but **if I go,** I will send him to you. ⁸And when he comes, he will convince the world of sin and of righteousness and of judgment: ⁹of sin, because they do not believe in me; ¹⁰of righteousness, because **I go to the Father,** and you will see me no more; ¹¹of judgment, because the ruler of this world is judged.

¹²"I have yet many things to say to you, but you cannot bear them now. ¹³When the Spirit of truth comes, he will guide you into all the truth; for he will not speak on his own authority, but whatever he hears he will speak, and he will declare to you the things that are to come. ¹⁴He will glorify me, for he will take what is mine and declare it to you. ¹⁵All that **the Father** has is mine; therefore I said that he will take what is mine and declare it to you.

(c)   ¹⁶"A little while, and you will see me no more; again a little while, and you will see me." ¹⁷Some of his disciples said to one another, "What is this that he says to us, 'A little while, and you will not see me, and again a little while, and you will see me'; and, 'because I go to the Father'?" ¹⁸They said, "What does he mean by 'a little while'? We do not know what he means." ¹⁹Jesus knew that they wanted to ask him; so he said to them, "Is this what you are asking yourselves, what I meant by saying, 'A little while, and you will not see me, and again a little while, and you will see me'? ²⁰Truly, truly, I say to you, you will weep and lament, but the world will rejoice; you will be sorrowful, but your sorrow will turn into joy. ²¹ When a woman is in travail she has sorrow, because her hour has come; but when she is delivered of the child, she no longer remembers the anguish, for joy that a child is born into the world. ²² So you have sorrow now, but I will see you again and your hearts will rejoice, and no one will take your joy from you.

(b′)   ²³"In that day **you will ask nothing of me.** Truly, truly, I say to you, if you ask anything of **the Father,** he will give it to you in my name. ²⁴Hitherto you have asked nothing in my name; ask, and you will receive, that your joy may be full.

²⁵"I have said this to you in figures; the hour is coming when I shall no longer speak to you in figures but tell you plainly of **the Father.** ²⁶In that day you will ask in my name; and I do not say to you that I shall pray **the Father** for you; ²⁷for **the Father** himself loves you, because you have loved me and have believed that I came from **the Father.** ²⁸I came from **the Father** and have come into the world; again, **I am leaving the world and going to the Father.**" ²⁹His disciples said, "Ah, now you are speaking plainly, not in any figure! ³⁰Now we know that you know all things, and **need none to question you;** by this we believe that you came from God."

(a')   ³¹Jesus answered them, "Do you now believe? ³²**The hour is coming, indeed it has come,** when **you will be scattered,** every man to his home, and will leave me alone; yet I am not alone, for **the Father** is with me. ³³**I have said this to you,** that in me you may have peace. In the world **you have tribulation;** but be of good cheer, I have overcome the world."

Parallelism is created in (a) and (a') by speaking about persecution (cp. 16:2-3 with 16:32) and by repeating word for word such phrases as "I have said all this to you" in vv 1 and 33 and "the hour is coming" in vv 2 and 32.

In (b) and (b'), John creates parallelism by repeating in each the words "I am going" (vv 5 and 28) and by beginning both with a statement about asking (questioning) Jesus (cp. vv 5 and 23). The center (c) is set off from (b) and (b') by a description of the sorrow the apostles will experience when Jesus goes away and the joy they will feel when he returns. It is perhaps of some significance that joy is the subject of the center (c) both in section B' (15:26–16:33) and section C (15:1-25).

Commentary

Since section B' has been composed by the author in order to parallel section B (13:33–14:31), the reader may expect repetition of much that has already been said in section B and at the same time clarification of things said less clearly in section B.

(a) The time of persecution is coming (15:26–16:4).

15:26-27   the Counselor . . . will bear witness to me; and you also are witnesses. These two verses must be taken together. They assert, along with what follows, that in time of persecution the apostles will be assisted in their witness to Jesus by the Holy Spirit (cf. Acts 5:32; 6:10; 15:28). Here that assistance is mentioned first, and then the persecution. In Mt 10:16-20, the same is said in reverse order—first a prediction of persecution (Mt 10:16-18) and then the promise of assistance: "When they deliver you up, do not be anxious how you are to speak or what you are to say; for what you are to say will be given you in that hour; for it will not be you who speak, but the Spirit of your Father speaking through you" (Mt 10:19-20).[20]

In section B (13:33–14:31), where parallel references to the Counselor are found (cf. 14:16-17; 14:26), the promises that the Counselor would be with the apostles to assist them were more general. Here the assistance is more specific. The Counselor will help them in time of persecution (cf. 16:1-4 and 16:31-33) and in the specific work of witnessing to Jesus before the world.[21] In 16:7-14, the role of the Counselor in assisting the apostles will be amplified to include a further forensic activity in indicting and condemning the world, which does not accept Jesus.

15:27b because you have been with me from the beginning. In John's Gospel, the apostles appear on the scene from the very beginning (cf. Jn 1:35-51; 2:11-12). Being with Jesus from the beginning is important because it qualifies them as *witnesses* to all that Jesus said and did in the course of his ministry (cf. Acts 1:21-22: "So one of the men who have accompanied us during all the time that the Lord Jesus went in and out among us, beginning from the baptism of John until the day when he was taken up from us— one of these men must become with us a witness to his resurrection).''

16:1 I have said all this to you to keep you from falling away. One purpose of the farewell discourse is to prepare the apostles and the Church for the persecutions they will encounter after the resurrection. In view of the persecutions mentioned in 16:2-3, the warnings here are certainly realistic. The literal meaning of the word used for "falling away" is "being scandalized," a verb that has the meaning of something placed in the path of a person to make him or her stumble and fall. The stumbling envisioned here is another way of speaking about defection from the faith. Expulsion from the synagogue was only one of the pressures put upon Christian Jews by the synagogue.[22] In many cases they were excluded from the community, separated from their spouses and families, scourged, and imprisoned. The words of Jesus in Mt 10:16-38 describe very realistically the precarious position of Jews who converted to Christianity.

16:2-3 put you out of the synagogues. There is good evidence that in the late eighties, the synagogue authorities enacted an excommunication called the *Birkat ha-Minim* against those Jews who converted to Christianity.[23] John is probably referring to this excommunication both here and in 9:22 and 12:42. **Whoever kills you.** There is no evidence that the synagogue had a policy of putting Christians to death, but the persecution of Paul by the Jews, recorded in the Acts and mentioned by Paul himself in 2 Cor 11:23-24, would indicate that the synagogue took strenuous steps to discourage Jews from abandoning the synagogue to enter the Christian community.

16:4b when their hour comes. Persecution of the apostles and the Church did not take place during the ministry of Jesus but in the years following the resurrection when the apostles went out and witnessed to their faith in Jesus.

(b) I am going to him who sent me (16:5-15).

16:5 But now I am going to him who sent me. The going away theme, so elaborately developed in 13:33–14:7 and 14:28-31, is here taken up again, but this time in relation to the sending of the Counselor to help and guide the apostles in time of persecution.

16:7 it is to your advantage that I go away. In 14:28, it is *better for Jesus* that he goes to the Father; here it is *better for the apostles* because it is only when Jesus goes to the Father that he sends the Counselor. It is better because, as Brown says, "only through the internal presence of the Paraclete do the disciples come to understand Jesus fully."[24] It is significant that when Jesus meets his apostles after the resurrection, the first thing he does is breathe upon them and say, "Receive the Holy Spirit" (cf. 20:22).

16:8-11 He will convince the world of sin and of righteousness and of judgment. Here Jesus emphasizes the effect of the Counselor's presence in relation to the mission of the apostles to the world. Acting as prosecuting attorney against the world, the Counselor convicts the world of sin because it brought about the death of Jesus and refused to believe in him (cf. 12:37; 3:16-20). The Counselor also convinces the world of justice, not in the Pauline sense, but in the sense that Jesus will be vindicated as the innocent one who has died for others. Finally, the Counselor convinces the world of judgment inasmuch as the world opposed to Jesus is shown to have loved the darkness (cf. 3:17-21) and therefore brought itself into judgment, in the Johannine sense that the prince of this world no longer has power over Christians.[25] Such activity by the Counselor gives the apostles greater confidence in carrying out their mission to the world. All of this is said in the context of Jesus' return to the Father (cf. 16:5-7), which, as Hoskyns says, "is God's *imprimatur* upon the righteousness manifested in the life and death of his Son."[26]

16:12 many things to say to you. In vv 5-11, the Counselor enables the apostles to understand how Jesus' death has been his victory over the forces of evil in the world and thus fortifies them to go forth and bear witness to Jesus. In vv 12-15, the Counselor does something more—he enables the apostles to understand in depth the teaching they have heard from Jesus (cf. the parallel statement in 14:26).

16:13a he will guide you into all the truth. In 2:22; 12:6; and 13:7, Jesus spoke about this later, deeper understanding without mentioning the Counselor as its source. Here he explains how the Counselor is the source of the fuller understanding the Church (and this Gospel in particular) claims to have of Jesus and his teaching. It is not, therefore, new truth or a future new revelation, but a fuller understanding of what Jesus had already taught. In 15:15, Jesus had said, ". . . all that I have heard from my Father I have made known to you." The Counselor's function, as a consequence, is not to bring new revelation but to lead Christians to understand better what Jesus had taught and to apply it to their day-by-day living.

16:13b he will not speak on his own authority. The Counselor is another Jesus. What he speaks, therefore, is based on the authoritative teaching of Jesus rather than on any new revelation.

16:13c   he will declare to you the things that are to come. This is not a promise of new revelation but rather a promise that in the things that are to come, i.e., in new situations, the Counselor will assist the apostles to understand the significance of what Jesus had taught. Brown says, "The best Christian preparation for what is coming to pass is not an exact foreknowledge of the future but a deep understanding of what Jesus means for one's own time."[27] That this is not a promise of new revelation is confirmed by what follows.

16:14-15   he will take what is mine and declare it to you. The proper function of the Counselor is to be another Jesus, not a source of new revelation. He enables the Christian to understand and live what Jesus has taught.

(c) A little while, and you will see me no more (16:16-22).

16:16-20   A little while. In 13:33-14:31, the parallel of section B' (15:26-16:31), Jesus began the farewell discourse with the words "Yet a little while I am with you" (13:33) and then went on to speak of the apostles' sadness because of his departure (14:18-19). Here the theme of the "little while" is taken up again and developed at length. As in 13:33-14:31, the apostles again question Jesus, but this time they question him as a group. In view of the fact that so much is said about the Counselor in both section B and section B', it is probable that the seeing referred to here is not only the brief seeing of Jesus after his resurrection, but also the seeing of him through the Counselor, who is another Jesus who will be with them, as promised earlier in vv 8-15. Thus, the "little while" covers not only the time between Jesus' death and resurrection but also the whole of the future, when the apostles and all Christians will experience the continued presence of Jesus through the Counselor.

16:21-22   When a woman is in travail. The pains of childbirth (cf. the use of this analogy in Is 26:17-18; 54:1-2; 66:7-10; Mi 5:3) are likened to the time of anguish when Jesus dies, followed by the time of joy when he rises. The emphasis here is on the time of joy. In 3:1-21, the chiastic counterpart of chs 13–17 in the Gospel as a whole, mother and childbirth are mentioned in 3:3-7, thus paralleling 16:21-22, the only other mention of that subject.

(b') I am leaving the world and going to the Father (16:23-30).[28]

16:23a   In that day you will ask nothing of me. Because of the presence of the Counselor, the apostles will be able to understand Jesus' teaching and will no longer have need to ask questions. In v 30, the parallel of v 23a, this is exactly the conclusion the apostles draw from Jesus' words. Barrett explains the distinction between the two verbs for "ask" in vv 23ff as follows: "The interpretation here depends upon the meaning of *erōtan*. In classical usage it is distinguished from the partial synonym *aitein* in that it means 'to ask a question,' while *aitein* means 'to ask for something.' In later Greek, however, *erōtan,* while retaining its original meaning, is sometimes used in the same sense as *aitein.* ''[29]

It is disputed whether v 23a goes with what precedes or with what follows. Brown opts for what precedes, but the chiastic parallelism of vv 23-30 suggests that v 23a goes more properly with what follows. [30] The parallelism goes as follows:

Text

(aa) 16:23 In that day you will ask (*erōtēsete*) nothing of me. Truly, truly, I say to you, if you ask anything of the Father, he will give it to you in my name. [24]Hitherto you have asked nothing in my name; ask, and you will receive, that your joy may be full.

(bb) [25]"I have said this to you **in figures;** the hour is coming when I shall no longer speak to you **in figures** but tell you **plainly** of the Father.

(cc) [26]"In that day you will ask in my name; and I do not say to you that I shall pray the Father for you; [27]for the Father himself loves you, because you have loved me and have believed that I came from the Father. [28]I came from the Father and have come into the world; again, I am leaving the world and going to the Father."

(b'b') [29]His disciples said, "Ah, now you are speaking **plainly, not in any figure!**

(a'a') [30]"Now we know that you know all things, and need none to **question** (*erōta*) you; by this we believe that you came from God."

16:23b-24 if you ask anything of the Father. Besides not having to ask questions (v 23a), the apostles will also have the privilege, because of their union with Jesus, of going directly to the Father with their requests, in the sure confidence that their prayers will be heard in the name of Jesus. This will be the case "in that day," i.e., after the resurrection mentioned implicitly in vv 16-22. What is said in vv 23b-24, 26 parallels what was said earlier in 14:13-14, 15-17; 15:7.

16:25 I have said this to you in figures. The reference in the immediate context is to the mysterious saying "A little while" in vv 16-19 and to the parabolic similitude of the travail and joy of the woman who gives birth in vv 21-22. It would probably also include such allegories as the wind in 3:8; the shepherd and the gate in 10:1ff; the saying about Lazarus' death in 11:11-12; the saying about seeing the Father in 14:7; and the vine and the branches in 15:1ff, all of which presented difficulties to the hearers (cf. 3:9; 10:24; 11:14; 14:8-9).

16:26-27 In that day you will ask in my name. After the resurrection, when the imperfect faith of the apostles has given way to full faith in Jesus as the one who came from the Father and has returned to the Father, the apostles and all believing Christians will be so united in mutual love with the Father and the Son that the Father will hear them as asking in unison with the Son (cf. 17:20-23).

16:28 I came from the Father. While these words constitute a summary of the Christian faith in Johannine terms, they nevertheless express nothing that has not already been said in the Gospel. Their purpose here is to exemplify what is meant by the words "I shall no longer speak to you in figures but tell you plainly of the Father" (v 25), and at the same time lead up to the impetuous and boastful declaration of the apostles in vv 29-30.

16:29-30 now you are speaking plainly . . . . Now we know . . . by this we believe. With typical Johannine irony, the apostles as a group boast, like Peter in 13:36-38, about their faith in Jesus. Their faith, however, will remain quite inadequate until it has experienced the crucible of the passion.

(a′) The time of persecution is coming (16:31-33).

16:31 Do you now believe? What Jesus said about Peter's boasting in 13:36-38 is now, in substance, said about the faith of all the apostles. When the hour of the passion arrives, their faith will be severely tried; indeed, they will come close to losing all faith in Jesus.

16:32a The hour is coming . . . when you will be scattered. In contrast with vv 25-27, where Jesus spoke about the more distant future, he now speaks about the immediate future—the time of betrayal when he will be arrested in the garden and abandoned by all except the Beloved Disciple (18:1-12).

16:32b yet I am not alone, for the Father is with me. It is possible, as Barrett says, "that John is here combating a misunderstanding of Mark 15:34" (Jesus' words on the cross: "My God, my God, why hast thou forsaken me?").[31]

16:33a that in me you may have peace. As in section B (13:33–14:31), Jesus promises peace (cf. 14:25). All that he has said in the farewell discourse has been said in order to sustain the faith of the apostles and the Church in time of persecution. The promised peace is that special support given by Jesus through the Counselor, embracing the certitude of faith in Jesus and the sustaining joy that goes with that faith even and especially in time of persecution.

16:33b I have overcome the world. Section B (13:33–14:31) terminated with the words ". . . the ruler of this *world* is coming. He has no power over me" (14:30). The language of 14:30 is more mythological than here; but in substance the meaning is the same in both places: Jesus has decisively conquered the forces of evil. These words return the reader to the words about persecution from the world in 15:26ff and distill in a concentrated form the overall message of apocalyptic literature in general. The farewell discourse, which began in 13:33 (preceded by 13:1-32 as an introduction), ends here. What follows in ch 17 is not addressed to the apostles but to the Father and constitutes an epilogue, just as 13:1-32 constitutes an introduction or prologue.

Section A' (17:1-26): Jesus prays for the Church.

Jesus' prayer for the Church summarizes much that was said in the introduction to the discourse in 13:1-32. In fact, it has so many parallels with 13:1-32 that it serves as an extended inclusion-conclusion to the whole discourse.

Parallel structure

(a) Jesus prays to the Father to glorify him with the **glory** he had **before the world was made** (17:1-5).

(b) Jesus speaks about his apostles, **to whom he has given the Father's word** (17:6-8).

(c) Jesus prays for his apostles (17:9-13).

(b') Jesus again prays for his apostles, **to whom he has given the Father's word** (17:14-19).

(a') Jesus prays for all believers and concludes by speaking about the **glory** the Father gave him **before the foundation of the world** (17:20-26).

Text

(a) 17:1 When Jesus had spoken these words, he lifted up his eyes to heaven and said, "**Father,** the hour has come; **glorify** thy Son that the Son may **glorify** thee, ²since thou hast given him power over all flesh, to give eternal life to all whom thou hast given him. ³And this is eternal life, that they **know** thee the only true God, and Jesus Christ **whom thou has sent.** ⁴I **glorified** thee on earth, having accomplished the work which thou gavest me to do; ⁵and now, **Father, glorify thou me in thy own presence with the glory which I had with thee before the world was made.**

(b) ⁶"I have manifested thy name to the men whom thou gavest me out of **the world;** thine they were, and thou gavest them to me, and they have kept **thy word.** ⁷Now they know that everything that thou hast given me is from thee; ⁸for **I have given them the words** which thou gavest me, and they have received them and know **in truth** that I came from thee; and they have believed that **thou didst send me.**

(c) ⁹"I am praying for them; I am not praying for the world but for those whom thou hast given me, for they are thine; ¹⁰all mine are thine, and thine are mine, and I am glorified in them. ¹¹And now I am no more in the world, but they are in the world, and I am coming to thee. Holy Father, keep them in thy name, which thou hast given me, that they may be one, even as we are one. ¹²While I was with them, I kept them in thy name, which thou hast given me; I have guarded them, and none of them is lost but the son of perdition, that the scripture might be fulfilled. ¹³But now I am coming to thee; and these things I speak in the world, that they may have my joy fulfilled in themselves.

(b') ¹⁴"I have given them thy word; and **the world** has hated them because they are not of **the world,** even as I am not of **the world.** ¹⁵I do not pray that thou shouldst take them out of **the world,** but that thou shouldst keep them from the evil one. ¹⁶They are not of **the world,** even as I am not of the world. ¹⁷Sanctify them in the **truth; thy word** is **truth.** ¹⁸As **thou didst send me** into **the world,** so I have sent them into **the world.** ¹⁹And for their sake I consecrate myself, that they also may be consecrated **in truth.**

(a′) ²⁰"I do not pray for these only, but also for those who believe in me through their word, ²¹that they may all be one; even as thou, **Father,** art in me, and I in thee, that they also may be in us, so that the world may believe that thou hast sent me. ²²**The glory** which thou hast given me I have given to them, that they may be one even as we are one, ²³I in them and thou in me, that they may become perfectly one, so that the world may **know** that thou hast sent me and hast loved them even as thou hast loved me. ²⁴**Father,** I desire that they also, whom thou hast given me, may be with me where I am, to behold **my glory which thou hast given me in thy love for me before the foundation of the world.** ²⁵O righteous **Father,** the world has not **known** thee, but I have **known** thee; and these **know that thou hast sent me.** ²⁶I made **known** to them thy name, and I will make it **known,** that the love with which thou hast loved me may be in them, and I in them."

John creates parallelism between (a) and (a′) by a repetition of the word "glory" and by a reprise of the motif "before the world was made" in v 5 with the words "before the foundation of the world" in v 24. The parallel use of the word "glory" is particularly important, since it returns the reader's mind to the end of section A (13:1-32), where Jesus first spoke of his glory (13:31-32), and because it illuminates the meaning of the word "glory" in v 22 ("The glory which thou hast given me I have given to them") as being almost equivalent to Jesus' demonstration of his love unto the end in 13:1-32.

In (b) and (b′), parallelism is achieved by repeating the words "world" in vv 6, 14, 15, 16, 18 and "your word" (message) in vv 6, 14, 17, and by designating Jesus as the one "sent" into the world in vv 8 and 18. In (c) and (b′), Jesus prays for his apostles, who have received the Father's message through him. In (a′), he brings his prayer to a close by praying that all who come to him through the preaching of the apostles (and presumably their successors) will share in his glory and be one with him as he is one with the Father. It is the perfect climax for an ecclesial prayer.

Commentary

Jesus' prayer constitutes a Johannine "Our Father" and has remarkable parallels with the "Our Father" prayers of Matthew (Mt 6:9-13) and Luke (Lk 11:2-4). To begin with, it is addressed to the Father (17:1, 5, 11, 21, 24, 25). It speaks implicitly of the "hallowing" of the Father's name (17:6, 11, 12, 26). It is concerned overall with the coming of the kingdom, i.e., with the completion of the work that the Father gave to the Son and that the Son has now given to the Church. And finally, it is concerned with the protection of the apostles and the Church from the evil one (17:12-15).³²

The ecclesial content of the prayer is particularly evident from the context and the division of the prayer. The context is found in 16:32-33, **where**

Jesus has just spoken about the time when the apostles "will be scattered" and will have tribulation in the world. The prayer begins with a pointed reference back to "these words": "When Jesus had spoken *these words*" (17:1). Following what he said about tribulation and scattering, Jesus begins his prayer for the apostles and the Church *in the world*. The division of the prayer follows the ecclesial development from Jesus to the apostles to the Church, speaking first about Jesus' work (17:1-5); then about Jesus and the apostles (17:6-8); then about the work of the apostles alone (17:9-13 and 17:14-19); and finally about the work of the Church, i.e., those who come to believe through the teaching and preaching of the apostles (17:20-26).

Chapter 17 has been called the "priestly prayer" of Jesus, but it is as much an instruction for the community on the subject of ecclesiology as it is a prayer of petition, and it is as much a revelation to the community of Jesus' union and communion with the Father as it is a prayer of praise. The Jesus who prays, moreover, is no longer of this world. He speaks from beyond the grave to Christians of all times. The Jesus of the priestly prayer, by his emphasis on his "power over all flesh" (17:2), on his work of revelation to the apostles (17:4-8), on the mission of the apostles (17:18), on the communion of Christians with the Father and the Son (17:22-25), and on his continued presence with his Church (17:25), resembles in Johannine clothing the Jesus of the great missionary mandate in Mt 28:18-20, and his prayer incorporates the major themes of Matthew's authoritative mission mandate.[33]

(a) Jesus prays to the Father to glorify him with the glory he had before the world was made (17:1-5).

17:1a   When Jesus had spoken these words. The reference is to the words about scattering and tribulation in 16:32-33 and signals a transition from teaching to prayer, which is indicated by the words "he lifted up his eyes to heaven."

17:1b   the hour has come. Note the parallel with 13:1, 31-32, where "the hour" is clearly the hour of Jesus' passion and death. **Glorify thy Son.** Speaking in the context of the hour, Jesus asks the Father to glorify him, for the Son is glorified when he brings salvation to men. At the same time, the Son glorifies the Father when he brings men to salvation, for he thus does the work of the Father (cf. 4:34) and manifests the Father's salvific love for men (cf. 7:39; 9:3; 11:4; 12:16, 23, 28).

17:2   since thou hast given him power . . . to give eternal life. The power of Jesus to give life had been emphasized in 5:21-30, but especially 5:26-27. It is precisely by giving eternal life that Jesus glorifies the Father (cf. 3:14-17) and does the work of the Father (cf. 4:34).

17:3   this is eternal life. This very Gnostic-sounding declaration loses its Gnostic import when the word "know" is interpreted in the Old Testament sense of the word as loving knowledge, as in Hosea and in the prophets in general. In Gnosticism, eternal life is achieved by leaving the body and the world. In Jn 17:14, 16, eternal life is given to Christians while they are in this world and in the flesh. In Gnosticism, knowledge is all; in John, love is all (cf. 13:1ff; 13:33ff and all that is said in the farewell discourse about the love commandment).

17:4-5 I glorified thee on earth. Verses 4 and 5 go together. Since Jesus has completed the work for which the Father sent him into the world (cf. 3:14-16; 4:34; 19:30), namely, the work of giving himself over to death in the passion, it follows that now the Father should glorify Jesus. That this glorification should be with the glory Jesus had with the Father "before the world was made" need not be understood in a Gnostic sense, but rather in the Jewish Christian sense, which likened Jesus to personified wisdom in the books of Proverbs and Wisdom (e.g., Prv 8:23, where it is said that wisdom existed *before the earth was created,* and Wis 7:25, where wisdom is said to be a pure effusion of God's glory).

(b) Jesus speaks about his apostles, to whom he has given the Father's word (17:6-8).

17:6 to the men whom thou gavest me out of the world. As proof that he has "accomplished the work" that the Father gave him to do (v 4), Jesus cites his success with the apostles: first, because he has manifested to them the name of his Father (v 6), probably the name Yahweh, which is implicit in Jesus' frequent references to himself as "I am" (cf. 6:20; 8:24, 28, 58; 18:5, 6, 18); and second, because he has successfully taught them the Father's words (revelation) and the substance of that revelation which they have believed, namely, that Jesus came from the Father and was sent by the Father (vv 7-8).

(c) Jesus prays for his apostles (17:9-13).

17:9 I am praying for them . . . not . . . for the world. The world envisaged here is not the world (all humanity) that God so loved that he gave his only Son (3:16), but that part of humanity opposed to and persecuting the Church. It is the world as described in 15:18-25; 16:1-4, 8-11, 20, 32-33. In sequence 4 (3:1-21), the chiastic parallel of sequence 18 (chs 13–17), this portion of the world is described as those who love the darkness and refuse to come to the light (cf. 3:19-21).

17:10 I am glorified in them. Jesus is glorified through the apostles inasmuch as they do his will as he did the Father's will (cf. 4:34) by fulfilling the mission he sends them to accomplish (cf. 17:18-20). The thought here is much like that of 15:1ff, where Jesus speaks of the apostles bearing "much fruit" (15:8) when they remain in union with him as the branch with the vine.

17:11 that they may be one, even as we are one. Jesus prays that the apostles, left in the world when he goes to the Father, may be one as Father and Son are one, i.e., united with the Father and the Son in a unity of self-sacrificing love (cf. vv 21-23).

17:12 none of them is lost but the son of perdition. The reference is to Judas and parallels nicely with what was said about him and about the fulfillment of the scriptures in section A (13:1-32), especially 13:2, 11, 18, 27-30.

(b') Jesus again prays for his apostles, to whom he has given the Father's word (17:14-19).

17:14 I have given them thy word. The reference is to the revelatory message of the Father that Jesus has brought to the world (cf. 5:31-47; 7:16-19; 8:26-29; 12:44-50 and the parallel to these words in 17:6).

17:15 that thou shouldst keep them from the evil one. The Greek (*ek tou ponerou*) could be translated "keep them from evil," but the parallelism of 17:1-26 with 13:1-32 suggests that the "evil one" here contemplated is the same as the devil of 13:2 and the Satan of 13:27.

17:17-18 Sanctify them. To "sanctify" means to set aside a thing for God or to set aside a person for a sacred calling. In the context of v 18 ("As thou didst send me into the world, so I have sent them into the world"), the sanctification of the apostles must be referred to the apostles' being set aside or called for the same mission as Jesus was (cf. 10:36). In short, Jesus prays for them as the ones commissioned to continue his work in the world by preaching in word and deed the word (message) of the Father's love (cf. 13:15-16; Mt 28:18-20).

17:19 For their sake I consecrate myself. Again, it is the context—in this case the broader context of the whole farewell discourse given on the night before Jesus *died*—that suggests he is speaking here of his own imminent death. Since the verb "consecrate" (*hagiazein*) can refer either to the thing set aside for sacrifice or to a person set aside for a sacred calling, it is this verse more than any other that suggests that Jesus prays here in ch 17 as the high priest who sacrifices himself. It is for this reason that the prayer is aptly called the "priestly prayer." Jesus consecrates himself so that they, the apostles, may be consecrated "in truth," i.e., as in v 17, in the truth of God's word (message) of love for the world.

(a') Jesus prays for all believers and concludes by speaking about the glory the Father gave him before the foundation of the world (17:20-26).

17:20 for those who believe in me through their word. A distinction is made between the apostles and those future Christians who come to believe in Jesus through the preaching of the apostles and their successors. John has in mind here all Christians, but especially his own community at the end of the first century (cf. 20:29).

17:21   that they all may be one. The unity here envisioned is a unity in self-sacrificing love similar to the unity in love of the Father and the Son. Where this unity is present, it will be a sign and proof to the world that the Father has sent Jesus. The same thing had been said in other terms in 13:1-17 and encapsulated in the words of 13:35, "By this all men will know that you are my disciples, if you have love for one another," and the words of 15:13, "Greater love has no man than this, that a man lay down his life for his friends. You are my friends if you do what I command you."

17:22-23   The glory which thou hast given me I have given to them. The glory given to Jesus was that manifested by his perfect unity of will with the Father, especially as that unity of will was manifested in Jesus' death. Jesus now gives this glory to his apostles, in the sense that when they die for one another, they show their unity of will with Jesus and with the Father. Where this happens, the world is led to recognize that the Father has indeed sent Jesus and has given to the faithful a share of that love with which he loves Jesus. Lindars puts it nicely: "The witness of the Church's united life is not merely a confirmation of the revelation of God in Jesus, but also a sign that the object of that revelation is being achieved. It displays and effects God's love for mankind . . . . The point is that the Father's unity with Jesus, and his unity with the Church, leads to the conclusion that 'thou . . . hast loved them even as thou hast loved me.' "[34]

17:24a   Father, I desire that . . . they may be with me. The prayer envisages the future when all will be one with Jesus and the Father in heaven. It presupposes an intervening time of suffering and death for the Church such as there will be in the immediate future for Jesus himself and for Peter later, as predicted in 13:36. It presupposes also Jesus' promise in 14:2 that he goes to prepare places for his apostles "in my Father's house."

17:24b   to behold my glory. In heaven the apostles will see Jesus in the splendor of his divinity and in that unity of love with the Father that has existed before the foundation of the world. As Barrett perceptively expresses it: "The ultimate root of the final hope of men lies in the love of the Father for the Son, that is in the eternal relationship of love which is thus seen to be of the essence of the Holy Trinity."[35]

17:25-26   O righteous Father. This final petition sums up much of John's theology: first, the mutual knowing (loving) of Father and Son; second, the success of Jesus in bringing people (the apostles) to believe that he was sent by the Father (v 25); third, the continuation of Jesus' work with people (through the Counselor) in making known the Father; fourth, the purpose of Jesus and the Church: that men and women may share in the mutual love of Father and Son and thus complete a circle of indwelling unity in love. Lindars comments: "The prayer ends with the substance of the new commandment of 13:34f, now raised to the status of the theological justification for the entire work of redemption . . . ."[36]

Themes

Unlike previous sequences of the Gospel, the farewell discourse does not concentrate on the themes of witness, response, and replacement, but on a new theme—the theme of discipleship, namely, what is required for a person to be a true follower of Jesus. Unlike Matthew (5–7; 10; 13; 18; 23–25), Mark (8:31–10:52), and Luke (9:51–19:27), who expound the theme of discipleship in detail and at length, John is satisfied to let Jesus expound discipleship only in substance.

For John, the substance of discipleship consists in three interconnected realities. First, the disciple must follow Jesus' example of "love unto the end," as expounded in the symbolism of the footwashing and as demonstrated in Jesus' own sacrifice of himself to death in the passion. Second, the disciple must remain intimately united with Jesus and the Father as the branch is united with the vine (15:1ff). Third, the disciple must work with the guidance and help of the Counselor to carry on Jesus' work in the world by "bearing much fruit," i.e., by bringing many to believe in Jesus as the one sent by the Father for the salvation of the world.

The substance of discipleship is summed up in the new commandment that the apostles (and all Christians) love one another "even as I have loved you" (13:34-35) and is expressed in the same commandment even more cogently in the words: "This is my commandment, that you love one another as I have loved you. Greater love has no man than this, that a man lay down his life for his friends" (15:12-13). Other commandments are mentioned (cf. 14:15, 21) and Jesus' revealed message as a whole is mentioned (cf. 17:6-8, 14), but only the love command and its ramifications are emphasized.

The more usual themes—witness, response, and replacement—are present but in no way stressed. Jesus witnesses to his unity with the Father and the Holy Spirit. The apostles respond positively by believing in Jesus; the Jews respond negatively by persecuting Jesus and the Church. This latter leads to an oblique reference to the theme of replacement in the allegory of the true vine versus the false vine in 15:1-6, 18-25. The little John has to say about these themes probably reflects his satisfaction with having dealt with them adequately in the first seventeen sequences of his Gospel.

Chiastic parallels with sequence 4 (3:1-21)

There are many parallels between the discourse to Nicodemus and the Last Supper discourse to the Twelve. Some are loud and clear. Some are faint and subtle. Some may appear to be, and indeed be, purely accidental, but the sheer number of parallels proves of itself that John intended to re-echo in the farewell discourse the many interlocking themes of the first major discourse in his Gospel. These themes are: God's love, eternal life, the sending and the "giving" of the Son, the necessity of faith in the Son, the

Holy Spirit and baptism, etc. The following arrangement in columns will help to bring out the number and strength of the parallels.

3:1-21	*13:1–17:26*
3:2 Nicodemus . . . came to Jesus by **night.**	13:30 So, after receiving the morsel, he (Judas) immediately went out; and it was **night.**
3:4 Can he enter a second time into his **mother's womb and be born?**	16:21 When a **woman is in travail . . .** but when she is delivered of **the child.**
3:5 **Unless one is born of water** and the **Spirit,** he **cannot** enter the kingdom of God.	13:8 **If I do not wash you, you have no part in me.**
3:6 That which is born of the **Spirit** is spirit. 3:8: So it is with everyone who is born of the **Spirit.**	14:16 . . . another Counselor . . . even the **Spirit** of truth . . . 14:26: The Counselor, the Holy **Spirit . . .**will teach you . . . 15:26: But when the Counselor comes . . . even the **Spirit** of truth . . . 16:7-15: When he comes (v 8). When the **Spirit** of truth comes . . . (v 13)
3:11 . . . we speak of what we **know.**	16:30 Now we **know** that you **know** . . .
3:13 No one has ascended into heaven but he who **descended from heaven . . .**	16:28 I . . . **have come into the world;** again, I am leaving the world and **going to the Father . . .**
3:15b. . . that whoever believes in him may have **eternal life.**	17:2 . . . thou hast given him power . . . to give **eternal life** to all whom thou hast given him.
3:17 For God **sent the Son into the world,** not to condemn the **world,** but that the **world might be saved** through him.	15:18-19 If the **world** hates you . . . If you were of the **world;** 17:18: As thou didst **send me into the world,** so I have **sent them into** the **world.**
3:16 For God so **loved** the **world** that he gave his only Son . . .	14:31. . .I do as the Father commanded me, so that the **world** may know that I **love** the Father.

Sequence 19

PASSION, DEATH, AND BURIAL

18:1–19:42

Parallel structure

Section A (18:1-12):	Arrested **in a garden,** Jesus is **bound** and led away to trial.
Section B (18:13-27):	Jesus, **the true high priest,** is put on trial before Caiaphas. The **Beloved Disciple** is present.
Section C (18:28–19:16):	Jesus, the king of Israel, is judged by Pilate and rejected by his own people.
Section B' (19:17-30):	As **true high priest,** Jesus, like Isaac, carries the wood of his own sacrifice. The **Beloved Disciple** is present.
Section A' (19:31-42):	**Bound** with burial cloths, Jesus is buried **in a garden.**

John divides his passion account, as he did the Last Supper discourse, into five sections, each composed according to the laws of parallelism. Parallelism in sections A and A' is created by paralleling the garden of the betrayal with the garden of the burial, and by paralleling the binding of Jesus' hands after his arrest with the binding of his body with burial cloths after being taken down from the cross.

In sections B and B', parallelism is achieved in two ways: first, by showing Jesus is the true high priest: in section B by contrasting him with Caiaphas; in section B' by comparing him to Isaac, who carried the wood of his own sacrifice just as Jesus carries his own cross; second, by introducing the Beloved Disciple into both sections. Section C is the climactic center of the whole passion account. It shows Jesus, the true judge of all the world, judged by Pilate and rejected as king by his own people in favor of Caesar.

In commenting on John's passion narrative, we presuppose that he works up selected elements of the broad oral tradition of the passion in his own typical and artistic manner rather than that he works from a written source or sources. We do not eliminate the possibility that John knew at least the Gospels of Mark and Luke, but we do not think that it has been proved that he used them as written sources.[1]

On the basis of this presupposition, we further presuppose that a vertical rather than a horizontal approach will provide the greater insight into John's passion account, i.e., the reader will understand the passion narrative better in the light of the Gospel as a whole and in the light of the evangelist's characteristic style and viewpoint (the vertical approach) than against its differences when compared with the passion accounts of the synoptic Gospels (the horizontal approach). Confirmation for these presuppositions is found in the overall structure of the passion narrative and in the pervasive presence throughout the narrative of John's characteristic style, dramatic techniques, and theological point of view.[2]

The characteristic style is unmistakable from beginning to end and needs no demonstration. The characteristic dramatic techniques stand out sharply in all parts of the account. John's technique of staging is immediately apparent in section B (18:13-27), where Peter's denial of Jesus plays front stage to Jesus' interrogation before Annas and Caiaphas. Staging is blatantly evident in the center of the narrative in section C (18:28-19:16), where the action is divided into three scenes on front stage with Pilate and the Jews, three scenes on back stage with Pilate and Jesus alone, and one scene on a middle stage with neither Pilate nor the Jews present but only Jesus and the soldiers mocking him as king of the Jews.

Characteristic of the Johannine theological point of view are the following: first, the elimination of the agony in the garden because it conflicts with the passion as the hour of Jesus' glory; second, the repeated "I am he" (three times) in the arrest scene (18:1-12); third, the emphasis on the nature of Jesus' kingship (18:33-38); fourth, the double meanings of such sayings as "It is finished" (19:30) and "he gave up his spirit" (19:30).

To the above should be added the numerous theological points made by means of the Sophoclean irony with which the author suffuses the whole account.[3] Judas, for example, who went out into the darkness in 13:32, returns now in the darkness with soldiers bearing lanterns to find "the light of the world." Caiaphas is continually called the high priest, but the audience knows that Jesus is the true and only high priest of the new covenant. John's readers are well aware of the irony implicit in Pilate's attempting to judge Jesus, the judge of the whole world. They know as well the kind of kingdom of which Jesus is king when Pilate asks, "Are you a king?" Likewise when Pilate asks, "What is truth?" the audience knows what Pilate does not—that Jesus himself is the way, the truth, and the life, and that the answer to Pilate's question stands immediately in front of his unseeing eyes. Again, when Pilate says, "Here is the man!" John's readers know what Pilate cannot even suspect, namely, that Jesus is man indeed but God as well. Finally, when the soldiers, with mocking irony, say to Jesus, "Hail, King of the Jews!" the reader of John's Gospel knows that there is a double irony here: the intended irony of the unbelieving soldiers and the double irony of which the soldiers are totally unconscious, namely, that he whom they ironically hail as king of the Jews is, ironically, truly the king of the Jews!

If these presuppositions are correct, then the purpose of John's passion narrative stands out clearly. He writes to show: (1) that Jesus is the true messianic king of the Jews, the true high priest, the true judge, the true temple, and the true lamb of God of the permanent Passover; (2) that Jesus was in sovereign control of everything that happened in his passion (cf. 18:4); (3) that Jesus was consciously fulfilling the will of the Father in going to his death (cf. 18:11); (4) that the Jews, as representatives of the forces of the evil world, had been responsible for bringing about the death of Jesus (cf. 18:8–19:16); (5) that Jesus' death was the demonstration of his love "unto the end" (cf. 19:30 and cp. 13:1-2). In sum, the purpose of the passion account is to show that Jesus' passion was in reality the hour of his glory.

Finally, in commenting on John's passion narrative, we take for granted the substantial historicity of the account as a whole. This can be demonstrated by a comparison with the synoptic passion narratives. We also take for granted, however, that John has taken considerable liberties in the telling of the story and that he has both highly dramatized and profoundly theologized it. In short, we take for granted that for John the historical level of the tradition serves as the basis for the dramatic level, and the dramatic level serves as the basis for the theological level. It is the latter that constitutes John's primary interest and excuses the considerable liberties he takes in telling the story. He is more interested in the theological truths that underlie the events than he is in the events themselves.

Section A (18:1-12): Arrested in a garden, Jesus is bound and led away to trial.

Parallel structure

 (a) A **band of soldiers** and some **officers of the Jews** come to arrest Jesus (18:1-3).
 (b) Jesus declares, "**I am he**" (18:4-5).
 (c) When Jesus says, "I am he," the soldiers draw back and fall to the ground (18:6).
 (b′) A third time Jesus declares, "**I am he**" (18:7-9).
 (a′) The **band of soldiers** and **the officers of the Jews** arrest Jesus (18:10-12).

Text

(a) 18:1 When Jesus had spoken these words, he went forth with his disciples across the Kidron valley, where there was a garden, which he and his disciples entered. ²Now Judas, who betrayed him, also knew the place; for Jesus often met there with his disciples. ³So Judas, procuring **a band of soldiers** and **some officers** from the chief priests and the Pharisees, went there with lanterns and torches and weapons.

(b)   ⁴Then Jesus, knowing all that was to befall him, came forward and said to them, **"Whom do you seek?"** ⁵They answered him, **"Jesus of Nazareth."** Jesus said to them, **"I am he."** **Judas,** who betrayed him, **was standing with them.**

(c)   ⁶When he said to them, "I am he," they drew back and fell to the ground.

(b′)   ⁷Again he asked them, **"Whom do you seek?"** And they said, **"Jesus of Nazareth."** ⁸Jesus answered, "I told you that **I am he;** so, if you seek me, let these men go." ⁹This was to fulfil the word ·which he had spoken, "Of those whom thou gavest me **I lost not one."**

(a′)   ¹⁰Then Simon Peter, having a sword, drew it and struck the high priest's slave and cut off his right ear. The slave's name was Malchus. ¹¹Jesus said to Peter, "Put your sword into its sheath; shall I not drink the cup which the Father has given me?" ¹²So **the band of soldiers** and their captain and **the officers of the Jews** seized Jesus and bound him.

John creates parallelism in (a) and (a′) by repeating in each the words "band of soldiers" and·"officers" (vv 3 and 12); in (b) and (b′), by repeating almost word for word the dialogue between Jesus and the officers. The parallelism of v 5b, which mentions Judas, with v 9b, which mentions the other eleven apostles, will be explained in the commentary.

Commentary

(a) A band of soldiers and some officers of the Jews come to arrest Jesus (18:1-3).

18:1 When Jesus had spoken these words. "These words" refers back to the farewell discourse in chs 13–17. The Kidron valley, not mentioned by the Synoptics, is a wadi running down the eastern side of Jerusalem, separating the city from the Mount Olivet area. It has flowing water only during the winter rainy season. In view of the fact that John has so much to say in his passion account about Jesus as the messianic king of Israel, it is not unlikely that he intends to remind his readers that King David, a thousand years before Jesus, had also crossed the Kidron when he fled from Jerusalem following the rebellion of his son Absalom (cf. 2 Sm 15:14). That the garden where Jesus and his disciples were accustomed to go is the garden of Gethsemane mentioned by Mark (14:32) and Matthew (26:36) is a more than reasonable deduction.

18:2-3 Now Judas, who betrayed him, also knew the place. John had already identified Judas as the traitor (cf. 6:64, 71; 12:4; 13:2, 11, 21, 31-32). Since he had been with Jesus in the garden, he was able to lead the Roman soldiers and the Jewish officers to the place. The lanterns and torches were undoubtedly necessary for an arrest at night. John's readers, however, would be alert to the irony of the fact that Judas, who had last been mentioned as going out into the darkness of night (cf. 13:21-32), comes out of the darkness with lanterns and torches to find "the light of the world."

(b) Jesus declares, "I am he" (18:4-5).

18:4 Then Jesus, knowing all that was to befall him. Jesus' foreknowledge of events is a typical Johannine theme (cf. 12:42, 48; 6:6; 13:1). Prefacing the passion as it does here, the remark constitutes a theological comment that places the whole of the passion under the initiative of Jesus. It also reminds the reader that in taking the passion upon himself freely, Jesus is deliberately doing the work for which the Father had sent him into the world (cf. 3:16; 4:34; 10:18; 17:4; 19:30). It is noteworthy in passing that John eliminates Judas' kiss of betrayal (cf. Mt 26:49). For John, the initiative for the passion rests entirely in the hands of Jesus.

18:5a They answered him, "Jesus of Nazareth." The same sequence of question and answer recurs in vv 7-8 and thus creates perfect parallelism between vv 4-5 (b) and vv 7-9 (b'). Jesus' answer, "I am he," which is repeated in vv 6 and 8, is intended by John to be understood in the sense of the divine name Yahweh (cf. 6:20; 8:24, 58).

18:5b Judas, who betrayed him, was standing with them. A second reference to Judas seems unnecessary after v 2 but can be plausibly explained on the basis of the parallelism that John wishes to create with v 9. In v 9, John quotes the words of Jesus, "Of those whom thou gavest me I lost not one." The quotation seems to be from 17:12b, but actually the exact words are found nowhere in John's Gospel. A good explanation would be that the evangelist says here that "Judas . . . was standing *with them,*" i.e., with the forces of the world, in order to exclude Judas from those (the Eleven) whom the Father had given Jesus according to 17:12b. Understood in this sense, the combined meaning of vv 5 and 9 would be equivalent to the meaning of 17:12b: "I have guarded them, and none of them (the Eleven) is lost but the son of perdition, that the scripture might be fulfilled." Judas, thus, was never part of those given to Jesus by the Father but, as mentioned in v 5b, "was [always] standing *with them.*"

In regard to the much argued question of different redactions of John's Gospel, it is of some interest to note that the author's allusion in 18:5b to 17:12 is a good indication that ch 17 was already a part of the Gospel when the passion narrative was composed and tells against those who consider ch 17 a later interpolation into the Gospel.

(c) When Jesus says, "I am he," the soldiers draw back and fall to the ground (18:6).

18:6 When he said to them, "I am he," they drew back and fell to the ground. This verse is so profoundly theological that one may seriously doubt the historicity of what is described. Rough soldiers would hardly fall to the ground before a lone figure identifying himself as the one they sought to arrest. If, however, one postulates that the soldiers understood Jesus' words "I am he" in the divine sense intended by John, then it is not difficult to imagine their reaction of awe and helplessness. What John appears to have done is to borrow the thought of Ps 56:9, "Then my enemies will be *turned back* in the day when I call," and the thought of Ps 27:2, "When evildoers assail me, uttering slanders against me, my adversaries and foes, they shall *stumble and fall,"* to express what the reaction of the soldiers in the garden would have been if they had known who it was they were attempting to arrest. This, of course, would be perfectly understandable to John's Christian readers.

(b′) A third time Jesus declares, "I am he" (18:7-9).

18:7-9 Again he asked them, "Whom do you seek?" These verses are almost identical with vv 4-5 of section (b) except for the reference in v 9 to the fulfillment of Jesus' word: "Of those whom thou gavest me I lost not one" (17:12). For the explanation, see the comment on 18:5.

(a′) The band of soldiers and the officers of the Jews arrest Jesus (18:10-12).

18:10-11 Then Simon Peter, having a sword, drew it. This little incident, mentioned in the synoptic Gospels (Mk 14:47; Mt 26:51; Lk 22:50) but without the identification of the names Peter and Malchus (v 10), is brought in by John in order to form a preface for the declaration of obedience to the Father implicit in the rhetorical question ". . . shall I not drink the cup which the Father has given me?" (v 11b). Peter is rebuked not so much for violence but because he is trying to interfere with the destiny decreed for Jesus by the Father, who "so loved the world that he gave his only Son" (cf. 3:16). In a number of places in the Gospel, John and/or Jesus makes allusions to the fact that Jesus' destiny was to die in order to prove the love of God and Jesus for the world (cf. 3:14, 17; 10:17-18; 11:49-52; 12:23-24; 13:1; 17:4; 19:30).

18:12 So the band of soldiers and their captain and the officers of the Jews seized Jesus and bound him. This verse forms a parallel with v 3 of (a). At the same time, it uses a verb, "bound," that will be repeated in section A′ when Joseph of Arimathea and Nicodemus take the body of Jesus from the cross and "bind" it in linen cloths (19:40). Thus John parallels section A (18:1-12), in which Jesus is arrested in a "garden" (18:1) and "bound" (18:12), with section A′ (19:31-42), in which Jesus is "bound" with linen clothes (19:40) and buried in a "garden" (19:41-42). The parallels can hardly be accidental. None of the Synoptics mentions that Jesus was arrested in a garden and buried in a garden. Nor do they say that when Jesus was arrested, his captors "bound" (*edēsan*) him. The Synoptics mention that Jesus' body was "wrapped" (*enetylixen*). They do not use the verb "bound" (*edēsan*), which is proper to John alone.

Section B (18:13-27): Jesus, the true high priest, is put on trial before Caiaphas. The Beloved Disciple is present.

Parallel structure

   (a) **Peter,** at the house of **Annas,** the father-in-law of **Caiaphas, denies Jesus** a first time (18:13-18).

   (b) **The high priest questions Jesus** about his teaching (18:19).

   (c) Jesus defends his teaching (18:20).

   (b′) **Jesus questions the high priest** (18:21-23).

   (a′) While Jesus is being sent from **Annas** to **Caiaphas, Peter denies Jesus** a second and a third time (18:24-27).

Text

(a)   18:13 First they led him to **Annas;** for he was the father-in-law of **Caiaphas,** who was **high priest** that year. ¹⁴It was **Caiaphas** who had given counsel to the Jews that it was expedient that one man should die for the people. ¹⁵**Simon Peter** followed Jesus, and so did another disciple. As this disciple was known to the **high priest,** he entered the court of the **high priest** along with **Jesus,** ¹⁶while **Peter** stood outside at the door. So the other disciple, who was known to the **high priest,** went out and spoke to the maid who kept the door, and brought **Peter** in. ¹⁷The maid who kept the door said to **Peter, "Are not you also one of this man's disciples?"** He said, **"I am not."** ¹⁸Now the **servants** and officers had made a charcoal fire, because it was cold, and they **were standing and warming themselves; Peter** also was with them, **standing and warming himself.**

(b)   ¹⁹The **high priest** then **questioned Jesus** about his disciples and his teaching.

(c)   ²⁰Jesus answered him, "I have spoken openly to the world; I have always taught in synagogues and in the temple, where all Jews come together; I have said nothing secretly.

(b′)   ²¹"Why do you **ask** me? **Ask** those who have heard me, what I said to them; they know what I said." ²²When he had said this, one of the officers standing by struck **Jesus** with his hand, saying, "Is that how you answer the **high priest?"** ²³Jesus answered him, "If I have spoken wrongly, bear witness to the wrong; but if I have spoken rightly, why do you strike me?"

(a′)   ²⁴**Annas** then sent him bound to **Caiaphas** the **high priest.** ²⁵Now **Simon Peter was standing and warming himself.** They said to him, **"Are not you also one of his disciples?"** He denied it and said, **"I am not."** ²⁶One of the **servants** of the **high priest,** a kinsman of the man whose ear **Peter** had cut off, asked, "Did I not see you in the garden with him?" ²⁷**Peter** again denied it; and at once the cock crowed.

Parallelism is created in (a) and (a′) by a repetition of the same cast of characters: Annas and Caiaphas, Peter and Jesus, and the servants; by a repetition of the same question and answer: "Are not you also one of this man's disciples?" followed by the same reply, "I am not" (cf. vv 17 and 25); and by a repetition of the comment that Peter was "standing and warming himself" by the charcoal fire (cf. vv 17 and 25). Significantly, in both

(a) and (a') the words "the high priest" are repeated almost excessively—three times in (a) and twice in (a'). The extraordinary emphasis on the words "high priest," as we shall see, helps to explain the relationship by parallelism between section B' (18:13-27) and section B' (19:17-30), in the latter of which Jesus shows himself to be the true high priest by bearing his own cross as Isaac bore the wood of his own sacrifice.

Parallelism is achieved in (b) and (b') by reversing the questioning. In (b) the high priest questions Jesus; in (b') Jesus questions the high priest. It should be noted that in both the same Greek verb (*erōtaō*) is used, a similarity that is erased by the RSV's use of the synonym "asked" in v 21.

Commentary

John's account of the trial before the high priest contains much that is similar to Mark's account (cf. Mk 14:53-72) and suggests either dependence on a common oral source or John's dependence on Mark's Gospel. The two accounts, however, differ significantly in their emphases. Mark emphasizes the trial and condemnation; John emphasizes Peter's threefold denial of Jesus, says almost nothing about the trial, and nothing at all about the death sentence passed by the Sanhedrin. John's lack of interest in the trial is easily explained. He had already anticipated the trial in the bitter controversies between Jesus and the leaders of the Jews (cf. 7:31-52; 8:48-58; 9:39–10:39). He had also anticipated the death sentence (cf. 11:45-54).

John's real interest in the account is theological and is revealed, not by the brief and inconsequential trial (vv. 19-23), but (1) by his emphasis on the title "high priest" (repeated eight times in the singular and not used thereafter in the rest of the Gospel); (2) by his emphasis on Peter's threefold denial of Jesus (vv 15-18 and 24-27); and (3) by his emphasis on Jesus as a true prophet whose foretelling of Peter's denial (cf. 13:38) was fulfilled to the letter (18:27). This true foretelling is contrasted with the unwitting foretelling of Jesus' death by the high priest, Caiaphas (cf. 11:50 and 18:14).

By his frequent repetition of the title "high priest" and by his contrast between Jesus, the prophet whose word is fulfilled, and Caiaphas, the high priest whose word is not fulfilled in the manner in which he meant it, John subtly forces the reader to deduce and proclaim that Jesus, rather than Annas or Caiaphas, is the true high priest of Israel. This deduction is borne out by the parallelism between section B' (18:13-27) and section B' (19:17-30), the section in which John describes Jesus' crucifixion and death. In 19:17-30, which parallels 18:13-27, Jesus is described as the high priest of his own sacrifice. He, the only Son of the Father, takes up the wood of his sacrifice, the cross, just as Isaac, the only son of Abraham, took up the wood of his sacrifice (cf. Jn 19:17 and Gn 22:6). Like Isaac, Jesus goes forth to the place of his sacrifice, where he will offer himself as "the Lamb of God, who takes away the sin of the world" (1:29).

In relation to the significance of the eightfold repetition of the word "high priest" in 18:13-27, it is of some interest to note that John uses the same technique of repetition to emphasize the kingship of Jesus in section C (18:28–19:16). In section C, John repeats the title "king" nine times and at the same time plays ironically on the meaning of the title to Pilate, the Jews, and even the Roman soldiers (cf. 18:33, 37; 19:3, 12, 14, 15). The end result is that John uses his repetition of the title in section C in order to inculcate his contention that Jesus is the true king of the Jews, just as he inculcates by repetition of the title "high priest" in section B that Jesus is the true high priest of Israel. If this argument is plausible, then the five scenes of the passion have been purposely arranged to form the following chiastic emphasis: A (18:1-12): Jesus is arrested and bound **in a garden;** B (18:13-27): Jesus is **the true high priest;** C (18:28–19:16): Jesus is the true king of Israel; B' (19:17-30): Jesus is **the true high priest;** A' (19:31-42): Jesus is **bound** and buried **in a garden.**

In addition, as we shall see, John insinuates in section B (18:13-27) that Jesus is the true prophet, and in section C (18:28–19:16) that Jesus is the true judge of all the world, including Pilate. Thus, in his passion account John presents Jesus as true high priest, true prophet, true king, and true judge of the world. This, of course, would be entirely characteristic. He had already presented Jesus as the true "Lamb of God, who takes away the sin of the world" (1:29), the true temple (2:18-21), the true water of life (4:10-14), the true judge of the world (5:21-23), the true bread of eternal life (6:35-58), the true light of the world (8:12), the true shepherd of the flock (10:11), the true source of resurrection and life (11:25-26), and finally the true vine (15:1).

(a) Peter, at the house of Annas, the father-in-law of Caiaphas, denies Jesus a first time (18:13-18).

18:13-14 First they led him to Annas. Annas had been high priest from 6 to 15 A.D., when he was deposed by the Roman procurator Gratus. Since such a deposition would have no validity for the Jews, it is likely that Annas was still considered a true high priest. If this deduction is correct, there can be no objection to a preliminary hearing before Annas such as that described in vv 19-23. This was followed by a second hearing before Caiaphas, a hearing about which John says nothing beyond the fact that Annas sent Jesus bound to Caiaphas (v 24). This would fit with Mark's mention of a first trial at night (Mk 14:53-64) followed by a second trial early in the morning (Mk 15:1).

That John is referring to two hearings, one before Annas and another before Caiaphas, is supported by the parallelism between vv 13 and 24. In addition, the parallelism of vv 13 and 24 eliminates the necessity of considering v 24 as either a gloss or an interpolation by a confused scribe. That Caiaphas, who was appointed high priest by the Roman procurator Gratus in the year 18 A.D., was high priest in "that year" need not mean that he had been appointed that year or that a new high priest was appointed yearly. It is probably John's way of pointing out that Caiaphas was high priest in that most memorable of all years—the year of Jesus' passion and death.

18:14　It was Caiaphas who had given counsel to the Jews. The reminder that Caiaphas had counseled that it "was expedient that one man should die for the people" is a reference back to 11:50, where John, with the subtlest of irony, pointed out how Caiaphas unwittingly had spoken the truth about Jesus even though he meant his words in a completely different sense. In 11:50, Caiaphas counseled Jesus' death in order to save the people from the Romans. Jesus, as John knew, would indeed be put to death, but to save the Jewish people from sin and not to save them from the Romans.

Thus, the high priest Caiaphas was proved a false prophet, whereas, as John will demonstrate in vv 15-18 and 25-27—the description of Peter's threefold denial of Jesus—Jesus, the true high priest, had shown himself to be a true prophet by foretelling accurately Peter's threefold denial before cockcrow (cf. 13:38). It is this theme rather than the trial theme that dominates the account. And it is the reference to Caiaphas' counsel concerning the necessity of Jesus' death (v 14) that points the way toward the development of this theme in 18:13-27.

18:15-16　Simon Peter followed Jesus, and so did another disciple. The other disciple is almost certainly the Beloved Disciple mentioned at the Last Supper (13:23-25), beneath the cross (19:26-27), with Peter at the tomb (20:2-10), and with the other disciples when Jesus appeared to them at the Lake of Galilee (21:7, 20-24). With one exception, his presence beneath the cross (19:25-27), he is always associated with Peter. Whoever he is—and we will deal with his identity in our commentary on ch 21—he is well enough known to Annas the high priest to have free access to his house (v 15b) and sufficient influence to gain entry for Peter as well (v 16).

18:17-18　The maid who kept the door said to Peter. The maid's question, Peter's denial, and the remark about Peter standing and warming himself at the charcoal fire are all repeated in 18:24-27 (section a′), creating perfect parallelism between the two sections (cp. vv 17-18 with v 25). In Mark's Gospel, Peter warms himself at the fire (Mk 14:54) and is questioned in the courtyard (Mk 14:66-72), while Jesus is tried and condemned by the Sanhedrin inside the house (Mk 14:55-65). Thus, both John and Mark use the dramatic technique of staging (outside and inside stages) to contrast Jesus' avowal of his innocence with Peter's avowal of denial.

(b) The high priest questions Jesus about his teaching (18:19).

18:19　The high priest then questioned Jesus. John's purpose in recounting the brief interrogation before Annas is to establish the innocence of Jesus. He does the same in the trial before Pilate, where Pilate expressly declares,

"Behold, I am bringing him out to you, that you may know that I find no crime in him" (19:4).

The hearing before Annas is neatly divided into three parts: first, in section (b), Annas questions Jesus about his disciples and his teaching, implying that there is something subversive about them (v 19); second, in section (c), Jesus defends himself against the charge of subversion by pointing to the public nature of his teaching (cf. 7:26; 11:54) and by asserting that he has "said nothing secretly" (v 20); third, in section (b'), Jesus questions Annas (the verb translated "questioned" in v 19 and "ask" in v 21 is the same in the Greek—*erōtaō*) and appeals to the testimony of those who have heard him teach in the synagogues and in the temple (v 21), thus countering the implied accusation that he has been teaching subversion.

(c) Jesus defends his teaching (18:20).

18:20 Jesus answered him. It is notable that Jesus speaks only about his teaching and says nothing in answer to Annas' question about his disciples (v 19). In all likelihood, John does not have Jesus bother replying to the implied charge that his disciples have been plotting subversion (cf. 11:48; 12:19). He has already shown that Jesus would have nothing to do with enthusiasts who sought to make of him a political Messiah (cf. 6:15; 12:14; 18:10-11). In the trial before Pilate, he will show Jesus denying unequivocally any claim to an earthly kingdom (cf. 19:33-36).

(b') Jesus questions the high priest (18:21-23).

18:21-23 Why do you ask me? Jewish law recognized the impropriety of asking an accused person to convict himself by his own testimony. Jesus' response, therefore, is both a question and an accusation, since it implies injustice on the part of the high priest (v 21). This injustice is compounded by the officer who strikes Jesus for so accusing the high priest (v 22). The officer (v 21) can no more provide witness that Jesus has spoken wrongly than Annas can provide witness that Jesus has spoken wrongly in secret. John, in short, proves Jesus innocent in every way. He will do the same in the trial before Pilate (18:28–19:16).

(a') While Jesus is being sent from Annas to Caiaphas, Peter denies Jesus a second and a third time (18:24-27).

18:24 Annas then sent him bound to Caiaphas the high priest. It is not known where Caiaphas was in residence, whether in his own palace or in another wing of Annas' house, and nothing is said about the trial before Caiaphas. John's silence about the trial can be explained in two ways. First, he takes for granted that his readers know the nature and outcome of that trial (cf. Mk 14:53-65; Mt 26:57-68; Lk 22:63-71). Second, his primary theological purpose in the whole of section B (18:13-27) is not to give details about Jesus' trial and condemnation but to emphasize the fulfillment of Jesus' prophecy (cf. 13:38) that Peter would deny him three times before cockcrow, the prophecy we see fulfilled in 18:27.

18:25   Now Simon Peter was standing and warming himself. This comment reflects back to v 18, where, at the end of section (a), Peter was standing and warming himself at the charcoal fire. Peter's first denial had been recorded in v 17, when the maid asked, "Are not you also one of this man's disciples?" Here the identical question is repeated, and Peter replies as he had in v 17, "I am not," thus denying Jesus for a second time.

18:26-27   One of the servants of the high priest. The third accusation is the most damaging because it comes from one who was in the garden when Peter struck Malchus (18:10). Peter's third denial follows and "at once the cock crowed" (v 27). Cockcrow in Jerusalem, whether it refers to the natural crowing of roosters before dawn or to the trumpet signal given at the close of the third watch of the night, would indicate that the interrogations of Jesus before Annas and Caiaphas were concluded about three or four o'clock in the morning. John, however, is not interested in clock time. He is interested in the theological aspect of Peter's denials, in establishing the fact that Jesus' prophecy about Peter's denials before cockcrow was fulfilled to the letter.

For Christian readers of the Gospel, John has made two points: first, that, historically speaking, Jesus was innocent and therefore unjustly condemned by the high priests and the Sanhedrin; second, that, theologically speaking, the true high priest of Israel was neither Annas nor Caiaphas but Jesus, whose prophecy, unlike that of Caiaphas, was fulfilled exactly as he had predicted (cf. 13:38).

Section C (18:28–19:16): Jesus, the king of Israel, is judged by Pilate and rejected by his own people.

Parallel structure

(a) **Outside,** the Jews ask **Pilate to condemn Jesus to death** (18:28-32).
(b) **Inside,** Pilate **questions Jesus about kingship** (18:33-38a).
(c) **Outside,** Pilate declares, "**I find no crime in him**" (18:38b-40).
(d) **Inside,** Jesus is scourged and mocked by the soldiers as "King of the Jews" (19:1-3).
(c′) **Outside,** Pilate declares, "**I find no crime in him**" (19:4-8).
(b′) **Inside,** Pilate **questions Jesus about power** (19:9-11).
(a′) **Outside, Pilate** gives in to the **Jews** and **condemns Jesus to death** (19:12-16a).

Text

(a)	18:28 Then they led Jesus from the house of Caiaphas to the praetorium. **It was early.** They themselves did not enter the praetorium, so that they might not be defiled, but might eat the **passover.** ²⁹So **Pilate went out to**

them and said, "What accusation do you bring against **this man?**" ³⁰They answered him, "If **this man** were not an evildoer, we would not have **handed him over.**" ³¹Pilate said to them, "Take him yourselves and **judge** him by your own law." The Jews said to him, "It is not lawful for us to put any man to death." ³²This was to fulfil the word which Jesus had spoken to show **by what death he was to die.**

(b)   ³³**Pilate entered the praetorium again and called Jesus, and said to him,** "Are you the King of the Jews?" ³⁴Jesus answered, "Do you say this of your own accord, or did others say it to you about me?" ³⁵Pilate answered, "Am I a Jew? Your own nation and **the chief priests have handed you over to me;** what have you done?" ³⁶Jesus answered, "My **kingship** is **not of this world;** if my **kingship** were of this world, my servants would fight, that I might not be handed over to the Jews; but my **kingship** is **not from the world.**" ³⁷Pilate said to him, "So you are a king?" Jesus answered, "You say that I am a king. For this I was born, and for this I have come into the world, to bear witness to the truth. Every one who is of the truth hears my voice." ³⁸ᵃPilate said to him, "What is truth?"

(c)   ³⁸ᵇAfter he had said this, **he went out to the Jews again,** and told them, "**I find no crime in him.** ³⁹But you have a custom that I should release one man for you at the Passover; will you have me release for you the King of the Jews?" ⁴⁰**They cried out** again, "Not this man, but Barabbas!" Now Barabbas was a robber.

(d)   19:1 Then Pilate took Jesus and scourged him. ²And the soldiers plaited a crown of thorns, and put it on his head, and arrayed him in a purple robe; ³they came up to him, saying, "Hail, King of the Jews!" and struck him with their hands.

(c′)   ⁴**Pilate went out again, and said to them,** "Behold, I am bringing him out to you, that you may know that **I find no crime in him.**" ⁵So Jesus came out, wearing the crown of thorns and the purple robe. Pilate said to them, "Here is the man!" ⁶When the chief priests and the officers saw him, **they cried out,** "Crucify him, crucify him!" Pilate said to them, "Take him yourselves and crucify him, for **I find no crime in him.**" ⁷The Jews answered him, "We have a law, and by that law he ought to die, because he has made himself the Son of God." ⁸When Pilate heard these words, he was the more afraid;

(b′)   ⁹**he entered the praetorium again and said to Jesus,** "Where are you from?" But Jesus gave no answer. ¹⁰Pilate therefore said to him, "You will not speak to me? Do you not know that I have **power** to release you, and **power** to crucify you?" ¹¹Jesus answered him, "You would have no **power** over me unless it had been given you **from above;** therefore **he who delivered me to you** has the greater sin."

(a′)   ¹²Upon this Pilate sought to release him, but the Jews cried out, "If you release **this man,** you are not Caesar's friend; every one who makes himself a king sets himself against Caesar." ¹³When Pilate heard these words, he **brought Jesus out** and sat down on the **judgment** seat at a place called The Pavement, and in Hebrew, Gabbatha. ¹⁴Now it was the day of Preparation of the **Passover; it was about the sixth hour.** He said to the Jews, "Here is your King!" ¹⁵They cried out, "Away with him, away with him, **crucify**

him!'' Pilate said to them, "Shall I **crucify** your King?" The chief priests answered, "We have no king but Caesar." ¹⁶Then he **handed him over to them to be crucified.**

Here, for the first and only time in the Gospel, the evangelist substitutes a seven-part format (*abcdc'b'a'*) in place of his customary five-part format (*abcb'a'*). One must clutch at straws to explain this extraordinary exception, and only one straw is reasonably plausible. In the Johannine school, Rome is symbolized as the great prostitute of Babylon (Rv 17:1-7), who sits on *seven* hills (Rv 17:9) and wars against the Lamb, the King of kings (Rv 17:14). In Rv 17, the allusions are all to Rome, the great world power, located beside the Tiber on seven well-known hills, which wars against Christ by persecuting Christians. In Jn 18:28–19:16a, it is noteworthy that Jesus is judged by Pilate, a Roman governor (18:28ff); there is a discussion of true kingship (18:33-38) and of true power (19:9-11); Caesar is mentioned (19:12, 15); and the "Lamb," the "King of kings," is condemned to die on a cross, which is the Roman manner of capital punishment (18:32; 19:16). In the Johannine school, in which symbolism played so large a part, it is at least plausible at this juncture of the Gospel, where a Roman official figures so prominently, that John might well have substituted a seven-part format for a five-part format in order to symbolize the beginning of the great prostitute's persecution of Christ and his Church.

In addition to his parallelism of outside stages (a) and (a'), (c) and (c') and inside stages (b) and (b'), John creates parallelism between (a) and (a') by repeating the following words: "it was early" (18:28) and "it was about the sixth hour" (19:14); "Passover" (18:28 and 19:24); "this man" (18:29 and 19:12); "handed him over" (18:30 and 19:16); "judge" (18:31) and "judgment seat" (19:13); "by what death he was to die" (18:32); and "he handed him over to be crucified" (19:16).

In (b) and (b'), John creates conceptual parallelism by balancing a discussion of kingship that is not of this world in 18:36-37 with a discussion of power from above in 19:10-11. In each, there is a reference to those who handed over Jesus to Pilate (18:35 and 19:11).

In (c) and (c'), John uses two exact verbal parallels: "I find no crime in him" (18:38b and 19:4, 6) and "they cried out" (18:40 and 19:6).

Commentary

Commentators agree that John has both highly dramatized and highly theologized the traditional and well-known account of Jesus' trial before Pilate. As early as 1962, A. Janssens de Varebeke noted the seven-part dramatic format with its chiastically balanced outside (1, 3, 5, 7) and inside (2, 4, 6) scenes.⁴ When one adds to this inside-outside staging of scenes the removal of the scourging from the end (cf. Mt 27:26; Mk 15:15) to the middle of the trial (Jn 19:1-3), the high incidence of John's theological vocabulary, and the typical Johannine technique of having Jesus dialogue about theological themes (in this case, his dialogues with Pilate about true kingship and true power from above), one comes to only one conclusion: John has used the trial before Pilate as a vehicle for his theological teaching that Jesus is the only true king and the only true judge of all the world, and that the Jews primarily and the Romans secondarily have been responsible for his death.

Scholars agree with this conclusion.[5] Readers should expect, therefore, to find in John's version of the trial before Pilate, as in other sections of his Gospel, a preponderance of theology over history, symbolism over fact, and dramatics over reality. John knew well the basic historical facts about the trial; he even seems to have based his account on Mark's passion narrative (cf. Mk 15:1-20). But it was the transcendent truths that underlay the trial rather than the mundane facts that concerned John. To bring them to the attention of his readers at the end of the first century, he resorted to his usual literary techniques: staging, dialogues, irony, and subtle innuendo. Nothing less could have done justice to the crushing irony of a petty Roman procurator judging and condemning to death the true judge of all the world, the true king of all the nations, and the true source of eternal life for all mankind.

(a) Outside, the Jews ask Pilate to condemn Jesus to death (18:28-32).

18:28a Then they led Jesus from the house of Caiaphas to the praetorium. Nothing is said about Jesus' trial before Caiaphas (cf. 18:24). From all that has been said about the Jews seeking to kill Jesus (cf. 5:18; 8:59; 10:30b; 11:47-54; 18:14), John can take for granted that his readers know that Caiaphas and the Sanhedrin had condemned Jesus to death (cf. Mk 14:55-64; Mt 26:54-66), a supposition confirmed by vv 29-31. **The praetorium,** which was the name for the official residence of the Roman governor, was at Caesarea ordinarily, but on the occasion of great feasts it was customary for the Roman governor to come to Jerusalem to be on hand in case disturbances broke out. The remark "It was early," which is paralleled in (a') by the remark "It was about the sixth hour" (19:14b), sets the time around 6 A.M., the time indicated by the word "early," a translation of *proi,* the Greek word for the last watch of the night, following cockcrow.

18:28b They themselves did not enter the praetorium. John's remark is ironical. The Jewish leaders have condemned to death the innocent Jesus but are scrupulous about contact with Pilate, since such contact with a Gentile would have rendered them ritually "unclean" according to the law and therefore unfit to eat the Passover lamb. The remark presupposes that the trial and the crucifixion took place on the day before the Passover, a chronology impossible to reconcile with the chronology of the Synoptics, who place the crucifixion a day later, i.e., on the fifteenth rather than the fourteenth of Nisan. There is no good explanation of this apparent contradiction.

18:29-31 So Pilate went out to them. The dialogue between Pilate and the Jewish leaders presupposes that the Sanhedrin's death sentence against Jesus was not known to Pilate. Pilate's statement "Take him yourselves and judge him by your own law" lays the burden of guilt on the Jews (v 31a). The Jews reply, "It is not lawful for us to put any man to death" (v 31b), and the fact that Jesus was subsequently crucified by the Romans would appear to support this contention. The point, however, is much disputed, especially in view of the stoning of Stephen (Acts 6). What seems reasonably clear historically is that the Sanhedrin might have had Jesus stoned to death but preferred to have the blame for his death placed on the Romans.

18:32 It was to fulfil the word. In 12:32 (cf. also 3:14; 8:28; 21:19), Jesus spoke of his death as being "lifted up from the earth," a patent allusion to crucifixion. John sees this as a prediction that Jesus would die by crucifixion. The statement in (a') that Pilate "handed him over to be crucified" (19:16) serves as a clarifying parallel to the words "by what death he was to die."

(b) Inside, Pilate questions Jesus about kingship (18:33-38a).

18:33-35 Pilate entered . . . called Jesus . . . and said to him, "Are you the King of the Jews?" The question implies that Pilate had heard that Jesus claimed to be the King of the Jews. Jesus' answer, "Do you say this of your own accord, or did others say it to you about me?" (v 34), puts Pilate on the defensive and at the same time sets the stage for a clarification of the nature of Jesus' kingship. Pilate's answer, "Am I a Jew?" evades Jesus' question and tries to blame everything on the Jews and their chief priests, who have "handed over" Jesus (cf. the parallel to this statement in 19:11 of section (b'), where Jesus declares that "he who delivered [handed over] me to you has the greater sin").

18:36 Jesus answered, "My kingship is not of this world." Jesus ignores Pilate's last question, "What have you done?" (v 35c). Instead, he explains the nature of his kingship. Since it "is not of this world," it can in no way be construed as a menace to Rome (the sense in which the Jews wanted Pilate to understand it). If it were of this world, Jesus' servants (followers) would have fought to prevent his arrest. Since they did not, it is clear that Jesus' kingship "is not from the world."

It should be noted that in 6:15 Jesus fled to the mountains when the Galilean Jews wanted to make him a political king, and in 12:12-19 he objected to similar overtures from the Jerusalem Jews by going out of his way to enter Jerusalem humbly on a donkey, in fulfillment of the prophecy of

Zech 9:9-10 (cf. 12:14-16). Thus, Jesus has been perfectly consistent, and Pilate has no justification for condemning him. It should be noted that in section (b′), the parallel to this section, the same discussion will be taken up again, but with the word "power" in place of "kingship" (19:10-11) and the words "from above" in place of "not from the world" (19:11).

18:37-38 Pilate said to him, "So you are a king?" The question presumes an affirmative answer, but Jesus' reply, "You say that I am a king," is purposely ambiguous, since what Pilate means by a king and what Jesus means by a king are far from the same. Leaving aside the question of kingship, Jesus explains the purpose of his birth and his coming "into" the world. He has come to witness to the truth, which the Gospel has already abundantly expounded (cf. 3:14-17; 4:13-14, 34; 5:21-30; 6:44-51; 8:12; 10:7-9, 14-18; 11:25-27), that the Father has sent him "into" the world to die for the world and thus to manifest his own and Jesus' love for all people.

Pilate's lame reply, "What is truth?" serves two purposes for John. First, it prepares the way for the judgment of Pilate the judge (cf. 19:11), who, despite his belief in Jesus' innocence, goes on to condemn him (cf. 18:38b; 19:4, 6, 16). Second, it alerts John's readers to the massive irony of Pilate's asking "What is truth?" with Jesus, "the way, the truth, and the life," standing directly in front of him.

(c) Outside, Pilate declares, "I find no crime in him" (18:38b-40).

18:38b I find no crime in him. The same words will be repeated in 19:4, 6 of section (c′) to form a perfect parallel with section (c). More than any other words, these words condemn Pilate the judge out of his own mouth. Thus, John lays the odium of Jesus' death not only on the chief priests (18:30; 19:11, 15) but on Rome's representative as well.

18:39-40 But you have a custom. Whether the custom of granting amnesty was usual at the feast of Passover (a fact that cannot be established) or usual in the sense that periodically amnesty might be declared on the occasion of a great feast is not known for certain. The latter is likely; the former is not entirely unlikely. The irony of the Jews' choosing the release of the robber Barabbas, whose name means "son of the father," rather than the release of the true Son of the Father would not have been lost on John's Christian readers (v 40).

(d) Inside, Jesus is scourged and mocked by the soldiers as "King of the Jews" (19:1-3).

19:1 Then Pilate took Jesus and scourged him. Normally, scourging preceded crucifixion (cf. Mk 15:15). John has transferred it to the middle of the trial for dramatic reasons. First, it testifies to the contradiction inherent in Pilate's declaration "I find no crime in him" and then having him scourged. Second, it prepares the way for the scene in section (c′) in which

Pilate presents Jesus wearing the crown and the purple robe with the words "Here is the man!" (19:5). Third, it serves as the centerpiece of John's chiastic *abcdc'b'a'* format and thus focuses his readers' attention on the kingship of Jesus, which is so central to the whole of section C (18:28–19:16).

19:2-3 And the soldiers plaited a crown of thorns. The crown and the purple robe (the royal color) contribute to the immense double irony of the soldiers' hailing Jesus as "King of the Jews." The double irony is that while the soldiers by no means truly consider Jesus a king and only hail him as such ironically, John's readers know that what the soldiers consider false is, ironically, absolutely true—Jesus is the king of the Jews and indeed of all the world.

(c') Outside, Pilate declares, "I find no crime in him" (19:4-8).

19:4-8 Pilate went out again. Pilate hopes that the sight of Jesus scourged and mocked will arouse the pity of the Jews and induce them to relent. His words "Here is the man!," meant to arouse compassion, are understood by John as ironic. He whom Pilate speaks of as "man" is actually the Son of God. The Jews are made to pick up on this irony by admitting to Pilate their real reason for seeking Jesus' death: "We have a law, and by that law he ought to die, because he has made himself the Son of God" (v 7).

In the trial before the Sanhedrin according to the Synoptics (cf. Mk 14:55-64; Mt 26:47-56; Lk 22:47-53), it is precisely on the charge of blasphemy that Jesus was condemned to death. Although this is the real reason for the Jews' opposition to Jesus, they have not pressed it up to the present because in Roman law, unlike Jewish law, it would not have provided grounds for a death penalty. The Jews' pressing of this charge at this moment in the trial was undoubtedly to arouse the superstitious fears of Pilate, a purpose amply accomplished, for "when Pilate heard these words, he was the more afraid" (v 8).

(b') Inside, Pilate questions Jesus about power (19:9-11).

19:9 He entered the praetorium again and said to Jesus, "Where are you from?" Pilate's question re-echoes a central theme of the Gospel—Jesus' origin from the Father (cf. 3:31-36; 6:32-40, 50-51; 7:27ff, 40-43; 8:14-16, 52; 9:29, 33; 16:26-28; 17:7, 25-26). Jesus gives no answer. He has already spoken about the origin of his kingship in 18:36-38 of section (b), and Pilate has shrugged him off with the question "What is truth?" (18:38).

19:10-11 Pilate therefore said to him . . . "Do you not know that I have power to release you, and power to crucify you?" In 18:36b, Jesus had said, "My kingship is not from the world." Implicit in the question of kingship is the question of power. Jesus acknowledges Pilate's power to crucify him but instructs Pilate on the true origin of all worldly power: "You would have no power over me unless it had been given you from above" (v 11a). Jesus has not answered the question "Where are you from?" in v 9, but here, implicitly at least, he answers it by identifying the place whence power comes—namely, "from above"—with the place whence his own kingly power comes (cp. 19:11a with its parallel in 18:36-37).

19:11b   therefore he who delivered me to you has the greater sin. Commentators debate the identity of the one "who delivered" Jesus to Pilate, whether Judas or the Jews. The parallelism of 19:11b in (b') with 18:35 in (b), where the same verb is used in both cases for "hand over" (*paredōkan* in 18:35 and *paradous* in 19:11b, both from *paradidōmi*), suggests strongly that the evangelist is thinking of the Jews, and especially the chief priests. Both Pilate and the Jews have sinned, therefore, but the Jews have the "greater sin." This conclusion is consistent with John's whole account of the trial, in which the Jews sin out of hatred and Pilate out of weakness. The true judge of all judges has given his verdict on both.

(a') Outside, Pilate gives in to the Jews and condemns Jesus to death (19:12-16a).

19:12a   Upon this Pilate sought to release him. Pilate understands well the truth of Jesus' verdict on him in 19:11b and makes a last attempt to exculpate himself from the justness of that verdict.

19:12b   If you release this man. The Jews are ready for Pilate. If the charge is brought against him that he has sided with one "who makes himself king," the political implications might well be immense for the vacillating procurator. Caesar (in this case it is Tiberius Caesar) demanded unwavering loyalty from his subordinates and was well known for his suspicious character. Pilate is concerned now with his own fate, not Jesus' fate.

19:13   When Pilate heard these words. It is most likely that Pilate himself "sat down" on the judgment seat, but the verb for "sit" can have both a transitive and an intransitive sense, and it may be that the evangelist means to say that Pilate sat Jesus on the judgment seat. If this is allowed, then it is certainly Jesus, not Pilate, who silently gives the final judgment on both Pilate and the Jews for what they are about to bring to pass. The place "called The Pavement" (*lithostrōtos*) may be the pavement made up of large paving blocks discovered by archaeologists in the lower levels of the fortress Antonia, but no certainty is possible. **Gabbatha** probably means an elevated place or ridge, and there is some evidence that the fortress Antonia stood on an elevated section in the northeast corner of Jerusalem.

19:14a   Now it was the day of preparation of the Passover. John last mentioned chronology in 18:28 of section (a). Here the parallels with 18:28 are obvious. The only difference is in the hour. In 18:28 it is the early or last watch (*proi*) of the night and therefore around 6 A.M. Here it is the sixth hour, i.e., noon, six hours after daybreak. John mentions the day and the hour not only to create parallelism between sections (a) and (a'), but also to focus attention on the Passover and the slaughter of the Passover lambs, which began in the temple at noon of the day before Passover. In section B′ (19:17-30), he will tell the story of Jesus' crucifixion in terms that depict Jesus as the Lamb of God sacrificed on the cross for the sins of the world.

19:14b-16 He said to the Jews, "Here is your King!" Pilate's last-ditch attempt to save Jesus fails. In reply, the Jews declare, "We have no king but Caesar." In the mouth of Jews, the words are almost blasphemous. It may be John's intent in recording these words to remind his readers that the Jews, since they have rejected Jesus their true king, indeed have no king but Caesar. The words "he handed him over" in v 16 hark back to the beginning of the trial, where the Jews declare, "If this man were not an evildoer, we would not have handed him over," thus framing the whole account with a significant inclusion-conclusion.

Section B′ (19:17-30): As true high priest, Jesus, like Isaac, carries the wood of his own sacrifice. The Beloved Disciple is present.

Parallel structure

(a) Jesus carries his own **cross** (19:17).
(b) The **soldiers** crucify Jesus (19:18).
(c) Pilate writes: "Jesus of Nazareth, the King of the Jews" (19:19-22).
(b′) The **soldiers** cast lots for Jesus' garments (19:23-24).
(a′) Jesus dies on the **cross** (19:25-30).

Text

(a) 19:17 So **they** took Jesus, and he went out, bearing his own **cross,** to the place called the place of a skull, which is called in Hebrew Golgotha.

(b) [18]There **they crucified him,** and with him two others, **one** on either side, and Jesus between them.

(c) [19]Pilate also wrote a title and put it on the cross; it read, "Jesus of Nazareth, the King of the Jews." [20]Many of the Jews read this title, for the place where Jesus was crucified was near the city; and it was **written** in Hebrew, in Latin, and in Greek. [21]The chief priests of the Jews then said to Pilate, "Do not **write,** 'The King of the Jews,' but 'This man said, I am King of the Jews.' " [22]Pilate answered, "What I have **written** I have **written."**

(b′) [23]When **the soldiers had crucified Jesus** they took his garments and made four parts, **one** for each soldier; also his tunic. But the tunic was without seam, woven from top to bottom; [24]so they said to one another, "Let us not tear it, but cast lots for it to see whose it shall be." This was to fulfil the scripture, "They parted my garments among them, and for my clothing they cast lots."

(a′) [25]So **the soldiers** did this. But standing by the **cross** of Jesus were his mother, and his mother's sister, Mary the wife of Clopas, and Mary Magdalene. [26]When Jesus saw his mother, and the disciple whom he loved standing near, he said to his mother, "Woman, behold, your son!" [27]Then he said to the disciple, "Behold, your mother!" And from that hour the disciple took her to his own home. [28]After this Jesus, knowing that all was now finished, said (to fulfil the scripture), "I thirst." [29]A bowl full of vinegar stood there; so they put a sponge full of the vinegar on hyssop and held it to his mouth. [30]When Jesus had received the vinegar, he said, "It is finished"; and he bowed his head and gave up his spirit.

John creates parallelism in (a) and (a') by repeating the word "cross" (vv 17 and 25); in (b) and (b'), by repeating "they [the soldiers] crucified him" (vv 18 and 23) and "one" (vv 18 and 23). The center (c) is set off from (b) and (b') by a change of characters (Pilate and the Jews) and a change of subject (the title put on Jesus' cross).

Commentary

In a Gospel in which the events of Jesus' life are so consistently and so highly theologized, no event is more thoroughly theologized than the death of Jesus. The brief fourteen verses of section B' might be interpreted as no more than a laconic account of the carrying of the cross, the title placed on the cross, the crucifixion itself, the casting of lots for Jesus' garments, and the last words and death of Jesus. But that would be to ignore the embarrassment of theological richness and symbolism John has poured into this brief account of the climactic event of Jesus' life on earth.

Here in these few verses, John brings to a searing focus all that he said about Jesus' mysterious hour; all that Jesus himself said about the destruction of the temple of his body (2:19-21); the lifting up of the Son of man as Moses lifted up the serpent in the wilderness (3:14); the Father's "giving" of his only Son so that whoever believes in him should not perish but have eternal life (3:10); the hour when the Jews will have lifted up the Son of man and will know that he is "I am he" (8:28); the hour when no one takes Jesus' life from him but when he lays it down of his own accord (10:18); the hour when the grain of wheat falls into the earth, dies, and bears much fruit (12:24); the hour when Jesus is lifted up from the earth and draws all to himself (12:32-33); the hour, finally, when Jesus, knowing that his time had come to depart out of this world to the Father, having loved his own who were in the world, loves them to the end (13:1).

In view of all this and along with almost all commentators on John's passion account, we feel more than justified in going beyond the literal sense of John's words to attempt to grasp the deeper symbolic and theological nuances he has built into his portrayal of Jesus' crucifixion.

(a) Jesus carries his own cross (19:17).

19:17 So they took Jesus. The "they" is ambiguous. It could refer to the Jews of 19:16, but more likely, in view of the prominent part given to the soldiers in vv 18, 23-25, 29, it refers to the Roman soldiers.

he went out, bearing his own cross. In Mk 15:21, Simon of Cyrene assists Jesus. This can be squared with John's account if one accepts that Jesus started out alone bearing his cross and, when he later weakened, was assisted by Simon. This is possible, but more probably John wishes to stress Jesus' initiative in taking upon himself the work the Father had given him to do (cf. 4:34; 10:17-18; 13:1-7; 18:11). On a deeper and typically Johannine level, it is quite probable that John expects his readers to see here an allusion to Isaac, who, according to Gn 22:6, carried the wood for his own sacrifice. This fits with the theme of Jesus the true high priest (cf. 18:13-27) who offers his life for the sheep (10:11, 15, 17-18); who has been consecrated (i.e., set aside for sacrifice) by his Father (10:36); who has been hailed as the Lamb of God (1:29, 35); and whose legs were not broken on the cross that the scripture concerning the paschal lamb might be fulfilled in him: "Not a bone of him shall be broken" (19:36).

the place of a skull, which is called in Hebrew Golgotha. Probably so called because of its shape, Golgotha had to be outside the city walls because Jewish law required that a burial ground be outside the city lest its use render the city unclean. In the fourth century, Constantine cleared away most of the hill to build the Church of the Holy Sepulchre. Part of the skull-shaped hill is preserved at the southeast corner of the present church.

(b) The soldiers crucify Jesus (19:18).

19:18a   they crucified him. John gives no details. It was customary that criminals to be crucified carried the crossbar, which was then attached to a permanent vertical stake at the site of the execution. The remains of a first-century crucifixion victim found recently near Jerusalem show that the nails were placed, not in the palm of the hands, but between the bones of the forearm, just above the wrists.[6]

19:18b   and with him two others, one on either side, and Jesus between them. John says nothing about the penitent thief (Lk 23:40-43) nor about the fact that the two were robbers (Mk 15:27). Barrett suggests that John mentions the two "only in order that it may later (vv 31-37) be emphasized that no bone of Jesus was broken, and that from his side there flowed blood and water."[7] This may very well be true. J. Gerhard, however, suggests a more intriguing explanation. He sees in the words "one on either side, and Jesus between them" an allusion to the building of the propitiatory in Ex 25:17-24, and especially v 22: "There I will meet with you, and *from above the mercy seat, from between the two cherubim* that are upon the ark of the testimony, *I will speak with you* of all that I will give you in commandment *for the people* [*sons*] *of Israel.*" Thus, Jesus on the cross is the new Holy of Holies, the new tabernacle-temple of Israel and, like Yahweh above the ark and between the cherubim, he speaks to the sons of Israel. In 19:26-27, Jesus will speak from between the two crucified with him to the Beloved Disciple, representing the sons of Israel, and to Mary, representing mother Israel.

The suggestion is not as fanciful as it seems. Jesus' assertion "Destroy this temple [meaning his body] and in three days I will raise it up" (2:19) is found in sequence 3 (2:13-25), which constitutes the chiastic counterpart of sequence 19 (18:1-19:42) in the Gospel as a whole. Here, then, with the raising up of Jesus on the cross between the "two others," we see the beginning of the raising up of the new temple that is Jesus' body, the tabernacle of the new covenant (cf. 1:14 and 7:1-8:58 *passim*). Very significantly, as Gerhard points out, the same verb (*teleō*) is used by Jesus when he finishes his work ("It is *finished*"—19:30) as was used of Moses when he finished the building of the first tabernacle ("So Moses *finished* the work"—Ex 40:33).[8]

(c) Pilate writes: "Jesus of Nazareth, the King of the Jews" (19:19-22).

19:19-20 Pilate also wrote a title and put it on the cross. It was customary to attach to the cross of a crucified criminal a title indicating the crime for which he was being punished.[9] Pilate, bested by the Jews in his attempt to save Jesus (19:12-16), words the title in such a way, and in three languages for all the world to read, that the Jews who have declared "We have no king but Caesar" (19:15) are now presented with Jesus as their king.

19:21-22 The chief priests of the Jews then said to Pilate. The ironic truth of the title is clear to John's Christian readers. That it is meant as an insult is clear to the Jews. Their attempt to have it changed is fruitless. They bested Pilate in the trial of Jesus; they will not best him here. John emphasizes the incident, not just because it happened (cf. Mk 15:26; Mt 27:37; Lk 23:38), but because it gave him the opportunity to reiterate once more what the Jews were vehemently disputing at the end of the first century, namely, that Jesus was indeed the long-awaited Messiah of Israel (cf. 1:49; 4:25-26; 7:25-31, 40-43; 11:27; 12:12-15; 19:33-38).

In addition, there is the emphasis on the word "write" (*graphein*), which is repeated five times and which is regularly used for the scripture, i.e., the writings. In view of the fact that John is about to cite the fulfillment of the scriptures about Jesus' death (19:24, 28), this emphasis on what has been written serves to prepare the way for the fulfillment of the scriptures at Jesus' death.

(b') The soldiers cast lots for Jesus' garments (19:23-24).

19:23-24 they took his garments and made four parts. Much is made of this apparently trivial episode, primarily because it fulfilled what was said in Ps 22:18: "they divide my garments among them, and for my raiment they cast lots." The Synoptics adverted to the text of Ps 22:18 (Mk 15:24; Mt 27:35; Lk 23:35) but said nothing about the number of parts, nothing about the tunic without seam, and nothing expressly about the fulfillment of the scripture. John, on the contrary, goes out of his way to emphasize all three. One must ask why.

To begin with, it is known that the garments of the condemned were considered the perquisite of the executioners. Thus, John tells us nothing new
in mentioning the fact. But the text of Ps 22:18 mentioned "garments" in
the first half of the verse and "raiment" in the second half. As a Jew, John
certainly knew that this amounted to parallelism of members and that, at
least in this case, the second half of the verse was simply repeating what was
said in the first half. Why then did he choose to have each half say something
different? The answer would appear to lie in John's love for symbolism. The
four parts indicate implicitly that there were four soldiers. The number four,
however, also symbolizes universality. What happens in Jesus' death happens for the sake of all—he is "the Lamb of God, who takes away the sin
of the world."

Secondly, what happens in Jesus' death happens according to the scriptures because Jesus came not only to fulfill the Father's will but to fulfill
what the Father had written about him in the scriptures. Thus, as Jesus comes
to the end of his work on earth, it is important to note that what he did
was done in fulfillment of the scriptures.

Lastly, John saw a special significance in using the second half of v 18
of Ps 22 to refer to the tunic without seam.

19:23b-24   the tunic was without seam, woven from top to bottom. Many
commentators see something symbolic about the tunic without seam. They
disagree, however, about the nature of the symbolism.[10] Some see the tunic
as symbolizing the priesthood of Jesus, since it was well known that the high
priest wore such a garment (Lv 16:4).[11] Others see it as symbolizing the unity
of the Church (cf. 10:16; 11:52; 17:21-24), in the manner of the net that did
not tear even though filled with 153 fish (21:11). Schnackenburg sees it as
symbolic of Jesus' utter degradation inasmuch as he is deprived of all his
earthly possessions.[12] Lindars says the tunic is said to be without seam simply
to explain why the soldiers had to cast lots for it.[13]

Of all the explanations, the symbolism of the tunic without seam per-
taining to the priesthood of Jesus fits the context best. It fits with Jesus,
like Isaac, carrying the wood of his own sacrifice (19:17) and with what is
said in the Gospel about Jesus being consecrated by the Father as the Lamb
of God who lays down his life freely for the sin of the world (1:29; 10:17-18)
and whose bones, like those of the paschal lamb, are not broken (19:36).
Finally, it fits with the words of the soldiers, "Let us not tear it," a remark
that suggests a deeper meaning when one recalls that according to Lv 21:10
the high priest was forbidden to rend (tear) his garments.

(a') Jesus dies on the cross (19:25-30).

19:25   So the soldiers did this. The Greek (*men* followed by *de*) indicates
that this brief statement goes with what follows, in the sense that while the
four soldiers were doing this, namely, dividing up Jesus' garments, something

else was going on between Jesus and those beneath the cross. **But standing by the cross.** It is difficult to determine whether there are three or four women beneath the cross. Schnackenburg opts for four, the first two women without names, the last two with names. He is probably right.[14]

19:26-27 he said to his mother, "Woman, behold, your son!" Then he said to the disciple, "Behold, your mother!" Some see in these words an adoption formula as in Ps 2:7, where God says to the Davidic king, "You are my son, today I have begotten you." This would fit with the idea of Jesus making sure that his mother would be cared for after his death and with the words "The disciple took her to his own home."

So simple an explanation, however, seems out of place in the theologically charged atmosphere of John's crucifixion account. Commentators, as a result, see symbolism here and give interpretations of the symbolism. Some see Mary as representative of either Judaism or Jewish Christians, and the Beloved Disciple as representative of either Christianity or gentile Christians.

Others—Catholic Mariologists in particular—see Mary as given a maternal and mediatory role in relation to the Beloved Disciple as representative of the Church and individual Christians. They contrast her special role here at the hour of Jesus' death with her more physical role at Cana, where Jesus answered her implicit request for wine with the words "O woman, what have you to do with me? My hour has not yet come" (2:4).

Still others see Mary, not as representative of Judaism, but as representative of all those in Israel who down the centuries had been true to Yahweh and so constituted the true, as opposed to the false, Israel.[15] In this case, the Beloved Disciple would represent those many Jews and Gentiles who by believing in Jesus now constituted the Christian community, the continuation of the true Israel of old. In view of the fact that Jesus himself said to the Samaritan woman, ". . . salvation is from the Jews," this interpretation has much to commend it and fits with the following explanation, which we think sees an even deeper and more elaborate explanation of John's mother-son symbolism.

This deeper explanation sees Mary as the woman of Gn 3:15, who is also called the woman and of whom God says to the serpent, "I will put enmity between you and the woman, and between your seed and her seed; he [her seed] shall bruise your head, and you shall bruise his heel." The text envisages those sons of mother Israel who will conquer the forces of evil in the world. Jesus in John's Gospel is that descendant of mother Eve who conquers the prince of this world (cf. 14:30 and 16:33) and entrusts to his brothers and sisters in the Church the continuation of his work of conquest (cf. 17:20-26). John, therefore, who is consigned to Mary as her son, represents all Christians who by believing in Jesus have become sons and daughters of God and brothers and sisters of Christ. Mary represents the faithful old Israel, and John the new.

This interpretation fits with the overtones of the book of Genesis in (1) the opening words of the prologue, "In the beginning" (1:1); (2) the references to creation (1:2-3); (3) the possible playing on the seven days of creation in Gn 1-2; and (4) Jesus' addressing his mother as "woman" (Jn 2:4). It fits also with the words of the prologue ". . . he gave power to become children of God" (1:12) and with Jesus' words at the end of the Gospel ". . . but go to my brethren and say to them, I am ascending to my Father and your Father, to my God and your God" (20:17)—words which imply that Jesus' followers are adopted brothers/sisters and therefore sons/daughters of the same Father.

19:28 After this Jesus, knowing that all was now finished, said (to fulfil the scripture), "I thirst." Just as the Johannine Jesus "knew that his hour had come to depart out of this world to the Father" (13:1), so now he knows that all is finished and that he has completed the work his Father sent him to do. To emphasize the completion of his work, he seizes upon the words of the sufferer in Ps 69:21: "for my thirst they gave me vinegar to drink." J. Marsh aptly remarks, "We should misinterpret John . . . were we to think that at this moment of his life Jesus was trying to think of what he had to do in order to make his actions conform to the predictions (so called) of scripture. John is not so naive as that."[16] Psalm 69, like Ps 22:15, which may also be alluded to here, ends up with the deliverance and the triumph of the psalmist. Jesus quotes and fulfills the words of the psalm to indicate that the moment of his triumph is at hand. In full control of his passion from beginning to end (cf. 10:17-18; 13:1, 31-32; 18:11), Jesus receives the vinegar, says "It is finished," then deliberately bows his head and dies.

Considering the context, which deals with the completion of Jesus' work, it is not impossible that John means Jesus' words "I thirst" in a still deeper sense. When the disciples in 4:31 ask Jesus to eat, he replies, "I have food to eat of which you do not know. . . . My food is to do the will of him who sent me, and to accomplish his work." Not only Jesus' food but his drink as well would be to accomplish the work of the Father. "I thirst" might very well mean "I thirst to complete my Father's work."

19:29 they put a sponge full of the vinegar on hyssop and held it to his mouth. John here records the fulfillment of the words of Ps 69:21b: "for my thirst they gave me vinegar to drink." His choice of the word "hyssop," however, is strange. The Synoptics use the word "reed" (cf. Mk 16:36). Hyssop was a small bushy plant used, according to Ex 12:22, to sprinkle the blood of the Passover lamb on the doorposts at the time of the exodus. In choosing the word "hyssop," John is almost certainly alluding to Jesus as the Lamb of the new Passover, whose blood is shed for the salvation of Israel and all the nations (cf. 11:51-52).

Such an interpretation fits with the Baptist's words "Behold, the Lamb of God, who takes away the sin of the world" (1:29); with Jesus, like Isaac, carrying the wood of his own sacrifice (19:17); with the hour when Jesus died, the same hour that the Passover lamb was sacrificed in the temple; and with the fulfillment of the scripture, "Not a bone of him [the Passover lamb] shall be broken," in reference to the fact that Jesus' legs were not broken on the cross (19:36).

19:30 he said, "It is finished." The Greek text has only one word (*tetelestai*), with an indefinite subject. In view, however, of 4:34, "My food is to do the will of him who sent me, and to accomplish (*teleiōsō*) his work," and 17:4, "I glorified thee on earth, having accomplished (*teleiōsas*) the work which thou gavest me to do . . . ," there can be little doubt that the implied object of the verb is the "work" the Father gave Jesus to do, which is completed with his death on the cross. **And gave up his spirit.** The words may mean quite simply that Jesus expired. They may also mean that at his death Jesus gave the Holy Spirit, as he had promised when he said, ". . . it is to your advantage that I go away, for if I do not go away, the Counselor will not come to you; but if I go, I will send him to you" (16:7). This interpretation is possible but dubious, in view of the fact that John records explicitly Jesus' giving of the Spirit to his apostles in the upper room on the evening of the day he rose from the dead (cf. 20:22).

Section A' (19:31-42): Bound with burial cloths, Jesus is buried in a garden.

Parallel structure

(a) **The Jews ask Pilate** that their legs might be broken, and that they might **be taken away** (19:31).

(b) They did not **break** his legs, but one of the soldiers **pierced** his side with a spear (19:32-34).

(c) The witness of the Beloved Disciple (19:35)

(b') Not a bone of him shall be **broken.** They shall look on him whom they have **pierced** (19:36-37).

(a') **Joseph of Arimathea asks Pilate** that he might **take away** the body of Jesus (19:38-42).

Text

(a)   19:31 Since it was **the day of Preparation,** in order to prevent the **bodies** from remaining on the cross on the sabbath (for that sabbath was a high day), **the Jews asked Pilate** that their legs might be broken, and that they **might be taken away.**

(b)   [32]So the soldiers came and broke the legs of the first, and of the other who had been crucified with him; [33]but when they came to Jesus and saw that he was already dead, **they did not break his legs.** [34]But one of the soldiers **pierced** his side with a spear, and at once there came out blood and water.

(c)   [35]He who saw it has borne witness—his testimony is true, and he knows that he tells the truth—that you also may believe.

(b')   ³⁶For these things took place that the scripture might be fulfilled, **"Not a bone of him shall be broken."** ³⁷And again another scripture says, "They shall look on him whom they have **pierced."**

(a')   ³⁸After this Joseph of Arimathea, who was a disciple of Jesus, but secretly, for fear of **the Jews, asked Pilate** that he **might take away the body** of Jesus, and **Pilate** gave him leave. So he came and **took away his body.** ³⁹Nicodemus also, who had at first come to him by night, came bringing a mixture of myrrh and aloes, about a hundred pounds' weight. ⁴⁰**They took the body** of Jesus, and bound it in linen cloths with the spices, as is the burial custom of **the Jews.** ⁴¹Now in the place where he was crucified there was a garden, and in the garden a new tomb where no one had ever been laid. ⁴²So because of **the Jewish day of Preparation,** as the tomb was close at hand, they laid Jesus there.

In (a) and (a'), John creates verbal parallelism by repeating the words "asked Pilate," "take away," and "day of Preparation." In (b) and (b'), he uses both verbal and conceptual parallelism by balancing the actions of the soldiers (they do not *break* the legs of Jesus, but one of them pierces his side) with the words of Ex 12:46 concerning the bones of the paschal lamb and the prophecy of Zech 12:10 concerning the piercing of the Messiah. The witness of the Beloved Disciple (c) clearly separates (b) from (b').

Commentary

(a) The Jews ask Pilate that their legs might be broken, and that they might be taken away (19:31).

19:31 Since it was the day of Preparation. Jesus was crucified on Friday, the day before the Passover, which in that year took place on a sabbath. It was on this day, the vigil of the feast, that the lambs for the feast of Passover were slaughtered in the temple. John notes the time because, as v 36 clearly implies, Jesus is the paschal lamb of the new exodus and the new covenant. He also notes the time because it helps explain the Jews' request that Jesus' legs be broken.

in order to prevent the bodies from remaining on the cross on the sabbath. According to Dt 21:22, a crucified person was considered accursed by God. The law prescribed, therefore, that the body of such a one be buried on the same day lest the dead body render the land unclean. In order to hasten Jesus' death and burial before the sabbath, the Jews ask Pilate to have Jesus' legs broken, a punishment known as the crurifragium. While the breaking of the legs was an act of mercy, since it brought about a quicker end to the torture of crucifixion, the Jews request it not as an act of mercy but to ensure that Jesus would not linger on and die on the sabbath.

(b) They did not break his legs, but one of the soldiers pierced his side with a spear (19:32-34).

19:32-33 So the soldiers came and broke. Since the breaking of the legs was intended to hasten death, and Jesus was already dead, the soldiers did not break his legs. John notes the fact because he intends to explain its theological significance in v 36. He notes the piercing of Jesus' side for the same reason. Why Jesus died so quickly has never been adequately explained. Victims of crucifixion sometimes lingered on in agony for several days. Explanations such as that he died of a broken heart or chose to die at the same time that the Passover lambs were slaughtered in the temple (between noon and 6 P.M. on the vigil of the feast) are plausible but hardly compelling.

19:34 But one of the soldiers pierced his side with a spear. Explanations for the piercing of Jesus' side are: (1) the soldier did it as a way of determining whether Jesus was alive or dead, in which case he presumably pierced the side of Jesus to see whether Jesus would react; or (2) he did it to ensure that Jesus was dead. Both explanations are plausible. **And at once there came out blood and water.** Whatever the medical explanation of this extraordinary phenomenon, John records it for theological reasons—his own if he himself is the Beloved Disciple (cf. 21:24); if he is not, then because of the significance the Beloved Disciple saw in it, prompting him to witness to the fact (v 35) for the spiritual benefit of his community.

The theological significance of the flow of blood from Jesus' side is easier to explain than the flow of water. The Baptist spoke of Jesus as the "Lamb of God, who takes away the sin of the world" (1:29). John presents Jesus as the Passover Lamb put to death at the same time (between noon and 6 P.M. on the vigil of the Passover) as the lambs were slaughtered in the temple. He also presents him as high priest. Like Isaac, Jesus carries the wood for his own sacrifice (19:17). Like the high priest, he wears a tunic without seam (19:23). In a context so transfused with the concepts of priesthood, sacrifice, and the feast of Passover, John almost certainly sees blood as the blood of Jesus' sacrifice. The conclusion is supported when we recall that Jewish law demanded that the blood of the sacrificial victim *flow* so that it could be poured out on the altar. What the Beloved Disciple sees in the flow of blood from Jesus' side, therefore, is the blood of Jesus shed to take away the sin of the world (cf. Jn 1:7; 2:2; 3:5; 4:10; Mt 23:35; Acts 5:28; Heb 9:12).

The flow of water is not so easily explained. Does it symbolize baptism, or the Holy Spirit, or possibly even the flow of life-giving water from Ezekiel's new temple (Ez 47:1-12)? Most likely it symbolizes baptism. In 3:5 and 13:9-10, water is symbolic of baptism, just as here in 19:34 the blood is symbolic of Jesus' sacrificial death. Significantly, Jesus associates both baptism and his death in his discourse to Nicodemus (3:1-21). Persons are born anew through water and the Holy Spirit (3:5), but, as Jesus declares in answering Nicodemus' question "How can this be?" (3:9), this comes about through his being lifted up (on the cross) so that whoever believes in him may have eternal life (3:14-15). In view of this intimate connection between water and the death of Jesus in the Nicodemus discourse, we believe that the water that flowed from Jesus' side symbolizes baptism. If this is granted, then it would follow that while the flow of blood symbolizes Jesus' sacrificial death, it also symbolizes the Eucharist (cf. 6:51-58).

A number of authors see the water as symbolic also of the Holy Spirit,[17] citing 7:37-39 and 3:5. But in 3:5 the water and the Spirit are distinct, and in 7:37-39 it is not at all clear that the words "Out of his heart will flow rivers of living water" refer to the heart of Jesus and not to that of the believer. The following words, "Now this he said about the Spirit, which those who believed in him were to receive; for as yet the Spirit had not been given, because Jesus was not yet glorified," show clearly that water is symbolic of the Spirit and that the giving of the Spirit is contingent on the death-glorification of Jesus. If this be true, then the water as symbolizing the Holy Spirit should probably be associated with 19:30: ". . . and he bowed his head and gave up his *spirit.*" But in either case, since Jesus bestows the Spirit on his apostles only after the resurrection (cf. 20:22), the giving of the Spirit can at the most be a proleptic giving.

We have mentioned the possible allusion to the life-giving water that flowed from Ezekiel's new temple (Ez 47:1-12) because John made it clear in sequence 3 (2:13-25) that Jesus' body is the new temple. John might easily have seen the cleansing, life-giving water that flowed from Ezekiel's new temple as the prototype of the water that flowed from Jesus' side and symbolized the cleansing, life-giving effects of the sacrament of baptism.

(c) The witness of the Beloved Disciple (19:35)

19:35ab He who saw it has borne witness. It is assumed that the one who bore witness was the Beloved Disciple mentioned in 19:26. It is not clear, however, whether he bears witness as author of the Gospel (cf. 21:24) or whether he communicated this information to the author, who then saw in it the symbolism of baptism and the sacrificial death of Jesus. In either case, if the Beloved Disciple is the author, then he himself vouches for the truth of what he saw in the words "his testimony is true, and he knows that he tells the truth." If the Beloved Disciple is not the author, then the author himself vouches for the truth of what the Beloved Disciple witnessed. In either case, the author is emphasizing both the fact and the significance of the flow of blood and water.

19:35c that you also may believe. John here turns to his audience, both Christian Jews on the fence and Jewish Christians in danger of falling away from Christianity because of the persecution by the synagogue and the theological arguments of the synagogue theologians against Christianity. He speaks to them now as he will in 20:31, where he says ". . . but these are written that you may believe that Jesus is the Christ, the Son of God, and that believing you may have life in his name." One must ask, then, why such an emphasis on the symbolism of the flow of blood and water? In 20:31, John explains why he wrote about Jesus' miracles. Here he speaks about the flow of blood and water for the same reason. In some way, therefore, the flow of blood and water has a witness value similar to that of Jesus' miracles.

We would suggest that this probative value goes back to what was said in the discourse to Nicodemus about the necessity of baptism in association with the death of Jesus (cf. 3:5, 14-16) and to what Jesus said about the necessity of the Eucharist in the discourse on the bread from heaven (6:51-58). In 3:1-21 and 6:51-58, John was refuting the Jewish theologians' arguments against the Christian position on baptism and the Eucharist. John emphasizes the flow of blood and water, therefore, because his audience, both Christian Jews and Jewish Christians, can readily see in the flow of blood and water a symbolic witness to the efficacity of the sacraments of baptism and Eucharist.

The extraordinary flow of blood and water, in short, provided for John's audience corroboration for what had been said about baptism in 3:5, "Unless one is born of *water* and the Spirit, he cannot enter the kingdom of God," and about the Eucharist in 6:53, "Unless you eat the flesh of the Son of man and drink his *blood,* you have no life in you." Barrett suggests that what John wants to say is, "You" (the readers of the gospel) "are not merely to believe that blood and water did in fact issue from the side of the crucified, but to believe in the full Christian sense."[18]

(b′) Not a bone of him shall be broken. They shall look on him whom they have pierced (19:36-37).

19:36 Not a bone of him shall be broken. John uses this first proof from Scripture, as he does also the second, to provide an exquisite parallel with the words of the (b) section: "they did not break his legs" (v 33) and "the soldiers pierced his side with a spear" (v 34). The quotation probably comes from Ex 12:10 and refers to the paschal lamb. It thus reinforces John's contention that Jesus is the sacrificial Passover Lamb of the new covenant (cf. 1:29; 19:17, 23b, 29b) who is sacrificed on the cross at the same time that the Passover lambs are being sacrificed in the temple.[19]

19:37 They shall look on him whom they have pierced. The quotation comes from a translation of the Hebrew rather than the Septuagint text of Zech 12:10. The meaning of Zech 12:10 is vague, but the appropriateness of the words to refer to the piercing of Jesus' side is more than obvious, and it is in this that John is interested. He may also see the words "look on him" as a fulfillment of what Jesus said about his death in 3:14-15: "And as Moses lifted up the serpent in the wilderness, so must the Son of man be lifted up, that whoever believes in him may have eternal life" (cf. Nm 21:8-9).

(a′) Joseph of Arimathea asks Pilate that he might take away the body of Jesus
   (19:38-42).

19:38 Joseph of Arimathea. In 12:32, Jesus had said, "And I, when I
am lifted up from the earth, will draw all men to myself." With Joseph,
a respected member of the council (Mk 14:43) and a disciple of Jesus, but
"secretly" for fear of the Jews, there begins the fulfillment of Jesus' prediction. Joseph goes to Pilate, openly for all the Jews to see, takes and buries
the body of Jesus in his own new tomb (Mt 27:59).

19:39 Nicodemus also. Like Joseph, Nicodemus had probably been a
secret disciple of Jesus (cf. 3:1ff; 7:50-52). He too now comes openly to Jesus.
A mixture of myrrh and aloes. The weight of the spices used in the preparation of Jesus' body for burial is lavish. Brown suggests that this was John's
symbolic way of signifying that Jesus was buried with royal honors, since
only kings were buried with such lavish amounts of oils and spices.[20]

**19:40 They took the body of Jesus, and bound it in linen cloths with
the spices.** It is difficult to harmonize this statement with Mark's statement
that the women on Easter morning brought aromatic oils to anoint the body
of Jesus (Mk 16:1 and cf. Lk 23:55-56; 24:1). The two traditions can be rec-
onciled only if one presupposes that though the women knew about the lavish
burial accorded Jesus by Joseph and Nicodemus, they naturally wished, out
of love and devotion, to add their personal touch to what had been done
by the men—a not unlikely but hardly provable presupposition.

19:41-42 Now in the place where he was crucified there was a garden.
Only John mentions the garden, just as he alone spoke of the place where
Jesus was arrested as a garden (18:1). The designation of the place as a garden
does not seem to have any symbolic intent, unless it is meant to prepare the
way for the nuptial language from the Song of Songs used in the account
of the resurrection appearance of Jesus to Mary Magdalene in 20:11-17.[21]
Apart from such a possibility, mention of the garden serves as a subtle
inclusion-conclusion to the whole passion account. In 18:1-12, Jesus was arrested and bound in a garden; here his body is bound and buried in a garden.

Themes

The primary theme of John's passion account is the kingship of Jesus.
It runs throughout the trial before Pilate (18:28–19:16). It is emphasized by
the crowning with thorns, by the soldiers' mockery of Jesus as king of the
Jews, and by the title Pilate has written for Jesus' cross. If the great amount
of myrrh and aloes brought by Nicodemus for Jesus' burial symbolizes royal
burial, then the theme is carried on right to the end of the passion account.

The secondary theme of the passion account is the priesthood of Jesus.
He, not Caiaphas, is the true high priest (18:13-27). He, like Isaac, carries
the wood of his own sacrifice (19:17). He wears the tunic without seam worn
by the high priest (19:23). He gives up his life in sacrifice at the same time

that the Passover lambs are sacrificed in the temple (19:14), and like a true sacrificial victim, his blood flows from his body (19:34).

Chiastic parallels with sequence 3 (2:13-25)

The parallels between Jesus' cleansing of the temple and John's passion account are highly conceptual but remarkably clear. To begin with, both take place at the same time—at the feast of the Passover. Both deal with the end of the Jewish sacrificial system. In 2:13-25, Jesus drives out of the temple the sheep and the oxen used as sacrificial victims (2:15). In the passion account, Jesus himself is high priest and paschal lamb sacrificed for the salvation of the world. With his death the old Passover is superseded. Finally, in sequence 3, when Jesus says, "Destroy this temple, and in three days I will build it up," John goes on to remark, "But he spoke of the temple of his body" (2:21). In sequence 19, John tells the story of how the Jews brought about the destruction of the temple of Jesus' body. Thus, the two sequences deal with the same basic concepts and balance beautifully.

Sequence 20

MARY AT THE TOMB

20:1-18

Parallel structure

(a) **Mary Magdalene comes** to the tomb (20:1).

(b) Mary tells the **two** disciples, **"They have taken the Lord out of the tomb, and we do not know where they have laid him"** (20:2-9).

(c) Then the disciples went back to their homes (20:10).

(b') Mary tells **two** angels, **". . . they have taken away my Lord, and I do not know where they have laid him"** (20:11-17).

(a') **Mary Magdalene comes** to the disciples (20:18).

Before presenting the text of 20:1-18, something must be said about the way John lays it out. He divides it into brief opening and closing scenes: (a) Mary coming (20:1) and (a') Mary departing from the tomb (20:18), and two longer scenes: (b) Peter and the other disciple at the tomb (20:2-9) and (b') Mary, the two angels, and Jesus at the tomb (20:11-17). He uses the center (c) to provide a hinge between the two longer scenes and at the same time to get Peter and the other disciple off the stage by remarking, "Then the disciples went back to their homes."

In the longer scenes (20:2-9 and 20:11-17), John creates secondary *abcb'a'* formats in such a way that (aa) balances with (a'a') and (bb) balances with (b'b'). Scholars have found difficulties in the text of 20:1-18, seeing in it unnecessary repetitions and a patchwork of sources and redactions.[1] John's use of parallelism in (b) and (b') explains the repetitions and diminishes considerably the cogency of source and redaction conclusions.

Text

(a)   20:1 Now on the first day of the week **Mary Magdalene came** to the tomb early, while it was still dark, and **saw** that the stone had been taken away from the tomb.

(b)   ²So she ran, and went to Simon Peter and the other disciple, the one whom Jesus loved, and said to them, **"They have taken the Lord out of the tomb, and we do not know where they have laid him."** ³Peter then came out with the other disciple, and they went toward the tomb. ⁴They **both** ran,

but the other disciple outran Peter and reached the tomb first; ⁵and **stooping to look in,** he saw the linen cloths lying there, but he did not go in. ⁶Then
Simon Peter came, following him, and went **into the tomb;** he saw the linen
cloths lying, ⁷and the napkin, which had been on his **head,** not lying with
the linen cloths but rolled up in a place by itself. ⁸Then the other disciple,
who reached the tomb first, also went in, and he saw and believed; ⁹for as
yet **they did not know** the scripture, that he must rise from the dead.

(c)   ¹⁰Then the disciples went back to their homes.

(b′)   ¹¹But Mary stood weeping outside the tomb, and as she wept she **stooped
to look into the tomb;** ¹²and she saw **two** angels in white, sitting where the
body of Jesus had **lain,** one at the **head** and one at the feet. ¹³They said
to her, "Woman, why are you weeping?" She said to them, **"Because they
have taken away my Lord, and I do not know where they have laid him."**
¹⁴Saying this, she turned round and saw Jesus standing, but **she did not know**
that it was Jesus. ¹⁵Jesus said to her, "Woman, why are you weeping? Whom
do you seek?" Supposing him to be the gardener, she said to him, "Sir,
**if you have carried him away, tell me where you have laid him, and I will
take him away.**" ¹⁶Jesus said to her, "Mary." She turned and said to him
in Hebrew, "Rabboni!" (which means Teacher). ¹⁷Jesus said to her, "Do
not hold me, for I have not yet ascended to the Father; but go to my brethren
and say to them, I am ascending to my Father and your Father, to my God
and your God."

(a′)   ¹⁸**Mary Magdalene went** and said to the disciples, "I have **seen** the Lord";
and she told them that he had said these things to her.

John creates parallelism in (a) and (a′) by repeating in vv 1 and 18 the
same name, Mary Magdalene, the same verb for *"came-went"* (*erchetai*),
and the same meaning for the verbs for "saw" (*blepei* in v 1 and *heōraka*
in v 18).

In (b) and (b′), he parallels "They have taken the Lord . . ." in v 2
with the same words in vv 13 and 15; "both" *(dyo)* disciples in v 4 with "two"
(dyo) angels in v 12; "stooping to look into the tomb" in v 5 with the same
in v 11; and finally "they did not know" in v 9 with "she did not know"
in v 14.

Commentary

(a) Mary Magdalene comes to the tomb (20:1).

20:1 Mary Magdalene came to the tomb early, while it was still dark.
Magdalene's presence at the tomb is mentioned by all four evangelists, but
only John mentions her as alone at the tomb. In the synoptic accounts, other
women accompany her (cf. Mt 28:1; Mk 16:1; Lk 24:1-12). Luke mentions
her as one "from whom seven demons had gone out" (8:2). Some authors
identify her with the sinful woman of Lk 7:38, who wept over Jesus' feet
and dried them with her hair. A few identify her with Mary of Bethany (Jn
12:3-8). Nothing is certain. The most one can say is that for reasons of his

own John has reduced to Magdalene alone the group of women who came to the tomb on Easter morning. As Brown points out, "This editorial reduction is an instance of the Johannine tendency to individualize for dramatic purposes, and is also designed to prepare the way for the Christophony in 14-18."[2] That there were other women is clear from v 2, where Magdalene says, ". . . and *we* do not know where they have laid him."

(b) Mary tells the two disciples, "They have taken the Lord out of the tomb, and we know not where they have laid him" (20:2-9).

With v 2, John begins the first of his two balanced scenes at the tomb: (1) Mary and the two disciples (vv 2-9); (2) Mary, the two angels, and Jesus (vv 11-17). Each scene is laid out according to John's usual *abcb'a'* format.

Parallel structure of 20:2-9

(aa)   20:2 So she ran, and went to Simon Peter and **the other disciple,** the one whom Jesus loved, and said to them, "They have taken the Lord out of the tomb, and we do not know where they have laid him." [3]Peter then **came out** with **the other disciple,** and they went toward the tomb. [4]They both ran, but **the other disciple** outran Peter and **reached the tomb first;**

(bb)   [5]and stooping to look in, **he saw the linen cloths lying** there, but he did not go in.

(cc)   [6a]Then Simon Peter came, following him, and went into the tomb;

(b'b')   [6b]**he saw the linen cloths lying,** [7]and the napkin, which had been on his head, not **lying with the linen cloths** but rolled up in a place by itself.

(a'a')   [8]Then **the other disciple,** who **reached the tomb first,** also **went in,** and he saw and believed; [9]for as yet they did not know the scripture, that he must rise from the dead.

20:2-3 So she ran, and went to Simon Peter and the other disciple. John leaves it to the reader's imagination to deduce that Mary had looked into the tomb before announcing to Peter and the other disciple that "they have taken the Lord out of the tomb." John is interested in getting the two disciples to the tomb and in recording their reactions to the position of the burial cloths. Simon Peter and the other disciple, the one whom Jesus loved, are mentioned together on several occasions in John's Gospel: (1) at the Last Supper (13:23-25); (2) at the court of the high priest (18:15-16); (3) in the boat when the haul of fish was made (21:7); (4) on the lakeshore when Peter asked Jesus, "Lord, what about this man?," speaking about the disciple whom Jesus loved (21:20-23).

In view of the fact that John is dramatizing the whole account, it is banal to ask such questions as: (1) Did or did not Mary look into the tomb before running to Peter and the Beloved Disciple? (2) Were Peter and the Beloved Disciple in hiding with the other apostles in the upper room at this time (cf.

20:19)? (3) Why did the other apostles not run to the tomb also? (4) Did Peter and the Beloved Disciple run so fast that they left Mary behind and subsequently departed without telling her about the position of the linen cloths? One might ask a multitude of questions, but they would all be beside the point in view of John's obvious intent to dramatize.

20:4 They both ran, but the other disciple outran Peter and reached the tomb first. Much has been made of the superior speed of the other disciple as well as of the fact that he waited to allow Peter to precede him into the tomb (v 6a). It was not because he was younger that he ran faster than Peter. This might be true but it is also trivial. John has the Beloved Disciple run faster for the same reason that he mentions him as "lying close to the breast of Jesus" at the Last Supper (13:23), for the same reason that he calls him "the disciple whom Jesus loved" (*passim*), and for the same reason that he has him alone recognize from afar that it is Jesus who stands on the shore of the lake (21:7). Love makes the eye more keen and the feet more fleet. The Beloved Disciple is not only the hero of the Johannine community; he is also the symbolic representative of what every Johannine Christian is expected to be.

20:5-6a but he did not go in. The Beloved Disciple allowed Peter to precede him into the tomb in order to show his respect for the apostle whom Jesus appoints as vicar-shepherd of his sheep (cf. 21:15-17) and who later, like Jesus himself, will lay down his life for the sheep (cf. 21:18-20). Without ch 21, which many consider an addition to the completed Gospel, the Beloved Disciple's behavior is not as easily explained.

20:6b-7 he saw the linen cloths lying. According to v 5, the Beloved Disciple had already seen the linen cloths. Now Peter sees them. But as v 8 will tell us, it will be only the Beloved Disciple who recognizes the significance of the position of the linen cloths and the napkin that had been on Jesus' head. Why, then, does John have Peter witness and verify the position of the cloths? Most likely for the same reason that he had the Beloved Disciple let Peter precede him into the tomb. Peter's witness, because of his position as vicar-shepherd of Jesus' flock, is important as testimony to any evidence in relation to the resurrection. Only the Beloved Disciple believes on the basis of this evidence (v 8b), but Peter's eyewitness testimony verifies the reality and factual content of the evidence. Thus, as Hoskyns says, "the weight of the evidence for the empty tomb" rests "upon the accurate testimony of two chief disciples, rather than upon the witness of the women. . . ."[3]

The probatory value of the position of the linen cloths and the napkin is explained in various ways. One explanation is that if grave robbers had taken away the body of Jesus, they would not have left behind the valuable burial linens. Since the linens were still there, and Jesus' body had not been stolen from the grave, it must be that he had risen from the dead. This makes some sense except for the conclusion, but it is hardly what John wanted to say by emphasizing the position of the linens. More likely John wanted to draw attention to the way the linens were disposed on the ground.

This leads to two possibilities: (1) the linens were folded neatly, indicating that Jesus himself had removed them from his body as he rose from the dead and, unlike Lazarus who came forth from the tomb still wearing his burial linens (because, theoretically, he would still have need of them), Jesus would no longer have need of them;[4] (2) the linens were so disposed on the ground that they still held the outline of the body, and the napkin that had been tied under Jesus' chin and over the top of his head still remained in the circular position it had when it was tied over Jesus' head. This is the more probable explanation, though how Mary and Peter could have missed its import is not at all clear.

20:8 the other disciple . . . saw and believed. Where Magdalene came to a wrong conclusion in thinking that Jesus' body had been stolen from the tomb, and where Peter apparently drew no conclusion at all, the Beloved Disciple sees and believes! Presumably he believes on the basis of the evidence provided by the position of the linen cloths and the napkin. How the evangelist knew that the Beloved Disciple believed requires some explanation. There are two possibilities. First, the evangelist himself is the Beloved Disciple (cf. 21:24), and he here testifies to the insight that brought him to faith. Second, the evangelist is not the Beloved Disciple but knows from the Beloved Disciple that this was his reaction to the position of the cloths.

If the latter explanation is true, then one must ask why the evangelist went out of his way to mention the Beloved Disciple's faith in the resurrection. Here one can only suggest that the evangelist is again emphasizing the pre-eminence of love. Love for Jesus made the Beloved Disciple run to the tomb faster than Peter. Later, love for Jesus enables the Beloved Disciple to see from afar what the other apostles do not see, namely, that the stranger on the shore of the sea is the Lord (21:17).

20:9 for as yet they did not know the scripture. After the resurrection, the early Christians searched the scriptures and found what they considered ample evidence for the foretelling of the resurrection of Jesus (cf. Ps 16:10; Ps 22:22-31; Ps 110:2; Hos 6:2; Is 53:10-12). Why John makes this observation at this point in his narrative is best explained by interpreting it in relationship to the faith of the Beloved Disciple. The Beloved Disciple believed prior to, and independent of, those texts of scripture that later Christians (the "they" of the remark) called upon as support for their belief in the resurrection of Jesus (cf. Lk 24:25-27 and Acts 2:22-36).

(c) Then the disciples went back to their homes (20:10).

This remark serves to get the disciples off the stage, leaving it clear for the scene that follows. John used a similar dramatic technique in the story of the Samaritan woman, where he got the disciples off the stage in 4:8 and then returned them to the stage in 4:27 following upon the exit of the Samaritan woman. Since the disciples are found together in the upper room in 21:1ff, the "homes" they went back to are presumably the place at which they were staying in Jerusalem rather than their homes in Galilee.

(b′) Mary tells two angels, ". . . they have taken away my Lord, and I do not know where they have laid him" (20:11-17).

Parallel structure of 20:11-17

(aa)   20:11 But Mary stood weeping outside the tomb, and as she wept she stooped to look into the tomb; [12]and she saw two angels in white, sitting where the body of **Jesus** had lain, one at the head and one at the feet.

(bb)   [13]**They said to her, "Woman, why are you weeping?"** She said to them, "Because **they have taken away** my Lord, and I do not know **where they have laid him."** [14]Saying this, she **turned** round and saw Jesus standing,

(cc)   [14b]but she did not know that it was Jesus.

(b′b′)   [15]**Jesus said to her, "Woman, why are you weeping?** Whom do you seek?" Supposing him to be the gardener, she said to him, "Sir, if you **have carried him away, tell me where you have laid him,** and I will take him away." [16]Jesus said to her, "Mary." She **turned** and said to him in Hebrew, "Rabboni!" (which means Teacher).

(a′a′)   [17]**Jesus** said to her, "Do not hold me, for I have not yet ascended to the Father; but go to my brethren and say to them, I am ascending to my Father and your Father, to my God and your God."

20:11-13 But Mary stood weeping outside the tomb. In fine dramatic fashion, John says nothing about the arrival of Mary at the tomb and nothing about any report she might have had from Peter and the Beloved Disciple concerning the burial cloths. John is concerned only with Mary's anguish over the apparent stealing of Jesus' body from the tomb. Like the Beloved Disciple (v 5), she stoops to look into the tomb, but instead of seeing the burial cloths, she sees two angels; and instead of coming to believe in the resurrection of Jesus, she continues to think that his body has been stolen from the tomb (cf. v 13). The two angels, like the two disciples, witness to the empty tomb. Two men instead of two angels are mentioned in Mk 16:5 and Lk 24:4, but the meaning is the same.

20:14-16 she turned round and saw Jesus standing. Mary does not know it is Jesus even when he speaks to her. That she supposed he might be the gardener fits with the mentioning of a garden as the place in which Jesus was buried (19:41) and with the fact that in other appearances of Jesus after his resurrection, he was not immediately recognizable (cf. 21:4; Lk 24:30-31). When Jesus calls her by name (v 16), it is different—she recognizes him immediately. The title she uses, "Rabboni," is another form of the word "rabbi" and, as John explains, both here and in 1:38, means "Teacher." By stressing the fact that Mary recognized Jesus only when he called her by name, John is probably reminding his readers of what Jesus said about the good shepherd: ". . . the sheep hear his voice, and he calls his own sheep by name and leads them out" (10:3).

20:17a Do not hold me, for I have not yet ascended to the Father. Whatever the manner of Mary's holding Jesus, whether embracing him or clinging to his feet, Jesus' words "I have not yet ascended to my Father" remind Mary and, through her, the reader of much that Jesus had said in his farewell discourse. There, as here, he had talked about absence and presence, about going away and returning, about going to the Father and sending the Counselor.

In part V of the Gospel (12:12–21:25), this sequence (sequence 20) is the chiastic parallel of sequence 18 (chs 13–17). It is very legitimate, therefore, to interpret Jesus' words "I have not yet ascended to the Father" in the light of what he says about going to the Father in the farewell discourse. As Brown asks, "Why would Mary try to hold on to Jesus, and why would he tell her not to do so on the grounds that he had *not yet* ascended?"[5] Without recognizing the chiastic parallelism of sequences 18 and 20, Brown nevertheless rightly interprets Mary's actions and Jesus' words in relation to what Jesus had said in his farewell discourse about returning to the Father and sending the Counselor.[6] In brief, Mary thinks that Jesus has fulfilled the promise he made in 14:18-19 when he said, "I will not leave you desolate; I will come to you"; and when he later said, "So you have sorrow now, but I will see you again and your hearts will rejoice, and no one will take your joy from you" (16:22).

When the reader recalls these and so many other statements in the farewell discourse about Jesus' going to the Father and returning (cf. 13:1, 3, 36; 14:1-3, 18-19, 25-28; 15:26; 16:5-7, 10, 16-22, 28; 17:13), it is not too difficult to see that what Jesus is doing here is correcting a misunderstanding on the part of Mary. (We have already seen John frequently using the misunderstanding technique.) Jesus' permanent return will be via the Counselor. Mary misunderstands, thinking that Jesus has returned and will remain physically. He must remind her, therefore, and his brethren as well (v 17b), that he has yet to ascend to the Father. When he has ascended to the Father, he will send the Counselor. It is the Counselor who will be with them permanently as another Jesus.

This is a different scenario from that in Acts 1–2, where Luke dramatizes the sending of the Spirit in his own inimitable way. It is even different, in a sense, from the ordinary Johannine scenario, which more properly envisions Jesus' death, exaltation, and return to the Father as happening on the cross. But it is not un-Johannine. In 17:1-26, John has Jesus pray to the Father from beyond the grave in words that speak in the past tense about what he had done on earth. Here, for purposes of dramatization, he has Jesus speak as if he had not yet ascended to the Father in order to remind Mary and his followers that his work would only be completed when he had sent the Spirit (cf. 16:7). As so often, Brown expresses beautifully this complex situation:

> The vehicle for this reinterpretative dramatization of the resurrection is the appearance to Magdalene, a story that came down from early times but was not part of the official preaching. As we have explained, by clinging to Jesus Mary acts out the misapprehension that the Jesus who had come forth from the tomb has fulfilled God's plan and is ready to resume the closeness of earthly relationship to his followers. Jesus answers by explaining that resurrection is part of ascension, and his enduring presence in the Spirit can be given only when he has ascended to the Father. And so, when in the next scene he appears to the disciples, he is the glorified Jesus who gives the Spirit (xx 22—a glorification is implied, for vii 39 stated that there could be no gift of the Spirit until Jesus had been glorified).[7]

20:17b but go to my brethren. Most commentators consider the "brethren" to be the same as the disciples mentioned in v 18, and this is more than likely. Yet it cannot be denied that the brethren of Jesus are mentioned elsewhere (cf. 2:12 and 7:3) and that it is not unfitting that Jesus should send such a message to them. Supportive of this possibility is the fact that Jesus' brethren and Jesus' disciples are clearly distinguished in 2:11-12 of sequence 2, which is the chiastic parallel of sequence 20 in the Gospel as a whole.

to my Father and to your Father, to my God and your God. As early as the prologue, John had said, "But to all who received him . . . he gave power to become children of God" (1:12). This has come about because of Jesus' work, which he completes in the hour of his passion, death, and resurrection-ascension. Now that the brethren are about to become children of God, Jesus can speak to them by anticipation about "my Father and your Father, my God and your God" (for the same formula, see Ru 1:16). Once they are born of the Spirit (3:5), they become children of God.

(a') Mary Magdalene comes to the disciples (20:18).

20:18 Mary Magdalene went and said to the disciples. With these words John ends his account with an inclusion-conclusion. In v 1, he said, ". . . Mary Magdalene *came (erchetai)* to the tomb . . . ." Here he repeats the same name and the same verb: "Mary Magdalene *went (erchetai)* to the disciples . . . ." In v 1, she *"saw (blepei)* that the stone had been taken away from the tomb." Here she tells the disciples, "I have *seen (heōraka)* the Lord . . . ." The verbs are different, but the meaning is the same.

Themes

The usual themes of witness and response recur. The resurrection is the greatest witness to the truth of Jesus' claims. Both the Beloved Disciple and

Mary respond to Jesus. There is no negative response and no replacement theme. More interestingly, the absence-presence and going-coming themes of the farewell discourse recur, but in a different form. Mary cannot find Jesus. Eventually he comes to her. But she misunderstands his coming to her and has to learn the importance of his going to the Father.

Chiastic parallels with sequence 18 (13:1–17:26)

In the five sequences of part V (12:12–21:26) of the Gospel, sequence 20 parallels sequence 18. Apart from the parallelism of Peter and the Beloved Disciple, who appear together both in 13:23-25 and in 20:2-9, the remaining parallels are almost entirely conceptual. In the farewell discourse, Jesus speaks of his going away to the Father and returning, of his absence for a little while and his returning in a little while, and of the necessity of going to the Father in order to send the Counselor. In 20:1-18, the recurring lament "They have taken my Lord away" emphasizes the theme of absence. This is then counterbalanced by the presence of Jesus in the garden and his words implying further absence: "Do not hold me, for I have not yet ascended to the Father."

Chiastic parallels with sequence 2 (2:1-12)

In the Gospel as a whole, sequence 20 is balanced by sequence 2. There are several simple parallels. In each, a Mary is addressed as "Woman" (cf. 2:4 and 20:13, 15). In each, both the brethren and the disciples are mentioned (cf. 2:11-12 and 20:17-18). In each, a specific day of the week is mentioned (in 2:1, it is the *third day;* in 20:1, it is the *first day*). In 2:11 it is said, ". . . his disciples *believed* (*episteusan*) in him"; and in 20:8 it is said of the Beloved Disciple, ". . . he saw and *believed* (*episteusen*). Less obvious and perhaps unintentional is the parallel between the "six stone jars [which] were *standing* (*keimenai*) there" (2:6) and "the linen cloths *lying* (*keimena*) there" (20:5-7); and the parallel between the steward of the feast who *"did not know* (*ouk ēidei*) where it [the wine] came from" (2:9) and the disciples who *"did not know*˙ (*oudepō gar ēideisan*) the scripture" (20:9) and Mary who *"did not know* (*ouk ēidei*) that it was Jesus" (20:14). Equally less obvious but perhaps not at all unintentional is the parallel between "My hour has *not yet* (*oupō*) come" (2:4) and "Do not hold me, for I have *not yet* (*oupō*) ascended to the Father" (20:17). The "not yet" (*oupō*) in both places has to do with an element of Jesus' hour and in each case is addressed to a "woman"—Jesus' mother in 2:4 and Mary Magdalene in 20:17.

Besides these simple parallels, there is the intriguing possibility that John has utilized in 20:1-18 the nuptial language of the Canticle of Canticles (especially 3:1-4) in order to create a broad parallel with the nuptial situation described in 2:1-12. Two authors, M. Cambe and A. Feuillet, have drawn attention to the echoes of the Song of Solomon in 20:1-18.[8]

In the Canticle, it is night (3:1). The woman goes about the city seeking her beloved (3:2a). She says, "I will seek him whom my soul loves. I sought him but found him not" (3:2b). She asks the watchmen, "Have you seen him whom my soul loves?" (3:3). Finally, she says, "Scarcely had I passed them, when I found him whom my soul loves. I held him and would not let him go" (3:4).

In 20:1-18, it is early (the end of the night). Mary goes to the tomb seeking the body of Jesus. She does not find it. She sees two angels (the watchmen?). Immediately after her words with the angels, she turns, sees Jesus, thinks he is the gardener, then recognizes him, holds on to him, and does not want to let him go.

The parallels are fairly close. If we add to the above the mention in the Canticle of Canticles of gardens (4:12; 5:1; 6:2; 8:13); of brothers (1:6; 8:1, 8); of running (2:8; 8:14); and perhaps even myrrh and aloes (4:14; 5:1), the overall nuptial parallels between 20:1-18 and the Canticle of Canticles become even closer.

Sequence 21

JESUS APPEARS TO HIS DISCIPLES

20:19–21:25

Parallel structure

(a) Jesus **commissions** the apostles (20:19-23).
(b) **Jesus' presence** is required for the conversion of Thomas (20:24-29).
(c) The purpose of the signs (20:30-31)
(b') **Jesus' presence** is required for the catch of fish (21:1-14).
(a') Jesus **commissions** Peter (21:15-25).

Text

(a)   20:19 On the evening of that day, the first day of the week, the doors being shut where **the disciples** were, for fear of the Jews, **Jesus came** and stood among them and said to them, "Peace be with you." ²⁰When he had said this, he showed them his hands and his side. Then **the disciples were glad** when they **saw the Lord.** ²¹Jesus said to them again, "Peace be with you. **As the Father has sent me, even so I send you.**" ²²And when he had said this, he breathed on them, and said to them, "Receive the Holy Spirit. ²³If you forgive the sins of any, they are forgiven; if you retain the sins of any, they are retained."

(b)   ²⁴Now **Thomas,** one of the twelve, **called the Twin,** was not with them when **Jesus came.** ²⁵So **the other disciples** told him, "We have seen **the Lord.**" But he said to them, "Unless I see in his hands the print of the nails, and **place** [*balō*] my **finger** [*daktylon*] in the mark of the nails, and **place** my hand in his side, I will not believe."
²⁶Eight days later, **his disciples** were again in the house, and **Thomas** was with them. The doors were shut, but **Jesus came** and **stood** among them, and said, "Peace be with you." ²⁷Then he said to **Thomas,** "Put your finger here, and see my hands; and put out your hand, and **place** it in my side; do not be faithless, but believing." ²⁸**Thomas** answered him, "My **Lord** and my God!" ²⁹Jesus said to him, "Have you believed because you have seen me? Blessed are those who have not seen and yet believe."

(c)   ³⁰Now Jesus did many other signs in the presence of the disciples, which are not written in this book; ³¹but these are written that you may believe that Jesus is the Christ, the Son of God, and that believing you may have life in his name.

(b')   21:1 After this Jesus revealed himself again to the **disciples** by the Sea of Tiberias; and he revealed himself in this way. ²Simon Peter, **Thomas called**

the Twin, Nathanael of Cana in Galilee, the sons of Zebedee, and two others of **his disciples** were together. ³Simon Peter said to them, "I am going fishing." They said to him, "We will go with you." They went out and got into the boat; but that night they caught nothing.

⁴Just as day was breaking, **Jesus stood** on the beach; yet **the disciples** did not know that it was Jesus. ⁵Jesus said to them, "Children, have you any fish?" They answered him, "No." ⁶He said to them, **"Cast** [*balete*] the **net** [*diktyon*] on the right side of the boat, and you will find some." So they **cast** it, and now they were not able to haul it in, for the quantity of fish. ⁷That **disciple** whom Jesus loved said to Peter, "It is **the Lord!"** When Simon Peter heard that it was **the Lord,** he put on his clothes, for he was stripped for work, and sprang into the sea. ⁸But **the other disciples** came in the boat, dragging the net full of fish, for they were not far from the land, but about a hundred yards off.

⁹When they got out on land, they saw a charcoal fire there, with fish lying on it, and bread. ¹⁰Jesus said to them, "Bring some of the fish that you have just caught." ¹¹So Simon Peter went aboard and hauled the net ashore, full of large fish, a hundred and fifty-three of them; and although there were so many, the net was not torn. ¹²Jesus said to them, "Come and have breakfast." Now none of **the disciples** dared ask him, "Who are you?" They knew it was **the Lord.** ¹³**Jesus came** and took the bread and gave it to them, and so with the fish. ¹⁴This was now the third time that Jesus was revealed to **the disciples** after he was raised from the dead.

(a′)   ¹⁵When they had finished breakfast, Jesus said to **Simon Peter, "Simon, son of John,** do you love me more than these?" He said to him, "Yes, **Lord;** you know that I love you." **He said to him, "Feed my lambs."** ¹⁶A second time he said to him, **"Simon, son of John,** do you love me?" He said to him, "Yes, **Lord;** you know that I love you." He said to him, **"Tend my sheep."** ¹⁷He said to him the third time, **"Simon, son of John,** do you love me?" **Peter was grieved** because he said to him the third time, "Do you love me?" And he said to him, **"Lord,** you know everything; you know that I love you." Jesus said to him, **"Feed my sheep.** ¹⁸Truly, truly, I say to you, when you were young, you girded yourself and walked where you would; but when you are old, you will stretch out your hands, and another will gird you and carry you where you do not wish to go." ¹⁹(This he said to show by what death he was to glorify God.) And after this he said to him, "Follow me."

²⁰**Peter** turned and **saw** following them the disciple whom Jesus loved, who had lain close to his breast at the supper and had said, **"Lord,** who is it that is going to betray you?" ²¹When **Peter saw** him, he said to Jesus, **"Lord,** what about this man?" ²²Jesus said to him, "If it is my will that he remain **until I come,** what is that to you? Follow me!" ²³The saying spread abroad among the brethren that this disciple was not to die; yet Jesus did not say to him that he was not to die, but, "If it is my will that he remain **until I come,** what is that to you?"

²⁴This is the disciple who is bearing witness to these things, and who has written these things; and we know that his testimony is true. ²⁵But there are also many other things which Jesus did; were every one of them to be written, I suppose that the world itself could not contain the books that would be written.

Conceptual parallelism is achieved in (a) and (a′) by the recurrence of the theme of commissioning: first, the apostles as a group in (a) and then Peter in (a′) as vicar-shepherd of the good shepherd's flock (cf. 10:1ff). In 20:20, the disciples are glad. In 21:17, Peter is grieved. There are also a few verbal parallels: "saw," "Lord," and "come" (coming to the disciples in 20:19, and the second coming in 21:22-23).

In (b) and (b′), conceptual parallelism is achieved by emphasizing the necessity of Jesus' presence for bringing people to believe. Thomas in (b) believes only when Jesus is present; the apostles in (b′) catch no fish (do not bring people to believe) when Jesus is absent but catch a multitude when he is present (cf. 15:1-7). Verbal parallels are: "Lord," "Thomas called the Twin," "disciples," "stood," and "place" or "cast" (the same Greek verb *ballō* is used for "place" in 20:25, 27 and for "cast" in 21:6).

The center (c) continues the theme of believing in Jesus by reminding the reader that the purpose of the signs is "that you may believe that Jesus is the Christ, the Son of God, and that believing you may have life in his name" (20:31).

As the inclusion-conclusion of part V of the Gospel (12:12–21:25), sequence 21 looks back to sequence 17 (12:12-50) by speaking about signs (cp. 20:30-31 and 12:37ff), about "being lifted up" (cp. 21:19 and 12:32-33), and by speaking about Jesus' coming—his coming to Jerusalem in 12:12-19 and his second coming in 21:20-23.

The sequence not only looks back to the introductory sequence (12:12-50) of part V of the Gospel (12:12–21:25), but it also looks back to its chiastic parallel in sequence 1 of the Gospel (1:19-51). In both sequences, Jesus is with his apostles; Nathanael and Peter are present again, and so are the two unnamed disciples; and in both sequences Peter (who is called Simon, son of John, only in sequences 1 and 21) is commissioned shepherd of Jesus' flock, thus explaining why Jesus looked at him in sequence 1 and called him "Rock" (cf. 1:42).

Commentary

In sequence 21 (20:19–21:25), we have included the whole of ch 21, thus indicating our conviction that this much disputed chapter is integral not only to sequence 21 but to the whole of the Gospel. Critics, on the contrary, have almost unanimously agreed that ch 21 is an addition to the completed Gospel, added to it by the final redactor. As our commentary will indicate, it is impossible to accept John's parallelism and at the same time exclude ch 21 as a later addition. The material in the chapter is essential not only for the parallelism of sequence 21 itself (20:19–21:25) but also for the chiastic parallelism of sequence 21 with sequence 17 (12:12-50) and with sequence 1 (1:19-51). Following the commentary, we will indicate these parallels that prove indubitably that ch 21 belonged to the Gospel from the beginning.

(a) Jesus commissions the apostles (20:19-23).

20:19 On the evening of that day. "That day" is the day mentioned in 20:1, namely, "the first day of the week," when early in the day Jesus appeared to Mary Magdalene. **The doors being shut . . . for fear of the Jews.** Fear of the Jews would be sufficient reason for the doors being closed, but as Barrett points out, "John's motive . . . for mentioning that the doors were shut was to suggest the mysterious power of the risen Jesus, who was at once sufficiently corporeal to show his wounds and sufficiently immaterial to pass through closed doors."[1] **Peace be with you.** Here Jesus, as he had promised in 14:27 and 16:33, bestows upon his apostles that peace which the world cannot give.

20:20 he showed them his hands and his side. Before commissioning the apostles (20:21-22), Jesus shows them the marks of the nails in his hands and the spear wound in his side (cf. 19:14) to prove to them that he is truly the resurrected one who had died on the cross.

20:21 As the Father has sent me, even so I send you. The theme of Jesus' having been sent by the Father runs throughout the Gospel (3:17; 5:36; 6:29; 8:42; 10:36; 11:42; 17:3 and *passim*). With these words, Jesus commissions his apostles as a group. Presumably only ten apostles are present, since Thomas is absent (cf. 20:24) and Judas has joined the enemies of Jesus (cf. 18:5b). The reference to the "twelve" (20:24) suggests that those referred to here as "disciples" (20:19) are the smaller group known as the apostles rather than the larger group known generally as the disciples of Jesus. The commissioning of the apostles had been foreshadowed in Jesus' farewell discourse (cf. 13:12-17 and 17:6-9, 14-18, 20-22). The wording of the commission is similar to Mt 10:40, and the actual commissioning is the Johannine version of the longer commissioning found in Mt 28:16-20.

20:22 he breathed on them, and said to them, "Receive the Holy Spirit." Just as Jesus acted in the power of the Spirit (cf. 1:32, where the Baptist declares, "I saw the Spirit descend as a dove from heaven, and it remained on him"), so now he invests with the power of the Spirit those whom he sends as the Father sent him. John says that Jesus "breathed" on them. This statement suggests a reference to Gn 2:7, where "the Lord God formed man of dust from the ground, and breathed into his nostrils the breath of life." Symbolically, John is speaking about the commission of the apostles as a new creation—a new beginning and a new world. It is worthy of note that the Gospel began with a reference to the first creation in the prologue (1:1-3); here it ends with a reference to the new creation brought about by Jesus' passion, death, and resurrection.

The functions of the Holy Spirit in the life of the apostles and the Church had already been described in the farewell address (cf. 14:16-17, 25-26; 16:7-15). The only one of these functions mentioned here is the function of judging [the world], either forgiving or convicting of sin those who do not accept and believe in Jesus.

20:23 If you forgive the sins of any, they are forgiven; if you retain the sins of any, they are retained. In sequence 1 (1:19-51), the chiastic parallel of sequence 21 (20:19–21:25), the Baptist hails Jesus as "the Lamb of God, who takes away the sin of the world" (1:29, 36) and then goes on to say, "He on whom you see the Spirit descend and remain, this is he who baptizes with the Holy Spirit" (1:33). Here in 20:22-23, the Lamb of God who takes away the sin (*hamartian*) of the world and who baptizes with the Holy Spirit first invests his apostles with the power of the Holy Spirit (20:22) and then empowers them to forgive or retain sins (*hamartias*).

If the reader recalls that Jesus bestows this power on his apostles immediately after saying to them, "As the Father has sent me, even so I send you" (20:21), then at least three conclusions are possible. First, the apostles are to continue Jesus' work of taking away the sin of the world. Second, the work is done through the Holy Spirit and baptism (cf. 1:33; 3:5). Third, the sin of the world which the Father sent Jesus to "take away" and which Jesus sends the apostles to "take away" or retain is the sin of unbelief in Jesus.

Confirmation for these conclusions comes from the Gospel as a whole. In 3:5, Jesus says, "Truly, truly, I say to you, unless one is born of *water* and *the Spirit,* he cannot enter the kingdom of God." He then goes on to say in 3:17-18: "For God *sent* the Son into the *world,* not to condemn the world, but that the world might be saved through him. He who *believes in him* is not condemned; he who does not *believe* is condemned already, because he has not *believed* in the name of the only Son of God."

In the rest of the Gospel, everything depends on a response or lack of response to faith in Jesus. The Samaritan woman, the Samaritan townspeople, and the royal official believe (ch 4). The Jerusalem Jews (5:1-47) and the Galilean Jews do not believe (6:1-15). When the Jews ask Jesus, "What must we do, to be doing the works of God?" Jesus replies, "This is the work of God, that you believe in him whom he has sent" (6:28-29). In chs 7–8, the Jews at the feast of Tabernacles refuse to believe in Jesus and Jesus tells them, "I go away, and you will seek me and die in your sin" (8:21). In ch 9, the man born blind believes in Jesus (9:38); the Pharisees refuse to believe (9:41). The theme of unbelief is summed up in 12:37-43, beginning with the words "Though he had done so many *signs before them,* yet *they did not believe* in him." The theme of belief is summed up in 20:30-31 in the words "Now Jesus did *many other signs in the presence of the disciples,* which are not written in this book; but these are written *that you may believe* that Jesus is the Christ, the Son of God, and that *believing* you may have life in his name."

Since belief and unbelief are so central to John's Gospel, it seems best to interpret the power given to the apostles at the very least as a power to admit or exclude from baptism those who have heard the gospel and either believe or refuse to believe. In this sense, it will correspond to the power of the keys given to Peter in Matthew's Gospel (cf. Mt 16:17-19 and see also 18:18). That this power extends to sins committed after baptism is more than probable and is supported by the fact that the Gospel appeals in a special way not only to Christian Jews afraid to leave the synagogue but also to Jewish Christians who have either apostatized or are in danger of apostasy, e.g., the many disciples who, after hearing Jesus' discourse on the Eucharist, "drew back and no longer went about with him" (6:66) and those other sheep of whom Jesus says, "I must bring them also, and they will heed my voice. So there shall be one flock, one shepherd" (10:16). That this power to forgive sins included sins committed after baptism is taken for granted by the author of 1 John, who tells the members of his community that "If we confess our sins, he is faithful and just, and will forgive our sins and cleanse us from all unrighteousness."[2]

(b) Jesus' presence is required for the conversion of Thomas (20:24-29).

Parallel structure of 20:24-29

(aa)   20:24 Now **Thomas,** one of the twelve, called the Twin, was not with them when **Jesus** came. [25]So the other disciples told him, "We have **seen** the **Lord.**"

(bb)   [25b]But he said to them, "Unless **I see in his hands** the print of the nails, and place my **finger** in the mark of the nails, and **place my hand in his side,** I will not **believe.**"

(cc)   [26]Eight days later, his disciples were again in the house, and Thomas was with them. The doors were shut, but Jesus came and stood among them, and said, "Peace be with you."

(b'b')   [27]Then he said to Thomas, "**Put your finger** here, and **see my hands;** and put out your **hand,** and **place it in my side;** do not be faithless, but **believing.**"

(a'a')   [28]**Thomas** answered him, "My **Lord** and my God!" [29]**Jesus** said to him, "Have you believed because you have **seen** me? Blessed are those who have not **seen** and yet believe."

20:24   Now Thomas, one of the twelve, called the Twin. Thomas is mentioned in 11:16; 14:15; and 21:2. John uses him in this episode as a concrete example of the doubt manifested by some of Jesus' disciples concerning the resurrection (cf. Mt 28:17 and Lk 24:11, 25, 41).

20:25-26   Unless I see in his hands the mark of the nails. Thomas will not be satisfied with the testimony of others, nor will he be satisfied with a spiritual body or some kind of an apparition. He will be satisfied only by the physical evidence that assures him the risen Jesus is the same as the crucified Jesus.

20:27   Then he said to Thomas, "Put your finger here, and see my hands." There is no indication that Thomas actually touched the body of Jesus. The presence of Jesus was enough to dispel his doubts and elicit his well-known act of faith both in the physical resurrection and in the divinity of Jesus.

20:28   Thomas answered him, "My Lord and my God!" The words are equivalent to the Old Testament title "Yahweh Elohim" and form a chiastic parallel with Nathanael's profession of faith, "Rabbi, you are the Son of God" (1:49; cf. also 1:1, 34). Thomas' witness could be interpreted as a powerful apologetic argument for the resurrection of Jesus and as a refutation of Gnostic arguments against the resurrection. More likely, however, John uses the episode to dramatize for his audience in the nineties the importance of faith in Jesus, whether that faith comes through sight or through hearing the gospel. This is brought out in the next verse.

20:29   Jesus said to him, "Have you believed because you have seen me? Blessed are those who have not seen and yet believe." Some, like Barrett,[3] consider v 29a to be a statement rather than a question, but comparison with the Nathanael parallel in 1:48-50, where Jesus first questions Nathanael before replying to his profession of faith, suggests that here too Jesus first questions Thomas and then replies to his profession of faith.

It is disputed whether Jesus' reply, "Have you believed because you have seen me?" means that faith without sight is superior to faith with sight. Brown denies that faith without sight is better.[4] Lindars argues more cogently that this is precisely the point John is making. He says, "Being absent when Jesus appeared to the disciples on Easter night, Thomas was virtually in the position of the Christian who has not seen the risen Jesus, and he should not have needed a further appearance in order to come to faith. Obviously John has the reader in mind in making this point."[5]

One is reminded here of Jesus' words to Nathanael, "Because I said to you, I saw you under the fig tree, do you believe?" (1:50), and of his words to the royal official, "Unless you see signs and wonders you will not believe" (4:51). That faith without signs is superior to faith with signs would seem also to be the meaning of the beatitude "Blessed are those who have not seen and yet believe" (v 29b). This does not mean that either Jesus or John did not take seriously the historical value of the signs as testimony (cf. 1:51; 2:11; 5:36; 10:25, 32, 37-38; 12:37). It only means that the point John is making here has more to do with faith than with the historical value of the signs.

(c) The purpose of the signs (20:30-31)

20:30   Now Jesus did many other signs in the presence of the disciples, which are not written in this book. By the words "many *other* signs," John clearly implies that the resurrection sign, the subject of the dialogue with Thomas, is to be understood as one of the signs performed by Jesus. These many other signs not written in this book were well known to John's readers either from the oral tradition or from the synoptic Gospels.

The signs are mentioned as done "in the presence of his disciples" because his disciples have been commissioned to carry on the work of Jesus (20:19-23 and cf. 21:1-14), and witnessing to his signs will be part of that work (cf. 15:27 and see also Acts 1:21-22). They are also mentioned as done "in the presence of his disciples" to distinguish them from the signs done in the presence of other disciples and even the Jews, signs that did not, as in the case of the resurrection appearances, already result in the faith of those who saw them (cf. 2:23-25; 3:2; 6:14-15; 9:1ff; 12:37-43).

The resurrection sign, given here in 20:19-29 first to the group and then to Thomas, is the great sign that leads to faith. John said in 2:22, "When therefore he was raised from the dead, his disciples remembered that he had said this; and they believed the scripture and the word which Jesus had spoken." Other signs not written in this book are important, but none ranks with the great sign of the resurrection.

20:31 but these are written that you may believe that Jesus is the Christ, the Son of God, and that believing you may have life in his name. The verb for "believe" could be understood either as an aorist or as a present subjunctive.[6] Translated as a present subjunctive (*pisteuete*), it would mean "that you may continue to believe." Translated as an aorist subjunctive (*pisteusete*), it would mean "that you may believe" or "that you may come to believe." Since the argumentation and tone of the whole Gospel deal with believers on the fence—whether Jews in the synagogue who believed in Jesus but were afraid to profess their faith for fear of being expelled from the synagogue, or Jewish Christians in danger of apostasizing because of the influence of the synagogue—it is more likely that the verb is to be understood as a present subjunctive and should therefore be translated "that you may continue to believe." That Jesus is the Christ, the Son of God, and that believing you may have life in his name has been the central message of the Gospel from the prologue (cf. 1:1, 12-13) to the very end.

Authors, with the exception of Hoskyns and Lagrange, have contended for years that vv 30-31 constitute the original ending of John's Gospel and that the contents of ch 21 constitute a later addition either by the author himself or by a disciple-editor. This contention, based upon the presupposition that the Gospel was written according to the laws of narrative rather than according to the laws of parallelism, is so firmly held by scholars that an author of the caliber of Lindars can go so far as to declare that Hoskyns "perversely argues that this is not the end of the book, but merely a summary of the chapter . . . ."[7]

We, on the contrary, will argue in the remainder of our commentary that far from being perverse, Hoskyns was extraordinarily perceptive. These verses (vv 30-31) constitute the (c) section of sequence 21 (20:19–21:25), and the sequence can come to its conclusion only when the author has supplied (b') and (a') sections to balance his (b) section in 20:24-29 and his (a) section in 20:18-23. The fact that he does supply these (b') and (a') sections, just as he supplied them in every other sequence of the Gospel, constitutes a massive argument for the unity and originality of all the material in sequence 21 (20:19–21:25). Hoskyns and Lagrange, for all that they wrote more than half a century ago, were more perceptive than perverse.[8]

(b') Jesus' presence is required for the catch of fish (21:1-14).

Leaving aside arguments from style,[9] upon which authors are divided, with some in favor and others against the Johannine style of the chapter, two arguments strongly favor the proposition that ch 21 comes from the same hand as the rest of the Gospel: first, the typical *abcb'a'* format of 21:1-14, which has been demonstrated to be the key literary characteristic of the author of the rest of the Gospel; second, the parallelism of the whole of sequence 21 (20:18–21:25) in itself, then with its chiastic parallel (12:12-50) in part V of the Gospel (12:12–21:25), and finally with its chiastic parallel (1:19-51) in the Gospel as a whole. We deal with the first argument immediately by demonstrating the chiastic parallelism of 21:1-14. We deal with the second argument following the commentary on the whole of sequence 21 (see pp. 310ff).

Parallel structure of 21:1-14

(aa)   21:1 After this Jesus **revealed** himself again **to the disciples** by the Sea of Tiberias; and he **revealed** himself in this way.

(bb)   [2]**Simon Peter,** Thomas called the Twin, Nathanael of Cana in Galilee, the sons of Zebedee, and two **others of his disciples** were together. [3]**Simon Peter** said to them, "I am going fishing." They said to him, "We will go with you." **They went out** (*exēlthon*) **and got into** (*enebēsan*) **the boat;** but that night they **caught** nothing. [4]Just as day was breaking, Jesus stood on the beach; yet **the disciples did not know that it was Jesus.** [5]Jesus said to them, "Children, have you any **fish?**" They answered him, "No." [6]He said to them, "Cast the **net** on the right side of the boat, and you will find some." So they cast it, and now they were not able to **haul** (*helkysai*) it in, **for the quantity of fish.**

(cc)   [7]That disciple whom Jesus loved said to Peter, "It is the Lord!" When Simon Peter heard that it was the Lord, he put on his clothes, for he was stripped for work, and sprang into the sea.

(b'b') [8]But **the other disciples came** (*ēlthon*) **in the boat,** dragging the **net full of fish,** for they were not far from the land, but about a hundred yards off. [9]When **they got out** (*apebēsan*) on land, they saw a charcoal fire there, with **fish** lying on it, and bread. [10]Jesus said to them, "Bring some of the **fish** that you have just **caught.**" [11]So **Simon Peter went aboard** (*anebē*) and **hauled** (*heilkysen*) the **net** ashore, **full of large fish, a hundred and fifty-three of them;** and although there were **so many,** the **net** was not torn. [12]Jesus said to them, "Come and have breakfast." Now none of the **disciples** dared ask him, "Who are you?" **They knew it was the Lord.** [13]Jesus came and took the bread and gave it to them, and so with the **fish.**

(a′a′)   [14]This was now the third time that **Jesus was revealed to the disciples** after he was raised from the dead.

John creates parallelism in (aa) and (a′a′) by repeating the words "Jesus," "revealed," and "to the disciples." In (bb) and (b′b′), he repeats the words "Simon Peter," "disciples," "boat," "net," "haul," "fish," and the two concepts: quantity of fish (vv 6 and 8, 11), and the disciples' knowing or not knowing it was Jesus on the shore (vv 4 and 12). Section (cc) deals with Peter and the disciple whom Jesus loved and clearly separates section (bb) from section (b′b′).

21:1   After this Jesus revealed himself again . . . in this way. The words "again" and "in this way" link Jesus' third appearance to his disciples with his first and second appearances, already described in 20:19-29. In those appearances Jesus revealed himself by coming through the doors of the upper room in Jerusalem and standing, easily recognizable, in their midst.

His "way" of revealing himself in this third appearance is significantly different in three ways. First, Jesus is at a distance on the shore of the sea, and the disciples do not know that it is he (v 4). Second, Peter and the Beloved Disciple are the first to know "it is the Lord" (v 7). Third, the disciples' failure to catch any fish by themselves and their success in catching a huge quantity of fish when Jesus is present (vv 6, 8, 11), added to the Eucharistic actions and words of Jesus on the shore, finally reveal to the disciples also that "it is the Lord" (v 12).

The words "in this way" (rather than the other way he revealed himself) thus qualify this third revelation of Jesus to his disciples. They prepare the reader to scrutinize more intently and question more theologically the significance of the disciples' success in catching a large quantity of fish when Jesus was present and directing their endeavors (vv 4-6), and the significance of the disciples' recognizing that "it was the Lord" only when they saw that Jesus had prepared a meal for them "and took the bread and gave it to them, and so with the fish" (vv 12-13). It is not too much to expect of John's readers that the disciples' success in fishing when Jesus was present would remind them of his words "apart from me you can do nothing" (15:5), and that the words "Jesus came and took the bread and gave it to them" would remind them of what he had done on the mountain when he multiplied the loaves and the fishes for the multitude (6:1-13).

21:2   Simon Peter, Thomas called the Twin, Nathanael of Cana in Galilee, the sons of Zebedee, and two others of his disciples were together. Four of the seven disciples listed here are mentioned in sequence 1 (1:19-51): Simon Peter (1:40-41); the two unnamed disciples (1:37), of whom one is identified as Andrew (1:40) and the other is left nameless; and Nathanael.

The return of these four at the end of the Gospel indicates that John in sequence 21 is directing his reader's mind back to sequence 1 (1:19-51) and thus forming a grand inclusion-conclusion for the whole of his Gospel. Only in sequence 21 and in sequence 1 is Peter called Simon, son of John, and are the two unnamed disciples and Nathanael mentioned. Thomas called the Twin is mentioned in order to form a parallel with 20:24-29.

Why the sons of Zebedee are mentioned is difficult to explain, unless John wishes to symbolize by the number seven the universal scope of this symbolic fishing trip. In view of the number 153 in v 11, which almost all commentators consider another symbol of the universal scope of this symbolic fishing trip, this explanation is not improbable.

21:3 Simon Peter said to them, "I am going fishing." Whatever the actual circumstances of this fishing trip (cf. Lk 5:1-11 for a different version), John tells the story in such a way that Peter's leadership is emphasized. He is the one who says, "I am going fishing" and is then followed by the others. He, along with the Beloved Disciple, is the first to recognize Jesus on the shore (v 7). It is he who first goes to Jesus (v 7c). And it is he who hauls ashore the net "full of large fish, a hundred and fifty-three of them" (v 11). John's purpose in emphasizing the leadership of Simon Peter is to prepare the reader for Jesus' commission of Peter to be the vicar-shepherd of his flock in 21:15ff.

21:4-6 Just as day was breaking, Jesus stood on the beach. The presence of Jesus makes all the difference in the world for the success of the disciples' fishing endeavors. Without him, they catch nothing (v 3b); with him, they catch a quantity of fish so great that they cannot haul in the net (v 6). Almost all commentators agree in interpreting the fishing trip as symbolic of the apostolic mission to "catch" men and women (cf. Mk 1:17; Mt 4:19; Lk 5:10). Jesus had said, "Apart from me, you can do nothing" (15:5). Here the truth of that saying is demonstrated in relation to the apostolic mission.

21:7 That disciple whom Jesus loved said to Peter, "It is the Lord." This little aside indicates that the Beloved Disciple was in the boat and therefore must have been one of the disciples mentioned in v 2—either one of the sons of Zebedee or one of the two unnamed disciples. Andrew is identified in 1:40 as one of the two unnamed disciples. There is some evidence that Philip is the other unnamed disciple. Here the Beloved Disciple is the first to recognize Jesus, just as he was the first to believe in the resurrection when he saw the position of the burial cloths (20:8).

Simon Peter accepts the word of the Beloved Disciple. That he should put on clothes before jumping into the water seems incongruous. Most likely the meaning is, as Brown suggests, not that he put on clothes, but that he was naked under his outer garment, which he tucked up (rather than "put on") in order to swim more easily to shore.[10] Peter's haste to go to Jesus is perhaps meant to remind the reader how much Peter has changed since he so hastily and energetically denied Jesus at the time of the passion (cf. 18:17-27). This would anticipate 21:15-18, where Peter three times asserts his love for Jesus and thus atones for his threefold denial.

21:8-10   But the other disciples came in the boat. The scene that greets the other disciples as they arrive with the net full of fish is reminiscent of the loaves miracle in 6:1-15. There Jesus took bread and fish and distributed them to the multitude. Here he does the same to the disciples (v 13) and thus gives them as a group, as he had given to Thomas as an individual, another clear indication that, though risen from the dead, he is the same Jesus who before his passion and death had multiplied the loaves and fishes for the multitude.

21:11   So Simon Peter went aboard and hauled the net ashore. Peter's initiative in hauling the net ashore is similar to his earlier initiative in leading the fishing trip in v 3. **Full of large fish, a hundred and fifty-three.** The emphasis on a huge and quasi-miraculous catch of fish is continued here from vv 6 and 8. Whatever the actual size of the haul of fish, exegetes agree that it is symbolic of the apostolic ministry, which is to be "fishers of men," and that it represents, therefore, the success of the Christian mission to the world. Brown says, "It is not too great an exaggeration to say that the catch of fish is the dramatic equivalent of the command given in the Matthaean account of the Galilean appearance: 'Go therefore and make disciples of all nations' (Matt xxviii 19)."[11] Explanations for the exact number of one hundred and fifty-three fish vary. First, most explain it, with St. Jerome, as coinciding with the conclusion of Greek zoologists that there were one hundred and fifty-three different kinds of fish. Others explain it as a number symbolic of completion or perfection. Brown suggests that it was the actual number; that the fish were counted by the Beloved Disciple, who here, as in other places in the Gospel, gives eyewitness accounts (cf. 19:35; 20:7; 21:24); and that later it was kept to add to the symbolism of the story to indicate "the magnitude of the results for the disciples' mission."[12]

the net was not torn. This remark is similar in symbolism to the remark made about Jesus' tunic without seam which the soldiers did not tear (19:23-24). It is symbolic of the unity of the flock of the good shepherd (cf. 10:16), a theme that will be taken up in another way when Jesus says to Peter, "Feed my sheep" (21:15-17). It should be noted that John forges a clear conceptual parallel here between the haul of fish, representing the success of the apostolic fishers of souls, and the words of Jesus in 12:32, "and I, when I am lifted up from the earth, will draw all men to myself." In 21:11, the verb for "hauled" is *heilkysen,* from *helkyein;* in 12:32, the verb for "draw" is *helkysō.* The concept and the verb *helkyein* in 21:11 thus parallel the concept and the verb in 12:32. The fact that 21:11 occurs in sequence 21 (20:19–21:25), which is the chiastic parellel of sequence 17 (12:12-50) in part V of the Gospel as a whole, is another confirmation of the authenticity of ch 21. Whoever wrote the one also wrote the other.

21:12-13 Jesus said to them, "Come and have breakfast." The disciples, who "did not know that it was Jesus" in v 4, now know that it is the Lord. They do not dare to ask him because, like Thomas (20:28-29), they are filled with awe. The remark "they knew it was the Lord" is almost certainly prompted by the disciples' recollection of the loaves and the fishes, now distributed to them as they once were to the multitude on the mountain (cf. 6:1-15). The whole incident is reminiscent of Lk 24:13-35, where the disciples on the road to Emmaus told how "he was known to them in the breaking of the bread" (Lk 24:35).

The Eucharistic overtones of this little episode are not insignificant in relation to the missionary work of the apostles, nor are they out of place following the symbolic catch of fish. The words *"Follow me,* and I will make you fishers of men" (Mt 4:19) imply that the success of the apostolic ministry is intimately bound up with following Jesus. But following Jesus means dying with Jesus. Since the Eucharist commemorates the death of Jesus, mention of a Eucharistic meal in relationship to the catch of fish is the equivalent in broad terms of saying, "Follow me and [then] I will make you fishers of men."[13]

The sequence of ministry and Eucharist (death of Jesus) used here in relation to the work of the apostles will be used again immediately in John's account of the commission of Peter, who is first told to "feed my sheep" (21:15-17) and then told that he will follow Jesus to the cross (21:18-19).

21:14 This was now the third time that Jesus was revealed to the disciples after he was raised from the dead. This verse clearly parallels v 1. It also links Jesus' appearance to the disciples in Galilee with his two previous appearances to them in Jerusalem (20:19-29) and further confirms the authenticity of ch 21. There are four appearances of Jesus after his resurrection— one to Mary Magdalene and three to the disciples. This has been the third "to the disciples."

(a′) Jesus commissions Peter (21:15-25).

In the (a′) section (21:15-25) of sequence 21 (20:19–21:25), John creates a clear conceptual parallel with the (a) section (20:19-23), in which he described Jesus' commissioning of the apostles as a group. Here he describes Jesus' commissioning of Simon Peter to be his vicar-shepherd of the flock as a whole. Here also he clarifies expectations and anticipations raised earlier in the Gospel concerning both the position of Peter in the Church and the death of Peter.

In 1:42, John raised his readers' expectations concerning Peter's future position in the Church by pointing out that when Andrew brought Peter to Jesus, "Jesus looked at him, and said, 'So you are Simon the son of John? You shall be called Cephas' (which means Peter)." Matthew explained the name Cephas in Jesus' words, "You are Peter [rock], and on this rock I will build my church" (Mt 16:18). John clarifies the name "rock" here in 21:15-18 by showing Jesus commissioning Peter as vicar-shepherd of his flock, which is equivalent to designating him as shepherd of his flock, the Church (cf. Jn 10:16).

Concerning Peter's death, Jesus had said to Peter, "Where I am going you cannot follow me *now;* but you shall follow *afterward"* (13:36). Here in 21:18-19, Jesus speaks about Peter's death, and John explains Jesus' cryptic words by saying, "This he said to show by what death he [Peter] was to glorify God" (21:19).

It should be noted that if ch 21 had not been part of the original Gospel, the author would have grievously failed his readers by capriciously arousing their expectations and anticipations concerning Peter and then failing to fulfill them.[14] The same, of course, can be said for the Beloved Disciple, although not to the same degree. John makes the Beloved Disciple one of the central characters of the last part of his Gospel. It is he who rests his head on the chest of Jesus at the Last Supper (13:23-25). He intercedes to get Peter admitted to the court of the high priest (18:15-16). He stands at the foot of the cross and receives into his care the mother of Jesus (19:27). He witnesses to the blood and water flowing from Jesus' side (19:35). He runs with Peter to the tomb on Easter morning and is the first to believe in Jesus' resurrection (20:8). He alone recognizes Jesus on the shore and tells Peter, "It is the Lord" (21:7). Finally, the function of the Beloved Disciple as witness to Jesus is attested to in the last words of the Gospel (21:24-25).

So much about Peter had to be clarified and is clarified in 25:15-19. But the same is true of the Beloved Disciple. If ch 21 had not been part of the original Gospel, so much that was said about the Beloved Disciple would have remained unresolved. His last appearance in the Gospel would have been at the tomb, where he saw the position of the burial cloths and believed (20:10). This, however, can hardly be the last word concerning the Beloved Disciple. In short, it is fitting, if not demanded, that John, who has said so much about Peter and the Beloved Disciple, and who has shown the two associated at the supper, in the court of the high priest, and in the race to the tomb on Easter morning, should not conclude his Gospel without clarifying the positions of these two intimately associated disciples. As we see from the following parallel structure of this final section of the Gospel, this is precisely what John does.

Parallel structure of 21:15-25

(aa) Peter's **function** as **vicar-shepherd** of Jesus (21:15-17)
(bb) John **affirms** that Jesus told Peter he **would die** (21:18-19).
(cc) Peter and the Beloved Disciple (20:20)
(b'b') John **denies** that Jesus told Peter the Beloved Disciple **would not die** (20:21-23).
(a'a') The Beloved Disciple's **function** as **witness** to Jesus (20:24-25)

Text

(aa)   21:15 When they had finished breakfast, Jesus said to Simon Peter, "Simon, son of John, do you love me more than **these?**" He said to him, "Yes, Lord; you know that I love you." He said to him, **"Feed my lambs."** [16]A second time he said to him, "Simon, son of John, do you love me?" He said to him, "Yes, Lord; you know that I love you." He said to him, **"Tend my sheep."** [17]He said to him the third time, "Simon, son of John, do you love me?" Peter was grieved because he said to him the third time, "Do you love me?" And he said to him, "Lord, you know everything; you know that I love you." Jesus said to him, **"Feed my sheep."**

(bb)   [18]"Truly, truly, I say to you, when you were young, you girded yourself and walked where you would; but when you are old, you will stretch out your hands, and another will gird you and carry you where you do not wish to go." [19](This he said to show by what **death** he was to glorify God.) And after this he said to him, **"Follow me."**

(cc)   [20]Peter turned and saw following them the disciple whom Jesus loved, who had lain close to his breast at the supper and had said, "Lord, who is it that is going to betray you?"

(b'b')   [21]When Peter saw him, he said to Jesus, "Lord, what about this man?" [22]Jesus said to him, "If it is my will that he remain until I come, what is that to you? **Follow me!**" [23]The saying spread abroad among the brethren that this disciple was not to **die;** yet Jesus did not say to him that he was not to **die,** but, "If it is my will that he remain until I come, what is that to you?"

(a'a')   [24]This is the disciple who is **bearing witness** to **these things** and who has written these things; and we know that his **testimony** is true. [25]But there are also many other things which Jesus did; were every one of them to be written, I suppose that the world itself could not contain the books that would be written.

As we have seen in so many other sections of his Gospel, John creates parallelism by paralleling either words or concepts or both. Here the primary parallelism is conceptual. In (aa) and (a'a'), he speaks of the functions first of Peter as vicar-shepherd of Jesus' flock (21:15-17) and then of the Beloved Disciple as the one who bears witness to Jesus through the Gospel he has written (21:24-25). In (bb) and (b'b'), he deals with the concept of death. He affirms that the Lord did indeed speak about Peter's death (21:18-19). He denies, however, that Jesus said anything concerning the Beloved Disciple's death (21:21-33). The (cc) section serves as a perfect hinge, bringing together Peter and the Beloved Disciple, the two disciples with whom the whole section is concerned. There are very few parallel words—possibly the word "these" (*toutōn*) in vv 15, 24; and certainly the words "death-die" in vv 19, 23 and the phrase "Follow me" in vv 19 and 22.

The importance of establishing this typical *abcb'a'* Johannine format will become evident when we deal with the question of the authorship of the Gospel. To anticipate, whoever wrote this last little section in an *abcb'a'* format also wrote the whole of sequence 21 (20:19–21:25), and whoever wrote sequence 21 also wrote the whole Gospel. The parallelism of this final section (21:15-25) of sequence 21 (20:19–21:25) gives good reason to believe that that person was none other than the Beloved Disciple who testifies in 21:24-25 not only to his function as a witness to Jesus but also to the manner in which he carried out that function: "This is the disciple [the Beloved Disciple mentioned in vv 20-23] who is bearing witness to these things, and who has written these things."

21:15a When they had finished breakfast, Jesus said to Simon Peter, "Simon, son of John, do you love me more than these?" The words "when they had finished breakfast" serve to provide continuity with the previous section, where Peter had led the fishing expedition, was the first to go to Jesus on the shore, and was the one who hauled in the net with the huge catch of fish symbolizing the success of the "fishers of men" as long as Jesus was with them. The words "son of John" are found only here and in 1:42 and create one of the many parallels between this sequence and sequence 1 (1:19-51).

Do you love me more than these? The "these" is ambiguous. It could mean Peter's boat and fishing gear and the life that went with it, but more likely the "these" are the other disciples. Jesus asks this question three times to impress upon Peter the importance of self-sacrificing love. Many interpret the threefold question as Jesus' reminder to Peter of his threefold denial. This is not improbable, but the primary emphasis is on Peter's sincere avowal of his love for Jesus. Such love is required of the one who is to be commissioned vicar-shepherd of Jesus' flock.

One must recall, when interpreting this threefold question, Jesus' own love unto the end (13:1), symbolized by the washing of the feet (13:2-11) and given as an example for his disciples (13:12-20). One must remember also Jesus' new commandment, "that you love one another; even as I have loved you, that you also love one another" (13:34), and the words that serve as a commentary on the new commandment, "Greater love has no man than this, that a man lay down his life for his friends" (15:13). To be the true vicar-shepherd of Jesus' flock, one must love as Jesus loved. That Peter loved as Jesus loved is proved by his martyrdom (cf. 21:18-19).

21:15b-17 Feed my lambs. With these words, repeated three times with variations on the word for "lambs," Jesus commissions Peter as vicar-shepherd of his flock, the Church.[15] What this means and what this calls for is explained in 10:1-21, where Jesus speaks of himself as the good shepherd who lays down his life for his sheep (10:15) and has "other sheep . . . not of this fold" that must be brought into the fold so that "there will be one flock, one shepherd" (10:16). For the full import of Peter's commission as vicar-shepherd, the reader should study carefully Ez 34, which provides the background in the Old Testament for the shepherd parable in Jn 10:1-21.

Much has been written about the ecclesial significance of Peter's commission to be Jesus' vicar-shepherd of the sheep.[16] For those who hold that ch 21 is not an original part of the Gospel but rather the work of a so-called ecclesiastical redactor, the chapter was added in order to bring the Gospel into line with the teaching of the developing early Catholic Church. Our view is that ch 21 was always part of the Gospel, is in no way the work of a redactor, and provides the original and only conclusion of the Gospel.

There is good reason for our view. First, the verses dealing with Peter's commission occur in the (a') section (21:15-25) of sequence 21 and parallel the (a) section (20:19-23), thus proving that the same author wrote both sections. Second, the commissioning of Peter looks back at, parallels conceptually, and fulfills the expectations aroused by, Jesus' words to Peter in 1:42: " 'So you are Simon the son of John? You shall be called Cephas' (which means Peter)." Again, one can argue that whoever wrote 1:42 also wrote 21:15-17. Third, the author takes for granted that the reader of 21:15-17 will understand the metaphor of the vicar-shepherd of the sheep against the background provided by the good shepherd parable in 10:1-21. This is true not only for the vicar-shepherd metaphor of 21:15-17 but also for the death of Peter foretold in 21:18-19, because Peter, the vicar-shepherd, will die just as the good shepherd does in 10:11, 15-16. Finally, as we will show (see p. 310), sequence 21 (20:19-21:25) parallels chiastically with sequence 17 (12:12-50) of part V (12:12-21:25). Whoever wrote sequence 17 must also have written sequence 21.

There is every indication, therefore, that the section on Peter as the vicar-shepherd of Jesus is not the addition of an ecclesiastical redactor but the work of the original Johannine author. Its ecclesial import, as a consequence, enjoys the full weight of the original inspired author's authority.

21:18 Truly, truly, I say to you, when you were young, you girded yourself and walked where you would. Jesus' mysterious statement foretells Peter's death by crucifixion. That this is the meaning of Jesus' words, however, is made clear only by the author's parenthetical remark in v 19. The only probable allusion to crucifixion in Jesus' statement is contained in the words "you will stretch out your hands." It is precisely because Jesus is not more explicit that John has to clarify by appending his explanatory comment in v 19. Why Jesus was not more explicit is hard to explain, unless he was simply using a proverbial saying about the freedom of the young contrasted with the helplessness of the old. If such was the case, then the full import of Jesus' words became clear only after Peter's death by crucifixion.

21:19 (This he said to show by what death he was to glorify God.) And after this he said to him, "Follow me." This parenthetical remark parallels and harks back to 12:33, where John made an identical parenthetical remark about Jesus' words "and I, when I am lifted up from the earth, will draw all men to myself" (12:32). John's remark in 12:33, "He said this to show by what death he was to die," explains the words "lifted up" as referring to Jesus' crucifixion. His words here, "by what death he was to glorify God," indicate that Peter would glorify God as Jesus did—by doing the will of God even when it entailed crucifixion (cf. 13:31-32, 36-37; 15:8; 17:4, 22).

Very significantly, Jesus then says to Peter, "Follow me," words that parallel what Jesus said in 12:26, "If any one serves me, he must *follow* me; and where I am, there shall my servant be also." Thus, what following Jesus will mean for Peter is best explained in 12:23-32, which occurs in sequence 17 (12:12-50), the chiastic parallel to sequence 21 (20:19-21:25) in part V (12:12-21:25) of the Gospel as a whole.

21:20 Peter turned and saw following them the disciple whom Jesus loved. This verse provides the hinge in the *abcb'a'* format of 21:15-25 by bringing together the two disciples whose functions and destinies constitute the subject matter of section (a'). The words "who had lain close to his breast at the supper and had said, 'Lord, who is it that is going to betray you?' " serve as a cross-reference to 13:23-25 and provide, if the reader recalls John's liking for cross-references (cf. 4:46; 6:26; 7:21-23; 10:21; 11:2; 18:14, 26; 21:14), another small proof that the author of ch 21 is the same author who wrote the rest of the Gospel.

21:21 When Peter saw him, he said to Jesus, "Lord, what about this man?" Jesus has just told Peter that his destiny is to follow him to death on the cross (21:18-19). Peter's question, therefore, would appear to pertain to the destiny of the Beloved Disciple. Is the Beloved Disciple to follow Jesus to death on the cross? Jesus refuses to answer Peter's question and reiterates his command, "Follow me" (cf. v 19). Implied but not stated is the deduction that the Beloved Disciple will not die as Peter will die, i.e., by crucifixion.

21:23 The saying spread abroad among the brethren that this disciple was not to die. The brethren have misunderstood the meaning of Jesus' words "If it is my will that he remain until I come, what is that to you?" The words seem to imply that the Beloved Disciple will remain alive until Jesus' second coming; and since those alive at the second coming will not die at all, the brethren's false deduction is that the Beloved Disciple will not die. John corrects their false deduction. Jesus, he says, "did not say to him that he was not to die . . . ." The Beloved Disciple, therefore, like Peter, will die. The only difference is that the manner of Peter's death (crucifixion) is described. Nothing is said about how the Beloved Disciple will die.

Those who hold the view that ch 21 is the work and addition of a redactor interpret this episode to mean that the Beloved Disciple has also died. Against this view there are several arguments. First, the misunderstanding technique that is so obvious here is a typical and much used Johannine technique (cf. the use of the misunderstanding technique in the discourse to Nicodemus [3:3-4], in the discussion with the Samaritan woman [4:13-15], in the Eucharistic discourse [6:41], and many other places [e.g., 2:19-21;

8:56-58; 11:11-15; 13:6-7; 14:7-9]). Typically, Jesus makes a mysterious statement. The statement is misunderstood. Jesus or the author gives the correct
understanding of the mysterious statement. That is exactly what happens here.

Second, if the Beloved Disciple lived to a very great age, one can understand why the rumor might have spread that he was not to die. One can also
understand why the author would want to correct this rumor lest, when the
Beloved Disciple eventually died, some should claim that Jesus falsely
predicted that he would not die.

Third, and most important, the author indicates by the parallel structure
he gives to 21:15-25 that he intends in the (aa) section to describe the function of Peter, and in the (a'a') section to describe the function of the Beloved
Disciple. This he faithfully does, describing the function of the Beloved Disciple in vv 24-25 to be that of witnessing to Jesus by writing this Gospel.
He cannot, therefore, have died until after the Gospel was written.

**21:24a This is the disciple who is bearing witness to these things and
who has written these things.** This statement serves two purposes. First, it
identifies the Beloved Disciple as the author of the Gospel. Second, it specifies
the function of the Beloved Disciple. In the (aa) section (21:15-17), Peter's
function was specified as vicar-shepherd of Jesus' flock. Here in the parallel
(a'a') section, the Beloved Disciple's function is specified as witness to Jesus.
Peter carried out his function by feeding Jesus' sheep; the Beloved Disciple
carried out his function by writing his Gospel.

21:24b   and we know that his testimony is true. The testimony (*martyria*)
referred to is the witness to Jesus given by the Beloved Disciple in the Gospel
he has written and is now bringing to a conclusion. Since the witness he gives
is primarily a faith-witness, and since the members of his community share
with him in his faith-witness to Jesus, the Beloved Disciple does not hesitate
to include himself along with them in the avowal that "we know that his
testimony is true."

It should be noted that the same expression "we know" (*oidamen*) occurs regularly in the first letter of John (cf. 1 Jn 3:2, 14; 5:15; 18:20) and
refers to the whole Johannine Church. It is not, therefore, unusual for an
author in the Johannine community to profess his faith in union with his
community. He had done the same in the prologue when he included himself
in the statement "And the Word became flesh and dwelt among *us,* full of
grace and truth; *we* have beheld his glory, glory as of the only Son from
the Father" (1:14); and in the further statement "And from his fulness have
we all received, grace upon grace" (1:16). The recurrence of the "we" in
21:24 makes it quite possible, considering the author's great love for inclusion-
conclusion, that the "we" here is meant to take the reader's mind back to
the "we" in the prologue. In that case, one might well consider 21:24-25
as a short epilogue written to balance with the prologue and to conclude the
Gospel as the prologue began it.

In regard to the "witness" the Beloved Disciple gives to Jesus in his Gospel, it is important to distinguish between eyewitness and faith-witness. The Beloved Disciple gives massive faith-witness to Jesus beginning with the prologue and continuing regularly in almost every sequence of the Gospel. He gives very little eyewitness testimony and designates it as eyewitness testimony on only one occasion, when he states concerning the flow of blood and water from Jesus' side, "He who saw it has borne witness—his testimony is true, and he knows that he tells the truth" (19:35). The statement is similar to what he says in 21:24, but there is one important difference. In 19:35, he says, ". . . and *he* knows that he tells the truth." In 21:24, he says, ". . . and *we* know that his testimony is true." In 19:35, he must say "he" because he is giving his own eyewitness testimony. In 21:24 he says "we" because he is giving his own and his community's faith-witness rather than eyewitness testimony to Jesus.

Unlike most,[17] we have identified the Beloved Disciple as the author of the Gospel. We have done so for several reasons. First, whoever wrote v 24 explicitly designates the Beloved Disciple as the one "who has written these things." Second, the parallelism of 21:15-25 proves that whoever wrote v 24 also wrote 21:15-25. Third, since 21:15-25 is parallel to 20:19-22, whoever wrote 21:15-25 also wrote the whole of 20:19–21:25. Finally, as we will see, the whole of 20:19–21:25 (sequence 21) is parallel to 1:19-51 (sequence 1). It follows, therefore, that whoever wrote sequence 21 also wrote sequence 1 and all the other chiastically balanced sequences that make up the Gospel as a whole. The literary evidence points to one author for the Gospel as a whole, and that one author identifies himself as the Beloved Disciple.

21:25 But there are also many other things which Jesus did. The author concludes with the hyperbolic statement that if all the things that Jesus did were written down, "the world itself could not contain the books that would be written." The claim is vastly exaggerated if one understands by it the limited historical deeds and words of Jesus. It is less exaggerated if one understands the author to be speaking about the significance of the things that Jesus did. This book, added to the multitude of books on the Fourth Gospel in the last fifty years alone, testifies in its own small way to the magnitude of that significance and to the seemingly endless flood of books it continues to inspire.

Themes

The final sequence of the Gospel continues the usual witness and response themes. Jesus witnesses to himself by appearing three times to his disciples and by directing their fishing endeavors to a miraculous catch of fish. The disciples and Thomas respond by belief in the risen Jesus. In addition to these themes, there is the theme of mission: the disciples as a group are commissioned, and Peter as an individual is commissioned. Like Matthew, who ends his Gospel with the great mission charge (Mt 28:18-20), John too ends with Jesus' commissions for ministry and with the miraculous catch of fishes, symbolic of the success of that ministry.[18]

Chiastic parallels with sequence 17 (12:12-50)

The first and last sequences of part V (12:12–21:25) of the Gospel parallel both verbally and conceptually. An arrangement in columns makes the few but important parallels more easily recognizable.

20:18–21:25	*12:12-50*
20:30: Now Jesus **did many** other **signs in the presence of his disciples . . .** but these are written **that you may believe . . .**	12:37: Though he **had done** so **many signs before them,** yet **they did not believe . . .**
20:30b: ". . . and that believing you may have **life in his name."**	12:50: "And I know that his commandment is **eternal life."**
21:6b: they were not able to **haul** (*helkysai*) it in, for the **quantity** of fish.	12:32: ". . . and I, when I am lifted up from the earth, will draw (*helkysō*) **all men** to myself."
21:19a: This **he said to show by what death** he was to glorify God.	12:33: **He said this to show by what death** he was to die.
21:19b: And after this he said to him, **"Follow me."**	12:26: "If any one serves me, he must **follow me."**
21:22: "If it is my will that he remain **until I come** [second coming], what is that to you?"	12:13b: "Blessed is he who **comes** in the name of the Lord." 12:15: "Fear not, daughter of Zion . . . your king is **coming . . .**" 12:46: "**I have come** as light into the world" [first coming]. 12:47b: ". . . for I did not **come** to judge the world but to save the world."
21:19: This he said to show by what **death** he was to **glorify** God.	12:23: "The hour has come for the Son of man to be **glorified."** 12:24: ". . . unless a grain of wheat falls into the earth and **dies,** it remains alone; but if it **dies** it bears much fruit."

Chiastic parallels with sequence 1 (1:19-51)

The number of verbal and conceptual parallels that link the last with the first sequence is so great that one is almost forced to deduce that John wrote sequence 21 as a grand inclusion-conclusion for the whole Gospel. Some of the parallels could be fortuitous, though this is unlikely considering the author's studied endeavor throughout the Gospel to designedly create parallels, but such a multitude of parallels cannot possibly be fortuitous. There are at least seventeen parallels. We present them, as usual, in columns.

20:19–21:25

1:19-51

20:19: Jesus came and **stood among** (*estē eis to meson*) them . . .

1:26b: ". . . but **among you stands** (*mesos hymon stekei*) one whom you do not know . . ."

20:22: he breathed on them, and said to them, "Receive **the Holy Spirit**."

1:32: "I saw **the Spirit** descend . . ."
1:33: "He on whom you see **the Spirit** descend and remain, this is he who baptizes with the **Holy Spirit**."

20:23: "If you forgive the sins (*hamartias*) of any . . . if you retain the **sins** (*hamartias*) of any . . ."
20:28: Thomas answered him, "**My Lord and my God!**"

1:29: "Behold, the Lamb of God, who takes away the **sin** (*hamartian*) of the world!"
1:34: "And I have seen and have borne witness that this is **the Son of God**."
1:49: Nathanael answered him, "Rabbi, you are **the Son of God!**"

20:27b: ". . . do not be faithless, but **believing**." 20:29: Jesus said to him, "**Have you believed because you have seen me?**"
21:2: **Simon Peter . . . Nathanael . . .** and **two others of his disciples** . . .

1:50: "**Because I said to you, I saw you under the fig tree, do you believe?**"

1:37: The **two disciples** heard him say this . . . 1:41: He first found his brother **Simon** . . . 1:47: Jesus saw **Nathanael** coming to him . . .

21:1: After this Jesus **revealed** (*ephanerōsen*) himself again to the disciples . . . 21:14: This was now the third time that Jesus was **revealed** (*ephanerōthē*) to the disciples . . .

1:31b: ". . . but for this I came baptizing with water, that he might be **revealed** (*phanerōthē*) to Israel."

21:4: Jesus **stood** on the beach; yet **the disciples did not know** that it was Jesus.
21:12: Now none of the disciples dared ask him, "**Who are you?**"
21:15a: Jesus said to Simon Peter, "Simon, **son of John,** do you love me more than these?"
21:15c: He said to him, "**Feed my lambs.**"

1:26: ". . . but among you **stands** one whom **you do not know** . . ."
1:19: sent priests and Levites from Jerusalem to ask him, "**Who are you?**"
1:42b: "So you are Simon **the son of John . . .**"

1:42c: Jesus looked at him, and said, "You shall be called **Cephas**" (which means Peter).

21:19: And after this he said to him, "**Follow me.**"

1:37: The two disciples heard him say this, and they **followed Jesus**. 1:43: And he found Philip and said to him, "**Follow me.**"

21:20: Peter **turned** (*epistrapheis*) and saw following them . . .

1:38: Jesus **turned** (*strapheis*), and **saw** them **following**.

21:22: "If it is my will that he **remain** (*menein*) . . ."	1:39b: They came and saw where he was **staying** (*menei*); and they stayed (*emeinan*) with him that day.
21:22: Jesus said to him, "If it is my will that he remain **until I come** [second coming], what is that to you?"	1:23: 'Make straight the way of the Lord' [first coming] . . . 1:27: ". . . even he who **comes** after me . . ." 1:29: The next day he saw Jesus **coming** toward him . . . 1:30: 'After me **comes** a man who ranks before me, for he was before me.'
21:24: This is the disciple who is **bearing witness** (*martyrōn*) to these things . . . and we know that his **testimony** (*martyria*) is true.	1:19: this is the **testimony** (*martyria*) of John . . . 1:32: And John **bore witness** (*emartyrēsen*) . . . 1:34: And I have seen and **have borne witness** (*memartyrēka*) that this is the Son of God.
21:24: This is the disciple . . . who has **written** these things . . . 21:25: were every one of them to be **written** . . . the world itself could not contain the books that would be **written.**	1:45: "We have found him of whom Moses in the law and also the prophets **wrote.**"
21:25b: the **world** itself could not contain the books that would be written.	1:29: "Behold, the Lamb of God, who takes away the sin of the **world.**"

The Gospel ends as it began. It began with the witness of the Baptist; it ends with the witness of the Beloved Disciple. It began with the first coming of Jesus; it ends with a reference to his second coming. It began with the Lamb of God who takes away the sin of the world; it ends with the Lamb of God giving to his apostles the authority to forgive or retain sins. It began with Jesus looking at Peter and saying, in anticipation of his commission as vicar-shepherd of the flock, "You shall be called Cephas" (Rock); it ends with Jesus saying to Peter, "Feed my sheep." It begins at the waters of the Jordan when five disciples follow Jesus and witness to him; it ends at the waters of the Sea of Tiberias when four of the same disciples are back with Jesus again and Peter and the Beloved Disciple follow him. It begins with the Baptist's and Nathanael's witness to Jesus as the Son of God; it ends with the undying witness of Thomas, "My Lord and my God."

This in conclusion is the genius of John, whom we may now with some confidence identify as the Beloved Disciple, that he who rested his head on the loving heart of Jesus has witnessed through his Gospel to that so great love of the Father that he gave his only-begotten Son, and to that so great love of the Son that he gave his life for the world. Through his Gospel the Beloved Disciple now calls upon the world not only to believe in the Son but to follow in his footsteps by loving as he loved—unto the end.

Notes

Publication data for references given in these Notes can be found in the Bibliography, page 329.

INTRODUCTION—pages 1–18

1. Cf. C. K. Barrett, *The Fourth Gospel,* 83–88.
2. Cf. R. Brown, *The Community of the Beloved Disciple,* 33–34.
3. Cf. R. A. Culpepper, *The Johannine School.*
4. Cf. C. K. Barrett, *The Fourth Gospel,* 108.
5. Cf. R. Fortna, *The Gospel of Signs,* 221–234.
6. Cf. J. L. Martyn, *History and Theology in the Fourth Gospel* (2nd ed.), 164–166. See also, D. Moody Smith, "The Setting and Shape of a Johannine Narrative Source," *JBL* 95 (June 1976) 231–241.
7. Cf. B. Lindars, *Behind the Fourth Gospel,* 27–42.
8. Cf. B. Lindars, *Behind the Fourth Gospel,* 43–60.
9. Cf. C. K. Barrett, *The Fourth Gospel,* 111.
10. Cf. R. Brown, *John,* lxvii–lxxix.
11. Cf. J. L. Martyn, *The Gospel of John in Christian History,* 116–121.
12. Cf. R. Brown, *The Community,* 59–91; 165–169; see also J. L. Martyn, *The Gospel of John in Christian History,* 6–8; 90–121.
13. Cf. D. W. Wead, *The Literary Devices in John's Gospel;* R. Brown, *John,* cxxxv; R. Schnackenburg, *The Gospel According to John,* 105ff; J. Marsh, *Saint John,* 56–58; 66–68; C. H. Dodd, *Historical Tradition in the Fourth Gospel,* 315–334.
14. Cf. C. H. Dodd, *Historical Tradition,* 315–334.
15. Cf. P. F. Ellis, *The Yahwist: The Bible's First Theologian,* 118–127.
16. The division of our New Testament into chapters and verses was done by Stephen Langton in 1226 A.D.
17. Cf. C. H. Talbert, *Literary Patterns, Theological Themes and the Genre of Luke-Acts,* 67–82; N. W. Lund, *Chiasmus in the New Testament;* and P. F. Ellis, *Seven Pauline Letters,* in which Paul's regular use of an *aba'* chiastic format is demonstrated for all the major sections of 1 and 2 Cor, Phil, Gal, 1 Thes, and Rom.
18. Cf. D. Moody Smith, *The Composition and Order of the Fourth Gospel,* 238–249. For the present situation, see D. A. Carson, "Current Source Criticism of the Fourth Gospel: Some Methodological Considerations," *JBL* 97 (September 1978) 411–429.
19. Cf. D. M. Smith, *Composition,* 239.
20. Cf. R. Brown, *John,* xxivff; see also the commentaries of Lightfoot, Bultmann, Barrett, Dodd, Schnackenburg, Lindars, and Marsh.
21. Cf. H. M. Teeple, "Methodology in Source Analysis of the Fourth Gospel," *JBL* 81 (June 1962) 286.
22. The major part of what follows is dependent on the first draft of a doctoral disser-

313

tation by John Gerhard, S.J., entitled *The Literary Unity and the Compositional Methods of the Gospel of John.*

23. Quoted from J. Marsh, *John,* 43.
24. But see P. L. Shuler, *A Genre for the Gospels,* 88–106, concerning the flexibility of the laws of narrative in Gospel times.
25. Cf. C. H. Dodd, *The Interpretation of the Fourth Gospel,* 290.
26. Cf. C. H. Whitman, *Homer and the Heroic Tradition;* J. T. Shepherd, *The Pattern of the Iliad;* C. M. Bowra, *Tradition and Design in the Iliad;* J. L. Myres, "The Last Book of the Iliad," *JHS* 52 (1932) 264–296; G. E. Duckworth, *Structural Patterns and Proportions in Vergil's Aeneid.*
27. Cf. D. J. McCarthy, "Moses' Dealings with Pharaoh: Ex 7:8–10:25," *CBQ* 27 (1965) 336–347; "Plagues and the Sea of Reeds: Exodus 5–14," *JBL* 85 (March 1966) 137–158; B. Porten, "The Structure and Theme of the Solomon Narrative (1 Kings 3–11)," *HUCA* 38 (1967) 93–128; G. M. Landes, "The Kerygma of the Book of Jonah," *Int* 21 (1967) 3–31; A. G. Wright, "The Structure of the Book of Wisdom," *Biblica* 48 (1967) 168; P. W. Skehan, "Seven Pillars of Wisdom," *CBQ* 10 (1948) 125; J. T. Walsh, "Gn 2:4b–3:25: A Synchronic Approach," *JBL* 96 (July 1977) 161–177; S. E. McEvenue, *The Narrative Style of the Priestly Writer;* B. W. Anderson, "From Analysis to Synthesis: The Interpretation of Gn 1–11," *JBL* 97 (March 1978) 23–39; J. Cheryl Exum, "Promise and Fulfillment: Narrative Art in Judges 13," *JBL* 99 (March 1980) 43–59; C. H. Lohr, "Oral Techniques in the Gospel of Matthew," *CBQ* 23 (1961) 404–416; P. F. Ellis, *Matthew: His Mind and His Message,* 10–13; J. Dewey, *Markan Public Debate: Literary Technique, Concentric Structure and Theology in Mark 2:1–3:6;* C. H. Talbert, *Literary Patterns, Theological Themes, and the Genre of Luke-Acts,* 67–88; D. Deeks, "The Structure of the Fourth Gospel," *NTS* 15 (1968) 107–128; C. H. Talbert, "Artistry and Theology: An Analysis of the Architecture of John 1:19–5:47," *CBQ* 32 (1970) 341–366; M. E. Boismard, *Saint John's Prologue,* 76–81; R. A. Culpepper, "The Pivot of John's Prologue," *NTS* 27 (1980) 1–31; J. J. Collins, "The 'ABA' Pattern and the Text of Paul," in *Studiorum Paulinorum Congressus Internationalis Catholicus* (Rome, 1963); P. F. Ellis, *Seven Pauline Letters;* E. S. Fiorenza, "Composition and Structure of the Revelation of John," *CBQ* 39 (July 1977) 344–366; A. Vanhoye, *A Structural Translation of the Epistle to the Hebrews.*
28. Cf. C. H. Talbert, *Literary Patterns, Theological Themes, and the Genre of Luke-Acts,* 74.
29. For the criteria that determine parallels, see J. Dewey, *Markan Public Debate,* 35–39.

PROLOGUE (1:1-18)—pages 19-28

1. For the opinion that the prologue was an early Christian hymn adapted by John to serve as overture to his Gospel, cf. R. Brown, *John,* 18–23; J. T. Sanders, *The New Testament Christological Hymns,* 20–57.
2. Cf. C. H. Dodd, *The Fourth Gospel,* 263–295; R. Brown, *John,* 519–524.
3. Cf. R. Brown, *John,* 524.
4. Cf. R. A. Culpepper, "The Pivot of John's Prologue," *NTS* 27 (1980) 1–31.
5. C. K. Barrett, typical of those who defend the unity of the prologue, says: "The prologue is not a jig-saw puzzle but one piece of solid theological writing" (*The Prologue of John's Gospel,* 27).

6. With E. Käsemann (*New Testament Questions of Today,* 146, 166) and with R. A. Culpepper ("The Pivot of John's Prologue" 13–14), and on the basis of the parallelism between vv 4-8 (a) and vv 15-17 (a'), we believe there is good reason to see the earliest reference in the prologue to the historical Jesus in vv 4-5. This is supported by the clear reference to the historical Jesus in the witness of the Baptist in vv 6-8, also part of section (a).
7. Cf. C. K. Barrett, *John,* 132.
8. Cf. M. S. Boismard, *St. John's Prologue;* R. A. Culpepper, "The Pivot of John's Prologue," 15–16 and *passim.*
9. Cf. R. A. Culpepper, "The Pivot of John's Prologue," 14–17.
10. Cf. E. Hoskyns, *The Fourth Gospel,* 153.

SEQUENCE 1 (1:19-51)—pages 30-39

1. As R. Schnackenburg says: "The aim of the evangelist seems to be to show Jesus coming forth from concealment, with the help of the divinely inspired testimony of John (cf. 1:31), then introducing himself to his first disciples as the promised Messiah, surpassing and intensifying their hopes (1:50f) and finally beginning the revelation of his glory with the first 'sign' (2:11)." (*John,* 284).
2. On the "heaping up of titles," cf. G. MacRae, "The Fourth Gospel and *Religionsgeschichte,*" *CBQ* 31 (January 1970) 10–24.
3. For the chronological development of Christology, cf. E. Schillebeeckx, *Jesus,* 550ff; R. Brown, *The Birth of the Messiah* 29-32 and *passim.*
4. Cf. H. M. Teeple, *The Mosaic Eschatological Prophet,* 102ff.
5. Cf. R. Schnackenburg, *John,* 305–306; R. Brown, *John,* 57.
6. Cf. R. Brown, *John,* 84–85, who notes the parallelism but attributes it to "the result of editing and combining accounts." See also, J. L. Martyn, *The Gospel of John in Christian History,* 46–54.
7. Additions credited by Bultmann and others to an ecclesiastical redactor can all be explained as original to the Gospel when the Gospel is read according to the laws of parallelism. As we shall see from the numerous parallels between sequence 1 and sequence 21 (20:19–21:25), these two sequences had to belong to the Gospel from the beginning. There can be no question, therefore, of ch 21 being the later addition of an ecclesiastical redactor.
8. Cf. R. Schnackenburg, *John,* 313.
9. Cf. R. Brown, *John,* 87.
10. Cf. S. Mowinckel, *He That Cometh,* 293–294.
11. "Son of man" as a title for Jesus occurs thirteen times in the Gospel (1:51; 3:14; 5:27; 6:27, 53, 62; 8:28; 9:35; 12:23, 34 (bis); 13:31). R. Schnackenburg (*John,* 529–542) deals at length with its origin, its use in John, and the problems connected with it.
12. Cf. C. H. Dodd, *Interpretation,* 294, 296.

SEQUENCE 2 (2:1-12)—pages 40-44

1. While the symbolism of a new week of creation would not be alien to the deeper levels of John's theology, R. Brown rightly suggests caution: "The application

of the theology of *seven* days to John i 19–ii 11 is very attractive, but how can we possibly be sure that we are not reading into the Gospel something that was never even thought of by the evangelist or the redactor?'' (*John,* 106).

2. Commentators frequently end the Cana story with v 11. The parallelism of vv 11-12 with vv 1-2, however, indicates conclusively that the evangelist himself ended the story at v 12.

3. The reference to Jesus' brothers in 20:17 occurs in sequence 20 (20:1-18—the story of Mary at the tomb), the chiastic parallel of sequence 2 (2:1-12) in the Gospel as a whole, and is one of several parallels between the two sequences.

4. Cf. E. Hoskyns, *The Fourth Gospel,* 185–192; C. H. Dodd, *Tradition,* 223ff; B. Lindars, *John,* 123–135; A. Feuillet, *Johannine Studies,* 17–37.

SEQUENCE 3 (2:12-25)—pages 45-49

1. Sequence 3, the central sequence of part I (1:19–4:3), is in chiastic parallelism with sequence 19 (18:1–19:42), the central sequence of part V (12:12–21:25).

2. R. Brown, *John,* 116–122, and most other commentators go to great lengths to explain how the cleansing of the temple came to be moved up to the beginning of the Gospel.

3. E. Hoskyns, *The Fourth Gospel,* 196, grasps John's meaning perfectly: ''The earlier Evangelists seem to have seen in the incident no more than an attempt to purify the temple, the last Evangelist brings it into relationship with the advent of the new, spiritual worship of God, and sees its whole meaning in that relationship.''

SEQUENCE 4 (3:1-21)—pages 50-59

1. E. Hoskyns, *The Fourth Gospel,* 201.

2. R. Bultmann says: ''One can recognize in Nicodemus a shadow of the scribe in Mk 12:23ff., who is not far from the Kingdom of God and yet does not belong to it'' (*John,* 132).

3. In the Gospel as a whole, sequence 4 is chiastically paralleled by sequence 18 (13:1–17:26), the night discourse at the Last Supper.

4. C. H. Dodd, *Tradition,* 315–334; see also D. W. Wead, *The Literary Devices in John's Gospel.*

5. R. Bultmann, *John,* 132.

6. In John's theology, there is a profound parallelism and equivalence in the statements ''Unless one is born of water and the Spirit, he cannot enter the kingdom of God'' (3:5) and ''If I do not wash you, you have no part in me'' (13:8)—Jesus' words to Peter when Peter refused to be washed.

7. R. Schnackenburg, *John,* 376.

8. E. Hoskyns, *The Fourth Gospel,* 205.

9. In 17:20-23, John asserts that the work of the Church is to so manifest the love of Jesus and its own unity with Jesus in love that the world will know that the Father sent Jesus and, knowing this, will come to believe and be saved. As Jesus solemnly declares concerning the world: ''For God sent the Son into the world, not to condemn the world, but that the world might be saved through him'' (3:17).

10. E. Hoskyns, *The Fourth Gospel,* 203.
11. For the numerous parallels between sequence 4 and sequence 18 (13:1–17:26), see pp. 245–246.

SEQUENCE 5 (3:22–4:3)—pages 60–64

1. C. K. Barrett, *John,* 185, says about the "something given": "If the work of the former [Jesus] is eclipsing that of the latter [the Baptist], the will of God must require that it should be so."
2. The parenthetical correction ("although Jesus himself did not baptize, but only his disciples") is sometimes considered a gloss introduced by a copyist who wished to further distinguish Jesus from the Baptist, as if baptizing were too lowly an occupation for Jesus. In favor of the authenticity of the text, however, is the fact that it is found in all the manuscripts. In addition, the reference to the disciples provides a parallel with the mention of the disciples in 3:22 of (a). Finally, if Jesus' disciples baptized, it may well explain why baptism became a Christian rite of initiation immediately after Pentecost.

SEQUENCE 6 (4:4–38)—pages 66–76

1. C. K. Barrett, *John,* 193, considers the necessity here as referring to the need to go through Samaria if one wished to take the shortest route to Jerusalem and denies any theological significance to the statement.
2. Cf. D. Daube, "Jesus and the Samaritan Woman: The Meaning of *sygchraōmai,*" *JBL* 69 (1950) 137–147.
3. R. Schnackenburg, *John,* 438, gives five reasons for the newness of this worship.
4. C. K. Barrett, *John,* 201.
5. R. Schnackenburg, *John,* 453.
6. R. H. Lightfoot, *St. John's Gospel,* 120.

SEQUENCE 7 (4:39–45)—pages 77–81

1. E. Hoskyns, *The Fourth Gospel,* 247.
2. See p. 32.
3. Many authors, including Brown and Schnackenburg, consider 4:44 a gloss. Parallelism would indicate it is anything but a gloss.
4. R. Schnackenburg, *John,* 463.

SEQUENCE 8 (4:46–54)—pages 82–85

1. The literary question of the relation between John's account and those of Mt 8:5–13 and Lk 7:1–10 is not easily settled, but the similarities in all three accounts outweigh the differences and are so close that in all probability the three stories

constitute three different versions of the same miracle, with the differences accounted for by the different theological and redactional purposes of the authors. The interdependence would seem to be by way of the primitive tradition and not via dependence of John on either Matthew or Luke (cf. R. Schnackenburg, *John,* 469–477; R. Brown, *John,* 192–194; C. H. Dodd, *Tradition,* 188–195)).

2. Cf. R. Fortna, *The Gospel of Signs,* 41.
3. Cf. R. Schnackenburg, *John,* 469, 475–477.
4. R. Brown, *John,* 195, sees the pedagogy of faith here to be "not to lead the official away from a faith based on signs; rather, it was to lead him to a faith that would not be based on the wondrous aspect of the sign but on what the sign would tell him about Jesus." But this explanation does not seem to take into sufficient account the cumulative effect of vv 48 and 50b, where John makes the traditional story serve his own theology of faith. R. Schnackenburg, *John,* 475–477, sees this more clearly.
5. Cf. R. Fortna, *The Gospel of Signs,* 44; R. Brown, *John,* 194–195.
6. R. Brown, *John,* 197.

SEQUENCE 9 (5:1-47)—pages 86-99

1. Cf. C. K. Barrett, *John,* 209.
2. R. Brown, *John,* 208.
3. C. K. Barrett, *John,* 214.
4. Because of the almost identical terms, R. Brown, *John,* 219, considers vv 26-30 a "duplicate" of 5:19-25, speaks of "both forms of the discourse," and attributes the parallelism between vv 19 and 30 to "an editorial attempt to produce an inclusion binding the whole passage together."
5. Bultmann's well-known attribution of the passage to an ecclesiastical redactor because of the contrast between the realized eschatology of vv 24-25 and the final eschatology of vv 28-29 has been contested by many. It collapses entirely when one recognizes that the two passages are in perfect parallelism and could only, as such, have come from the one, thoroughly consistent author.
6. R. Brown, *John,* 224, rightly sees no real contradiction between 5:31 and 8:14 but doubts "if the same editor wrote both lines." As we shall see, the parallelism between 5:1-47 (sequence 9) and 7:1-8:59 (sequence 13) eliminates the need to call upon some later, careless editor and allows the author himself to eliminate any wrong impression his readers might get from a wrong interpretation of 5:31.
7. R. Brown, *John,* 228.

SEQUENCE 10 (6:1-15)—pages 100-106

1. R. Brown, *John,* 236-250; C. H. Dodd, *Tradition,* 196-222, but especially 218-222.
2. R. Brown, *John,* 284-303.
3. Cf. C. H. Dodd, *Tradition,* 201ff.
4. The major commentaries discuss the question at length, on the doubtful presupposition that John is interested in a correct historical narrative and a precise geographical setting.

5. B. Lindars, *John,* 243.
6. E. Hoskyns, *The Fourth Gospel,* 282–283.
7. The negative response of the Galilean Jews (cf. 4:44-45; 6:14-15; 6:60-66), compared with the vitriolic response of the Jerusalem Jews (cf. 5:1-47; 7:1-10:39; 11:45-54; 12:1-11, 37-43; 18:28-19:16), is tame and suggests that John puts the greater blame for the rejection of Jesus by his own people on the Jewish leaders in Jerusalem. In this he agrees with the Synoptics.

SEQUENCE 11 (6:16-21)—pages 109-111

1. Cf. C. H. Holman, *A Handbook to Literature,* 156ff.
2. The biblical evidence for works composed of two halves in inverted order around a centerpiece (in this case, the episode of the walking on the sea) has been amply documented by C. H. Talbert in his *Literary Patterns, Theological Themes and the Genre of Luke-Acts,* 75–79.
3. Besides the exodus account in Ex 12-24, John probably has in mind the poetic accounts of the exodus in Pss 78, 105, 106, 107, and Is 40-55.
4. R. Brown, *John,* 252.
5. Unlike all the other twenty sequences of the Gospel, sequence 11 stands alone without any chiastic parallel. This suggests strongly that John meant it to be the centerpiece and turning point or hinge of the whole Gospel.

SEQUENCE 12 (6:22-71)—pages 114-134

1. E. Hoskyns, *The Fourth Gospel,* 368.
2. P. Borgen, *Bread from Heaven,* 59–98.
3. A. Guilding, *The Fourth Gospel and Jewish Worship.* See also B. Lindar's critique of Guilding in *The Gospel of John,* 251, and R. Brown, *John,* 278ff.
4. R. Brown, *John,* 279.
5. Cf. Q. Quesnell, *The Mind of Mark,* 193–208; 257–266.
6. R. Brown, *John,* 271. See also, J. L. Martyn, *History and Theology in the Fourth Gospel,* 45–68.
7. In speaking about "food which endures," John uses the verb *menein.* It forms a parallel with 6:56: "He who eats my flesh and drinks my blood abides (*menei*) in me, and I in him." More significantly, it is John's verb for expressing, as R. Brown (*John,* 510) puts it, "the permanency of relationship between Father and Son and between Son and Christian." Since the Eucharist is the bread that brings about this relationship in 6:56, it is reasonable to believe that John is speaking about this same Eucharistic bread here in 6:27.
8. Cf. R. Brown, *John,* 255-266.
9. Cf. J. Craghan, "Mary's *Ante Partum* Virginity: The Biblical View," *AER* 162 (1970) 361–372.
10. Cf. P. F. Ellis, *Matthew: His Mind and His Message,* 56.
11. Cf. R. Brown, *John,* 510-512.
12. *Ibid.,* 272-274.
13. We would agree entirely with E. Hoskyns, *The Fourth Gospel,* 305, who with his usual perspicacity observes: "The dislocation of the discourse, on the assumption that it is possible to separate an original stratum from later interpolations

is only a learned method of saying that a scholar is unable to penetrate the author's meaning, and prefers to substitute two or more disjointed fragments for one homogeneous whole."

14. R. Brown, *John,* 294, attributes the parallels to a redactor who put parallel discourses side by side, and refuses to accept P. Borgen's thesis that the whole discourse is a unity, with vv 48-58 expounding the word "eat" of the homiletic text (v 31) upon which the whole homily is based.

15. It is perhaps significant that the parallel structure of 6:43-58 mirrors the parallel structure of the whole sequence. Thus, 6:41-43 is the *center* of the whole sequence (6:22-71) just as 6:52 is the *center* of 6:43-58. Each center portrays the Jews as quarreling about what Jesus has said. The literary artistry is extraordinary.

16. E. Hoskyns, *The Fourth Gospel,* 297-298.

17. R. Brown, *John,* 297.

18. Cf. W. Schmithals, *Gnosticism in Corinth,* 25-86; C. H. Dodd, *The Johannine Epistles,* xviii–xxvi; R. Brown, *The Epistles of John,* 59-68.

19. E. Hoskyns, *The Fourth Gospel,* 300.

20. In the Synoptics, the title "Son of man" is regularly used in the context of the passion and death of Jesus (cf. Mk 8:31; 9:31; 10:33; 14:21 [in the context of the Eucharist]; 14:62; Mt 26:2, 24, 45, 55, 64; Lk 22:22, 48, 69). It is significant that in both Mark and Matthew (Mk 8:31; Mt 16:21), Jesus' prediction of his passion and death follows the same sequence as in John: (1) loaves (Mt 15:32-39; Mk 8:1-9); (2) Peter's confession (Mt 16:17-19; Mk 8:27-30); (3) the suffering Son of man (Mt 16:21; Mk 8:31).

21. On the vexed question of the interpretation of this text, see E. Hoskyns, *The Fourth Gospel,* detached note 5, 304-307.

22. R. Brown, *John,* 301-302, lists the parallels between John, Mark, and Matthew and concludes: ". . . the picture in John where the Petrine material is scattered may be more primitive than the Matthaean picture, although we cannot, of course, be certain that John's localization of these individual sayings is always original."

23. R. Bultmann, *John,* 345, on the basis of the subsequent reference to Jesus' death in vv 70-71, sees the title as a reference to Jesus as a victim.

24. B. Lindars, *John,* 276.

25. E. Hoskyns, *The Fourth Gospel,* 368, agrees substantially with C. H. Dodd, *Interpretation,* 345, who says: "It seems, therefore, that the sequence of incidents [in 6:1-21] gives a progression parallel to that which we find in the discourse. If so, then the narrative of the Feeding of the Multitude is not only significant or symbolical in itself, but it constitutes, in conjunction with the two incidents following, a complex *semeion* which is elucidated, after the Johannine manner, in the appended discourse."

SEQUENCE 13 (7:1-8:59)—pages 135-157

1. The text of 7:1-11 is arranged according to an *abcb'a'* format: (aa) v 1; (bb) vv 2-4; (cc) v 5; (b'b') vv 6-8; (a'a') vv 9-11.

2. 7:14-30 also has a parallel structure: (aa) v 14; (bb) v 15; (cc) vv 16-24; (b'b') vv 25-27; (a'a') vv 28-30.

3. We bypass the arguments for and against changing the order of the chapters in Jn 5-7. The arguments for having ch 7 follow immediately upon ch 5 are for the most part based on the presupposition that John's Gospel should follow the strict laws of narrative. As we have tried to demonstrate, John's compositional

structure follows the laws of parallelism. According to these laws, chs 7–8 are exactly where they belong—chiastically balanced with sequence 9 (5:1-47) in part II (4:4–6:15) and chiastically balanced with sequence 15 (10:22-39) in part V (6:22–12:11).

4. E. Hoskyns, *The Fourth Gospel,* 319, interprets 7:33-36 as a condemnation of the Jews who do not believe in Jesus.

5. A. Guilding mentions a number of texts (e.g., Jer 2:13; Is 44:3) that took as their theme the water of divine help and were read at the feast of Tabernacles. It is not improbable that John has Jesus speak of himself as the source of living waters in order to inculcate in another way his teaching that Jesus replaces all the Jewish feasts.

6. In the RSV, the quotation is punctuated in such a way that the "his" becomes the believer and the rivers flow from the believer. It is impossible to resolve the ambiguity, but as E. Hoskyns observes, "each translation yields a Johannine sense. Where the living water flows from the believer, the Johannine sense would be that those who believe become disciples of Jesus and through their preaching and teaching become sources of faith and life for others" (*The Fourth Gospel,* 365–366).

7. The reference to the Spirit as future supports but does not confirm the conclusion that the "him" from whom the living waters will flow is the believer rather than Jesus (see the commentary on 7:37-38 and footnote).

8. For the ideological background of the word "light" in the Bible and in extrabiblical religions, cf. C. K. Barrett, *John,* 277–278, and C. H. Dodd, *Tradition,* 201–212.

9. The precise meaning of the Greek text (*tēn archēn ho ti kai lalō hymin*) has been endlessly argued (cf. C. K. Barrett, *John,* 283f, who prefers the translation: "I am from the beginning what I tell you"—a meaning that fits well with v 24 and with the line of John's argumentation).

10. C. K. Barrett, *John,* 285, and R. Brown, *John,* 354, attribute the line to a rather puzzled final redactor.

11. It should be noted that 8:31-41 falls into John's typical parallel structure: (aa) 31-32; (bb) 33; (cc) 34-36; (b'b') 37; (a'a') 38-41, with "truth" the parallel word in (aa) and (a'a'), and "Abraham's seed" the parallel words in (bb) and (b'b').

12. Cf. J. L. Martyn, *History and Theology in the Fourth Gospel,* for a good account of the opposition between Jews and Christians at the end of the first century and for the influence of the opposition on John's Gospel.

SEQUENCE 14 (9:1-10:21)—pages 158-170

1. See blind Bartimaeus (Mk 10:46-52; Lk 18:35-43; Mt 20:29-34); two blind men in Galilee (Mt 12:22-23 and possibly Lk 11:14); a blind man healed with the use of spittle (Mk 8:22-26 and Mt 15:30).

2. R. Brown, *John,* 378.

3. C. K. Barrett, *John,* 299.

4. E. Hoskyns, *The Fourth Gospel,* 362, and J. L. Martyn, who in his *History and Theology in the Fourth Gospel,* has developed these insights of Hoskyns into a full-fledged study of the Johannine community.

5. Cf. C. K. Barrett, *John,* 296.

6. Cf. R. Brown, *John,* 372-373.

7. Cf. R. Brown, *John,* 380. See also J. L. Martyn, *History and Theology, passim.*
8. R. Brown, *John,* 379–380. See also Brown's *The Community of the Beloved Disciple,* 72–73.
9. Cf. C. H. Dodd, *Interpretation,* 358ff.
10. Cf. R. Brown, *John,* 379.
11. *Ibid.,* 380ff.
12. Cf. E. Hoskyns, *The Fourth Gospel,* 363–365.
13. See the commentary on 3:1-21.
14. The two sections of 9:1–10:21 form a unity of narrative, discourse, and monologue very similar to the format of 5:1-47, where the evangelist uses the cure of the paralytic in 5:1-18 as a springboard for the discourse in 5:19-47, in which Jesus condemns the Jews of Jerusalem in a manner similar to the way he condemns the Pharisees in 9:39–10:21.
15. C. K. Barrett, *John,* 304.
16. R. Brown, *The Community,* 78, thinks that Jesus alludes to leaders of Christian groups: "The hirelings are shepherds of the sheep, which means leaders of Christian groups, perhaps of Jewish Christian churches. They have not distanced their flocks sufficiently from 'the Jews' who are trying to take them away (i.e., back to the synagogue) for they have not really accepted the Johannine thesis that Judaism has been replaced by Christianity."
17. J. L. Martyn, *The Gospel of John in Christian History,* 119, believes it refers primarily "to other Jewish Christians who, like those of the Johannine community, have been *scattered* from their parent synagogues by experiencing excommunication."

SEQUENCE 16 (10:40–12:11)—pages 177–193

1. The synoptic Gospels agree with John in attributing the plot against Jesus to the Jewish leaders' alarm when they perceive that many of the people are beginning to believe in and follow Jesus (cf. Mt 21:15; 26:4; Mk 11:18; Lk 19:47-48).
2. Cf. R. Brown, *John,* 414, 427f, 429.
3. C. K. Barrett, *John,* 329.
4. Cf. R. Brown, *John,* 425–426; E. Hoskyns, *The Fourth Gospel,* 403–405; C. K. Barrett, *John,* 332–333; J. Marsh, *John,* 435–438; B. Lindars, *John,* 398.
5. Cf. C. H. Dodd, *Interpretation,* 365.
6. Source analysis of the anointing pericope is difficult. C. H. Dodd, *Interpretation,* 162–173, considers all three narratives about the anointing (Mk 14:3-9; Mt 26:6-13; Lk 7:36-38; Jn 12:1-8) as reducible to one original event. R. Brown, *John,* 451, opts for two events conflated from the oral tradition: an incident in Galilee at the house of a Pharisee, as in Lk 7:36-38; an incident at Bethany, at the house of Simon the leper, with an almost pure form of the tradition given in Matthew and Mark. From these two traditions, Brown holds, John composed 12:1-8.
7. In a similar manner, John located the cleansing of the temple at the beginning of his Gospel (2:13-25) rather than just before the passion, where it occurs in the Synoptics, not because he did not know when it took place, but because he needed it at the beginning of his Gospel to form a chiastic parallel with the passion account in chs 18–19, where the destruction of the temple of Jesus' body, predicted in 2:18-19, actually took place. As so often in John's Gospel, parallelism takes precedence over chronology.
8. Cf. R. Brown, *John,* 453.

SEQUENCE 17 (12:12-50)—pages 197-208

1. E. Hoskyns, *The Fourth Gospel,* 420.
2. *Ibid.,* 422.
3. Most commentaries divide John's Gospel into two major parts, the first (1:19-12:50) entitled "The Book of Signs," concluded by 12:1-50, and the second (13:1-21:25) entitled "The Book of Glory," concluded by 20:1-31, with ch 21 considered an addition by the so-called ecclesiastical redactor. This division ignores the fact that if there is such a thing as a Book of Glory, it definitely would have to begin with Jesus' statement in 12:23 that "the hour has come for the Son of man to be glorified" and with his further statements, "Now is my soul troubled" (12:27) and "Now is the judgment of this world" (12:31). It also ignores the inclusion-conclusion formed by the numerous parallels of 12:12-50 with 20:19-21:25—an inclusion that frames the whole of part V of the Gospel and indicates as clearly as the author could that 12:12-50 is not a conclusion but a beginning—the introduction to the concluding part (12:12-21:25) of the whole five-part Gospel. If one is to speak about a Book of Glory in John's Gospel, it would be more correct to begin it at 12:12 than at 13:1.

   The whole concept, however, of a Book of Signs and a Book of Glory is dubious because, as has been frequently pointed out by commentators, John speaks of Jesus' signs not only in chs 1-12 but also in chs 20-21. Furthermore, if, as many hold, the passion, death, and resurrection constitute the great sign in John's Gospel, then this sign, along with the sign referred to in 20:30 and the final sign in 21:1-8, occurs well outside the boundaries of the so-called Book of Signs.
4. Cf. R. Schnackenburg, *John,* 389.
5. R. Brown, *John,* 477.
6. R. Brown, *John,* 479.
7. Cf. R. Schnackenburg, *John,* 419-421.
8. E. Hoskyns, *The Fourth Gospel,* 420, says, "The author does not draw out the emphasis of the action of Jesus [i.e., his humble entrance on a donkey] because the discourse which follows (vv. 23-36) makes sufficiently clear the distinction between the Messiahship of Jesus and the royal messiah whom the Jews supposed they were welcoming into the city. He is content merely to note that the disciples did not understand until later, after the glorification of Jesus, either the significance of His action or the precise nature of the misunderstanding of the crowd."

SEQUENCE 18 (13:1-17:26)—pages 209-246

1. In addition to the major commentaries, see D. M. Smith, Jr., *The Composition and Order of the Fourth Gospel.*
2. R. Brown, *John,* 562.
3. R. Brown, *John,* 568, explains the words "except for his feet" as an addition by a scribe who, "faced with the statement, 'The man who has bathed has no need to wash,' and not recognizing that the bath was the footwashing, thought that he had to insert an exceptive phrase to show that Jesus did not mean to exclude the footwashing when he said there was no need to wash. In so doing he unwittingly provided later theologians with an even richer sacramental doc-

trine, for the phrase could be interpreted as a reference to the necessity of Penance after the bath of Baptism."

4. Cf. C. H. Dodd, *Tradition,* 62–64.

5. C. H. Dodd, *Interpretation,* 397.

6. The association in 13:34 of the love command with Jesus' death (his "going away") reinforces the argument of those who hold for a unity of intent in the footwashing symbolism and in the words "For I have given you an *example . . .*" (13:15) against those who see the footwashing as an earlier stratum dealing with Jesus' death, followed by a later moralizing exhortation to humble service (cf. R. Brown, *John,* 562: "Such an understanding of 6-10 as primarily christological and only secondarily sacramental is one more reason for considering these verses as more original than 12-20 . . . .").

7. C. K. Barrett, *John,* 382.

8. R. Brown, *John,* 636. On prayer in the Fourth Gospel, cf. D. M. Stanley, *Jesus in Gethsemane,* 230–266.

9. Cf. R. Brown, *John,* 1141, and see his appendix V in vol. 29A; see also J. M. Robinson and H. Koester, *Trajectories in Early Christianity,* 258–259.

10. Cf. D. B. Woll, "The Departure of 'The Way': The First Farewell Discourse in the Gospel of John," *JBL* 99 (June 1980) 225–239.

11. We have begun the inclusion-conclusion of section B at v 21 because the references to commandments and love in vv 21, 24, 28, 31 hark back to the beginning of the discourse, where Jesus first began speaking about the love commandment (13:34-35). Other parallels with the introduction (13:33–14:4) can be found in v 23: "make our home (*monēn*) with him" (cp. 14:2: "In my Father's house are many rooms [*monai*]); 14:27: "Let not your hearts be troubled" (cp. 14:1); and 14:28: "You heard me say to you, 'I *go away,* and I will come to you'" (cp. 13:33, 36; 14:2-5).

12. R. Brown, *John,* 667–668.

13. R. Brown, *John,* 674, considers the motif contrasting Jesus and his followers "as the real vine with the false vine represented by the Jewish Synagogue" a motif that would "fit in with one of the main purposes for which the gospel was written, namely, apologetic against the Synagogue." He sees this reference to the false vine, however, as only a "secondary reference." He says "it does not seem . . . Jesus is directly polemicizing against a false vine . . . ," but he fails to see that the antithetic parallelism of vv 1-6 (a) with vv 18-25 (a') supports more firmly the opinion that "true" here is contrasted with "false." Similar contrasts are found in 2:1-12 (wine versus water); 2:13-25 (the temple of Jesus' body replacing the temple of Jerusalem); 3:1-21 (life from above versus life from below); 4:7-14 (the water of life that Jesus gives versus the water from Jacob's well); and especially 6:32ff, where Jesus speaks of himself as "the *true* bread from heaven." All these are examples of the replacement theme so pervasive in John's theology.

14. *Ibid.,* 679.

15. *Ibid.,* 681.

16. E. Hoskyns, *The Fourth Gospel,* 478.

17. *Ibid.,* 478.

18. Cf. J. Painter, *Reading John's Gospel Today,* 31.

19. The major commentators, with the exception of Hoskyns, almost all consider 15:26-16:33 to be a later addition to the Gospel.

20. The substance of Mt 10:16-20 is taken from Mk 13:9-13, where the situation envisaged is the same as in Mt 10:16ff and Jn 15:26ff, namely, when the apostles bear witness to Jesus and the gospel before the world and suffer as a consequence

the persecution and the hatred of the world, they are not to be anxious about what they say, "for it is not you who speak, but the Holy Spirit" (Mk 13:11).

21. In view of what was said about the synagogue as the false Israel in 15:18-25, the reference in 16:2 to putting the apostles out of the "synagogues" would indicate that John sees the assistance of the Counselor as particularly relevant to the ongoing polemic between the synagogue and the Christian community at the end of the first century.

22. Cf. D. R. A. Hare, *The Theme of Jewish Persecution of Christians in the Gospel according to St. Matthew,* 19-77; 146-171.

23. J. L. Martyn, *The Gospel of John in Christian History,* 92, says: "The number of points in the history of the Johannine community about which we may be virtually certain is relatively small, and we need to be clear about that. One of these relatively secure points is surely the highly probable correspondence to the *Birkat ha-minim* (Benediction Against Heretics) of the expressions 'to be put out of the synagogue' and 'to put someone out of the synagogue' which emerge in John 9:22, 12:42 and 16:2."

24. R. Brown, *John,* 711.

25. *Ibid.,* 711-714.

26. E. Hoskyns, *The Fourth Gospel,* 485.

27. R. Brown, *John,* 716.

28. Verses 23-30 are composed in parallel: (aa) 23-24 (*you will ask nothing of me*); (bb) 25-27 (*I have said this to you in figures*); (cc) 28 (I came from the Father . . . and am going to the Father); (b'b') 29 (*Now you are speaking plainly, not in any figure*); (a'a') 30 (*you . . . need no one to question you*).

29. C. K. Barrett, *John,* 412.

30. R. Brown, *John,* 722-723.

31. C. K. Barrett, *John,* 415.

32. In addition to the major commentaries, see E. Käsemann, *The Testament of Jesus;* J. M. Robinson and H. Koester, *Trajectories Through Early Christianity,* 256-260; V. P. Furnish, *The Love Command in the New Testament,* 132-148.

33. Cf. P. F. Ellis, *Matthew: His Mind and His Message,* 20-25.

34. Cf. B. Lindars, *John,* 531.

35. C. K. Barrett, *John,* 429.

36. B. Lindars, *John,* 533.

SEQUENCE 19 (18:1-19:42)—pages 247-279

1. For the merits of the presupposition, compare E. Haenchen's "History and Interpretation in the Johannine Passion Narrative," *Int* 23 (April 1970) 198-219, with R. Fortna's *The Gospel of Signs,* 113-158.

2. Cf. R. Brown, "The Passion According to John: Chapters 18 and 19," *Worship* 49 (March 1975) 126-134.

3. Cf. D. Wead, *The Literary Devices in John's Gospel,* 47-68.

4. Cf. A. Janssens de Varebeke, "La structure des scènes du recit de la passion en Joh., xviii-xix," *ETL* 38 (1962) 504-522.

5. Cf. R. Brown, *John,* 857-865; C. K. Barrett, *John,* 443; J. Marsh, *John,* 588-594.

6. See B. Lindars, *John,* 574.

7. C. K. Barrett, *John,* 456.

8. J. Gerhard, *Unpublished Notes,* 196-198.

9. Cf. C. K. Barrett, *John,* 456.
10. Cf. R. Brown, *John,* 920–922.
11. Josephus, *Ant.,* III, 161.
12. R. Schnackenburg, *John,* 274.
13. Cf. B. Lindars, *John,* 578.
14. R. Schnackenburg, *John,* 276–277.
15. See Rom 9–11 for the Pauline understanding of the remnant as constituting the fulfilment of God's promises to the Jews.
16. J. Marsh, *John,* 617.
17. Cf. R. Brown, *John,* 949–950.
18. C. K. Barrett, *John,* 463.
19. Cf. R. Brown, *John,* 952–953.
20. *Ibid.,* 960; see also Brown's article "The Passion according to John: Chapters 18–19," *Worship* (March 1975) 134.
21. See pp. 288–289.

SEQUENCE 20 (20:1-18)—pages 280-289

1. Cf. R. Brown, *John,* 995–1004.
2. *Ibid.,* 999.
3. E. Hoskyns, *The Fourth Gospel,* 540.
4. Cf. R. Schnackenburg, *John,* 311–312.
5. R. Brown, *John,* 1011.
6. *Ibid.,* 1012–1017.
7. *Ibid.,* 1014.
8. Cf. M. Cambe, "L'influence du Cantique des Cantiques sur le Nouveau Testament," *RThom* 62 (1962) 5–26; A. Feuillet, "La recherche du Christ dans la Nouvelle Alliance d'après la Christophanie de Jo 20,11-18," *L'homme devant Dieu,* Mélanges H. de Lubac (Paris: Aubier, 1963) 1:93–112.

SEQUENCE 21 (20:19-21:25)—pages 290-312

1. C. K. Barrett, *John,* 472.
2. For a detailed discussion of the meaning, extent, and exercise of the power to forgive sins, see R. Brown, *John,* 1040–1045.
3. C. K. Barrett, *John,* 477.
4. R. Brown, *John,* 1050.
5. B. Lindars, *John,* 616.
6. See the discussion in R. Schnackenburg, *John,* 338.
7. B. Lindars, *John,* 617.
8. For a defense of the position of Hoskyns and Lagrange that ch 21 is authentically Johannine, see P. Minear, "The Original Functions of John 21" *JBL* 102 (March 1983) 85–98.
9. Cf. R. Brown, *John,* 1079–1080; R. Schnackenburg, *John,* 349–351; B. Lindars, *John,* 621–624.
10. R. Brown, *John,* 1072.
11. *Ibid.,* 1098.
12. *Ibid.,* 1074–1076.

13. Cf. P. Meye, *Jesus and the Twelve,* for a discussion of "fishers of men."
14. Cf. P. Minear, "The Original Functions of Jn 21," *JBL* 102 (March 1983) 91–95.
15. For arguments concerning the authenticity of these words when compared with Mt 16:17-19 and Lk 22:31-32, cf. P. F. Ellis, *Matthew: His Mind and His Message,* 125–134.
16. Cf. R. Brown, *John,* 1112–1117.
17. Earlier authors favored the Beloved Disciple as the author. Most modern authors either consider the author anonymous or attribute the Gospel to John, the son of Zebedee.
18. Cf. E. Hoskyns, *The Fourth Gospel,* 550.

Bibliography

Barrett, C. K. *The Gospel According to John.* London: SPCK, 1967.

Boismard, M. E. *St. John's Prologue.* Westminster, Md.: Newman Press, 1957.

Borgen, P. *Bread from Heaven.* Leiden: Brill, 1965.

Brown, R. *The Gospel According to John.* 2 vols. New York: Doubleday, 1966-70.

_____. *The Epistles of John.* New York: Doubleday, 1982.

_____. *The Community of the Beloved Disciple.* New York: Paulist Press, 1979.

Cambe, M. "L'influence du Cantique des Cantiques sur le Nouveau Testament," *RThom* 62 (1962) 5-26.

Culpepper, R. A. *The Johannine School.* Missoula, Mont.: Scholars' Press, 1975.

_____. "The Pivot of John's Prologue," *NTS* 27 (1980) 1-31.

Dodd, C. H. *The Interpretation of the Fourth Gospel.* Cambridge: University Press, 1953.

_____. *Historical Tradition in the Fourth Gospel.* Cambridge: University Press, 1963.

Dewey, J. *Markan Public Debate.* Missoula, Mont.: Scholars' Press, 1980.

Ellis, P. F. *Seven Pauline Letters.* Collegeville, Minn.: The Liturgical Press, 1982.

_____. *Matthew: His Mind and His Message.* Collegeville, Minn.: The Liturgical Press, 1974.

Feuillet, A. "La recherche du Christ dans la Nouvelle Alliance d'après la Christophanie de Jo 20, 11-18." *L'homme devant Dieu.* Melanges H. de Lubac. Paris: Aubier, 1963, 1:93-112.

Fiorenza, E. S., "Composition and Structure of the Revelation of John," *CBQ* 39 (July 1977) 344-366.

Fortna, R. *The Gospel of Signs.* London: Cambridge University Press, 1970.

Gerhard, J. *The Literary Unity and the Compositional Methods of the Gospel of John.* Unpublished dissertation. Washington: The Catholic University of America, 1975.

Harner, P. B. *The "I Am" of the Fourth Gospel.* Philadelphia: Fortress Press, 1970.

Hoskyns, E. *The Fourth Gospel.* London: Faber and Faber Ltd., 1947.

Kugel, J. L. *The Idea of Biblical Poetry: Parallelism and Its History.* New Haven, Conn.: Yale University Press, 1981.

Kysar, R. *The Fourth Evangelist and His Gospel.* Minneapolis: Augsburg Publishing House, 1975.

Lightfoot, R. H. *St. John's Gospel.* London: Oxford University Press, 1960.

Lindars, B. *The Gospel of John.* London: Oliphants, 1972.

Marsh, J. *Saint John.* Baltimore: Penguin Books, 1968.

Martyn, J. L. *History and Theology in the Fourth Gospel.* Nashville: Abingdon Press, 1979.

_____. *The Gospel of John in Christian History.* New York: Paulist Press, 1978.

Meye, P. *Jesus and the Twelve.* Grand Rapids, Mich.: Wm. B. Eerdmans, 1968.

Minear, P. "The Audience of the Fourth Evangelist," *Interpretation* 31 (October 1977) 339-354.

_____. "The Original Functions of John 21," *JBL* 102 (March 1983) 85-98.

Mowinckel, S. *He That Cometh.* Oxford: Basil Blackwell, 1956.

Robinson, J. M., and Koester, H. *Trajectories Through Early Christianity.* Philadelphia: Fortress Press, 1971.

Sanders, J. T. *The New Testament Christological Hymns.* Cambridge: Cambridge University Press, 1971.

Schnackenburg, R. *The Gospel According to St. John.* 3 vols. New York: The Seabury Press, 1980–82.

Smith, D. M. *The Composition and Order of the Fourth Gospel.* New Haven, Conn.: Yale University Press, 1965.

Talbert, C. H. *Literary Patterns, Theological Themes and the Genre of Luke-Acts.* Missoula, Mont.: Scholars' Press, 1974.

_____. "Artistry and Theology: An Analysis of the Architecture of John 1:19–5:47," *CBQ* 32 (July 1970) 341–366.

Taylor, M. J. *A Companion to John.* New York: Alba House, 1977.

Windisch, H. *The Spirit-Paraclete in the Fourth Gospel.* Philadelphia: Fortress Press, 1968.

pg 43 ll "inchoatively"

abcba

1:38 "What do you seek?"

polemical - 4
chiasmic - 6
lapidary - 7